Practical
Advanced
Biology

Practical Advanced Biology

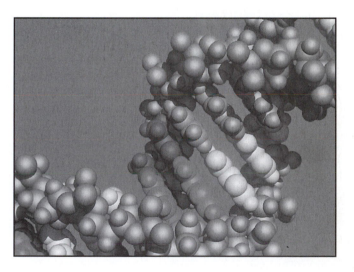

Tim King
Second Deputy Head of Abingdon School

Michael Reiss
Professor of Science Education, University of London Institute of Education

with

Michael Roberts
Formerly Head of Biology at Marlborough College and Cheltenham College

Published in 1994 by:
Thomas Nelson and Sons Ltd

Second edition published in 2001 by:
Nelson Thornes Ltd
Delta Place
27 Bath Road
CHELTENHAM
GL53 7TH
United Kingdom

01 02 03 04 05 / 10 9 8 7 6 5 4 3 2 1

A catalogue record for this book is available from the British Library

ISBN 0 17 448308 2

Illustrations by David Russell
Page make-up by Wearset Ltd

Printed and bound in Great Britain by The Bath Press

Contents

Note: Items of a biotechnological/microbiological nature are identified here, and within the Sections of this book, by the use of the flag ^{BM}.

Section 3

Regulation and defence 151

Section 4

Response and coordination 175

Section 8

Evolution of life   **295**

Appendix

Preface for teachers and technicians

The purpose of this book is to provide a comprehensive coverage of the practical element in all current advanced biology specifications. The book should also prove suitable for students pursuing introductory biology courses in universities and colleges of further education. With the exception of this preface, the reader is assumed to be a student. It is particularly important that students read the section *Introducing Practical Advanced Biology* before undertaking any of the practical work. It explains the rationale of the book and introduces the student to safety and other issues.

Each of the eight main sections of the book covers a particular area of biology and contains four different kinds of practical activity as follows:

- **Techniques** – structured activities which teach the student an important biological practical technique.
- **Practical exercises** – structured activities in which the student is led carefully through the activity, step by step.
- **Investigations** – more open-ended than practical exercises, giving students the opportunity to plan their work and evaluate their findings.
- **Projects** – even more open-ended, requiring students to undertake a piece of extended research, refine their ideas and design further investigations.

The **Appendix** contains a guide on how to carry out **statistical analysis** and a set of recipes for **biological reagents**.

The practical exercises, investigations and projects are of different lengths, difficulty and novelty, to enable teachers/lecturers and students to select the most appropriate ones for their specific needs and interests.

A list of requirements is given alongside each technique, practical exercise and investigation. The following abbreviations are used with respect to microscope slides: **WM** whole mount; **LS** longitudinal section; **VS** vertical section; **TS** transverse section; **HS** horizontal section; **VLS** vertical longitudinal section.

Standard icons are used throughout the book to draw students' attention to specific issues of health and safety (see p. 15).

Introducing Practical Advanced Biology

The purpose of this book is to help you, the student, carry out practical work for advanced level biology. Biology is a large subject and we have chosen to divide the main part of the book into eight sections. These sections correspond to the sections in M. B. V. Roberts, M. J. Reiss & G. Monger, *Advanced Biology*, NelsonThornes, 2000, and are as follows:

- Section 1 **Molecules to organisms**
- Section 2 **Respiration, nutrition and transport**
- Section 3 **Regulation and defence**
- Section 4 **Response and coordination**
- Section 5 **Reproduction, growth and development**
- Section 6 **Heredity and genetics**
- Section 7 **Organisms and their environment**
- Section 8 **Evolution of life**

In addition, there is an important appendix on **Statistical analysis**.

This chapter provides an introduction to the book as a whole. It is meant to help you to find your way around the book and get the most from it.

Within each section we have classified each practical activity into four *kinds* of practical activity, namely **techniques**, **practical exercises**, **investigations** and **projects**. We will now examine these four categories in more detail. We will show how they complement each other and can help you build up the skills and experiences needed by a scientifically rigorous biologist.

Techniques

Techniques are presented in boxes. The aim is to introduce you to fundamental biological practical techniques and pieces of apparatus, so that you are able to use these confidently and safely. For example, there are technique boxes on using a spirometer, on staining bacteria and on handling *Drosophila*. Techniques are subsequently used in practical exercises and investigations and are resources on which you can draw when undertaking projects.

Biologists need to be able to use many different types of apparatus, for example potometers (to measure water uptake by plants), respirometers (to measure oxygen uptake or carbon dioxide production), Petri dishes (for plating out bacteria and other microorganisms) and the light microscope (to magnify specimens). Many of the technique boxes are designed to help you derive the maximum benefit from a piece of apparatus.

Practical exercises

Practical exercises are structured activities through which you are led carefully, step by step. The aim is to enable you to carry out an important biology experiment, for example studying the effect of light intensity on photosynthesis or looking at the effect of pH on enzyme activity.

The great majority of these practical exercises can be completed in 90 minutes or less in the laboratory.

To get the most out of the practical exercises, you need to follow the instructions carefully. These instructions have been designed to provide you with experience in the following skills:

- Following instructions
- Making accurate observations
- Recording results in an appropriate form
- Presenting results in an appropriate form
- Drawing conclusions

We shall now look at each of these skills in more detail.

Following instructions

Instructions are provided in the order in which you need to carry them out. We would advise that, before carrying out the instructions, you read through the entire practical. This will help you to understand what you are doing and why you are doing it. In turn, this will help you to remember what you have learned.

In most cases we have presented each practical exercise under the following headings:

- **Introduction** – a few lines about the purpose of the practical exercise.
- **Procedure** – numbered steps that need to be carried out.
- **For consideration** – some questions to help you think carefully about the results you have obtained.
- **Requirements** – a list of the apparatus, chemicals and biological materials you need.

Making accurate observations

In most cases the practical exercise will make it clear what you need to observe, for example the time taken for a certain volume of gas to be evolved or the width of a sample of cells. Ensure that you know how to use any necessary equipment before starting the practical. Think carefully about the **precision** with which you will make your observations. Common sense is needed here. If you are measuring the length and width of tree leaves so as to produce a key, there's no need to use fractions of a millimetre.

Recording results in an appropriate form

Results can be recorded in various ways. Often it is helpful to record raw data in a **table**. Most data will be in the form of numbers, that is they will be **quantitative** data (also known as **numerical** data). However, some data, for example flower colour, will be **qualitative**.

One form in which some biological findings can be recorded is a **drawing**. You don't need to be a professional artist to make worthwhile biological drawings. If you follow the following guidelines, a drawing can be of considerable biological value:

- Ensure that your completed drawing will cover at least one-third of an A4 page.
- Plan your drawing so that the various parts are in proportion and

will not finish up too small. Small marks to indicate the length and breadth of the proposed drawing are a great help in planning, and a faint outline can be rapidly drawn to show the relative positions of the parts.

- The final drawing should be made with clean, firm lines using a sharp HB pencil and, if needed, a good quality eraser (not a white-out fluid). If important details are too small to be shown in proportion, they can be put in an enlarged drawing at the side of the main drawing.
- Avoid shading and the use of colour *unless* you are an excellent artist *and* they really help, for example when drawing soil profiles.
- When drawing structures seen with the naked eye or hand lens, use *two* lines to delineate such things as blood vessels and petioles. This will help you to indicate the relative widths of such structures (see, for example, Figure 2.37, p. 126).
- When drawing low power **plan drawings** under the light microscope, don't attempt to draw individual cells – just the extent of different tissues (see, for example, Figure 2.45A & B, p. 138).
- When drawing plant cells at high power under the light microscope, use two lines to indicate the width of cell walls, but a single line to indicate a membrane (see, for example, Figure 1.5, p. 35).
- Always put a scale on each drawing, for example ×10.

Presenting results in an appropriate form

Presentation of data is all about using graphs or other visual means to make it easier to see what your results tell you. The following four ways of presenting data are the most frequently used in biology: **line graphs**, **bar charts**, **histograms** and **scattergrams**.

Line graphs

Figure I.1 shows an example of a **line graph**, often simply called a **graph**. Points should be clearly marked. Encircled dots, ⊙, or crosses, ×, are appropriate. Whether the points should be joined by straight lines, as in Figure I.1, or by a smooth curve depends on how certain you are that a smooth curve would indicate the likely position of intermediate points better than a series of straight lines. Whenever you are unsure of the likely position of intermediate points, it is best to use straight lines. Notice also how the axes in Figure I.1 are labelled, and the use of a little gap bounded by short slanting lines on the vertical axis to indicate that the graph jumps from 0 to 50 mg blood glucose per 100 cm^3 of blood.

Bar charts

Figure I.2 shows an example of a **bar chart**. In a bar chart the horizontal axis shows **discrete categories**. In the example shown here these discrete categories are four different species of plants. The vertical axis gives a numerical measure such as **abundance** or **frequency**. In this particular example the vertical axis shows the number of species of butterfly that visited each plant during an hour's observation period. Conventionally, the blocks are of equal width and do not touch.

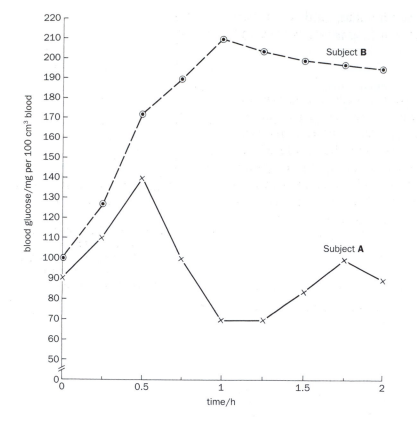

Figure I.1 An example of a graph showing blood glucose concentrations in mg per 100 cm³ blood for two human subjects, A and B.

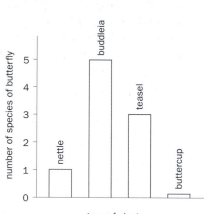

Figure I.2 An example of a bar chart showing the number of species of butterfly that visited each of four plants during an hour's observation period. Note that the blocks are separated, as is conventional with discrete categories.

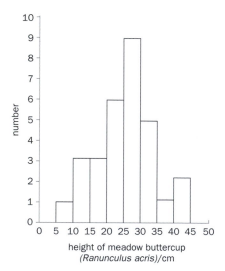

Figure I.3 An example of a histogram showing the heights of a collection of meadow buttercups. Note that the blocks touch each other, as is conventional with continuous categories.

Histograms

Figure I.3 shows an example of a **histogram**. In a histogram the horizontal axis shows **continuous categories**, represented by numbers. In the example shown here the horizontal axis shows the height of meadow buttercups. The vertical axis of a histogram, like that of a bar chart, gives a numerical measure such as abundance or frequency. Such histograms are sometimes referred to as **frequency distribution histograms**. Conventionally, the blocks touch.

Scattergrams

Figure I.4 shows an example of a **scattergram.** A scattergram is a useful way to show the relationship between two variables. The example given here shows the relationship between the height of different meadow buttercup plants and the number of pollinating insects they attract. If one of the variables is determined by the other, it is best to put the **independent variable** on the horizontal, x, axis and the **dependent variable** on the vertical, y, axis. In this example, the number of pollinating insects attracted is the dependent variable because it *depends* on the other (independent) variable, namely the height of the plant. When plotting the results of an experiment, what you *control* (e.g. light intensity, enzyme concentration) goes on the horizontal axis, and what you *measure* (e.g. rate of photosynthesis, rate at which substrate is used up) goes on the vertical axis.

Drawing conclusions

You will need to draw conclusions. If your practical exercise has involved the testing of a hypothesis, for example that the enzyme pepsin works better at low pHs than in neutral or alkaline conditions, your conclusion should indicate whether the hypothesis has been **refuted** (i.e. shown not to be the case) or **supported**. Of course, even if your hypothesis has been supported, it doesn't mean that it has been confirmed with 100% certainty – in other words, it isn't *proved*. Science proceeds more by showing that certain ideas are wrong than by showing that others are right (think about that!). Your conclusion might therefore include further ways of testing the original hypothesis, or might raise new possibilities to be investigated.

Often, you will only be able to arrive at your conclusions after statistically analysing your data. **Statistics** are so important in biology that we have given them an Appendix to themselves (see pp. 304–317).

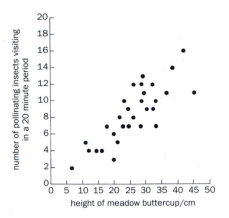

Figure I.4 An example of a scattergram, showing the numbers of pollinating insects (*y* axis) visiting different meadow buttercup plants of particular heights (*x* axis) over a period of 20 minutes.

Investigations

Investigations are more open-ended than practical exercises and give you more opportunity to plan your work. You are not told exactly what to do, but are given only general guidance. For example, you might investigate the distribution of woodland herbs in relation to light intensity, or you might design and use a questionnaire to study the incidence of cigarette smoking among people of different age and gender. Some of these investigations can be carried out in 90 minutes or less in the laboratory, but many take longer than this and are not laboratory-based. In most cases we have presented each investigation under the following headings:

*   **Introduction** – a few lines about the purpose of the investigation.
*   **Guidance** – some suggestions about issues you might consider, with ideas about how you might proceed.
*   **For consideration** – some questions to help you think carefully about the results you have obtained.
*   **Requirements** – a list of the apparatus, chemicals and biological materials which you may need.

By doing the investigations, you will gain experience in much the same skills as when doing practical exercises *and* in the following skill that is more specific to investigations:

*   planning investigations

Planning investigations

You may already have had considerable experience at planning and carrying out scientific investigations. The importance of careful planning cannot be overstated. Your results will be of value *whatever* they are – provided you have given careful thought to the design of your investigation. Here are the sorts of things that need to be thought about when planning an investigation:

- What hypotheses can you suggest?
- Are your hypotheses based on scientific knowledge rather than mere hunches?
- What testable predictions can you make from your hypotheses before obtaining any results?
- How can you ensure that any experimental tests you carry out are fair?
- Can you make any mathematical (quantitative) predictions?
- How many variables are you investigating?
- Are your variables discrete or continuous?
- How can you manipulate the independent variables?
- What, if any, controls do you need?
- How many **replicates** (i.e. repeat observations) will you need to carry out?
- How will you collect your results?
- What measurements are needed?
- What techniques will you use to obtain relevant information?
- Will you need to analyse your results statistically (see pp. 304–317)? If so, does this affect the numbers of observations you need to make?
- Is your intended procedure safe and does it show due regard for living organisms and the environment? Carry out a **risk assessment**.

Your investigation may require the use of a **questionnaire**. The design, testing and implementation of questionnaires is dealt with as Technique 3.14 on p. 169. Your teacher/lecturer will need to check your plan before you implement it.

Projects

Projects are even more open-ended than investigations, take more time and require you to refine your ideas as you proceed. Little or no guidance is given, though in some cases we suggest some useful reading. In all, about 250 possible projects are outlined in this book. Some of these would take, from start to finish, about 10 hours over a period of a few weeks. Others could take as much as 80 hours spread over 12 months. Some are laboratory-based, others involve field work or can be carried out at home. Examples include investigating the properties of the digestive enzyme rennin, studying factors affecting the reaction times of humans, dissecting conifer cones, and relating the patterns of mosses on walls to measured environmental variables.

A project differs from an investigation in the following ways:

- You have more choice in deciding what to study and how to proceed.
- They usually take longer and often involve a *series* of investigations. You may need to carry out more than one risk assessment.
- You will need to evaluate your findings as you proceed, and modify your work accordingly.

Projects give you the opportunity to be creative. A successful project can give you a flavour of what it is like to be a professional research scientist. It involves working in detail on one problem, adapting your approach as you go along.

Choosing a project

Some people find it very easy to think of projects to do; others, however good they are at biology, find it very difficult. At the end of each Section in this book various possible projects are suggested, often with some ideas to get you going. In many ways, though, it doesn't really matter *what* project you undertake, so long as it interests you. More important is *how* you undertake it. Having said that, several factors may help you to choose the subject of your project:

- You may have a special interest in a certain part of biology (e.g. conservation or sports science).
- You may possess a particular skill (e.g. electronics, bird identification or photography).
- An unusual opportunity may present itself (e.g. you live near a farm or get a holiday job working in a firm that makes biochemicals).
- You may by chance come across an interesting biological phenomenon (e.g. large chunks may be missing from the leaves of a certain plant).

To help you choose a possible project you may find the following approach useful:

- Make a list of those parts of biology that interest you.
- Make a list of any special experiences you have, for example: identifying a particular group of organisms; a relevant hobby or activity (such as keeping fish or regular child-minding); living in, or having access to, a distinctive place (such as the seashore).
- Make a list of things you might really like to do during your project if only they were feasible, for example climbing mountains or taking photographs.

Now draw together the above three lists to identify an area of biology in which you might realistically be able to do an original project. Don't worry about the precise title or detailed aims, just the subject area in which you might work.

Identifying the aims of your project

Having identified a possible project area, the next thing to do is to decide on your aims. Broadly speaking, this means getting an idea of what you are trying to find out, and identifying one or more key research questions you hope to answer. You may, tentatively, be able to suggest hypotheses and make some predictions to be tested.

  Here are a few examples:

- Suppose your project involves studying the succession of insects, fungi and other organisms on rotting fruits. Make a list of four questions your study might attempt to answer.
- Suppose your project involves investigating the reaction times of adult humans. Suggest four factors that might affect reaction times.
- Imagine your project involves identifying the invertebrates in a small river from near its source to the point where it enters the sea. Propose four hypotheses that you could test once you had collected suitable data.

- For two possible projects of your choosing, or suggested in this book, propose either four key questions that could be asked or four hypotheses that could be tested.

Designing projects

Once you have identified a possible project and begun to establish its aims, you may want to get going straight away. First, though, you must have some sort of **experimental design**. This will allow you to collect the data you need in an appropriate way.

Here are some examples:

- Suppose your project involves studying the succession of organisms on rotting fruits. Describe a possible experimental design.
- Suppose your project involves investigating the reaction times of adults. Outline the procedure you might adopt.
- Imagine your project involves identifying the invertebrates of a small river from near its source to the point where it enters the sea. Describe a possible design for the project.
- For two projects of your own choosing, or suggested in this book, outline possible experimental designs, ensuring that each allows appropriate data to be collected, suitable factors to be investigated or hypotheses to be tested.

Practical equipment

Make a list of the practical equipment you are likely to require for your project. Check with your teacher, lecturer or technician that what you need will be available when you require it – some things may need to be ordered in advance. If you need some laboratory space, ensure that this too will be available when you need it and for as long as you need it.

Modifying your project

As you proceed with your project, you should monitor your progress. Don't leave the analysis of your results to the very end. Instead, carry out preliminary analyses. These will enable you to modify your experimental design as you go along. There are several reasons why your experimental design may need modifying:

- You find you have bitten off more than you can chew and need to simplify your project. It is easy to underestimate the time required for project work.
- Unforeseen difficulties crop up, necessitating alterations.
- You find out something really interesting but unexpected, and decide to follow that up instead of your original aim.

All these are valid reasons for modifying your project. When it comes to sticking to your original experimental design, there's a fine line between showing perseverance (a virtue in science) and stubbornness (a vice). As a scientist you need constantly to evaluate your progress and think about whether to continue as you intended, or change tack.

Ethical considerations

Always consult your teacher/lecturer about what you intend to do before carrying out a project. In particular:

- Don't cause any distress or suffering to animals (including inverte-brates), for example by subjecting them to extremes of temperature or depriving them of food.
- Don't cause damage to the environment, for example by uprooting plants (illegal in the UK unless you have the landowner's permission) or by failing to return animals (e.g. woodlice) to the wild.
- Don't ask unduly personal questions of people when using question-naires
- When working with others, pay due regard to their opinions and contributions.

References

Albone, E., Collins, N. & Hill, T. *Scientific Research in Schools: A Compendium of Practical Experience.* Clifton Scientific Trust, Bristol, 1995.

Cain, N. W. *Animal Behavior Science Projects.* John Wiley & Sons, New York, 1995.

Chalmers, N. & Parker, P. *The OU Project Guide, 2nd edn.* The Field Studies Council, Preston Montford, 1989.

Dashefsky, H. S. *Insect Biology: 49 Science Fair Projects.* TAB Books, Blue Ridge Summit, PA, 1992.

Dockery, M. & Reiss, M. *Animal Behaviour: Practical Work and Data Response Exercises for Sixth Form Students.* Association for the Study of Animal Behaviour, Cambridge, 1996.

Eldridge, D. & Lock, R. *Revised Nuffield Advanced Science: Biology Projects and Investigations.* Longman, Harlow, 1994.

Hampton, C. H., Hampton, C. D., Kramer, D. C. and others. *Classroom Creature Culture: Algae to Anoles, revised edn – A Collection of Articles from the Columns of* 'Science and Children'. National Science Teachers' Association, Arlington, VA, 1997.

Hershey, D. R. *Plant Biology Science Projects.* John Wiley & Sons, New York, 1995.

National Centre for Biotechnology Education. *Practical Biotechnology: A Guide for Schools and Colleges.* University of Reading Department of Microbiology, Reading, 1993.

Reiss, M. J. (Ed.). *Living Biology in Schools.* Institute of Biology, London, 1996.

Wedgwood, M. *Tackling Biology Projects.* Macmillan Education, Basingstoke, 1987.

Williams, P. *Exploring with Wisconsin Fast Plants.* Kendall/Hunt, Dubuque, Iowa, 1995.

Key skills

Key skills are the general skills that can help you to improve your own learning and performance. They are relevant to what you do in education, training, work and life in general. Key skills are important in your learning because they can help you to focus on what you are learning and how you are learning, so you can get better results. Key skills will be important in your future career because they can help you to be flexible in whatever kind of work you will do. Employers are increasingly looking for key skills when recruiting and promoting people. These skills

- Use effective methods of exchanging information to support your purpose.
- Develop the structure and content of your presentation using the views of others, where appropriate, to guide refinements.
- Present information effectively, using a format and style that suits your purpose and audience.
- Ensure your work is accurate and makes sense.

Problem solving

At level 3 in **problem solving** you need to produce evidence to show you can:

- Explore the problem, accurately analysing its features, and agree with others on how to show success in solving it.
- Select and use a variety of methods to come up with different ways of tackling the problem.
- Compare the main features of each possible option, including risk factors, and justify the option you select to take forward.
- Plan how to carry out your chosen option and obtain agreement to go ahead from an appropriate person.
- Implement your plan effectively, using support and feedback from others.
- Review progress towards solving the problem and revise your approach as necessary.
- Agree, with an appropriate person, methods to check if the problem has been solved.
- Apply these methods accurately, draw conclusions and fully describe the results.
- Review your approach to problem solving, including whether alternative methods and options might have proved more effective.

Working with others

At level 3 in **working with others** you need to produce evidence to show you can:

- Agree realistic objectives for working together and what needs to be done to achieve them.
- Exchange information, based on appropriate evidence, to help agree responsibilities.
- Agree suitable working arrangements with those involved.
- Organise and carry out tasks so you can be effective and efficient in meeting your responsibilities and produce the quality of work required.
- Seek to establish and maintain cooperative working relationships, agreeing ways to overcome any difficulties.
- Exchange accurate information on progress of work, agreeing changes where necessary to achieve objectives.
- Agree the extent to which work with others has been successful and the objectives have been met.
- Identify factors that have influenced the outcome.
- Agree ways of improving work with others in the future.

References

Beare, R. & Hewitson, J. Asking and answering all sorts of scientific questions using spreadsheets. *School Science Review*, **77** (281), 43–53, 1996.

Davids, H., Frost, R. & Hemsley, K. *Science On-line: Practical Ideas for Using the World Wide Web*. British Educational Communications and Technology Agency, Coventry, 2000.

Garvin, J. W. *Skills in Advanced Biology: Investigating 3*. Stanley Thornes, Cheltenham, 1995.

Jones, A., Reed, R. & Weyers, J. *Practical Skills in Biology*. Longman Scientific & Technical, Harlow, 1994.

Pechenik, J. & Lamb, B. *How to Write about Biology*. HarperCollins, London, 1994.

Qualifications and Curriculum Authority. *Key Skills*. Qualifications and Curriculum Authority, London, 1999. www.qca.org.uk

Redfern, P. & Beattie, R. Click here: biology on the internet. *Biological Sciences Review*, **10** (2), 26–29, 1997.

Spark, P. An A-level biologist's guide to the world wide web. *Biological Sciences Review*, **10** (4), 26–29, 1998.

Whitehouse, M. (Ed.) [Special issue on IT in science education.] *School Science Review*, **79** (287), 15–113, 1997.

Assessment

Your teacher/lecturer will undoubtedly advise you about the precise **assessment requirements** of your particular Awarding Body. However, while there are differences, the schemes for practical assessment of the various Awarding Bodies also have a lot in common.

Every now and again in each Section of the book we have suggested how an investigation can be used to assess practical skills. We have divided practical skills into four categories:

- Planning
- Implementing a plan
- Analysing evidence and drawing conclusions
- Evaluation

Planning

Good **planning** involves:

- Retrieving and evaluating existing information from a variety of sources.
- Using this information to develop a strategy that is well structured, logical and links coherently to underlying scientific knowledge and understanding.
- Ensuring that your methods are such that any data you will collect will be suitable for statistical analysis.

Implementing a plan

Successful **implementation of a plan** involves:

- Using appropriate equipment and techniques to obtain and record relevant data.

- Taking precautions to ensure that the data are valid and reliable.
- Being able to modify the plan if needs be.
- Working safely and taking account of any ethical considerations such as the well-being of organisms and conservation needs of the environment.

Analysing evidence and drawing conclusions

Successful **analysis and the drawing of conclusions** involves:

- Demonstrating a high degree of competence in the presentation and display of the collected data.
- Recognising and interpreting trends in the data.
- Providing coherent, logical and comprehensive explanations of the findings in terms of appropriate biological knowledge.

Evaluation

Appropriate **evaluation** involves:

- Describing any errors or other shortcomings and assessing their impact on the data collected and conclusions drawn.
- Discussing how further practical work could be used to address any errors or shortcomings.

Reference

Adds, J., Larkcom, E., Miller, R. & Sutton, R. *Tools, Techniques and Assessment in Biology: A Course Guide for Students and Teachers.* Nelson, Walton-on-Thames, 1999.

Health and Safety

Surveys have shown that science laboratories are among the safest places to be. Nevertheless, this is no cause for complacency. On the occasions when something goes wrong and a person is injured, it is usually because one of the following common-sense rules has been broken:

- Always move slowly and carefully in a laboratory.
- Never put your fingers in your mouth or eyes after using chemicals or touching biological specimens until you have washed your hands thoroughly with soap and warm water, and dried them hygienically.
- Make sure glass objects (e.g. thermometers, beakers) cannot roll off tables or be knocked onto the floor.
- Wear eye protection whenever there is a risk of damage to the eyes. Situations of risk include: heating anything with a Bunsen burner; handling many liquids, particularly those identified as being corrosive, irritant, toxic or harmful; handling corrosive or irritant solids; some dissection work. Throughout this book, risks to eyes have been identified as far as possible, but in your own investigations and project work you will have to assess whether your activities pose any risks and check your plans with your teacher/lecturer before you start.
- Allow Bunsen burners, tripods, gauzes and beakers to cool down before handling them.
- Never allow your own body fluids (especially blood and saliva) to

come into contact with someone else, or theirs to come into contact with you.

- Keep long hair tied back and don't wear dangly earrings.
- Don't allow electrical equipment to come into contact with water.
- If you are unsure how to carry out a scientific procedure, ask your teacher/lecturer first.
- Make sure you understand *why* you are going to do something before you do it.
- Wear a lab. coat when using chemicals or handling any biological material except prepared slides or mounted specimens.
- Follow agreed procedures with regard to cuts, burns, electric shocks and other accidents (e.g. with chemicals).
- Follow all specific health and safety instructions given in this book or provided by your teacher/lecturer for particular practical work (e.g. use of gloves, disinfectant).
- When carrying out field work, work in pairs. That way, if something goes wrong for one of you, the other can help or obtain assistance.
- When carrying out field work, ensure you let your teacher/lecturer and parent(s)/guardian(s) know where you will be going. If you possess a mobile phone, take it with you.

With practice, these procedures should become second nature to you. They will enable you to carry out practical work in safety.

The following icons are used throughout the book to draw your attention to specific issues of health and safety:

Corrosive   Highly flammable   Risk of electric shock

Biohazard   Danger   Oxidising

Harmful or irritant   Toxic   Eye protection must be worn   Gloves should be worn

References

Association for Science Education. *Safeguards in the School Laboratory, 10th edn*. Association for Science Education, Hatfield, 1996.

Department for Education and Employment. *Safety in Science Education*. The Stationery Office, London, 1996.

National Association of Field Studies Officers (NAFSO). *Field Studies Centres: A Code of Practice – Quality, Safety and Sustainability.* National Association of Field Studies Officers (NAFSO), Stibbington, 1998.

Nichols, D. (Ed.). *Safety in Biological Fieldwork: Guidance Notes for Codes of Practice.* Institute of Biology, London, 1999.

Growth of plants in mineral salt cultures

This investigation extends over more than one practical session.

About 15 elements, which plants absorb from the soil or water as ions or as inorganic compounds, are essential for plant growth, but only seven of them are required in quantity. These are **nitrogen** (absorbed as nitrate or ammonium), **phosphorus** (absorbed as one of the types of phosphate ion), **sulphur** (absorbed as sulphate), **potassium**, **calcium**, **magnesium** and **iron**.

Two types of investigations on plant nutrition are frequently carried out. In the first, the same plant species is grown in a series of solutions containing nutrient ions, but – apart from a control that contains *all* the required nutrients – each solution lacks one specific element. In the second, all the plants receive a complete set of nutrient ions, but each receives a different amount of *one* of them, such as nitrate.

It is of course traditional to carry out such experiments with plants grown in jars or milk bottles, but here we suggest a successful method pioneered by John Hewitson and Richard Price (see reference); please refer to their paper for details.

Guidance

Radish plants are grown from seed, one per film container, in a medium consisting of equal proportions of silver sand and 'perlite'. Arrange the plastic film containers in a 3 × 3 array on top of the lid of a 1 kg margarine container (Figure 1.1). This is placed crossways across the top of an open 1 kg margarine container, which is filled with nutrient solution.

The nutrient solution is supplied to the growing plants in the film containers by capillary action. Before the growing medium is placed in the containers, a small hole is made in the base of each and a piece of fine capillary matting is pushed through it. After the containers have been filled with soil, they are placed on a larger piece of capillary matting. This extends across the top of the margarine container on which their bases rest, and hangs down into the nutrient solution.

One seed is planted in each container at a depth of 1 cm, and the plants are illuminated, as they grow, under a bank of fluorescent tubes, kept 15 cm above the tallest leaves. An experiment takes 2 weeks. During the experiment, examine and record any visible differences between the plants subjected to different treatments. After that time, the radishes can be harvested, air-dried, separated into shoots and roots, and weighed *individually* to determine their **dry mass**.

You can vary the nutrient ions as you wish. In their paper, Hewitson and Price list the composition of the solutions which they used, both to deprive the plants of one element at a time, and to test the effects of supplying increasing concentrations of nitrogen as nitrate.

Antifungal compounds on seeds

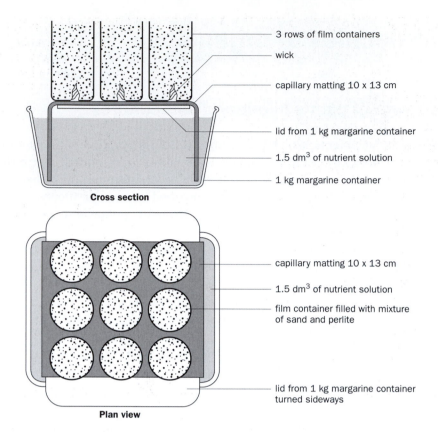

A suggested arrangement of radish plants in the nutrient culture experiment.

- 3 rows of film containers
- wick
- capillary matting 10 x 13 cm
- lid from 1 kg margarine container
- 1.5 dm³ of nutrient solution
- 1 kg margarine container

Cross section

- capillary matting 10 x 13 cm
- 1.5 dm³ of nutrient solution
- film container filled with mixture of sand and perlite
- lid from 1 kg margarine container turned sideways

Plan view

Figure 1.1 A suggested arrangement of radish plants in the nutrient culture experiment.

For consideration

1 When you began to grow the plants, were they entirely devoid of the seven main nutrient elements? If not, where did the nutrients come from?

2 What are the advantages and disadvantages of starting the experiment with seeds rather than with cuttings?

3 Suggest an advantage of growing the plants in plastic instead of glass containers.

4 Explain any visible differences exhibited by the plants in the different treatments, and any differences in the shoot to root ratios at the end of the experiment.

Reference

Hewitson, J. & Price, R. Plant mineral nutrition in the classroom: the radish, *Raphanus sativus* L. is a good plant for such studies. *School Science Review*, **76** (274), 45–55, 1994.

Chemical	Stock solution (g dm^{-3})	Quantity of stock solution per 2 dm^3 distilled water
Major nutrients		
Potassium nitrate (KNO$_3$)	101	35
Potassium chloride (KCl)	75	25
Sodium dihydrogen phosphate(V)	156	60
Calcium nitrate (Ca(NO$_3$)$_2$.4H$_2$O)	236	14
Magnesium suphate (MgSO$_4$.7H$_2$O)	246	48
Calcium chloride (CaCl$_2$)	110	106
Micronutrients		
Solution A		
Copper sulphate (CuSO$_4$.5H$_2$O)	0.12	1
Manganese sulphate (MnSO$_4$)	11.2	2.4
Zinc sulphate (ZnSO$_4$)	1.44	1
Solution B		
Ammonium molybdate ((NH$_4$)$_6$Mo$_7$O$_{24}$.4H$_2$O)	0.016	2.4
Boric acid (H$_3$BO$_4$)	1.3	1
Solution C		
EDTA, iron(III), monosodium salt	6.52	24

Potassium nitrate
Calcium nitrate

Calcium chloride
Manganese sulphate
Ammonium molybdate

✓ **Application of number:** Measure and record the dry masses of the plants. For the numerical data which you have collected, calculate the averages for each treatment, and use a t-test to determine whether any of these means differ significantly.

✓ **Information technology:** If you have merely omitted an element in each treatment, use the computer to draw a bar chart of your results. If you have examined the effects of an increasing concentration of a particular nutrient ion, use a graph-drawing program on the computer to produce a graph of your results.

Food tests

1.2 TECHNIQUE

This box describes methods of identifying the main classes of chemical compounds in a balanced diet. The compounds can be in ground-up tissue, intact cells, foodstuffs and extracted juices. Investigation 1.3 (p. 21) involves the use of these methods. You will need to wear your eye protection for these tests. It is safest to use water baths for heating.

Eye protection must be worn

Carbohydrates

Sugars (monosaccharides and disaccharides)

All monosaccharides (e.g. glucose, galactose, fructose) and certain disaccharides (e.g. maltose) will reduce copper(II) sulphate, producing a precipitate of copper(I) oxide on heating. Such sugars are known as **reducing sugars**, and can be tested for by heating with **Benedict's reagent**, which contains copper(II) sulphate. Add an equal quantity of

Benedict's reagent to the substance to be tested. Shake, and bring to the boil by heating the test tube in a water bath. A green precipitate indicates relatively little sugar, yellow somewhat more, brown even more and red the most.

The disaccharide sucrose, however, gives a negative Benedict's test. Its presence can be detected by Benedict's solution provided it is first hydrolysed into glucose and fructose, and then tested with Benedict's solution. This will yield a positive result.

To test for the presence of sucrose in a compound which has already tested negative with Benedict's solution, add a few drops of dilute (0.5 mol dm^{-3}) hydrochloric acid and boil. Neutralise with sodium hydrogencarbonate (check the pH with pH paper) and test with Benedict's reagent again.

Dilute hydrochloric acid

Starch

The addition of **dilute iodine solution** to a solution or a tissue containing starch yields a blue-black colour. If you are testing a foodstuff in water, the blue colour sometimes appears on the foodstuff itself, rather than in the solution, as starch is relatively insoluble.

Cellulose

Cellulose stains purple with **Schultze's solution** (chlor-zinc iodide).

Schultze's solution

Lipids

Shake a foodstuff in **absolute ethanol** in a test tube for 1 minute. Then pour the ethanol (not the foodstuff) into a test tube containing 7 cm^3 of water. A cloudy white emulsion indicates lipid. The density of the emulsion is proportional to the concentration of lipid in the substance being tested.

As lipids also take up the red stain **Sudan III**, another way to detect lipid in tissue that has been ground up is to transfer the tissue to a test tube containing water, and boil. If lipids are present, oil droplets will escape from the tissue and rise to the surface. To confirm that the droplets are lipid, add 2 cm^3 Sudan III, shake, and allow the oil to settle. The oil will now be stained red.

Ethanol

Lignin

Lignin, a hydrocarbon polymer characteristic of xylem tissue, stains red with **acidified phloroglucinol**. Add phloroglucinol first, and then a few drops of concentrated hydrochloric acid; or use a made-up solution of acidified phloroglucinol.

Phloroglucinol Concentrated hydrochloric acid

Phloroglucinol

Proteins

The **biuret test** is suitable for soluble proteins. Add a little potassium hydroxide to the solution until it clears. Then add a drop of dilute copper(II) sulphate solution down the side of the test tube. A blue ring at the surface of the solution indicates protein. On shaking, the blue ring disappears and the solution turns purple.

For insoluble proteins **Millon's reagent** is suitable, but you may not be allowed to use it because it is both toxic and corrosive. To a small amount (3 cm^3) of the solution or a suspension of the protein in a test tube in a water bath, add about six drops of Millon's reagent and boil

Millon's reagent

Millon's reagent

for 5 minutes. After cooling, add a few drops of 1% sodium nitrite to the reaction mixture. If protein is present, a brick-red precipitate appears on the surface of the substance being tested.

DCPIP

Vitamin C

Use the decolourisation of dichlorophenolindolephenol (**DCPIP**) as a quantitative test for vitamin C (see Investigation 1.9, p. 30).

Tests on intact tissue

The advantage of testing intact tissue is that the distribution of individual compounds within the cells can be studied in detail. Examples are as follows:

- The distribution of DNA and RNA in intact broad bean cells is investigated with methyl green–pyronin (Practical Exercise 6.8, p. 258).
- The chromosomes of dividing cells are shown up with orcein acetic (ethanoic) stain (Practical Exercise 5.1, p. 207).
- The cellulose in plant cell walls can be detected with Schultze's solution (this Technique, p. 20).
- The starch grains within onion cells are stained with dilute iodine solution (the Technique, p. 20).
- The lignified tissue within a plant root, plant stem or macerated tissue is stained with acidified phloroglucinol (Practical Exercise 5.3, p. 209).
- The waxy cuticle on a plant leaf, and the Casparian bands within the endodermis cell walls of a root, can be highlighted with Sudan III.

Requirements

Test tubes
Test tube rack
Bunsen burner
Pestle and mortar
Watch glass
Spatula
Eye protection
Lab. coat
Benedict's reagent
Copper(II) sulphate solution (1%)
DCPIP
Ethanol (absolute)
Hydrochloric acid, concentrated
Hydrochloric acid, dilute
Iodine solution
Methyl green–pyronin stain
Millon's reagent
Orcein acetic stain
Phloroglucinol (benzene-1,3,5-triol)
Potassium hydroxide (approx. 10–20%)
Schultze's solution
Sodium hydrogencarbonate
Sudan III stain
Litmus paper

Comparison of the chemical composition of various foodstuffs

1.3 INVESTIGATION

The relative concentrations of starch, reducing sugars, lipids and proteins in a variety of foodstuffs can be compared by using the techniques outlined in Technique 1.2 (p. 19) on food tests. Then you can relate the composition of the foodstuff to its function in the organism that produced it, or to the way in which the food was processed.

You can include almost any foodstuff in your investigation, but the following are suitable: milk, butter, cheese, apple, brown bread, white bread and meat.

Guidance

Test for starch with iodine solution, for reducing sugars with Benedict's solution, for lipids with the ethanol test and for proteins with the biuret test. You may also have time to test for lignin with acidified phloroglucinol. The methods are described in Technique 1.2 (p. 19).

Cut up the solids with a sharp knife or safety razor blade, or grind them up with a pestle and mortar if you feel that this is necessary. Try to make the tests as quantitative as possible. By standardising the amounts of foodstuffs to be tested, and the quantities of reagents, you will be able to make valid comparisons.

Sharp knife
Razor blade

Phloroglucinol

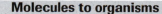

Ethanol

Eye protection
must be worn

Test tubes
Test tube rack
Test tube brushes
Sharp knife or razor blade
Ceramic tile
Spatula
Bunsen burner
Test tube holder
Safety spectacles
Iodine solution
Benedict's reagent
Ethanol (absolute)
Millon's reagent
Potassium hydroxide (dilute)
Copper(II) sulphate (1%)
Phloroglucinol
Concentrated hydrochloric acid
Meat (white meat, e.g. chicken, is best if
    Millon's test is used)
Milk
Cheese
Butter
Apple
White bread
Brown bread
Suspension of brewer's yeast

Apply the same test to all the foodstuffs, and compare the results, before you test for a different compound. Record the intensity of the colour produced (or, in the case of sugar, the actual colour itself) in each test on a five-point scale.

For consideration

1   Relate the composition of milk to its function. Account for the differences in composition between milk, cheese and butter in terms of the way in which cheese and butter are produced from milk.
2   Why does meat have such a high protein content? Which kind of proteins might be responsible? Can you name them?
3   Speculate on the advantages to an apple fruit of its high content of reducing sugars.

Key skills

✓   **Working with others:** To complete this investigation within one practical session, you will need to work in pairs. You will have to agree on a joint scale for recording and, as not all the pairs can do all the tests, organise at the start which tests are to be carried out by which pairs. At the end of the investigation, the data need to be pooled.
✓   **Communication:** Write an account of this investigation which can be easily understood by any of your classmates. Plan a talk to the others, with visual images, which is structured, easily understood and concise.

1.4 PRACTICAL EXERCISE   Quantitative food tests

In Technique 1.2 (p. 19) and Investigation 1.3 (p. 21), the food tests are largely **qualitative;** in other words, each positive test shows that the compound is present, but only very roughly conveys an impression of how much there is. An exception is the vitamin C test (Investigation 1.9, p. 30), which is **quantitative**, and so will not be repeated here. Also, Benedict's test can be made quantitative by drying the precipitate and determining its dry mass in order to assess how much reducing sugar is present. This, however, is somewhat time consuming.

Here, we shall describe quantitative tests for lipids, carbohydrates and proteins. These tests involve using a **colorimeter** equipped with a series of filters so that the absorbency of the precipitate can be determined at any particular wavelength. This can allow the concentration of the compound to be measured on a 100-point scale.

Lipids

To compare lipid concentrations, we suggest that you produce an emulsion as in Technique 1.2 (p. 20), shaking the foodstuff for exactly the same time with the same volume of absolute ethanol, and pouring it into $7\,cm^3$ of water in a test tube. Then measure the intensity of the white turbidity with a colorimeter. This only provides you with a relative, not an absolute, estimate of lipid concentration, but it is sufficient for most purposes.

If you wish to determine the absolute concentration, dissolve a small weighed mass of butter in the same volume of absolute ethanol and determine its absorbancy; repeat with smaller masses of butter to produce a calibration curve.

Ethanol

Starch

Starch can be determined quantitatively using the **iodine test**, with a colorimeter fitted with a red filter. Its concentration needs to be measured in studies of starch breakdown (e.g. by the enzyme amylase; Practical Exercise 2.33, p. 107) or starch synthesis (e.g. Practical Exercise 2.5, p. 63). The standard procedure is always to start with the same quantities of iodine solution and distilled water in a test tube – say $10\,cm^3$ of distilled water and $0.5\,cm^3$ of standard dilute iodine. You then add $0.5\,cm^3$ of reaction mixture, containing starch, taken at intervals from the start to the end of a reaction which is proceeding in a different test tube, to yield the blue colour.

A calibration curve allows the absolute concentration of starch to be determined. To the same mixture of iodine solution and distilled water, first add $0.5\,cm^3$ of 0.5% starch solution, and determine the absorbance with the colorimeter. Then repeat the process with the starch diluted twice, four times and eight times. Plot the calibration curve, and use it to determine the mass of starch in the solution at any time during the experiment.

Reducing sugars (e.g. glucose)

Clinistix reagent strips provide a semi-quantitative test.

To be more accurate, use a compound called 3,5-dinitrosalicylate (DNS). This compound (DNS) is reduced to a red compound (ANS) by glucose and fructose, and the colour density of ANS can be measured with a colorimeter. The composition of DNS solution, and that of the standard sugar solution used for calibration, are shown in the 'Requirements' box. The solutions you need are as follows:

DNS

1 A blank with no sugar: add $6\,cm^3$ of water to $2\,cm^3$ of DNS reagent in a test tube.
2 In a second tube, add $6\,cm^3$ of standard sugar solution to $2\,cm^3$ of DNS reagent.
3 To each of four more tubes, add $6\,cm^3$ of a dilution of the standard sugar solution to $2\,cm^3$ of DNS solution. The results produce a calibration curve.
4 Remove $6\,cm^3$ of each solution that you wish to test for reducing sugars, and add to $2\,cm^3$ of DNS solution in a separate test tube.

Eye protection must be worn

Requirements

Colorimeter with fitting colorimeter
   tubes (or spectrophotometer)
Test tubes
Pipettes, graduated (1 cm³, 5 cm³,
   10 cm³) with rubber bulbs
Stopclock
Water bath, heated
Test tube rack, metal
Marbles to fit into top of test tubes
Glass rods
Goggles
Ethanol, absolute
Iodine, dilute
Standard reducing sugar solution for
   DNS determination (Note 1)
DNS reagent (Note 2)
Protein standard (Note 3)
'Alkaline solution' for protein
   determination (Note 4)
Folin–Ciocalteau reagent

Notes: Preparation of solutions
1 Standard reducing sugar solution:
   Dissolve 0.15 g of glucose and 0.15 g
   of fructose in 1 dm³ of water.
2 DNS reagent: Make up and mix
   solutions A and B below, and make
   up the volume to 1 dm³ with water.
   Solution A: Dissolve 300 g of sodium
   potassium tartrate in about 500 cm³
   of water.
   Solution B: Dissolve 10 g of 3,5-
   dinitrosalicylate in 200 cm³ of
   2.0 mol dm⁻³ of sodium hydroxide
   solution.
3 Protein standard: Dissolve 0.1 g of
   either egg albumen or BSA (bovine
   serum albumin) in 100 cm³ of water.
4 'Alkaline solution': Mix (a) 1%
   aqueous CuSO₄, (b) 2% aqueous
   sodium potassium tartrate and (c)
   0.1 mol dm⁻³ sodium hydroxide with
   2% Na₂CO₃ dissolved in it, in the
   ratio 1:1:100.

Place all the tubes in a metal test tube rack. Then put a marble in the top of each tube to prevent water loss by evaporation, and put all the tubes at once into a boiling water bath for 5 minutes. Take out the rack and put it in cold water – the solutions have to be at room temperature to be read correctly.

Then read the absorbance in a colorimeter with a blue filter, after zeroing against the blank, or at 540 nm. If the absorbance of one of your test solutions is too high, try the procedure again after diluting it by a known factor, but always add 6 cm³ to 2 cm³ of DNS solution (or, at least, keep the ratio the same if there are limited volumes).

Proteins

The biuret test for protein (Technique 1.2, p.20) lacks sensitivity, and so a more sensitive modification of it, the Lowry method, is usually used. It gives a blue-purple colour, which is read at 600 nm.

Prepare four different dilutions of your protein standard solution (see 'Requirements' box). To separate test tubes, add (a) 1 cm³ of distilled water, (b) 1 cm³ of protein standard solution, (c) 1 cm³ of each of your dilutions of the protein standard solution or (d) 1 cm³ of each of your test solutions. Then add 5 cm³ of 'alkaline solution' (see 'Requirements' box) to each tube. Mix thoroughly and allow to stand for at least 10 minutes.

Then, to each tube, add 0.5 cm³ of Folin–Ciocalteau reagent, diluted 1:1 with distilled water on the day of use. Mix rapidly and thoroughly, but allow to stand for at least 30 minutes before reading the absorbance of the blue-purple colour.

For consideration

1 Find out about the main classes of lipids. Which of these classes will be detected by the test you have performed?

References

Adds, J., Larkom, E., Miller R. and others. *Tools, Techniques and Assessment in Biology*. Nelson, Walton-on-Thames, 1998. (For starch determination.)

Myers, A. *Preparation and Properties of Immobilised Invertase. Biochemistry Across the School Curriculum 3*. Biochemical Society, London, 1994. (For reducing sugar determination.)

Reed, R. H. Holmes, D., Weyers, J. and others. *Practical Skills in the Biomolecular Sciences*. Addison Wesley Longman, Harlow, 1998. (For protein determination.)

Sodium hydroxide   DNS   Sodium hydroxide
                                       with sodium carbonate

✓ **Application of number:** Throughout this exercise you will be measuring the masses and volumes of solids and liquids. You will need to draw calibration curves and to use them to calculate the concentrations of the various compounds in your solutions. Then you need to interpret the results.

✓ **Information technology:** The calibration curves might be best drawn on a computer.

Perception of sweetness in drinks and foods[BM]

Thousands of molecules are known to taste sweet, but only about 20 of them are permitted for use in food and drinks. Interestingly, sweetness is not restricted to any one class of biochemicals. Sweet molecules are found within **monosaccharides** (the various sugars), **peptides** (e.g. aspartame), **sulphimides** (e.g. saccharin) and other classes.

Guidance

1 Obtain a range of natural sweet substances, for example glucose, lactose and sucrose, and artificial sweeteners such as Canderel, Hermesetas and Sweetex.
2 Working in pairs, devise a method for comparing the relative sweetness of these compounds. This is likely to involve dissolving the substances in warm drinking water at a range of concentrations and carrying out taste tests.
3 Pay special attention to safety. Should the subject spit out the solution after tasting it, or swallow it? How should the palate be cleared before the next tasting?
4 Before undertaking your investigation, check your procedure with your teacher/lecturer.

For consideration

1 Draw up a table indicating the approximate comparative sweetness of the products that you have tested.
2 Are there any differences in taste between the compounds, aside from their sweetness?
3 Examine the ingredients lists of diet and non-diet soft drinks. Are there differences in the sweeteners used in these two types of products? If so, why do you think that this is?
4 What information did the tests provide about differences between humans in their ability to taste sweetness?

Reference

Birch, G. Sweet molecules. *Biological Sciences Review*, **9** (5), 39–41, 1997. (For background information on sweet molecules.)

Requirements

Disposable cups
Weighing scales (to 0.1 g)
Thermometer
Warm drinking water
Range of sweet molecules and sweeteners, e.g. glucose, lactose, sucrose, Canderel, Hermesetas, Sweetex
Cans (empty or full) of a range of diet and non-diet drinks

Analysis of the amino acids in a protein by paper chromatography

The purpose of this practical is to find which amino acids are present in the protein, albumen (egg white). The protein is first hydrolysed by treating it with the digestive enzyme, trypsin. The amino acids are then separated and identified by **paper chromatography**.

The principle behind paper chromatography is as follows. A small amount of solvent is put at the bottom of a jar. A strip of absorptive paper, with a concentrated spot of the mixed amino acids towards the bottom, is suspended in the jar so that its end dips into the solvent. The latter moves slowly up the strip of paper, carrying the amino acids with

This exercise extends over more than one practical session.

Butan-1-ol

Butan-1-ol

it. As the amino acids travel at different speeds, they separate from one another. The paper is then treated with a reagent that stains the amino acids so that they can be detected and identified.

Note: Chromatography solvents are usually highly flammable. Extinguish Bunsen burners.

Procedure

This experiment takes several days, so it is advisable to draw up a timetable.

1 To break down the protein, half fill a test tube with the trypsin solution provided. Then add the protein: either 2 g of egg white, or 5.0 cm³ of albumen. Finally, add a crystal of thymol to kill bacteria. Leave the mixture to incubate at 30 °C for 48–72 hours.

2 In a fume cupboard, pour the solvent into the jar to a depth of 3 cm. Put the lid on the jar so that the atmosphere inside becomes saturated with vapour.

3 Wash and dry your hands to remove amino acids. Handling the paper as little as possible, cut a strip of chromatography paper long enough for one end to dip into the solvent to a depth of about 5 mm, and the other end to stick out of the top of the jar by about 2 cm.

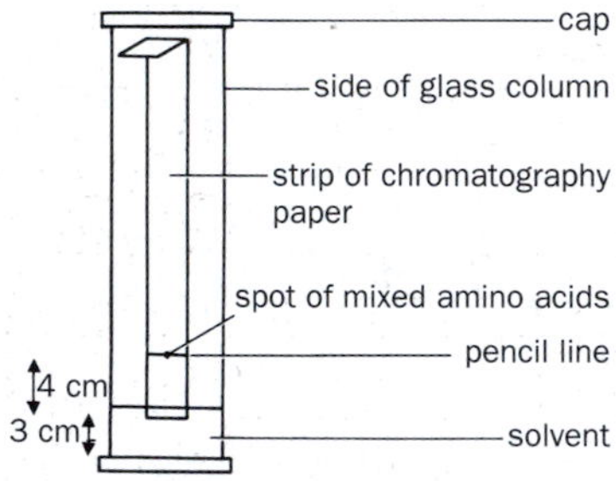

4 Draw a pencil line across the strip 4 cm from one end. Using a fine pipette, place a small drop of the amino acid mixture in the middle of the pencil line. Let this dry, place another drop on top of the first and dry again. Repeat this about six times, keeping the spot as small as possible.

5 Lower the strip carefully into the glass jar so that the bottom end dips about 5 mm into the solvent. Then bend the top end over and attach it to the lid (Figure 1.2). Leave the apparatus for 8–16 hours.

6 After 8–16 hours, remove the strip from the jar; the solvent should have risen 20–25 cm from the pencil line. Draw another line across the strip at the highest point reached by the solvent. Then hang the strip in a warm place to dry.

cap
side of glass column
strip of chromatography paper
spot of mixed amino acids
pencil line
4 cm
3 cm
solvent

Figure 1.2 Diagram of paper chromatography apparatus for the separation of amino acids.

Gloves should be worn

Ninhydrin   Ninhydrin    Ninhydrin

Developing the chromatogram

7 Developing the chromatogram involves staining the amino acids. This is done by means of a dilute solution of ninhydrin in butan-1-ol. Use a fume cupboard, wear gloves, and make sure that you do not spill the ninhydrin. Pour a small amount of the ninhydrin reagent into a glass crystallising dish and slowly draw the chromatography paper through the liquid. Ensure that the whole of the area between the two pencil lines is thoroughly soaked.

8 Dry the strip rapidly by holding it close to a source of heat, for example a hair dryer. Do not use a Bunsen flame; ninhydrin is flammable. If you continue to heat the strip after it is dry, purple spots will appear along its length. Continue heating until the colour in the spots is as dense as possible.

Interpreting the chromatogram

9 Each purple spot corresponds to one or more amino acids. To identify them, we make use of a measurement called the R_f, which stands for 'relative front'. This is the ratio of the distance moved by the spot to the distance moved by the solvent:

$$R_f = \frac{\text{distance moved by spot}}{\text{distance moved by solvent}}$$

10 Draw a horizontal line through each spot and calculate its R_f value. By comparing your R_f values with those listed in Table 1.1, try to identify the amino acid responsible for each spot in your chromatogram. On a separate sheet of paper, write down the name of each amino acid, together with its measured R_f value.

For consideration

1 According to your analysis, how many different amino acids occur in albumen?
2 Albumen is known to contain 15 amino acids (see Table 1.2). List several reasons why they do not all appear on your chromatogram.
3 Some of the spots are so close together that it is impossible to distinguish between them. How could you extend the chromatographic technique in order to show them?

Table 1.2 The amino acids present in the protein albumen (egg white), listed in order of decreasing concentration

Amino acid	Approximate % in albumen
Glutamic acid	16.5
Aspartic acid	9.3
Leucine	9.2
Serine	8.2
Phenylalanine	7.7
Valine	7.1
Isoleucine	7.0
Alanine	6.7
Lysine	6.3
Arginine	5.7
Methionine	5.2
Threonine	4.0
Tyrosine	3.7
Proline	3.6
Glycine	3.1

Table 1.1 The amino acids present in the protein albumen (egg white), listed in order of R_f value (in this solvent only)

Amino acid	R_f value
Lysine	0.14
Arginine	0.20
Aspartic acid	0.24
Glycine	0.26
Serine	0.27
Glutamic acid	0.30
Threonine	0.35
Alanine	0.38
Proline	0.43 (yellow)
Tyrosine	0.45
Methionine	0.55
Valine	0.60
Phenylalanine	0.68
Isoleucine	0.72
Leucine	0.73

Requirements

Fume cupboard
Boiling tube
Glass jar (approximately 40 cm high, 7 cm diameter; gas jar recommended)
Lid for glass jar
Strip of chromatography paper (about 40 × 2 cm)
Pencil and ruler
Dropping pipette with fine point
Measuring cylinder (10 cm³)
Adhesive
Kitchen gloves
Crystallising dish (12.5 cm diameter)
Hair dryer or small convector heater
Trypsin solution (10 cm³) (Note 1)
Thymol crystal
Solvent, 200 cm³ (Note 2)
Distilled water
Ninhydrin solution (sufficient to fill crystallising dish to a depth of 1 cm) (Note 3)
Egg white (2 g) or fluid albumen (5 cm³)

Trypsin

Ninhydrin

Glacial acetic acid

Notes: Making up solvent and solutions

1 Trypsin solution: Dissolve 2.0 g of trypsin in 100 cm³ of 1.0% sodium hydrogencarbonate.
2 Solvent: Mix 4 parts of butan-1-ol, 1 part of glacial acetic acid and 1 part of distilled water.
3 Ninhydrin reagent: make up a 1.0% solution of ninhydrin in butan-1-ol.

Separation of the pigments in red cabbage by two-way chromatography

This exercise extends over more than one session.

In Practical Exercise 1.6 (p. 25) and Technique 2.39 (p. 113), **chromatography** is often carried out 'one way'. This means that the substances are separated in just one dimension. However, this does not always separate the substances sufficiently for them to be readily identified. **Two-way chromatography** involves first separating the substances along one dimension, and then turning the chromatography paper through 90° and using another solvent to separate the substances further. In this practical you will use two-way chromatography to separate the pigments in red cabbage leaves.

Procedure

Carefully read Practical Exercise 1.6 (p. 25) and Technique 2.39 (p. 113). We suggest that you base your procedure on a refined version of Technique 2.39 (p. 113), but using red cabbage leaves rather than nettle leaves. Proceed as follows:

1   Homogenise 20 g of the red cabbage leaves and 200 cm³ of methanolic hydrochloric acid (1% concentrated hydrochloric acid in methanol) in a blender. Filter the homogenate.
2   Prepare a 10 × 10 cm sheet of chromatography or filter paper and a chromatography tank or other suitable closed container.
3   For your first solvent use a mixture of butan-1-ol, acetic acid and water. Let the chromatogram develop until the solvent has moved approximately 7 cm beyond the sample application line.
4   Remove the chromatography or filter paper from the tank and allow it to dry thoroughly. Remove the first solvent from the tank.
5   Turn the paper through 90° and for your second solvent use a mixture of propanone and petroleum ether.

For consideration

1   What is the advantage of using a second solvent after the chromatography paper has been turned through 90°?
2   How might the results differ if you reversed the order in which you used the two solvents?

Reference

Neilson, L. R. & Harley, S. M. Chemotaxonomy: simple tests for distinguishing between anthocyanins and betacyanins. *Journal of Biological Education*, **30**, 88–90, 1996.

Hydrochloric acid
Ethanoic acid

Methanol
Butan-1-ol
Propanone
Petroleum ether

Methanol

Butan-1-ol
Petroleum ether

Eye protection must be worn

Requirements

Blender
Filter funnel
Muslin *or* filter paper
Beaker (250 cm³)
Chromatography tank or other suitable closed container
10 × 10 cm sheet of silica-coated chromatography *or* filter paper
Goggles
Methanolic hydrochloric acid (200 cm³) – 1% concentrated (35–38%) hydrochloric acid in methanol
First solvent (mixture of butan-1-ol: glacial acetic acid:water in the ratio 4:1:5 (v/v/v))
Second solvent (1 part 90% propanone (acetone) to 9 parts petroleum ether (boiling point 80–100 °C))
Red cabbage leaves

Note: For the first solvent, mix the three liquids, allow the phases to separate, and use only the upper phase to a depth of about 1.5 cm in the tank.

One aim of this experiment is to determine which amino acids occur in casein, the major protein in milk. Another is to illustrate **paper electrophoresis**, an important technique for separating and identifying organic compounds in mixtures.

When a mixture of amino acids is placed on moist filter paper between two electrodes, and the current is switched on, the amino acids with no net charge will stay in place, the positively charged molecules will move towards the negative electrode, and the negatively charged molecules will move towards the positive electrode. When the current is switched off, the paper is dried and treated with a reagent that stains the amino acids so that they can be located and identified. To aid identification, solutions of known amino acids should be included in the experiment.

This exercise extends over more than one practical session.

Procedure

1 Take a 30 × 10 cm sheet of filter paper. Handle it carefully at the edges; do not finger the main bulk of the paper. Rule a pencil line across it halfway down, 15 cm from either end. Starting 1 cm from the edge, make nine pencil dots on this line, each 1 cm apart. Number these dots 1–9.

2 Dissolve 5 g of casein hydrolysate in 10 cm³ of water in a test tube. Stopper the test tube and shake thoroughly. After 5 minutes, use a dropping pipette with a fine point to pipette drops of this solution onto dots 3 and 6. Do not let the spots become larger than 3 mm in diameter.

3 Dry the spots by placing the paper some distance from a blow heater. Then add another drop of casein hydrolysate to each spot. Repeat this procedure another eight times.

4 Using a separate clean pipette in each case, add solutions of pure amino acids to the remaining dots as follows:
1 – arginine, 2 – lysine, 4 – glycine, 5 – aspartic acid, 7 – glutamic acid, 8 – valine, 9 – tryptophan. For each dot, about 10 applications of amino acid solution are needed.

5 To moisten the filter paper, first place some buffer solution in a crystallising dish in a fume cupboard. Draw both ends of the filter paper through the buffer so that the paper is wetted at both ends up to 2 cm from the pencil line, but remains dry in the centre.

6 Set up the paper in a tank as shown in Figure 1.3. Moisten the centre of the paper, but not the spots themselves, with buffer solution from a dropping pipette. Replace the top of the tank firmly.

7 Connect the electrodes to a 12–300 V d.c. supply. Run the current for half an hour (high voltage) or several hours (low voltage).

8 Switch off the current. Remove the paper from the jar, and hang it up to dry in a warm fume cupboard.

9 When the electrophoretogram is dry, you can stain it. In a fume cupboard, pour a small amount of ninhydrin solution into a glass crystallising dish. Slowly draw the electrophoresis paper through the liquid. Ensure that the whole of the area of the paper is thoroughly

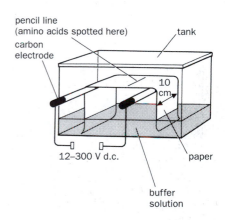

pencil line
(amino acids spotted here)
carbon electrode
tank
10 cm
12–300 V d.c.
paper
buffer solution

Figure 1.3 One type of apparatus for paper electrophoresis. Whatever the apparatus, the charged compounds to be separated are placed between the electrodes on a moist medium in a buffer solution that conducts electricity.

Current   Ninhydrin

Ninhydrin   Ninhydrin

Gloves should be worn

soaked. Then dry the paper in the fume cupboard and observe the stained amino acids.

10 Write (in pencil) alongside each spot the name of its amino acid.

11 List the amino acids that occur in casein.

For consideration

1 There are known to be 17 different amino acids in casein. Why do they not all appear in your electrophoretogram?

2 One possible answer to the previous question is that all the amino acids occur in your electrophoretogram, but some of the spots are so close to one another that it is impossible to distinguish between them. How could you extend the technique in order to investigate this possibility?

3 How do the charges on amino acid molecules originate?

4 If you altered the pH of the solution, would the pattern of spots obtained be the same? Explain your answer carefully.

5 Electrophoresis is frequently used to separate whole protein molecules. In protein synthesis, the amino groups of one amino acid join to the carboxylic acid groups of the next. Why then are proteins charged?

Reference

Brown, G. D. & Creedy, J. *Experimental Biology Manual*. Heinemann Educational, London, 1970.

Requirements

Fume cupboard
Electrophoresis apparatus with power supply
Chromatography or filter paper
Crystallising dish (diameter 12 cm or more)
Hair dryer or convector heater
Dropping pipettes (with fine points) ×10
Pencil and ruler
Glass beakers (50 cm³) ×8
Amino acids
Buffer solution (pH 3.6) (Note 1)
Ninhydrin solution (sufficient to fill crystallising dish to depth of 1 cm) (Note 2)
Casein hydrolysate (available from suppliers)

Notes: Making up solutions

1 Buffer solution: Carefully add 13.8 g of glacial acetic acid and 1.5 g of pyridine to 234.7 g of distilled water.

2 Ninhydrin reagent: Mix 200 mg of ninhydrin in 100 cm³ of propanone.

Propanone   Pyridine   Glacial ethanoic acid

1.9 INVESTIGATION

Vitamin C content of various fruits

Vitamin C prevents the deficiency disease scurvy, and is particularly abundant in citrus fruits such as oranges, lemons and limes. In this investigation you can compare the vitamin C contents of different fruits (or any other foodstuff) by a simple colour test, the decolourisation of the blue dye dichlorophenolindolephenol (**DCPIP**). Vitamin C is an antioxidant, and reduces DCPIP to a colourless solution (pink in the case of some fruits – it is the disappearance of the blue colour that you should look for).

First you estimate the volume of a known concentration of vitamin C solution required to decolourise 2 cm³ of a DCPIP solution. Then you determine the volume of fruit juice that decolourises 2 cm³ of DCPIP solution. This provides an estimate of the concentration of vitamin C in fruit juice, in units of 1 mg (see Guidance). This figure is then multiplied by the volume of the fruit to obtain its total vitamin C content.

DCPIP   DCPIP

Guidance

Using a pipette, add the vitamin C solution, drop by drop, to $2\,cm^3$ of the DCPIP solution in a test tube. Shake the tube gently after the addition of each drop and continue to add drops until the DCPIP solution is decolourised. Record the exact volume of vitamin C you added. Repeat the procedure and average the results.

You can now calculate the mass of vitamin C that is required to decolourise $2\,cm^3$ of DCPIP solution, knowing that the vitamin C solution was made up to contain 1 mg of vitamin C in $1.0\,cm^3$ of water.

Repeat this procedure with the fruit juice provided. This contains vitamin C at *unknown* concentration. If only one or two drops of fruit juice are required to decolourise DCPIP, dilute the juice five times and try again.

Using the same technique, compare the vitamin C contents of several different fruits or vegetables.

To determine the volume of your fruit, put it in a beaker and cover it with water. Mark the level of the meniscus on the outside of the beaker. Remove the fruit, make the water up to the mark with water from a measuring cylinder. The volume of water you add is equivalent to the volume of the fruit.

For consideration

1 Vitamin C (ascorbic acid) is derived from a 6-carbon sugar. Suggest why it is so abundant in fruits and vegetables. What functions might it serve?
2 List all the sources of error you can think of in calculating the vitamin C content of a fruit merely from its concentration in fruit juice and the volume of the fruit.
3 A typical adult human needs about 10 mg of vitamin C a day to prevent scurvy, and the British government recommends a daily intake of about 30 mg. To what extent can these needs be met by a single lemon or orange?

Requirements

Beaker ($100\,cm^3$)
Beaker ($500\,cm^3$)
Container to collect a small volume of lemon juice
Measuring cylinder ($250\,cm^3$)
Pipette or syringe to measure $2\,cm^3$ volume
Pipette or syringe to measure accurately volumes up to $1\,cm^3$
Test tube
Spatula
Distilled water ($50\,cm^3$)
Vitamin C (0.1%, fresh; 0.1% is 1 mg per cm^3 or l g per litre)
DCPIP (1% aqueous solution, freshly made up)
Fruit juice (for trying out the DCPIP test)
Fruits and vegetables

Assessment

- **Plan** your investigation. Do you have a testable hypothesis?
- **Implement** your plan. Make sure that you have taken enough repeated measurements on the same fruit juice to have confidence in your estimate of the average. If the endpoint is unclear, be prepared to dilute the fruit juice by a known factor.

- **Analyse your evidence** and **draw conclusions**. Take care over the calculations. If possible, use a t-test to test your hypothesis (see Statistical Analysis Appendix, p. 304).
- **Evaluate** your investigation. List limitations of the experimental techniques used and discuss the influence of these on your results.

Effect of storage on the presence of sugars and vitamin C

1.10 INVESTIGATION

Much of our food is stored for a long time before it reaches the shop counter, and even afterwards. What effect does this have on its content of vitamin C, sugars and other important constituents? You can find out

This exercise extends over more than one practical session.

by testing stored food and comparing it with fresh food. For instance, you can compare the vitamin C contents of fruit juices sold commercially with those of juice freshly extracted from fruits. Other food sources rich in vitamin C are spinach and peas.

You can also compare the effects of leaving food to decay naturally and of treating it in various ways – for example heating to different temperatures for different periods of time, chilling, refrigeration, deep freezing and/or pickling.

Guidance

If you are comparing, for example, the concentrations of compounds in fresh juice with those in commercial fruit juice, long-term pre-planning is unnecessary. However, if you want to find the effect of treating food, you may have to decide on a strategy for treating some of the food, and apply the treatment well before the practical session in which you carry out the analyses. Arrange things so that by *the start* of the analysis session all the foodstuffs are available to be analysed at the same time, and that your teacher or lecturer is aware of the equipment you need.

As you plan your investigation, bear in mind the principles of experimental design. One measurement per treatment is not enough. Take about four measurements for each treatment, so that you have the basis of a t-test to compare different treatments statistically (see Statistical Analysis Appendix, p.304). The number of different treatments that you can test is limited by the length of your practical session, but if different pairs work together and pool results, more can be accomplished.

You require the DCPIP test for vitamin C (Investigation 1.9, p.30). If no colorimeter is available, you will have to use Benedict's test for reducing sugars (Technique 1.2, p.20) and either compare the quantity of precipitate by eye, or be prepared to dry and weigh it. If, however, you have access to a colorimeter, the quantitative test for reducing sugars (Practical Exercise 1.4, p.23) is more rapid, convenient, objective and accurate.

For consideration

1 Explain the differences in concentration of vitamin C, reducing sugars or other constituents that you have tested in terms of the treatments to which the foods have been subjected.
2 What implications do these results have for the quality of the diet? How might the situation be improved?

Requirements

The analytical reagents required are listed under the relevant practicals: Investigation 1.9 (p.30) for vitamin C, Technique 1.2 (p.19) for food tests, including Benedict's test for reducing sugars, and Practical Exercise 1.4 (p.22) for quantitative food tests.

Key skills

✓ **Working with others:** In planning this investigation, you need to discuss with others which treatments to apply, who should carry out which tests, how many tests can be accomplished in the time available, and how you should pool the results at the end.

✓ **Application of number:** Once you have the individual results for each treatment, you will need to average them and to carry out a statistical test (e.g. a t-test) to determine whether or not the means are significantly different.

One of the best places from which to obtain animal cells for viewing under the microscope is the **epithelium** lining various organs in the body of a mammal. If the organ is a solid one, such as the kidney, the epithelium lining its outside may be used. In the case of hollow or tubular organs, such as the trachea, the epithelium lining the inside can be used.

The purpose of this investigation is to examine cells obtained from such sources in an attempt to build up a picture of a typical animal cell.

Guidance

Samples of epithelium can usually be removed by gently scraping the surface of the organ with a scalpel blade. The tissue thus obtained should be mounted in a drop of stain on a slide. A suitable stain is **methylene blue**.

Try taking scrapings from, for example, the inner surface of the trachea of sheep or pig. See if you can detect any cells. If you can, examine them under high power, using oil immersion if possible. Try other organs if available.

In some cases, for example the cornea of the eye, the epithelial cells come away so readily that all you need to do is touch the surface of a dry slide with the organ. Try this with a sheep's or pig's eye. Cells adhering to the slide may then be immersed in a drop of methylene blue and covered with a coverslip. (The eyes of cattle should not be used because of the slight theoretical risk of transmitting bovine spongiform encephalopathy (BSE).)

If you wish to examine human cells, the best source is the inner surface of the cheek. *To avoid possible transmission of disease, cheek cell sampling should be carried out only under the close supervision of a teacher or lecturer, using a sterile procedure such as that in Technique 1.12 (p. 34).*

Another source of human cells is the base of a hair. The cells come away with the hair when it is plucked.

A typical epithelial cell from the human cheek is shown in Figure 1.4. How do the cells that you have studied in this investigation differ from this one?

Mount a sample of epithelial cells in water instead of methylene blue. What difference does this make to how much you can see? Try observing the cells with dark ground illumination and, if available, phase contrast.

For consideration

1 How were your observations of animal cells helped by (a) staining and (b) different kinds of microscopy?

2 Were any structures shown in Figure 1.4 absent from the animal cells you looked at? If they were, suggest reasons.

References

Lewis, J. G. E. & Chester, M. F. Bullock's corneal cells: an alternative to human cheek cells. *School Science Review*, **70** (252), 74, 1989. (The instructions can be applied equally to sheep's or pig's eyes.)

Wells, J. Observing cells in plucked hair follicles. *Journal of Biological Education*, **25**, 3–4, 1991.

Biohazard

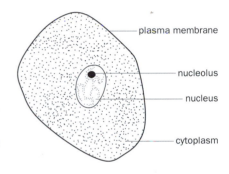

plasma membrane

nucleolus

nucleus

cytoplasm

Figure 1.4 A squamous epithelial cell from the inner lining of the human cheek, as seen under high power of the light microscope after staining with methylene blue.

Requirements

Microscope, if possible with phase contrast and/or oil immersion
Slides and coverslips
Scalpel
Methylene blue, 1%
Trachea of sheep or pig
Eye of sheep or pig
Other mammalian organs, as available

Note: Trachea and eyes of sheep and/or pig are available from the abattoir or butcher. Eyes can be refrigerated for up to 4 days beforehand. One eye is sufficient for making 10 slides.

Cheek cell sampling

The following safe procedure is recommended by the Institute of Biology. It should be carried out only under the close supervision of a teacher or lecturer.

Cheek cells

Sodium hypochlorite

1 Take a cotton bud from a newly opened pack.
2 Move the cotton bud over the inside of the cheek on one side of the mouth and along the outer lower side of the gum.
3 Smear the cotton bud over a small area of a clean microscope slide.
4 Place the used cotton bud immediately in a small volume of 1% sodium hypochlorite in a suitable container (e.g. $5\,cm^3$ of hypochlorite solution in a $10\,cm^3$ specimen tube).
5 Place 3 drops of 1% methylene blue from a teat pipette onto the smear and cover with a coverslip.
6 Observe the smear under the low power magnification of a microscope. When the cells are in focus, increase the power of the objective to achieve maximum magnification and resolution. The cytoplasm will be stained pale blue and the nucleus will be stained a darker blue.
7 After the cells have been observed, immerse the slide and coverslip in a beaker of laboratory disinfectant.
8 The teacher or lecturer or laboratory technician should place the used cotton buds in a polythene bag, which should be sealed and then disposed of in accordance with local regulations governing the disposal of laboratory waste.
9 Slides and coverslips should be washed thoroughly, dried and reused according to normal practice.

If the above safe procedure is followed, there are absolutely no reasons why any student, teacher or lecturer should be exposed to the risk of infection by the transmission of pathogens.

Requirements

Cotton bud, sealed
Slide and coverslip
Teat pipette
Sodium hypochlorite, $5\,cm^3$ of 1% in a $10\,cm^3$ specimen tube
Methylene blue, 1%
Disinfectant, in beaker
Polythene bag

Examination of plant cells

Plants provide excellent material for the study of cells. However, the features found in plant cells cannot all be seen in one cell. It is necessary to look at several different types of plant cell in order to build up a complete picture. This is what we shall do in this practical exercise. Before you start, it is useful to have in mind a theoretical concept of what a generalised plant cell looks like (Figure 1.5).

Procedure

1 Strip off a piece of epidermis from the inner lining of one of the fleshy scales of an onion, mount it in dilute iodine solution and observe one cell under low and high powers. Observe the granular cytoplasm surrounding the clear vacuole. The nucleus is located in the cytoplasm close to the cell wall.
2 Repeat step 1, but this time mount the piece of epidermis in water instead of dilute iodine solution. What difference does this make to

how much you can see? What does this tell you about the value of staining cells before you look at them under the microscope?

3   Open up one of the flowers of *Tradescantia* and remove a stamen. Mount the stamen in water and examine one of the hairs under high power. Adjust the illumination carefully or, better still, use phase contrast. The hair is a single cell. The nucleus is suspended in the centre of the cell by thin bridles of cytoplasm (Figure 1.6). Streaming of the cytoplasm, indicated by the movement of granules, can some-times be seen in these bridles and in the peripheral cytoplasm.

4   Neither of the cells examined so far contains chloroplasts. To see these organelles, mount a small leaf of moss in water and examine its cells under high power. The cells are so packed with chloroplasts that little else can be seen. What gives the chloroplasts their green colour?

5   Many plant cells store starch in the form of starch grains. Nowhere can these be better seen than in a potato tuber. Scrape some tissue from the cut surface of a potato tuber and mount it in water. Observe starch grains under low and high powers. They can be stained with dilute iodine solution by a technique called **irrigation** (Figure 1.7). Watch the starch grains turn blue as the stain moves across the slide. The starch grains are located inside tightly packed cells, the cell walls of which can just be seen. How would you describe the shape of these cells?

6   To see details of the cell wall, you need to examine cells with excep-tionally thick walls. Such cells can be seen in a transverse section of a pine needle (Figure 1.8). Layers of cellulose making up the secondary walls should be visible. The thin line between the cell walls of adjacent cells is the **middle lamella**. What does it consist of? Notice fine channels traversing the cell walls. They contain **plasmodesmata**, which connect adjacent cells.

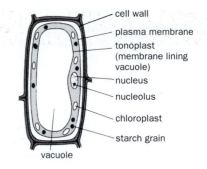

Figure 1.5 Drawing of a generalised plant cell. In reality there is no gap between the cell wall and plasma membrane: normally, the plasma membrane presses against the inner side of the cell wall, and it is so thin (8 μm) that it cannot be seen as a definite line.

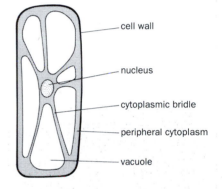

Figure 1.6 Staminal hair cell of *Tradescantia*, showing how the nucleus is suspended in the centre of the cell.

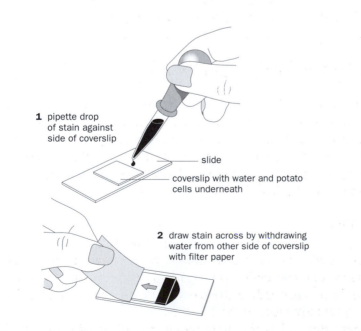

1   pipette drop of stain against side of coverslip

slide

coverslip with water and potato cells underneath

2   draw stain across by withdrawing water from other side of coverslip with filter paper

Figure 1.7 The technique of irrigation in which a stain is introduced under a coverslip.

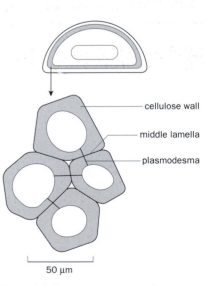

50 μm

Figure 1.8 Transverse section of a pine needle, showing where you can find cells with exceptionally thick walls.

For consideration

1 If you want to see the nuclei of plant cells it is better to look at onion cells rather than potato or moss leaf cells. Why?

2 There is no such thing as a typical plant cell. Explain.

3 Which structures, visible in typical plant cells, are absent from typical animal cells?

4 Suggest possible disadvantages of staining cells before viewing them under the microscope.

1.14 INVESTIGATION

The fine structure of cells

The **electron microscope** is much more powerful than the **light microscope**, but exactly how much more detail of cells does it reveal? In this investigation you will have an opportunity to find out.

Guidance

You will be given prepared slides of a transverse section of mammalian liver and a transverse section of a leaf.

Examine the slides under the light microscope, first under low power then high power. Concentrate on one particular cell; in the leaf, concentrate on a palisade cell, in the upper half of the leaf (see Figure 2.28, p. 112). Make a careful record of what you can, and cannot, see. If it is

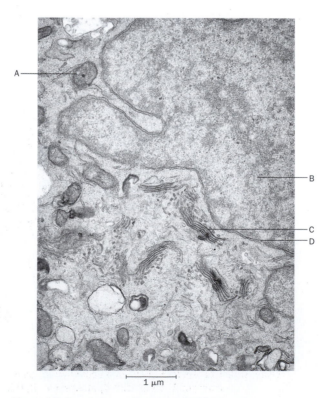

1 µm

Figure 1.9 An electron micrograph of part of a liver cell.

available, try using oil immersion to see if that helps. For an interpretation of the structures which you should be able to detect, see Figure 1.4 (p.33) and Figure 1.5 (p.35).

Then look at the electron micrographs in Figures 1.9–1.12. Identify as many structures and organelles as you can, using Figures 1.13–1.15 to

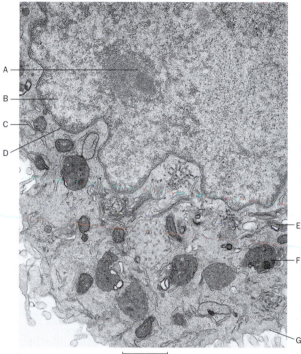

1 μm

Figure 1.10 Electron micrograph of a B lymphocyte cell from a chicken cell line.

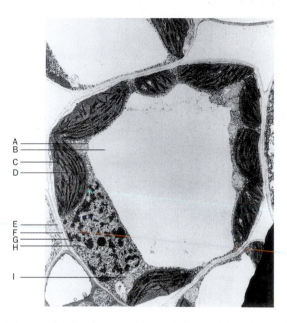

Figure 1.11 An electron micrograph (× 28, 800) of part of a photosynthetic cell from the leaf of the grass *Phleum pratense*. Can you identify the parts of the cell labelled A–I?

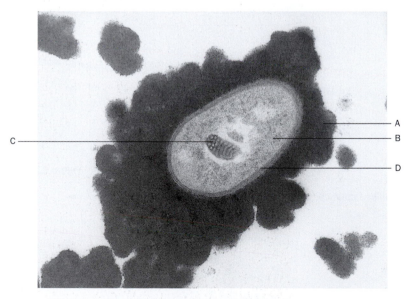

Figure 1.12 Electron micrograph of a bacterium. **A**, Slime capsule; **B**, cytoplasm; **C**, mesosome; **D**, cell membrane.

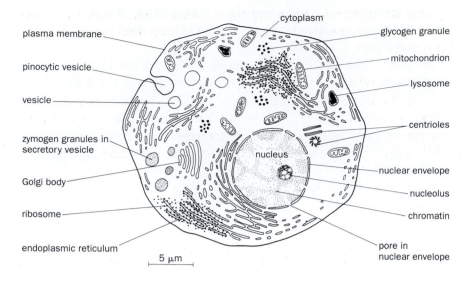

Figure 1.13 Diagram of a generalised animal cell as seen with the electron microscope.

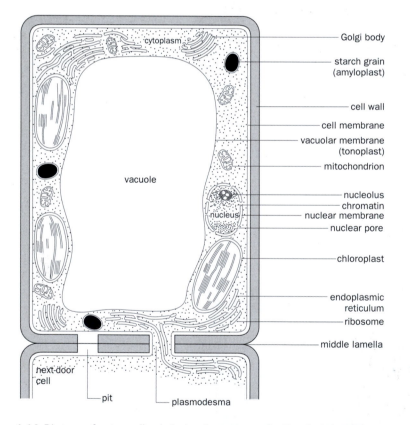

Figure 1.14 Diagram of a generalised plant cell as seen under the electron microscope.

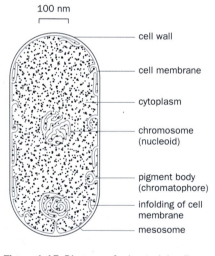

Figure 1.15 Diagram of a bacterial cell as seen under the electron microscope.

help you. By how many times are the animal and plant cells in Figures 1.9 and 1.11 more magnified in the electron micrograph than under your light microscope?

For consideration

1   Using the most effective method of presentation you can think of, compare the information about the structure of a cell provided by the electron microscope with that provided by the light microscope.
2   What are the advantages and disadvantages of examining cells with an electron microscope?
3   The detail revealed by the electron microscope is due to its *resolving power*. Explain.

Getting the best out of your microscope   1.15 TECHNIQUE

An immense amount of information can be obtained from the light microscope, but only if it is used properly. Its parts are shown in the Illustration. However, different types of microscope differ in their features. For example, some have built-in illumination and lack a mirror and/or condenser.

When setting up your microscope, start by cleaning the lenses. Then focus the object with correct illumination under low power. Then focus the object with correct illumination under high power. Practise using your microscope by examining a prepared slide of, for example, epithelial tissue. Proceed as follows.

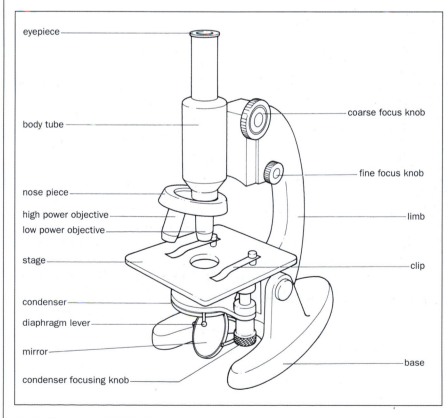

eyepiece
coarse focus knob
body tube
fine focus knob
nose piece
high power objective
low power objective
limb
stage
clip
condenser
diaphragm lever
mirror
base
condenser focusing knob

Illustration A typical light microscope.

Cleaning the lenses

A common reason why students fail to see things clearly under the microscope is that the lenses are dirty. So make sure that both the **eyepiece** and **objective lenses** are clean. Dirt and moisture should be removed by gently wiping them with **lens paper**. If necessary, remove the eyepiece and objectives from the microscope first, and moisten them if they are very dirty. **The condenser lens** should also be clean, as should the slide that you are going to examine.

Low power

Focusing

1 Rotate the **coarse focus knob** until the objective lenses are about 2 cm above the stage. Rotate the **nose piece** so that the low power objective lens is in line with the body tube. It should click into place.
2 Put the slide to be examined on the stage. Ensure that the object to be viewed is in the centre of the aperture in the stage, immediately beneath the objective lens. Clip the slide in position with both clips.
3 Looking at the microscope from the side, rack down the coarse focus until the low power objective is about 5 mm above the slide.
4 Now look down the microscope and rack the coarse focus upwards until the object is in focus.

Adjusting the illumination

The following instructions are based on microscopes which have a mirror and condenser and an external source of illumination.

1 Decide what source of light to use. The best source is natural daylight or a diffuse bulb. The whole field of view should be evenly illuminated. If a filament lamp is used, interpose a thin sheet of white paper between the bulb and the microscope.
2 The mirror has a flat side and a concave side. Using the flat side, adjust the angle of the mirror so that light from the source is transmitted through the microscope.
3 Focus the condenser. The purpose of the condenser is to bring rays of light from a wide angle to bear on the object. To focus the condenser, adjust its height until an object such as a pencil placed in front of the source of light, reflected by the mirror, is seen in focus at the same time as the object on the microscope slide.
4 If your microscope does not have a condenser, or if the condenser is not in use, use the concave side of the mirror to focus the light.
5 Open or close the **diaphragm** to the correct extent. The condenser should be used with the diaphragm as wide open as possible, without admitting too great an intensity of light. The definition of the image will then be at its best. If it is not possible to open the diaphragm widely without admitting too much light, place a sheet of white paper between the microscope and the lamp.

Caution

When looking down the microscope, never rack downwards to focus an object unless you know for certain that by focusing downwards only a very short distance the image will come into view. If you rack downwards, you run the risk of hitting the coverslip with the objective lens.

Caution

Always use the condenser focused. Never use the condenser with the concave mirror. The condenser lenses are designed to give optimum illumination only when focused with the flat mirror.

Caution

A common cause of poor definition is that the object is over-illuminated. Better definition is often obtained by cutting down the light, not by increasing it.

High power

1   Once the object is well defined under low power, move the slide so that the area which you want to observe in detail is in the centre of the field of view.
2   Rotate the nose piece until the high power objective clicks into place. The object should automatically come into focus, at least approximately. If it is not in focus, look at the microscope from the side and rack the fine adjustment downwards until the lens is about 1 mm from the slide. Then look down the microscope and focus by racking up.
3   With the object in view down the microscope, adjust the mirror and diaphragm until the illumination is correct and maximum clarity is obtained.

Magnification

The total magnification is the magnification of the eyepiece lens multiplied by the magnification of the objective lens. By using different combinations of lenses, different magnifications can be obtained.

Don't use a higher power than is necessary. More can be made out under low power with good illumination than under high power with poor illumination. Also, the larger the region of the object viewed, the easier it is to interpret what you see.

Identifying faults

If good definition is not obtained, ask yourself:

*   Is the slide clean?
*   Is the objective centred?
*   Are the lenses clean?
*   Is the source of illumination satisfactory?
*   Is the condenser focused?
*   Is the diaphragm adjusted correctly?

Special techniques in microscopy   1.16 TECHNIQUE

Oil immersion

If you require a particularly high magnification, **oil immersion** may be used. Fluid with the same refractive index as the objective lens is placed between a special objective lens and the coverslip so that it touches both. The fluid permits a larger cone of light rays to enter the objective from the specimen, and this increases the resolving power obtainable.

The fluid is usually cedar wood oil. Place a drop of oil on the coverslip above the specimen, then lower the objective until the lens comes into contact with the oil. View the object with appropriate illumination in the usual way.

Dark ground illumination

For small transparent objects, it is often best to view the specimen as a bright object against a dark background. This involves using **dark**

ground illumination. In this technique the light illuminating the object must not enter the objective lens; the only light rays entering the microscope must be those which have been reflected or scattered by the object itself.

Dark ground illumination can be achieved by illuminating the object obliquely from above and/or by interposing an opaque stop in the centre of the condenser.

Try looking at live unicellular organisms with dark ground illumination.

Phase contrast

Transparent structures, because of slight differences in their density and refractive index, produce invisible changes of phase in the light that passes through them. In **phase contrast microscopy** these changes in phase are converted into corresponding changes of amplitude, resulting in a high-contrast image in which the distribution of light rays is related to the changes in phase. As no staining is necessary, this technique can be used for showing up transparent structures in living material that would otherwise be difficult or impossible to see. Examining an object with phase contrast involves having a special annular disc beneath the condenser and an objective fitted with a phase plate. Microscopes with built-in phase contrast equipment are available.

Requirements

Microscope
Phase contrast microscope, if available
Lamp
Slide and coverslip
Thin sheet of white paper
Lens paper
Oil immersion objective
Cedar wood oil
Prepared slide e.g. of epithelial tissue
Unicellular organisms, live, in mixed culture

Note: The phase contrast microscope is best set up as a demonstration.

Measuring the size of an object under the light microscope

Objects can be measured under the microscope by means of an **eyepiece graticule**. This is a transparent scale mounted in the focal plane of the eyepiece, so it can be seen in the field of view at the same time as an object is being examined under the microscope.

Obviously, to be of any use, the eyepiece graticule scale must be calibrated. This can be done by placing a **stage micrometer** under the microscope. This is a glass slide on which is etched a series of vertical lines separated by distances of 1.0 mm, 0.1 mm and 0.01 mm – rather like a miniature transparent ruler. By superimposing the images of the eyepiece graticule and stage micrometer scales, it is possible to calibrate the graticule, so that the size of a given object viewed under the microscope can be estimated.

When calibrating, adopt the following procedure. Place the stage micrometer on the stage of the microscope, and bring its lines into focus. Move the stage micrometer until one of its lines coincides with one of the numbered lines on the eyepiece graticule. Count the number of lines on the eyepiece graticule that fill the space between the line that you have selected on the stage micrometer and the next one.

If the distance between the two lines on the stage micrometer is $100 \mu m$, and it is found that x divisions on the eyepiece graticule scale exactly fill this space, then the value of one eyepiece division is $100/x \mu m$.

Requirements

Microscope
Eyepiece graticule
Stage micrometer

Note: Graticules are available from biological suppliers, consisting of a $100 \mu m$ scale printed on transparent film. This can be used as an eyepiece graticule and/or a stage micrometer.

You won't always have time to measure the sizes of objects that you look at under the microscope. However, it is a good idea to get into the habit of doing so when possible, and to indicate the scale of any drawings you make. For example, if you draw a cell 500 times its natural size, the scale of drawing is ×500, and this should be written by the drawing.

Another way of indicating the size of an object in a drawing is to put a line by the drawing corresponding to a particular length. This is called a scale bar; an example is shown in Figure 1.9 (p. 36).

✓ **Application of number:** In order to calculate the size of an object in this way, you will need to be able to handle ratios and powers of 10.

Examination of animal tissues

The main purpose of this practical is to look at different types of animal tissue and relate their structure to the functions they perform. A secondary purpose is to learn how to recognise different types of animal tissue.

To recognise a tissue, four main features need to be considered:

- The type(s) of cell making up the tissue
- The positions of the cells relative to each other
- The presence of non-cellular inclusions in the tissue
- The position of the tissue in the organ

As you look at different tissues, be aware of the extent to which you depend on these five features in learning to recognise them.

Procedure

Epithelial tissue

Epithelial tissue (**epithelium**) is found lining the surface of the body and the cavities and tubes within it. Recognition depends mainly on the shapes of the cells.

1   First familiarise yourself with the different types of epithelia that exist (Figure 1.16).
2   Now look at prepared slides of some of the following organs, here listed in alphabetical order: gall bladder, kidney, peritoneum, rectum, small intestine, thyroid gland, trachea. In each case identify the type(s) of epithelium visible. Indicate if the epithelium has any special features such as **cilia**, **brush border** or **secretory cells** (e.g. mucus-secreting goblet cells). Try to relate these special features to the functions of the organs. To what extent do the epithelia depart from the simple patterns shown in Figure 1.16A?

Connective tissue

Connective tissue fills the spaces between other tissues and binds one tissue with another. It consists of various types of cells and non-living

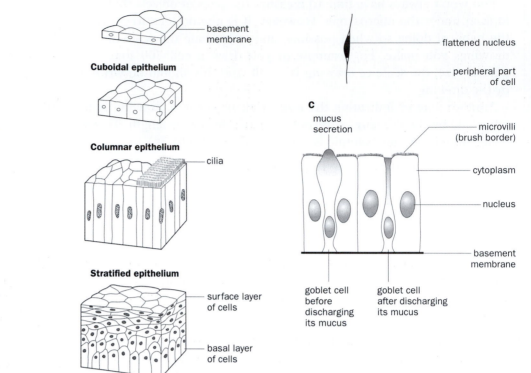

Figure 1.16 Epithelial tissue. **A** Four main types of epithelium found in humans and other mammals. Columnar epithelium is sometimes ciliated, as shown on the right-hand side of the drawing. **B** A squamous epithelial cell as it may appear in the wall of a capillary: the cells are so flat that, except in the region of the nucleus, they appear as no more than a thin line. **C** Detail of typical columnar epithelium, showing microvilli and goblet cells. The microvilli appear as a fuzzy line on the outer surface of the cells, the brush border. A brush border may also be visible on the surface of cuboidal epithelium. Goblet cells, so called because of their shape, secrete mucus.

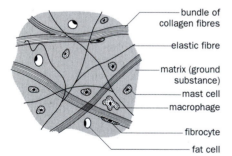

Figure 1.17 Areolar connective tissue as it appears in a typical microscopic preparation.

inclusions, and recognising different types of connective tissue depends on identifying these.

1   Examine a slide of **areolar tissue**, the weakest and most basic type of connective tissue. Use Figure 1.17 to help you identify its components. Note in particular the **collagen** and **elastic fibres**, which are widely dispersed in the gelatinous matrix (ground substance).

2   Examine longitudinal sections of a tendon and a ligament (Figure 1.18). In both cases the fibres are more densely packed than in areolar tissue and they lie parallel with one another. Tendons contain mainly collagen fibres, ligaments mainly elastic fibres. Relate this to the functions that tendons and ligaments perform in the human body.

3   Examine a section of adipose tissue. It consists almost entirely of densely packed **fat cells** (Figure 1.19). Whereabouts in the human body is this sort of tissue found, and what are its functions in these places?

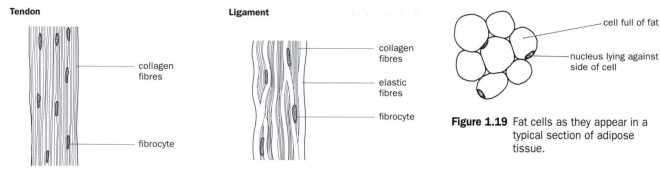

Figure 1.18 Longitudinal sections of tendon and ligament.

Figure 1.19 Fat cells as they appear in a typical section of adipose tissue.

Cartilage

Cartilage is associated mainly with the skeleton. It consists of **cartilage cells** (**chondrocytes**) embedded in a matrix. You can recognise cartilage tissue from the characteristic pattern of cartilage cells within the matrix (Figure 1.20).

1   Examine a section of **hyaline cartilage**, the most basic and the softest type of cartilage. Notice how the cells are arranged in the matrix. Does their grouping give any clues as to how they have been formed and what their function is?

2   In some places cartilage contains variable numbers of collagen or elastic fibres, making it tougher. Examine a section of **fibro-cartilage** from, for example, an intervertebral disc, and a section of **elastic cartilage** from, for example, the ear (pinna). What is the function of the cartilage in each of these locations?

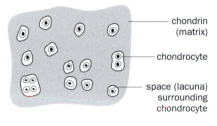

Figure 1.20 Hyaline cartilage as it appears in a typical microscopic section.

Smooth muscle

Smooth muscle is present in the walls of various organs and structures that move or change shape. Recognition depends mainly on the shapes of the cells, which are extremely long and spindly and have elongated nuclei (Figure 1.21).

1   Examine smooth muscle in the wall of the bladder and notice the shapes of the cells and their nuclei. What is the function of smooth muscle here?

2   Examine a section of the small intestine and try to locate smooth muscle in its wall. What is the function of the muscle in this situation?

Putting it all together

1   Look again at the organs you used for examining epithelia. In each case see if you can recognise any connective tissue, cartilage or smooth muscle. If they are present, explain their function(s) in the organ.

2   Examine sections of other organs of your own choice. See how many different tissues you can recognise in each one.

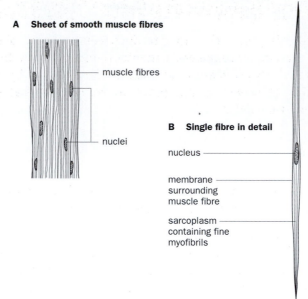

A Sheet of smooth muscle fibres

muscle fibres

nuclei

B Single fibre in detail

nucleus

membrane
surrounding
muscle fibre

sarcoplasm
containing fine
myofibrils

Figure 1.21 Smooth muscle tissue as seen in longitudinal section.

For consideration

1 To what extent does a knowledge of the function of a tissue enable you to make predictions about its structure? Give one example to illustrate your answer.

2 Now consider question 1 the other way round: to what extent does a knowledge of the structure of a tissue enable you to make predictions about its function? Again, give one example to illustrate your answer.

3 Think of the tissues that you have examined. Which features of each tissue do you consider to be particularly important in enabling you to recognise it?

Reference

Freeman, W. H. & Bracegirdle, B. *An Advanced Atlas of Histology.* Heinemann, London, 1976. (This book contains photomicrographs and explanatory drawings, an excellent aid to accurate identification and interpretation of tissues.)

Key skills

✓ **Application of number:** Using the method described in Technique 1.17 (p.42), calculate the sizes of some of the objects in the sections, for example the diameter of a glomerulus in a kidney nephron, and the height of a villus. In order to calculate the size of an object in this way, you will need to be able to handle ratios and powers of 10.

The object of this practical is to introduce you to some plant tissues which you will encounter repeatedly in later microscopic studies.

As with animal tissues, plant tissues can he investigated by examining prepared slides. However, in this practical we suggest that you make your own temporary slides.

Procedure

Epidermis

Epidermis lines the surface of leaves, stems and other parts of plants. It provides protection against physical damage and water loss.

1 Strip off a piece of epidermis from the lower side of a leaf of ivy-leaved toadflax (*Cymbalaria muralis*) and mount it in a drop of water or dilute iodine solution. Examine the epidermal cells, noting their shape and how they fit together. In passing, notice **stomata**, each one bordered by a pair of **guard cells**. They are dealt with in detail on p. 112.

2 Examine epidermal tissue obtained from other plants, stems as well as leaves, to gain some idea of how this tissue can vary.

Parenchyma (packing tissue)

Parenchyma fills up spaces inside stems, roots and leaves. Provided its cells are turgid, it provides strength and support.

1 Remove a small amount of the pulpy tissue from just beneath the skin of a tomato or grape. Place it in a drop of water on a slide and spread it out with needles. Add a coverslip and examine the parenchyma cells. Irrigate with fresh Schultze's solution. What effect does this stain have on what you can see?

2 Mount a small piece of the pulp of a potato tuber in Schultze's solution. What does the staining reaction suggest about one function of parenchyma tissue? (Hint: Schultze's solution is otherwise known as chlor-zinc iodine.)

3 How would you describe the shape of the potato cells? Make a plasticine model to show in three dimensions how the cells fit together.

Schultze's solution

Chlorenchyma (photosynthetic tissue)

Chlorenchyma is a modified form of parenchyma in which the cells contain chloroplasts and can therefore undergo photosynthesis. It is found mainly in leaves.

Mount a small leaf of Canadian pondweed (*Elodea canadensis*) in a drop of water on a slide and examine the cells packed with chloroplasts.

Collenchyma

Collenchyma is a type of strengthening tissue. Strength is derived from ribs of cellulose at the thickened corners of the elongated collenchyma cells.

A good place to see this type of tissue is in the stem of deadnettle (*Lamium* sp.) (Figure 1.22). Cut transverse and longitudinal sections of a deadnettle stem (see Technique 1.20, p. 49). Mount the sections in

Razor blade

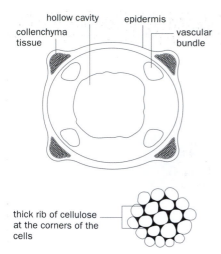

hollow cavity   epidermis

collenchyma   vascular
tissue   bundle

thick rib of cellulose — at the corners of the cells

Figure 1.22 Collenchyma tissue in a transverse section of the stem of deadnettle (*Lamium* sp.).

Acidified phloroglucinol Schultze's solution

Requirements

Microscope
Slides and coverslips
Razor blade with covered edge
Small paint brush
Dropper pipettes
Petri dish
Watch glass
Plasticine
Dilute iodine solution
Schultze's solution
Phloroglucinol, acidified
Ivy-leaved toadflax (*Cymbalaria muralis*)
Tomato or grape
Potato tuber
Canadian pondweed (*Elodea canadensis*)
Stem of deadnettle (*Lamium album*), fresh or preserved
Macerated woody twig

Note: Woody twigs can be macerated by prolonged immersion in a macerating fluid. Macerating fluids are available from suppliers.

Schultze's solution and make out as much as you can of the collenchyma tissue.

Sclerenchyma

Sclerenchyma is another type of strengthening tissue. However, in this case the cell walls are impregnated with lignin and the cells are dead. Most of the cells are elongated and are referred to as 'fibres'.

Mount a small quantity of macerated woody tissue in acidified phloroglucinol, which stains lignin red. Look for slender sclerenchyma fibres with tapering ends.

In passing, also notice lignified tubular elements in the xylem. These are **vessels** and/or **tracheids**. They have various sorts of thickening in their walls, which you may be able to see. They contribute mechanical strength to plants and also conduct water and mineral salts from roots to leaves (see Practical Exercises at the end of Section 2, e.g. Practical Exercise 2.51, p. 135).

For consideration

1   Relate the structure of the various plant tissues which you have looked at to the functions they perform within the plant.
2   Compare the epidermal tissue of plants with the epithelial tissue of animals, from both a structural and a functional point of view.

Reference

Clegg, C. J. & Cox, G. *Anatomy and Activities of Plants*. John Murray, London, 1978. (Photomicrographs with text and explanatory diagrams allow quick identification of plant tissues, with an understanding of their functions.)

Key skills

✓   **Application of number:** Using the method described in Technique 1.17 (p. 42), calculate the sizes of some of the objects in the sections, for example the diameter of a parenchyma cell, a sclerenchyma fibre and the length of a chloroplast in chlorenchyma. In order to calculate the size of an object in this way, you will need to be able to handle ratios and powers of 10.

If you want to examine the internal structure of a plant, it is usually necessary to cut thin sections and stain them. The stained sections can then be examined under the light microscope. The best procedure depends on which part of the plant you wish to investigate.

Stems

1 With a sharp scalpel, remove a short length of stem from between two nodes (Illustration 1).

Scalpel

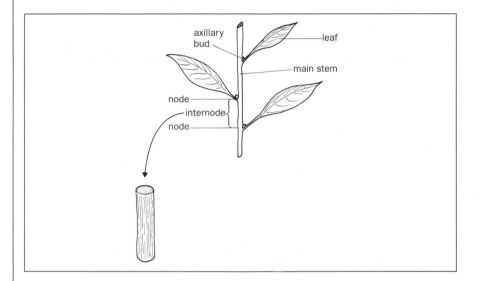

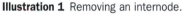

Illustration 1 Removing an internode.

2 With a new razor blade, cut thin transverse sections of the stem (Illustration 2A). Hold the piece of stem in one hand and the blade in the other. Keep the hand that you are holding the stem with well away from the cutting edge of the blade. Cut smoothly and

Schultze's solution

Eye protection must be worn

Razor blade

Illustration 2 Cutting (**A**) transverse and (**B**) longitudinal sections of a stem.

rapidly, constantly wetting the blade and surface of the stem with water. As the sections accumulate on the surface of the blade, transfer them with a small paint brush to a Petri dish of water.

3 Select your thinnest sections and transfer them to a watch glass of water. A section need not necessarily go right across the stem; often a thin wedge-shaped sliver is more useful than a complete section. Stain the sections in an appropriate stain for 10 minutes, then mount them in dilute glycerine. Alternatively, the sections can be mounted in the stain itself.

4 Try using different stains to see their effects. Each stain shows up a specific structure. Don't mix the stains: use a different one for each section. The main stains used are:
   • Dilute iodine solution, which stains starch grains blue-black
   • Schultze's solution, which stains cellulose purple
   • Acidified phloroglucinol, which stains lignin red

Note: Slides made as described above cannot be kept indefinitely. They are only temporary preparations. To make permanent preparations, see Box 5.5 p. 81 in M. B. V. Roberts, T. J. King & M. J. Reiss, *Practical Biology for Advanced Level*, Nelson, Walton-on-Thames, 1994.

Iodine solution   Acidified phloroglucinol

Eye protection must be worn

FABIL stain

Botanical razor or Razor blade

In addition, **FABIL stain** can be used to distinguish different tissues in one and the same section. It is toxic and messy to use, and gives variable results. However, it generally stains xylem elements brown, sclerenchyma pink, cellulose pale blue, cytoplasm and nuclei darker blue, and starch black.

5 To build up a complete picture of the three-dimensional structure of the stem and its constituent cells, cut longitudinal sections as well as transverse sections (Illustration 2B). Longitudinal sections can be stained and mounted in the same way as transverse sections. Oblique sections are often useful, too. When cutting such sections, always cut in a direction away from your hands.

Leaves

1 With small scissors, cut out the part of the leaf that you wish to investigate.
2 As the leaf is thin and flexible, it must be mounted in a firm position while the sections are being cut. Do this by inserting it into a vertical slit made down the centre of a piece of moistened elder pith or carrot tap root (Illustration 3).
3 Collect the sections, then stain and mount them as for the stem.

Roots

Roots, like leaves, are flexible, so they too must be mounted in elder pith or a carrot tap root before they can be sectioned. Proceed as for the leaf above.

Key skills

✓ **Problem solving:** In 'Stems' 5, you are expected to cut your stem in two or more planes and build up for yourself a three-dimensional picture of stem structure.

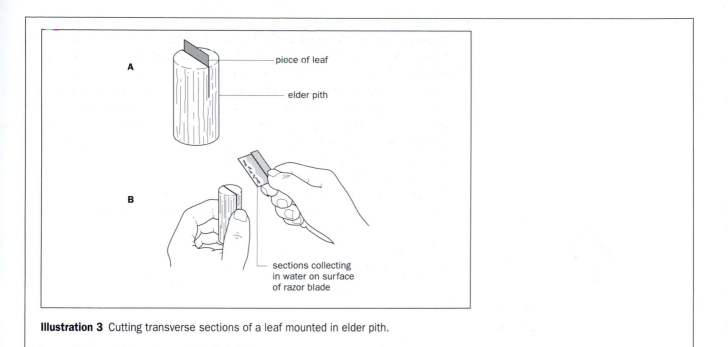

Illustration 3 Cutting transverse sections of a leaf mounted in elder pith.

Labels in illustration:
- piece of leaf
- elder pith
- A
- B
- sections collecting in water on surface of razor blade

Different kinds of structural organisation in organisms

Here are 10 different ways of describing the structural organisation of an organism:

- **Unicellular** (single-celled)
- **Multicellular** (many-celled) with undifferentiated cells (cells all of one type)
- Multicellular with **differentiated cells** (cells of more than one type)
- **Solitary** (separate from other individuals)
- **Modular** (made up of a variable number of identical parts)
- **Colonial** (linked to other individuals)
- **Asymmetrical**
- **Radially symmetrical**
- **Bilaterally symmetrical**
- **Cephalised** (possesses a head)

The purpose of this investigation is to look at a series of organisms and decide which of these descriptions apply to each one.

Guidance

First make sure that you understand the meaning of all the terms. Then try to decide which terms apply to each of the following organisms, listed in alphabetical order: *Amoeba*, creeping buttercup (*Ranunculus repens*), earthworm (*Lumbricus*), flatworm (*Planaria* or *Dendrocoelium*), *Hydra*, *Iris*, *Obelia*, *Paramecium*, *Pleurococcus*, *Spirogyra*.

In each case you will need to consider the whole organism and its microscopic structure. In the case of the earthworm, you will need to examine the inside of the animal by means of dissection and/or looking at a prepared transverse section.

Requirements

Microscope
Slides and coverslips
Teat pipette
Dissecting instruments
Amoeba, WM
Creeping buttercup (*Ranunculus repens*), entire with runners
Earthworm (*Lumbricus terrestris*), live, freshly killed and TS
Flatworm (*Planaria* or *Dendrocoelium*), live and TS
Hydra, live and TS
Iris, entire with rhizome
Obelia, preserved and WM
Paramecium, live and WM
Pleurococcus, live
Spirogyra, live

Extend the list to include other organisms if you wish. Present your conclusions in the form of a table.

For consideration

1 What other ways are there of describing the structure of organisms, besides those considered in this investigation?
2 Can you think of any non-structural ways of describing organisms, for instance according to their behaviour? Illustrate your answer by giving two contrasting examples.

The taxonomic hierarchy

Organisms can be classified into **species**, and species can be grouped together into **genera**, genera into **families**, families into **orders**, orders into **classes**, classes into **phyla** and phyla into **kingdoms**. This is called the **taxonomic hierarchy**.

As one progresses down the hierarchy, from kingdom to phylum to genus, fewer and fewer species are found within each group. At the same time, they have more in common. For example, the phylum Mollusca (molluscs) contains some 80000 living species which share certain fundamental features. Nevertheless, molluscs include such different organisms as slugs, clams and squids. However, within the phylum Mollusca, the genus *Patella* contains nothing but limpets, and it takes an expert to distinguish certain species of *Patella* from one another.

In this investigation you will examine some of the significant features used by taxonomists to classify certain plants. We shall begin with the genus *Ranunculus*, which includes the buttercups. The way one species in this genus fits into the taxonomic hierarchy is shown in Table 1.3.

Table 1.3 How the meadow buttercup (*Ranunculus acris*) fits into the classification of plants

Taxonomic category	Taxon
Kingdom	Plantae
Phlyum	Angiospermophyta
Class	Dicotyledoneae
Order	Ranales
Family	Ranunculaceae
Genus	*Ranunculus*
Specific epithet	*acris*
Species	*Ranunculus acris*

Procedure

1 Examine, either in the field or in the laboratory, at least some of the species of *Ranunculus* listed in Table 1.4, while they are in flower. Note similarities and differences between the different species.
2 From your observations, suggest (i) which features might cause all these species to be placed in the same genus; and (ii) which features distinguish one species from another.

Table 1.4 Scientific names, common British names and habitats of 11 species of *Ranunculus*

Scientific name	Common British name	Habitats
R. acris	Meadow buttercup	Grassland, especially damp and calcareous
R. aquatilis	Common water-crowfoot	Ponds, ditches, canals, slow rivers
R. arvensis	Corn buttercup	Cultivated ground, especially wheat fields
R. auricomus	Goldilocks	Woods, hedgebanks
R. bulbosus	Bulbous buttercup	Dry grassland, fixed dunes
R. flammula	Lesser spearwort	Wet places
R. ficaria	Lesser celandine	Damp meadows, woods, hedgebanks, beside streams
R. fluitans	River water-crowfoot	Rivers of moderate flow-rate
R. lingua	Greater spearwort	Marshes and pondsides
R. repens	Creeping buttercup	Wet grassland, woods, stream sides, marshes, dune-slacks, and as a weed of grassland and waste places
R. sceleratus	Celery-leaved buttercup	Marshy fields, ditches, ponds, stream sides

3   *Ranunculus* belongs to the family Ranunculaceae. This family contains many other genera besides *Ranunculus*. These genera include:
  - *Anemone*, e.g. *A. nemorosa* (wood anemone)
  - *Caltha*, e.g. *C. palustris* (marsh-marigold)
  - *Clematis*, e.g. *C. vitalba* (traveller's joy)
  - *Aquilegia*, e.g. *A. vulgaris* (columbine)
  - *Helleborus*, e.g. *H. foetidus* (stinking hellebore)

  Examine flowering and/or fruiting specimens of some or all of the above genera. Suggest which features distinguish one genus from another.

4   These genera, and therefore the species they contain, are placed in the same family because of certain similarities between their flowers. What features of the flowers do they share?

5   The Ranunculaceae is a family within the phylum Angiospermophyta (flowering plants). There are more than 200 families of angiosperms. These include the following: Asteraceae (e.g. daisy, thistles, groundsel); Brassicaceae (e.g. shepherd's purse, wallflower); Convolvulaceae (e.g. bindweed); Fabaceae, also known as Leguminosae (e.g. pea, clover, gorse); Lamiaceae, also known as Labiatae (e.g. deadnettle); Primulaceae (e.g. primrose, cowslip); Rosaceae (e.g. strawberry, roses); Scrophulariaceae (e.g. speedwells, foxglove, snapdragon); Violaceae (e.g. violets).

  Examine representatives of some or all of the above families. In what respects do they differ from the Ranunculaceae and from each other? What features do they have in common which cause them to be placed in the same phylum of the plant kingdom, the Angiospermophyta?

Ranunculus species (see Table 1.4) –
either live in the field or herbarium
specimens in the laboratory
Species belonging to some or all of the
following genera: *Anemone, Caltha,
Clematis, Aquilegia, Helleborus*
A few other angiosperms (see list in
step 5)
Hand lens

For consideration

1 With reference to the plants you have studied, is it true that the similarities between organisms increase as you go down the taxonomic hierarchy?

2 Can you suggest why characteristics of flowers and fruits are more widely used in the classification of plants than are vegetative characteristics, such as leaves?

1.23 PRACTICAL EXERCISE

Classification of organisms

At one time, the classification of organisms made up a substantial proportion of the time advanced level biology students spent on their course. Nowadays this is rarely the case unless you are studying an option concerned with the diversity of organisms. However, every student of biology, whatever their particular interests, should be able to classify organisms at least into their major groups. Accordingly, we present in Table 1.5 a classification of living organisms down to the level of phyla, sometimes classes, and invite you to use it to identify a number of specimens provided by your teacher or lecturer.

Table 1.5 The kingdoms and phyla (and some classes) of living organisms

KINGDOM PROKARYOTAE
Unicellular; lack nuclei and membrane-bound organelles.

KINGDOM PROTOCTISTA
Eukaryotic organisms which are not animals, plants or fungi; often unicellular.

Phylum Rhizopoda (rhizopods)
Pseudopodia for locomotion.

Phylum Zoomastigina (flagellates)
At least one flagellum for locomotion; heterotrophic.

Phylum Apicomplexa (sporozoans)
Multiple fission stages in the life history; mostly parasitic.

Phylum Ciliophora (ciliates)
Cilia for locomotion and/or feeding.

Phylum Euglenophyta (euglenoid flagellates)
Flagella; distinctive biochemistry (including paramylon as the cytoplasmic storage product); photosynthetic and non-photosynthetic members.

Phylum Oomycota (oomycetes)
Sexual reproduction by fertilisation of male and female gametangia; asexual sporangia produce biflagellate spores; hyphae non-septate (no cross walls).

Phylum Chlorophyta (green algae)
Photosynthetic, with green chlorophyll pigments as in plants; unicellular, colonial and filamentous.

Phylum Rhodophyta (red algae)
Photosynthetic, with plastids containing red pigments as well as chlorophyll.

Phylum Phaeophyta (brown algae)
Photosynthetic, with plastids containing brown pigments as well as chlorophyll.

KINGDOM FUNGI
Eukaryotic with a protective wall containing chitin; heterotrophic with absorptive methods of nutrition; usually organised into white thread-like multinucleate hyphae; spores without flagella.

Phylum Zygomycota (zygomycetes)
Sexual reproduction by gametangia producing a zygospore; hyphae non-septate.

Phylum Ascomycota (ascomycetes)
Sexual reproduction involving spore production inside a slender container (ascus); hyphae septate.

Phylum Basidiomycota (basidiomycetes)
Sexual reproduction involves spores produced externally on a basidium; hyphae septate.

KINGDOM PLANTAE
Eukaryotic, multicellular and photosynthetic; cell walls contain cellulose.

Phylum Bryophyta (bryophytes)
Conspicuous gametophyte generation; no true roots (body anchored by filamentous rhizoids).

Class Hepaticae (liverworts)
Body either a flat thallus or with leaves in three ranks; unicellular rhizoids; spore capsule opens by splitting into four valves.

Class Musci (mosses)
Leafy body with leaves spirally arranged; multicellular rhizoids; spore capsule with elaborate dispersal mechanism.

Phylum Lycophyta (club mosses)
Small spirally arranged leaves; sporangia usually in cones.

Phylum Sphenophyta (horsetails)
Leaves in whorls around the stem; sporangia in cones.

Phylum Filicinophyta (ferns)
Young leaves coiled in bud; sporangia in clusters (sori).

Phylum Coniferophyta (conifers)
Cone-bearing without flowers or fruits; ovules not surrounded by an ovary wall.

Phylum Angiospermophyta
(angiosperms – so called flowering plants)
Seed-bearing plants with flowers; seeds enclosed in a fruit.

Class Monocotyledoneae (monocots)
Leaves usually with parallel veins; embryos with one cotyledon; flower parts usually in multiples of three; vascular bundles scattered in stem; roots without a definite xylem 'star'.

Class Dicotyledoneae (dicots)
Net-veined leaves; embryos with two cotyledons; roots with two, four or five points on a xylem 'star'; secondary thickening present in trees and shrubs.

KINGDOM ANIMALIA
Eukaryotic, non-photosynthetic multicellular organisms with nervous coordination.

Phylum Cnidaria (coelenterates)
Two cell layers separated by a mesogloea; nematoblast (stinging) cells; radial symmetry with tentacles.

Phylum Platyhelminthes (flatworms)
Flat, unsegmented animals; often with a mouth, but lacking an anus.

Class Turbellaria (turbellarians)
Ciliated outer surface; free-living; aquatic.

Class Trematoda (flukes)
Non-ciliated outer surface; endoparasites; one or more suckers.

Class Cestoda (tapeworms)
Non-ciliated outer surface; endoparasites; scolex bearing suckers and hooks; flat, elongated body usually divided into sexually reproducing sections.

Phylum Nematoda (nematodes – also called roundworms)
Unsegmented cylindrical body; both a mouth and an anus.

Phylum Annelida (annelids – also called segmented worms)
Worm-like animals with clear segmentation.

Class Polychaeta (polychaetes – also called marine worms)
Distinct head; numerous chaetae on projections (parapodia); marine.

Class Oligochaeta (oligochaetes – also called earthworms)
No distinct head; few chaetae per segment and no parapodia; in fresh water and soil.

Class Hirudinea (leeches)
No distinct head; no chaetae or parapodia; usually ectoparasites or predators with two suckers.

Phylum Mollusca (molluscs)
Unsegmented, with a head, foot and visceral mass; often with a calcareous shell.

Class Gastropoda (snails and slugs)
Head, eyes and sensory tentacles; shell – if present – single, often coiled; radula used in feeding.

Class Pelycopoda (bivalves)
Head reduced, no tentacles; shell of two hinged valves; filter feeding.

Class Cephalopoda (octopods and squids)
Conspicuous head and tentacles; well developed eyes, beak and radula used in feeding; no shell in living forms.

Phylum Arthropoda (arthropods)
Hard exoskeleton; segmented; jointed limbs; bilaterally symmetrical.

Class Crustacea (crustaceans)
Head not clearly defined; two pairs of antennae; mostly aquatic.

Class Myriapoda (centipedes and millipedes)
Long body with many segments; distinct head; one pair of antennae; many legged; no wings; terrestrial.

Class Hexapoda (spiders, scorpions and mites)
Body divided into head, thorax and abdomen; three pairs of legs; head usually with compound eyes; frequently terrestrial; usually winged as adults.

Class Arachnida (arachnids)
Four pairs of legs attached to what appears to be a combined head and thorax; no true jaws; no compound eyes; terrestrial.

Phylum Echinodermata (sea urchins, starfish and brittlestars)
Spiny-skinned; water vascular system with tube feet; 5-way radial symmetry; marine.

Phylum Chordata (chordates)
Notochord; hollow dorsal nerve cord; visceral clefts; post-anal tail.

Class Chondrichthyes (cartilaginous fish)
Skeleton of cartilage; mouth ventral; fleshy fins; separate gill openings.

Class Osteichthyes (bony fish)
Skeleton of bone; mouth terminal; fins supported by rays; gills covered by a bony flap (operculum).

Class Amphibia (amphibians)
Soft skin; aquatic larvae with gills; land-living adults with lungs.

Class Reptilia (reptiles)
Scaly skin; usually limbed; lungs; eggs with shells.

Class Aves (birds)
Skin with feathers; winged; lungs; endothermic; eggs with shells.

Class Mammalia (mammals)
Skin with hair in follicles; lungs; endothermic; mostly viviparous; young fed on milk from mammary glands.

Microscope
Blunt seeker
Live specimens of some of the following organisms:
  Mucor
  Locusta or *Drosophila*
  Helix or *Arion* or *Cepaea* or *Achatina fulica*
  Daphnia or *Asellus* or *Gammarus*
  Euglena
  Lumbricus or *Allolobophora*
  Paramecium
  Poa or *Triticum* or *Lolium* or *Agrostis*
  Chlamydomonas or *Spirogyra*
  Amoeba
Prepared slides of some of the following organisms:
  Bryum or *Funaria* or *Mnium* or *Polytrichum*
  Plasmodium
  Fasciola
  Phytophthora
  Trypanosoma
Preserved specimens of some of the following organisms:
  Dryopteris or *Pteridium*
  Scyliorhinus
  Taenia
  Ascaris
  Clupea or *Salmo* or *Gadus*
  Rattus
  Asterias or *Ophiothrix*
  Fucus or *Laminaria*

Procedure

Assign each organism to its correct kingdom, phylum and – if appropriate – class, using the classification in Table 1.5. If any of the terms are unfamiliar to you, you will need to consult a standard textbook (e.g. M. B. V. Roberts, M. J. Reiss & G. Monger, *Advanced Biology*, Nelson, Walton-on-Thames, 2000), a dictionary of biology (e.g. M. Abercrombie, M. Hickman, M. L. Johnson & M. Thain, *The New Penguin Dictionary of Biology*, Penguin, Harmondsworth, Middx, 1990) or a book on the classification and identification of living organisms (e.g. G. Monger & M. Sangster, *Systematics and Classification*, Longman, Harlow, 1998). The classification in Table 1.5 is based on that provided in the 3rd edition of *Biological Nomenclature: Standard Terms and Expressions Used in the Teaching of Biology*, Institute of Biology, London, 2000.

For consideration

1 Explain why you found some of the organisms easier to classify than others.
2 One of the five kingdoms is generally thought to be less 'satisfactory' than the other four. Which do you suppose this is? In what way do you think it is less 'satisfactory'?

References

See under Procedure above.

Before starting a project, assess the risks inherent in your intended procedure and discuss your intended procedure with your teacher/lecturer.

1   Compare the distribution patterns of various chemical compounds within the seeds of various plant species, using the methods outlined in Technique 1.2 (p. 19) and Practical Exercise 1.4 (p. 22). Include both endospermic and non-endospermic seeds, some of which store carbohydrate and some of which store lipid. Separate the parts of the seed from one another and test them separately, or stain thin sections of the seeds and examine them under the microscope. Relate the distribution of the compounds to their functions in the seeds.

2   Investigate the effects of various detergents on the starch–iodine reaction. (Consult R. Hadi-Talab & R. Levinson, Rinse-aid and the starch–iodine reaction, *School Science Review*, **81** (297), 99–101, 2000.)

3   Compare, by paper chromatography, the range of pigments present in the petals of several closely related plant species, and explain why the petals are that particular colour. You might, for example, examine the range of coloured anthocyanin pigments in the petals or leaves of two or three closely related species, using two-way chromatography. (See R. Delpech, The importance of red pigments to plant life: experiments with anthocyanins, *Journal of Biological Education*, **34**, 206–210, 2000.)

4   Investigate the epidermis of the leaves of different species of flowering plant. Select leaves from plants growing in a range of environments and which differ in hairiness and colour. You might look at insectivorous plants. Look at, hairs, spines, stomatal density on both surfaces and any other epidermal structures you find. Relate your findings to the environments of the plants.

5   Water is 777 times more dense than air. Amongst plants growing in water, there might be less selection pressure for support tissue than amongst plants on land, as water plants are supported by the water itself. Test this hypothesis by comparing the quantity and arrangement of support tissue in transverse sections of stems, petioles and leaves of (a) plants submerged in water and closely related species growing on land (e.g. buttercups, see Practical Exercise 1.22, p. 52), and (b) parts of plants submerged beneath the water surface and similar parts in the air. To what extent do you think the presence and distribution of support tissues is genetically determined or environmentally determined?

6   Investigate the taxonomic hierarchy (see Practical Exercise 1.22, p. 52) using a variety of annelids (e.g. earthworms, lugworms, ragworms, fanworms and leeches). What characters are used to distinguish the different groups?

7   Find out about the principles of numerical taxonomy and attempt to use them to classify a group of organisms (e.g. different molluscs).

8   Compare the concentrations of lipids in various foodstuffs by hydrolysing the lipid and then determinining the 'saponification number' by titrating the free fatty acids with potassium hydroxide.

Potassium
hydroxide

✓ **Communication:** Make an oral presentation about your findings and conclusions. Speak clearly and adapt your style of presentation to suit your audience (probably your peers). Structure what you say so that the sequence of information and ideas may be easily followed. Use a range of techniques to engage your audience, including at least one image – this might be your graph of percentage changes against the molarities of the sucrose solutions, but need not be.

2.2 PRACTICAL EXERCISE — Determining the water potential of potato tuber cells by the density method

Suppose that we suspend some plant tissue in a sucrose solution for some time. Then we deposit beneath the surface a coloured drop of sucrose solution of equal concentration (molarity). If this drop neither rises nor falls, its water potential is equivalent to that of the solution *and the tissue suspended in it*. If, however, the tissue had previously gained water from the surrounding sucrose solution, making the solution more dense, the coloured drop would rise. If the tissue had previously lost water to the solution, making the solution less dense, the coloured drop, being more dense, would fall.

Suppose, therefore, that we suspend samples of a tissue in solutions of various strengths. We later add to each solution a coloured drop of the same concentration as the original solution. The original strength of the solution in which the drop shows least tendency to rise or fall corresponds most closely to the original water potential of the tissue.

Procedure

1 Arrange two rows of seven test tubes, one directly behind the other. Label the front row of test tubes, in order, 10, 15, 20, 25, 30, 50 and 70. Using a separate graduated syringe in each case, place $5\,cm^3$ of the appropriate sucrose solution in each of the front tubes: 0.10, 0.15, 0.20, 0.25, 0.30, 0.5 and $0.7\,mol\,dm^{-3}$ of sucrose.

2 From the test tube containing $0.1\,mol\,dm^{-3}$ of sucrose and labelled '10', pipette $3\,cm^3$ into the tube behind, leaving $2\,cm^3$ in the original front tube. Repeat the procedure with all the other sucrose solutions in turn, *using a different pipette in each case*. You will now have two rows of seven labelled test tubes, with the front ones containing $2\,cm^3$ of solution each and the back ones containing $3\,cm^3$ each of the same solution.

3 Place one drop of methylene blue into each of the front test tubes. This will colour the solution, but will not significantly alter its water potential.

Razor blade

4 Using a cork borer and a razor blade, prepare a cylinder of potato tuber tissue about $7\,mm$ diameter and $60\,mm$ long. Slice the cylinder into 30 discs of approximately equal ($2\,mm$) thickness.

5 Place four of the potato discs into each of the test tubes in the back row (those containing $3\,cm^3$ of solution). Manipulate the discs so that they are all covered with sucrose solution in each tube. Note the time.

6 After at least 25 minutes, pour off into a clean test tube the fluid from the tube containing potato discs in the 0.10 mol dm⁻³ solution. This tube of decanted solution should be placed in the test tube rack in the position previously occupied by the tube containing the potato discs immersed in 3 cm³ of 0.10 mol dm⁻³ sucrose.

7 Use a teat pipette to collect a small quantity of blue sucrose solution from the 0.10 mol dm⁻³ solution tube, labelled '10', at the front. Now, *with great care*, introduce a single drop of this blue fluid into the tube behind it – that is, the tube containing the decanted fluid that had been in contact with the potato slices. The drop should be released into the centre of the liquid about 5 mm below the surface.

8 Watch the drop. Note whether it remains in the same place, or rises, or sinks. Release another drop into the same solution and continue until you are certain that you have made the correct observation about the behaviour of the drop.

9 Repeat steps 6, 7 and 8 with the other six sets of tubes, using a clean pipette for each sucrose concentration.

10 Present your results in the form of a table.

For consideration

1 From your understanding of the factors that cause water to leave or enter plant cells, explain what has been happening in each of the sucrose concentrations. In each case account for the behaviour of the blue drops.

2 A 1.0 mol dm⁻³ solution of sucrose has a water potential of −3500 kPa. From your results, estimate the approximate water potential of the potato tissue.

3 Were you estimating the water potentials of the potato cells, or the water potentials of the solutions in their vacuoles? Explain your answer.

4 Consider very critically the instructions given for this practical exercise. Suggest how they might be improved.

Determining the solute potential of cell sap of plant epidermal cells

2.3 PRACTICAL EXERCISE

Water and other energy potentials in cells are given the symbol ψ, the Greek letter psi. The **water potential** of a plant cell (ψ_{cell}) is related to the **solute potential** of the sap (ψ_s) and the **pressure potential** (y_p) by the equation:

$$\psi_{cell} = \psi_s + \psi_p$$

The solute potential is the reduction in the water potential of the solution in the cell due to the presence of particles dissolved in the solution.

When a plant cell is surrounded by a solution of lower water potential it **plasmolyses** – that is, its cytoplasm loses water and contracts, gradually separating the plasma membrane from the cell wall until it rounds off in the centre. When plant cells are placed in a range of solutions of different concentrations, the solution just strong enough to make the plasma membrane separate from the cell wall in places (**incipient plasmolysis**) can be regarded as having the same solute potential as the

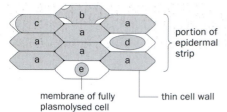

portion of epidermal strip

membrane of fully plasmolysed cell — thin cell wall

Figure 2.1 The appearance of onion epidermal cells at various stages of plasmolysis. Cells **a** are unplasmolysed, cells **b** and **c** exhibit incipient plasmolysis, and cells **d** and **e** show progressive plasmolysis as their plasma membranes separate from their cell walls.

Razor blade

cell sap. This is because, in the equation above, if no inward pressure is exerted by the cell wall ($\psi_p = 0$), the water potential of the cell (ψ_{cell}) equals the solute potential (ψ_s). This provides us with a way of estimating the solute potential of a plant tissue, which is the aim of this practical.

In practice, the cells in a piece of plant tissue plasmolyse at different rates (Figure 2.1). We can regard incipient plasmolysis as taking place when half the cells in the tissue exhibit visible plasmolysis.

Procedure

1   Into each of six specimen tubes, place about 10 cm^3 of a different sucrose solution (0.3, 0.4, 0.5, 0.6, 0.7 and 1.0 mol dm^{-3}) and label each tube appropriately.

2   Remove one of the fleshy scale leaves of an onion. With a razor blade, cut the inner epidermis (the outer epidermis is more suitable, but less easy to obtain) into 12 squares of side about 5 mm. The best results are obtained with epidermal strips one cell thick. Place two pieces of epidermis into each of the specimen tubes, stopper the tubes and gently shake the contents to submerge the tissue. Note the time.

3   After 20 minutes, remove one piece of epidermis from each tube and mount it on a labelled microscope slide, beneath a coverslip, in a drop of the solution in which it has been immersed. Observe under low power. Look for plasmolysed cells (Figure 2.1). If plasmolysed cells are not clearly visible in the more concentrated sucrose solutions, irrigate with dilute iodine solution to stain the cytoplasm, or view the second epidermal strips.

4   Count all the cells visible within the low power field of view. Now count all those that are plasmolysed. Include those that show a visible separation of the cell contents from the cell wall, however slight. If any reading is markedly at variance with the others, repeat the estimate with the second piece of epidermis.

5   Record the results in a table. Plot a graph of percentage plasmolysis against molarity of sucrose solution and join the points by straight lines.

6   Read off your graph the molarity of sucrose which corresponds to 50% plasmolysis. This solution may be regarded as having the same solute potential as the cell sap of the tissue. Use Table 2.1 to estimate the corresponding solute potential in kPa. Now you can breathe a psi of relief!

7   Finally, looking down the microscope as you do so, irrigate with distilled water a piece of epidermis which had been mounted in concentrated sucrose. Use filter paper to draw the water beneath the coverslip. Observe what happens and interpret the results.

For consideration

1   Explain the shape of your graph.

2   What are the major sources of inaccuracy in this method?

3   The epidermis of rhubarb and red cabbage has cells that contain a red pigment. How could you use the technique outlined in this practical to find out where the red pigment is located?

4   Why do not all the cells in the tissue have the same solute potential, and what might be the consequences of this?

The influence of water potential on dandelion scapes

The hollow **scapes** (flower stalks) of dandelion (*Taraxacum* sp.) exhibit various degrees of curvature when placed in sucrose or salt solutions of different water potential. The aim of this investigation is to quantify the effects of this, and suggest explanations, in terms of the anatomy of dandelion scapes and the differences in water potential between tissue and solution.

Guidance

To obtain the material for your investigation, split a scape longitudinally into six portions of length 5 cm. The strips immediately bend outwards. Immerse the strips in solutions of different water potentials for 15 minutes and record the results. If possible, devise a quantitative measure of curvature that takes the initial bending into account. You may also need to replicate your experiments, and to consider if you are justified in comparing strips from different scapes.

Why do the strips bend outwards as soon as they have been separated from one another? Investigate this by carefully cutting thin sections of a scape by hand and examining the anatomy of the stem (see Technique 1.20 on p. 49). You may wish to separate parts of the scape and determine the water potential of each one on its own, or you may be able to assess the degrees of curvature obtained when the inside layers or the outside layers of the scapes are exposed to various solutions on their own.

For consideration

Put your findings together to produce a full explanation of the degrees of curvature of the strips in the different solutions, using water potential terminology throughout.

Reference

Oxlade, E. L. & Clifford, P. E. The versatile dandelion. *Journal of Biological Education*, **33**, 125–129, 1999.

Razor blade

Requirements

Microscope
Ruler
Razor blade
Botanical razor
Pith *or* carrot tap root
Slides and coverslips
Large beakers
Supply of salt *or* sucrose solutions of various water potentials
Scapes (hollow peduncles) of dandelions (*Taraxacum* sp.)

Synthesis of starch using an enzyme extracted from a potato tuber

Potato tubers contain an enzyme which catalyses the synthesis of starch, a polymer of glucose units, from simple 'building blocks'. The aim of this practical is to find out which compounds the enzyme can act on to produce starch. You will investigate three possible substrates: **α-glucose**, **glucose-1-phosphate** (formed from a reaction between glucose and adenosine triphosphate (ATP)) and **maltose**, a disaccharide of two glucose units (Figure 2.2).

Procedure

Extracting the enzyme from potato tissue

1   Peel a medium-sized potato and cut it into small pieces. Grind a few pieces of potato in a pestle and mortar with some sand and 20 cm³ of water.

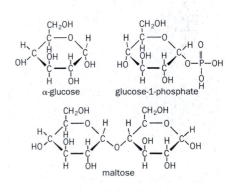

Figure 2.2 Three substrates from which starch might be made.

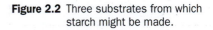

2 Pour the liquid part of the extract into two centrifuge tubes so that each contains an equal volume. Try not to let sand and solid matter get into the tubes – any which is added should be distributed equally between the two.

3 Spin the extracts in a centrifuge for a few minutes at 5000 rpm. The object is to deposit the starch, cell walls and other solid matter to the bottom of the centrifuge tubes. The starch-free liquid above the deposit should contain the enzyme.

4 Stop the centrifuge. Using a teat pipette, carefully withdraw from the centrifuge tube as much as possible of the clear enzyme solution, without disturbing the deposit beneath. Transfer it to a test tube.

5 This 'enzyme' solution must be starch-free. To check, transfer a few drops into a test tube containing $3 \, cm^3$ of iodine solution. If a blue colour appears, the solution contains some starch and the potato extract needs to be centrifuged again.

6 Distribute the enzyme solution equally between three test tubes.

Attempting starch synthesis

7 Label three clean test tubes G, G-1-P and M respectively. Using a separate syringe in each case, place $3 \, cm^3$ of glucose solution in the G tube, $3 \, cm^3$ of glucose-1-phosphate in the G-1-P tube, and $3 \, cm^3$ of maltose solution in the M tube.

8 To attempt starch synthesis, pour the contents of an enzyme tube into the substrate tube, mix well, note the time, and immediately withdraw one drop of the solution with a glass rod. Touch the drop onto a drop of fresh iodine solution on a white tile, stir and record the colour produced. Repeat at intervals of 1 minute for 15 minutes, recording the colour each time. Try to synthesise starch in the three tubes simultaneously. If and when you make starch, the extract will turn the iodine solution blue-black.

For consideration

1 The structural formulae of the three substrates are shown in Figure 2.2. What feature of the starch-synthesising substrate molecule might have been recognised by the starch-synthesising enzyme?

2 The synthesis of polymers such as starch requires metabolic energy. What was the energy source in the successful reaction?

3 The enzyme isolated from potatoes is known as **starch phosphorylase**. In the intact potato tuber it is also used to break down starch. How did conditions in the test tube favour starch *synthesis*? In what circumstances does the enzyme bring about starch synthesis in a potato?

4 In plant leaves, starch accumulates in chloroplasts. The synthesis of starch requires ATP. Where do you think this ATP comes from?

Requirements

Centrifuge and centrifuge tubes
Test tube rack
Pestle and mortar
Scalpel
Marker for writing on glass
Test tubes, ×7
Teat pipette
Syringes ($5 \, cm^3$), ×3
Glass rod
White tile
Glucose solution ($3 \, cm^3$, 1%)
Glucose-1-phosphate solution ($3 \, cm^3$, 1%)
Maltose solution ($3 \, cm^3$, 1%)
Iodine solution
Potato tuber

2.6 PRACTICAL EXERCISE

Effect of exposure to different temperatures on the molecular structure of an enzyme

Enzyme molecular structure is affected by temperature. To assess the effect of temperature on enzyme structure, you can expose samples of the enzyme to different temperatures for the same period of time, and then find how long each sample takes to catalyse its reaction under standard conditions.

In this experiment samples of **amylase**, a starch-digesting enzyme, are exposed to various temperatures for 5 minutes. The time required for each sample to digest the same quantity of starch at the same temperature is then estimated by using iodine solution (which turns blue-black in the presence of starch) as an indicator.

Procedure

1   Label five test tubes: room temperature (measure it!), 25 °C, 40 °C, 60 °C and 100 °C. Add 5 cm³ of amylase solution to each.
2   Keep the first tube at room temperature. Place each of the other tubes in the appropriate water bath for exactly 5 minutes. During this time, prepare a results sheet with time on the vertical axis and one column for each temperature.
3   Immediately remove the tubes from the water baths and cool them rapidly to room temperature with ice in a beaker (care!).
4   Once you are satisfied that the contents of each tube are at the same temperature, add 5 cm³ of starch solution to each and mix with a clean glass rod.
5   At intervals of 1 minute, test each tube for the presence of starch. Withdraw one drop of the starch–enzyme mixture, place it on a white tile and add one drop of iodine solution. Use a separate glass rod for each tube and a different one for the iodine solution.
6   Carefully record each result as it is obtained, in terms of a consistent colour scheme. Do not continue your observations for longer than 15 minutes. Note how long it takes in each case before a blue-black colour ceases to be obtained when iodine solution is added to the mixture.

For consideration

1   The assessment of the colour of an iodine solution is subjective. Can you think of a better way to compare reaction rates?
2   Speculate in detail on the influence of temperature on the molecular structure of the enzyme. What types of bond probably hold the molecule together and which is most likely to be broken by heat energy?

Eye protection must be worn

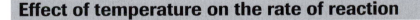

| Effect of temperature on the rate of reaction | 2.7 INVESTIGATION |

Design an experiment to assess the influence of temperature on the reaction rate, using the digestion of starch by the enzyme amylase as the enzyme–substrate system. Try to make the method as quantitative as possible, so that you can say how much faster the reaction occurs at one temperature than another.

In this investigation, the time required by amylase to digest the same quantity of starch at a series of different temperatures is estimated by using iodine solution as an indicator.

Guidance

Use a technique similar to that in Practical Exercise 2.6 on p. 64. Make sure that the starch and amylase solutions reach the temperatures of the water baths *before* you mix them.

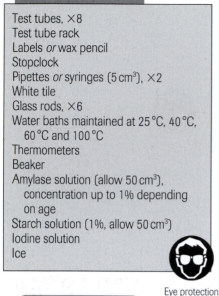

Test tubes, ×8
Test tube rack
Labels *or* wax pencil
Stopclock
Pipettes *or* syringes (5 cm³), ×2
White tile
Glass rods, ×6
Water baths maintained at 25 °C, 40 °C,
   60 °C and 100 °C
Thermometers
Beaker
Amylase solution (allow 50 cm³),
   concentration up to 1% depending
   on age
Starch solution (1%, allow 50 cm³)
Iodine solution
Ice

Eye protection
must be worn

Test each tube for the presence of starch at intervals of 1 minute. Carefully record in a table each result as it is obtained, in terms of a consistent colour scheme. Do not continue your observations for longer than 15 minutes.

For consideration

1 Suggest how you might relate the colour of the iodine to the proportion of the starch which has been broken down.
2 On the basis of the data you have collected, compare the rates of reaction at different temperatures.
3 Give two reasons why the rate of reaction increases with temperature, up to a point.
4 In conventional brewing, hot water is mixed with the mashed malt in order to stimulate the *rapid* breakdown of any remaining starch to maltose. What temperature of water would you advise the brewmaster to add?

Note: Beware of allergic reactions to amylase solution; avoid spills on the skin or rubbing eyes with contaminated fingers.

Assessment

- **Plan** your investigation. Identify and define the question you are attempting to answer. Explain the reasons for the procedures you have chosen.
- **Implement** your plan. Were you able to obtain and record an adequate range of valid observations and measurements?
- **Analyse your evidence** and **draw conclusions**. How can you best present your findings? Ensure you use appropriate scientific terminology when interpreting your findings.
- **Evaluate** your investigation. How adequate is the colour change of iodine solution as an indicator of the endpoint of the reaction? How could you make your measurements more precise?

2.8 INVESTIGATION

Effect of enzyme and substrate concentrations on the hydrolysis of sucrose

To investigate the effects of enzyme and substrate concentrations on the rate of a reaction, a convenient system is provided by the hydrolysis of the disaccharide sucrose by the enzyme **sucrase** into its constituent monosaccharides, glucose and fructose. On the basis of the information provided here, you can devise your own investigation.

The reaction is as follows:

$$C_{12}H_{22}O_{11} + H_2O \rightarrow C_6H_{12}O_6 + C_6H_{12}O_6$$
Sucrose   Glucose   Fructose

The progress of the reaction can be followed by testing for the substrates and products. Sucrose does not give a positive test when heated with Benedict's solution, but glucose and fructose both yield a yellow, brown or red precipitate.

Whatever experiment you attempt, it is probably best to measure the *initial* rate of the reaction – that is, the reaction over a short period of time, say 30 seconds. The rate of reaction declines with time, and if you measure the rate of reaction over a longer time than this, the effect of the decline of the reaction rate becomes confused with the effect of the enzyme or the substrate concentrations.

Guidance

Summary of the technique

Using a syringe, place $1\,cm^3$ of Benedict's solution in a test tube in a test tube rack. Then place $5\,cm^3$ of 2% sucrose in one test tube, $5\,cm^3$ of 1% sucrase in another, and put both into a water bath at 38 °C.

Leave both test tubes in the water bath for 5 minutes to allow their temperatures to reach the temperature of the water. Then, simultaneously, start the stopclock and pour the contents of the sucrase solution into the sucrose solution. Swirl the contents of the test tube and rapidly put it back into the 38 °C water bath.

After 30 seconds, remove $1\,cm^3$ of the reaction mixture with a syringe and squirt it into the test tube of Benedict's solution in the test tube rack. Now transfer this test tube to a water bath at 50 °C for 5 minutes, and during this time record both the timing of the colour changes and the approximate amount of precipitate formed.

Carrying out the investigation

Now plan and carry out an investigation, using dilutions of the sucrase and sucrose solutions provided, into the effect of altering the enzyme and substrate concentration on the rate of reaction. Write down your plan before you start. Keep detailed records of what you did and the results you obtained, and be prepared to modify your technique if necessary (e.g. by allowing the reaction to take place for 1 minute instead of 30 seconds) to obtain more satisfactory results.

For consideration

1 Examine your results. What relationship is there between the initial rate of reaction and the concentration of (a) enzyme and (b) substrate?

2 Explore ways of expressing your results in numbers which can be plotted on a graph. For example, if you calculate the rate of reaction as 1/reaction time for the first reducing sugars to be detected, you may find that a plot of this against enzyme or substrate concentration proves useful.

3 Explain your results in terms of the interactions between enzyme and substrate molecules.

Influence of pH on the activity of potato catalase   2.9 PRACTICAL EXERCISE

The activity of most enzymes, including **catalase**, is influenced by changes in pH. Catalase occurs in many plant and animal tissues. It breaks down toxic hydrogen peroxide, formed as a by-product of various biochemical reactions, into water and oxygen.

In this experiment, you can test the hypothesis that the optimum pH of catalase is about the same as the pH of potato cells (7.4). One way to do this is to place potato discs in hydrogen peroxide solutions of known pH and measure the rate at which oxygen is evolved. This reflects the activity of the catalase enzyme in the potato.

Procedure

1 With a cork borer, cut a cylinder of potato tuber tissue about 1 cm in diameter and at least 6 cm long. Slice the cylinder into discs 1 mm

Razor blade

thick and, as you do so, place them under water in a Petri dish. You require at least 60 discs.

2 Assemble the apparatus shown in Figure 2.3. Take particular care against breakage as you insert the manometer tube into the bung.

Glassware

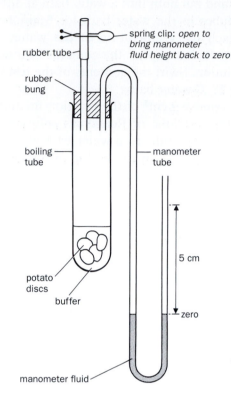

spring clip: *open to bring manometer fluid height back to zero*

rubber tube

rubber bung

boiling tube

manometer tube

5 cm

potato discs

buffer

zero

manometer fluid

Figure 2.3 Apparatus for measuring the rate of evolution of oxygen from hydrogen peroxide when living tissue is present.

Hydrogen peroxide solution

Eye protection must be worn

3 Remove the bung from the boiling tube. With a syringe, place into the boiling tube 5 cm³ of buffer solution at pH 3. Carefully add 10 potato discs. Then, with another syringe, add 5 cm³ of hydrogen peroxide solution. Wear eye protection.

4 Replace the bung immediately, making sure that it provides an airtight seal, and note the time. Mark on the right-hand manometer tube the position of the meniscus and draw a line 5 cm above it.

5 Gently agitate the boiling tube (why?). As the reaction begins and oxygen is produced, you should see the manometer fluid being pushed down the left-hand side of the manometer tube and rising on the right-hand side. Time how long it takes for the fluid to rise through 5 cm on the right-hand side.

6 Open the clip at the top of the boiling tube so that the manometer fluid returns to its original position. Then close the clip and time the production of a second 5 cm of oxygen. Work out the mean reading.

7 Remove the bung and thoroughly wash out the boiling tube.

8 Now carry out five further tests, each with a fresh set of 10 potato discs. Follow the same procedure, but with **buffer solutions** of pH 4, 5, 6, 7 and 8 in turn. Make sure that you use a *clean* syringe each time.

9 Take each of your mean readings and express the rate of reaction, in arbitrary units, by dividing 1000 by the time taken in seconds for a 5 cm rise in the manometer fluid.

10 Plot a graph of the rate of reaction (vertical axis) against pH.

For consideration

1 What is a 'buffer' solution? Why was it valuable to use buffer solutions in this experiment?

2 What was the relationship between the activity of potato catalase and pH?

3 Is the relationship between the activity of potato catalase and pH important for potato cells?

4 At the molecular level, how might pH affect the way an enzyme works?

5 Using the same apparatus, how would you measure the *volume* of gas given off per unit time?

Requirements

Razor blade
Cork borer
Ruler
Ceramic tile
Forceps
Boiling tube (with bored rubber bung)
Stand, bosses and clamps
Manometer tube (approx. 3 mm diameter)
Beaker
Syringes (5 cm³), ×2
Spring clip
Stopclock
Wax pencil
Potato tuber
Manometer fluid
Hydrogen peroxide solution ('20-volume')
Eye protection
Citric acid phosphate buffers, made up as shown below from Na_2HPO_4 ($0.2 \, mol \, dm^{-3}$) and citric acid ($0.1 \, mol \, dm^{-3}$) to give 100 cm³ of buffer in each case.

pH	Na_2HPO_4 (cm³)	Citric acid (cm³)
3.0	20.55	79.45
4.0	38.55	61.45
5.0	51.50	48.50
6.0	63.15	36.85
7.0	82.35	17.65
8.0	97.25	2.75

Effect of bead size on the activity of immobilised yeast or catalase[BM]

2.10 PRACTICAL EXERCISE

The **entrapment** of enzymes, yeast or other microorganisms in **beads** has become a standard technique in biotechnology. The beads can be easily replaced, removed, counted and handled; they can be cleaned with distilled water and used to create columns in which compounds are modified as they trickle down. Bead diameter influences surface area, which affects the rates of diffusion of compounds into and out of the beads.

In this practical exercise you will enclose yeast in alginate beads of different sizes, and use the rate of production of carbon dioxide gas as a measure of the rate of respiration. The same technique can be used to investigate the effect of bead size on the production of oxygen by the enzyme catalase acting on hydrogen peroxide. In this case it would be necessary to trap the *enzyme* in beads.

Procedure

1 Add 0.8 g of sodium alginate to 20 cm³ of distilled water, and stir this viscous liquid until it achieves an even consistency. Leave the solution to soak for 5 minutes.

2 Stir 1 g of yeast into 20 cm³ of distilled water and leave it to soak for 5 minutes.

3 Add the yeast suspension to the alginate solution and mix well with a glass rod.

4 Draw up 10 cm³ of the mixture into a syringe and drop the mixture, using a constant pressure so that the beads are all the same size, from a height of about 10 cm, into a beaker containing 100 cm³ of 1.4% calcium chloride solution.

5 Repeat this procedure twice more with different beakers of calcium chloride solution. In each case use a different speed of flow so as to produce beads of different sizes.

6 Allow the beads to stand in the calcium chloride solution for 20 minutes. Whilst they are standing, measure the average diameter of representative beads from each solution, with a ruler, under a binocular microscope, and then replace the beads. Strain with a tea strainer to remove the beads from the calcium chloride.

7 Set up three fermentation vessels as shown in Figure 2.4, with 3% sucrose solution and the beads. Investigate and record the relative rates of reaction.

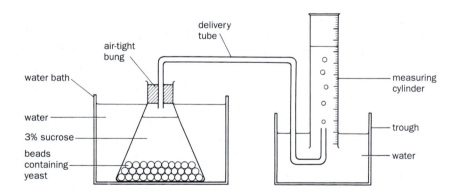

Figure 2.4 Simple apparatus for collecting carbon dioxide evolved from immobilised yeast, or oxygen from immobilised catalase acting on hydrogen peroxide.

Requirements

Beakers (250 cm³), ×4
Glass rod
Plastic syringe (10 cm³)
Tea strainer
Binocular microscope
Ruler
Fermentation apparatus (×3) as in Figure 2.4 (water bath, conical flask, bung and delivery tube, trough, 100 cm³ measuring cylinder)
Sodium alginate (2.4 g)
Distilled water
Calcium chloride solution (1.4%, 500 cm³)
Sucrose solution (3%, 750 cm³)
Dried yeast

For consideration

1 The volume of the beads is the same in all three solutions. Estimate the total surface areas of the beads in each solution, and the distance from the surface of a spherical bead to the centre.

2 Explain your results in terms of the ease with which sucrose enters a bead, the distance the molecules have to diffuse, and the average distance of the yeast cells from the surface of the bead.

About three-quarters of the world's human population are intolerant of **lactose** – milk sugar – in adulthood. This is one reason why milk may be treated with an enzyme, **lactase**: the enzyme breaks the disaccharide lactose into the monosaccharides glucose and galactose. The lactose content of milk can be reduced by passing it over lactase which has been immobilised in beads of alginate; the advantage of this procedure is that the encapsulated enzyme can be used again.

Procedure

1 Use a 10 cm³ syringe to transfer 8 cm³ of 2% sodium alginate solution to a small (50 or 25 cm³) beaker or plastic cup. Wear eye protection.
2 Use another 10 cm³ syringe to transfer 2 cm³ of lactase enzyme solution to the same beaker. Mix it thoroughly into the alginate solution.
3 Suck up the mixture into a third 10 cm³ syringe with a narrow outlet tube.
4 Gently add this mixture, a drop at a time, to 100 cm³ of 1.5% calcium chloride in a beaker. Hold the nozzle of the syringe 5 cm above the calcium chloride solution and press the plunger very gently. Make sure that the tip of the syringe does not touch the solution. Alginate beads, containing the enzyme, will appear in the solution. Try to make beads out of as much of the solution as possible. Then allow the beads to harden for 5 minutes.
5 During this time, clamp the empty syringe barrel (with the plastic tubing and Hoffman clip attached) to a vertical stand, with the base of the plastic tubing 15 cm above the bench surface. Place the small piece of nylon gauze at the base of the syringe barrel, so that it covers the entrance to the outlet.
6 Over a sink or a beaker, pour the alginate bead solution through a tea strainer to separate the beads. Transfer the beads to the clamped vertical syringe and gently tap them down to ensure that the milk cannot flow through them too rapidly.
7 Use a reagent strip to test the milk for glucose, and record the result.
8 Place a clean beaker beneath the plastic outlet tubing to the column. Begin to pour the milk down the column of beads. If you have time, you can close the Hoffman clip and allow the enzyme to work on the milk for a little while.
9 Collect the milk dripping from the base of the column, and test it for reducing sugar with the reagent strips, from time to time. Is there any difference from the result of your test on the milk at step 7?

For consideration

1 List as many advantages and disadvantages as you can of immobilising an enzyme in alginate beads.
2 Write an equation for the reaction, first in words and then in chemical symbols.
3 Suggest ways in which you could modify the apparatus to increase its efficiency on a commercial scale.

Lactase   Eye protection must be worn

Requirements

Small beakers (25 or 50 cm³), ×2
Beaker (250 cm³)
Syringes (10 cm³), ×3
Tea strainer
Retort stand, boss and clamp
Syringe barrel, 5 cm³ with plastic tubing and Hoffman clip attached
Nylon gauze (1–3 cm³)
Eye protection
Reagent strips, semi-quantitative, for determination of glucose (avoid touching the impregnated tip)
Milk (not UHT) (50 cm³ in a 100 cm³ beaker)
Lactase enzyme (available from NCBE)
Sodium alginate solution (2%, made up in distilled or deionised water, 8 cm³)
Calcium chloride solution (1.5%, 100 cm³)

Note: Beware of allergic reactions to lactase solution; avoid spills on the skin or rubbing eyes with contaminated fingers.

Reference

National Centre for Biotechnology Education. *Practical Biotechnology – A Guide for Schools and Colleges*. National Centre for Biotechnology Education, School of Animal and Microbial Sciences, University of Reading, Whiteknights, Reading RG6 6AJ.

2.12 PRACTICAL EXERCISE	**Removal of urea from solutions using immobilised urease[BM]**

In patients with kidney failure, urea accumulates in the blood rather than being excreted. One way to remove urea from the blood is to treat it with the enzyme **urease**, which decomposes urea into carbon dioxide and ammonia. This may be done in a reactor column containing the immobilised urease enzyme and 'activated' charcoal. **Immobilised enzymes** are enzyme molecules which have been trapped in beads of gelatine or on the surface of another compound to allow them to be handled more easily. The ammonia produced in this particular reaction is retained by the activated charcoal. The blood, free of urea, can then be returned to the patient. This practical simulates this process.

Procedure

Eye protection
must be worn

1   Mix 50 cm³ of urease solution and 50 cm³ of sodium alginate solution in a beaker. Wear eye protection. Draw this mixture into a plastic syringe. Inject it, drop by drop, into calcium chloride solution, in a beaker, to form about 300 uniformly sized beads. Remove the beads from the solution by straining through a tea strainer. Collect about 80 beads in boiling tubes, in groups of 10, ready for the calibration and estimation.

2   Set up the apparatus shown in Figure 2.5. First, remove the bottom of the plastic bottle, then turn it upside down and plug the neck with cotton wool. Place the neck of the inverted bottle in the jam jar (Figure 2.5A). Pack alternating layers of silver sand and activated

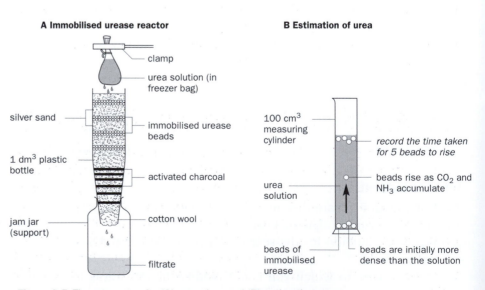

Figure 2.5 The apparatus for (**A**) removing, and (**B**) estimating urea.

charcoal into the bottom 10 cm of the bottle at the neck end. Then add alternating layers of silver sand and beads of immobilised urease to within 1–2 cm of the top.

3 Test and record the pH of the 2% urea solution provided. Pour about 150 cm³ of 2% urea solution into a freezer bag. Tie the bag with string. Clamp the bag above the inverted bottle. Prick the bag to establish a slow drip of urea solution through the apparatus.

4 Now establish a calibration curve. Fill a measuring cylinder to the 100 cm³ mark with 2% urea solution. Drop 10 beads of immobilised urease into the cylinder and note the time. The beads will sink, then slowly rise as they fill with carbon dioxide and ammonia, produced by the reaction between urease and urea. Record the time taken for five beads to rise to the surface (Figure 2.5B).

5 Repeat the procedure in step 4 using solutions containing 1.5, 1.0, 0.5 and 0.25% urea. In each case record the time taken for five beads to rise to the surface. Express the rate of reaction as 1000/time in seconds for the beads to rise. Plot a calibration curve showing the rate of reaction against the concentration of urea.

6 Now determine the concentration of the urea in the filtrate in the jam jar. Record the pH of the filtrate. Pour 100 cm³ of this filtrate into the measuring cylinder. (Keep the remaining filtrates.) Use 10 beads of immobilised urease, and your standard curve, to determine the concentration of urea.

7 Pass the remaining filtrate from the jam jar through the column a second time. Again, measure the pH, and find out how much urea the filtrate contains by repeating the measuring cylinder experiment and using the calibration curve.

For consideration

1 Did the passage of the urea solution through the column alter its pH, and if so, why?

2 Might this process have any use besides the treatment of blood by dialysis?

References

Freeland, P. W. *Focus on Biology: Micro-organisms in Action. Investigations*. Hodder & Stoughton, London, 1990.

Hawcroft, D. Simple studies on an immobilized enzyme. *Journal of Biological Education*, **31**, 141–145, 1997.

Requirements

Jam jar
Screw-top plastic bottle (1 dm³)
Scissors
Cotton wool
pH papers (pH 1–14)
Freezer bags, ×2
String
Clamp stand, boss and clamp
Pin
Beaker (250 cm³), ×2
Plastic syringe (10 cm³)
Tea strainer
Boiling tubes
Boiling tube rack
Measuring cylinder (100 cm³)
Glass rod
Eye protection
Urea solution (2%, 500 cm³)
Urease solution (60 cm³; see below)
Sodium alginate (3%, 75 cm³)
Calcium chloride (3%, 100 cm³)
Distilled *or* deionised water
Silver sand (500 g)
Activated charcoal (250 g)

Note: To make up the urease solution, crush 15 urease tablets in a polythene bag and dissolve the resulting powder in 1 dm³ of distilled water. Beware of allergic reactions to urease solution; avoid spills on the skin or rubbing eyes with contaminated fingers.

Use of pectinase in the production of fruit juice[BM]   2.13 PRACTICAL EXERCISE

Pectins are complex carbohydrates which are abundant in plant cell walls. In particular, they form the middle lamella layer – the 'glue' which sticks together adjacent plant cells in all plants, including apples. Apple juice is big business: millions of tons of apples are converted to juice each year. It is said that, by using enzymes called **pectinases** which break down pectins, the yield of apple juice from apples can be increased by 20%, even though as little as 150 cm³ of enzyme may need to be added to a ton of apples. This exercise enables you to test this claim.

Procedure

1. Label two 100 cm³ beakers, one 'pectinase' and the other 'control'. Check that a water bath set at 40 °C is available.
2. Using a knife, chop a medium sized apple into very small pieces on a ceramic tile. Add half to one beaker and half to another. Then check the masses of the two beakers on a balance. Adjust the pieces of apple until the masses of the two beakers are approximately equal.
3. Use a 5 cm³ syringe to collect 2.5 cm³ of pectinase enzyme from the supply provided. Use the same syringe to suck up another 2.5 cm³ of water from a beaker. Squirt the 5 cm³ of diluted enzyme onto the apple in the beaker marked 'pectinase'. Wear eye protection.
4. Using a different syringe, squirt 5 cm³ of water onto the apple pieces in the beaker marked 'control'.
5. Stir the contents of each beaker with a separate glass rod.
6. Incubate the beakers for 15–20 minutes in the water bath. Label two measuring cylinders 'pectinase' and 'control', and place in the top of each a filter funnel fitted with a coffee filter paper.
7. Pour the contents of the beakers into the filter funnels at the top of the appropriate measuring cylinders, and start the stopclock. Measure and record the volume of juice in each cylinder every 1 minute.
8. On the same piece of graph paper, plot graphs of the volume of juice collected against time for both treatments.
9. Determine the final volumes collected (in the same time interval) and combine the class results.

For consideration

1. Does the use of the pectinase enzyme have any effect on the volume of juice produced? Explain why this is.
2. What additional standardisation might you have carried out at the start of the experiment to enable you to compare the two sets of results for the class by a t-test (see Statistical Analysis Appendix, p. 304)?
3. What sorts of organisms might produce pectinases, and why?
4. Can you think of any other uses for pectinases?

Reference

National Centre for Biotechnology Education. *Practical Biotechnology – A Guide for Schools and Colleges*, 1993. National Centre for Biotechnology Education, School of Animal and Microbial Sciences, University of Reading, Whiteknights, Reading RG6 6AJ.

Eye protection must be worn

Knife

Pectinase

Requirements

Knife
Tile, ceramic
Marking pen for glass
Beakers (100 cm³), ×3
Balance, electrical
Syringes, plastic (5 cm³), ×2
Glass rods, ×2
Water bath, set to 40 °C
Measuring cylinders (100 cm³), ×2
Filter funnels, ×2
Coffee filter papers, ×2
Stopclock
Eye protection
Graph paper
Whole apples *or* tinned apple
Pectinase enzyme, e.g. available from NCBE

Note: Beware of allergic reactions to pectinase solution; avoid spills on the skin or rubbing eyes with contaminated fingers.

2.14 INVESTIGATION

The efficiency of various treatments intended to preserve milk[BM]

This experiment allows you to test the efficiency of different methods of **milk preservation**. Milk contains microorganisms, particularly *Lactobacillus* bacteria, which can reproduce rapidly at favourable temperatures. The lactic acid they produce in anaerobic respiration sours the milk and makes it unpalatable. The rate of microbial respiration in milk can be detected with resazurin dye and the accumulation of lactic acid can be estimated with a pH meter.

Several types of treated milk are commercially available, such as skimmed milk, semi-skimmed milk, ultra-heat-treated (UHT milk) and pasteurised milk. Unpasteurised milk ('green top') might serve as a control, though it is increasingly difficult to obtain. You can test these milks after they have been allowed to stand for various periods of time at room temperature. In addition, you can test the efficiency of your own methods of preservation, such as heat treatment, refrigeration, or the addition of sodium nitrite, vinegar or concentrated salt.

Sodium nitrite   Sodium nitrite

Guidance

A standardised test is required in order to assess the microbial activity in milk. The simplest is to mix the milk with resazurin dye at 37 °C and to record the rate at which the colour changes.

Add 1 cm³ of resazurin dye to each of a series of test tubes in a rack. Wear eye protection. Add 10 cm³ of milk to one of the tubes, replace the bung and, with your thumb on the bung, turn the tube upside down three times. Label the tube with the sample number and replace it in the rack. Repeat for the other tubes in turn. Record the colour of the contents of each tube, using the names blue, lilac, pink/mauve, pink and colourless. Record the colours every 5 minutes for 30 minutes. The more rapidly the colour changes, the greater the microbial activity in the milk.

Resazurin dye   Eye protection must be worn

The pH of milk samples can also be measured, preferably with a pH meter or probe but, failing that, with pH paper or universal indicator.

If you would like a more precise estimate of the numbers of microbes in milk, you can devise a **serial dilution** technique and estimate the numbers of colonies growing on china blue lactose agar.

For consideration

1. Why is milk particularly suitable for microbial growth?
2. Where do the *Lactobacillus* bacteria in milk come from?
3. Look up the various methods of pasteurisation used by dairies. How effective are they?
4. Try to find out the time that elapses between milk production and either its delivery to the doorstep, or its sale in a shop or supermarket. By how much would you expect its microbial population to increase during that time?
5. Can you find an effective preservative which does not alter the taste of milk? (Do not taste the milk.)

Requirements

Water bath at 37 °C
Test tubes with bungs
Test tube racks
Plastic syringes (2 cm³, 10 cm³)
Glass marker
Stopclock
pH meter with probe *or* pH paper *or* universal indicator
Eye protection
Various types of milk: skimmed, semi-skimmed, UHT, pasteurised and unpasteurised (if available)
Resazurin dye solution (instant)
Sodium nitrite
Spirit vinegar
Salt
China blue lactose agar

Key skills

✓ **Problem solving:** Explore the issue of how to test the efficiency of different methods of milk preservation. Suggest three options and justify the one you have selected. Plan how to carry out your chosen option and obtain agreement from your teacher/lecturer to go ahead. Implement your plan, obtaining and using feedback from others. These others might be your fellow students but you could, for example, approach people working in the food industry or in the microbiology department of a local university. Review progress towards solving the problem and revise your approach as necessary. Review your approach to problem solving, including whether alternative methods and options might have proved more effective.

Effect of age on the characteristics of milk[BM]

This investigation extends over more than one practical session.

The chemical composition of milk alters in subtle ways during its journey from the udder to your mouth. Sealed milk decomposes because of the enzymes produced by bacteria; bacteria remain, in small numbers, even after pasteurisation. Milk often remains in the refrigerator (or even outside it!) for some time, before being drunk. How does its quality as a foodstuff alter during this time? For background information, and for a method to assess the numbers of bacteria with time, see Investigation 2.14, p.74.

Guidance

In order to assess the amounts of reducing sugar, lipids or protein in milk samples you will need access to a colorimeter and the reagents in Practical Exercise 1.4 (p.22). Vitamin C, however, can be estimated without a colorimeter (Investigation 1.10, p.31), and semi-quantitative glucose test strips can be used to estimate lactose (multiply the glucose measurement by 1.92).

Design your experiment with care. Decide on at least three treatments, one of which is likely to be 'fresh' milk, the earliest you can obtain, and another of which is likely to be the same type of milk which has been kept at room temperature for a few days. If you intend to carry out all your measurements on one day, then several days before this you will need to begin to store your milk samples.

You need to decide whether to use only one storage condition, or to compare, say, storage in a refrigerator with storage at room temperature.

You also need to decide whether to store your samples sealed and unopened, or to open them to the air. To store them opened may introduce unpredictable numbers of bacteria; on the other hand, many people keep their milk open for some days until they finish the bottle, so this may both be more realistic and produce more dramatic results.

You should also plan how many samples of milk you will test in each storage condition. Single measurements, with only one test on milk of each age, are not scientifically respectable. If you carry out at least three tests for the same foodstuff on milk of each age, you may be able to compare the averages by using a t-test (see Statistical Analysis Appendix, p.304). You need to decide from the outset whether you will keep three or four bottles of the same age, or separate the milk of this age into three or four sterilised containers from the start, or whether it is sufficient merely to test one sample of milk three or four times.

Requirements

Apparatus and reagents for carrying out the quantitative food tests (Practical Exercise 1.4, p.22) or vitamin C tests (Investigation 1.10, p.31)
Fresh milk
Milk of the same sort stored in bottles or in sterilised glassware at room temperature (or in various places if the object is to compare different conditions) for different periods of time

For consideration

1 Why is milk such a valuable food for young mammals?
2 Explain your results. What enzymes might the bacteria be releasing, or could the bacteria be absorbing the compound you have been investigating? Have you enough evidence to justify the conclusion that the nutritional quality of milk does alter during storage?
3 Consider your family's own habits for storing milk. How might they be improved?
4 At what stage of storage might milk become unsafe to drink?

✓ **Application of number:** Compare the concentrations of the compounds you are testing in milk stored for different lengths of time by t-tests (see Statistical Analysis Appendix, p.304). Think about the appropriate level of accuracy for expressing your findings. Interpret the results of your calculations in terms of the numbers of bacteria present at different times.

✓ **Information technology:** Plot the graphs by using a computer graphical package. Ensure you present the information effectively, using a suitable format and style to combine text, image(s) and numbers.

✓ **Working with others:** If different individuals or pairs carry out different chemical tests, the class as a whole can accumulate more results, which can be shared. Milk storage also has to be organised. Discuss with one another, at the planning stage, the range of treatments, number of samples and storage methods you will use. Arrange between yourselves a schedule for milk purchase and storage, and have it checked by your teacher or lecturer.

Yoghurt production[BM]   2.16 PRACTICAL EXERCISE

Traditionally, yoghurt is made by incubating sterilised milk at about 45°C with the bacteria *Streptococcus thermophilus* and *Lactobacillus bulgaricus* in approximately equal proportions. After *S. thermophilus* has removed oxygen, creating anaerobic conditions, *Lactobacillus* anaerobically respires some of the milk sugar lactose to lactic acid. This acidifies the milk from pH 6.6–6.7 to a pH of 4.5–5.0. At this point the milk protein casein precipitates, forming a curd on the surface.

Procedure

1   Heat 1 litre of milk in a lidded saucepan to a temperature of 90°C. Then switch down the heat so that the milk remains at about 90°C for 10 minutes without boiling.
2   Leaving the lid on the container, cool the milk to 45°C.
3   Add 100 cm³ of natural, unpasteurised yoghurt to the milk and stir with a sterilised spoon or glass rod.
4   Pour the mixture into small sterilised containers which have sterilised lids, such as sterilised yoghurt cartons or sterilised glass jars with screw tops. Fill each container nearly to the top. Do not seal the lids, and leave screw tops loose. Alternatively, use clingfilm.
5   Place the yoghurt cultures in an oven at 30–45°C, or alternatively in a warm place.
6   After 18 hours, open the containers tentatively and examine them. Autoclave and throw away any that smell bad. Compare the pH of the final product with the original pH of the UHT milk. Do not eat any of the yoghurt.

Yoghurt

For consideration

1   Why was the milk heated to 90°C for 10 minutes at the start of the procedure?

Sterilised glass measuring cylinders
    (1 dm³, 100 cm³)
Saucepan, lidded
Hot plate *or* Bunsen burner and tripod
Thermometer
Spoon *or* glass rod, sterilised
Small cardboard cartons with lids *or*
    small screw-top jars, sterilised
    (100–250 cm³); alternatively, use
    clingfilm to seal
Oven (or water bath) at 45 °C
pH probe or pH paper
Skimmed or whole milk, UHT (1 dm³)
Natural, unpasteurised yoghurt culture
    (100 cm³)

2   When making yoghurt with fruit, would you add fruit at the beginning or the end? Give three reasons for your answer.
3   How would you produce a low-fat yoghurt?
4   Why are yoghurts resistant to bacterial decay?

References

Henderson, J., Knutton, S., Lally, V. and others. Biotechnology and the food industry. *Journal of Biological Education*, **25**, 95–102, 1991.

Stewart, P. E. Safely teaching Koch's postulates on the causation of infectious disease. *Journal of Biological Education*, **24**, 117–122, 1990.

2.17 INVESTIGATION

The optimum conditions for dry matter production by a fermenter[BM]

A **bioreactor** is a chamber in which defined conditions are maintained to encourage the production of useful compounds by the organisms inside. Several types of bioreactor are commercially available. Maintaining a pure culture of an organism inside a bioreactor for several weeks, with the continuous removal of the product, provides a useful insight into **commercial biotechnology**.

Another valuable exercise is to develop your own bioreactor and to test and refine various versions over several weeks. Some of the factors to be considered, and the problems to be overcome, are outlined here. The object is to attain a **continuous flow process**, in which some compounds are continually added and products are continually removed.

Guidance

Work in a group and share responsibilities.

1   The simplest bioreactor may be a boiling tube, with a cotton wool plug, containing an organism and its substrate, placed in a water bath.
2   **Contamination** with invading microorganisms is likely to be a problem, so all the materials should be autoclaved or disinfected with a dilute bleach solution.
3   To prevent contamination, it will be necessary to seal the top of the tube, but then the shortage of oxygen, the accumulation of waste gases or the pressure of accumulated gases may be a problem.
4   One solution to this would be to connect the reactor to an aquarium pump, connected to a cotton wool dust filter, and to provide an air exit, again with a filter to prevent the entry of foreign microorganisms. The entry of air must be slow, to avoid cooling the culture.
5   The addition of another glass tube to the cork at the top of the reactor would then allow sampling of the reaction mixture, and perhaps the harvesting of the products. A finger over the air exit builds up pressure sufficiently for some of the solution to pass through this sampling tube to be collected.
6   At this stage the circulation of the liquid within the reaction vessel

needs to be measured and improved. You may have to change the shape of the reaction vessel.

7   The addition of a further tube to the cork at the top allows the addition of extra nutrients or drops of acid or alkali to maintain a certain pH. If this can be done by drip feed under gravity, it begins to convert this process into a continuous one.

8   An additional degree of sophistication is provided by incorporating a motorised stirrer and internal aquarium-style heater into the reaction vessel. An infra-red detector allows the turbidity of the solution to be monitored, and a pH probe (linked to a computer with suitable data-logging software) allows a continuous read-out of pH to be obtained.

For consideration

1   How could you alter the conditions to maximise the output of useful product from your reactor?

2   What problems might you encounter in 'scaling up' the process a hundred thousand times to an industrial scale, and how might you overcome them?

Reference

Cowley, G., Lazonby, J., Brown, A. & Betts, B. A practical coffee-jar model of industrial fermentation. *School Science Review*, **81** (294), 103–107, 1999. (For another account of how to make your own fermenter.)

Requirements

This is an open-ended investigation and access to general laboratory glassware, bungs and glass tubing is required. It is valuable to have an autoclave (to sterilise glassware), an aquarium air pump and a water bath or aquarium heater with thermostat.
The reactor can be tried out with a variety of organisms. Examples include: *Saccharomyces cerevisiae* or *S. elipsoideus* in a sucrose- or glucose-containing medium (at 25–30 °C?) to produce ethanol and carbon dioxide; *Acetobacter aceti*, which produces vinegar when cultivated on dilute ethanol (at 30 °C?); *Alcaligenes eutrophus*, which produces polyhydroxybutyrate, a polymer to make plastic, when grown on dilute nutrient broth (at 30 °C?).

Key skills

✓   **Working with others:** Agree realistic objectives and suitable arrangements for working together. As an individual, organise and carry out your tasks so that you can be effective and efficient in meeting your responsibilities and produce the quality of work required. At the end of the investigation, agree, as a group, the extent to which the work was successful and, if appropriate, discuss ways of improving work with others in future.

✓   **Information technology:** Enter and bring together information in a consistent form, using automated routines where appropriate (e.g. data-logging of pH changes). Create and use appropriate structures and procedures to explore, develop and derive information (e.g. model the effect of changes in pH, temperature or oxygen concentration by setting up and running a simple spreadsheet). Use effective methods of exchanging information to support your purposes (e.g. e-mail your provisional findings to another group of advanced level biology students for them to comment on).

✓   **Communication:** During the investigation, make clear and relevant contributions, listen and respond sensitively to others and, if needs be, create opportunities for others to contribute to discussions. As a group, produce a report on the optimum conditions for dry matter production by a fermenter that uses a form of writing appropriate to the subject matter. Organise relevant information clearly and coherently, using specialist vocabulary where appropriate. Ensure your text is legible and the spelling, punctuation and grammar accurate, so that your meaning is clear. (Word processing and using a spell check will help here, but you may want to ask someone with good literary skills – ? a librarian or English teacher/lecturer – to read through one of your later drafts.)

Effect of temperature on the oxygen consumption of organisms

In organisms such as plants and arthropods, which have little or no control over their own body temperatures, the temperature inside the organism generally fluctuates with that of the environment. The respiration rate of such organisms changes accordingly. The aim of this experiment is to find out how temperature affects the rate of respiration of broad beans, mung beans, maggots, mealworms or woodlice. It also illustrates the principle of using an important piece of apparatus, the **respirometer**.

Principle

If a group of organisms is oxidising glucose by aerobic respiration, the volume of oxygen taken up equals the volume of carbon dioxide produced. In a closed vessel containing respiring organisms, the concentration of oxygen will decrease and the concentration of carbon dioxide will increase.

Suppose, however, that a compound which absorbs carbon dioxide is placed inside the closed vessel. The respiring organisms still absorb oxygen, and the rate at which the pressure decreases is a measure of the rate at which the organisms take up oxygen.

Two identical closed vessels are used. One contains living organisms, and the other (the control) contains either dead organisms or an equal volume of an inert material. The control is necessary because temperature changes affect the volumes of the gases. Any differences between the two vessels can then be attributed to gaseous exchange by the living organisms.

Procedure

Setting up the apparatus

1   If one is available, set a thermostatically controlled water bath to 20 °C. Alternatively, fill a beaker half full with cold water, to act as a water bath. Place it on a tripod and gauze and take the temperature of the water with a thermometer. If it is below 20 °C, heat the beaker gently with a Bunsen burner until it reaches 20 °C.

2   Label two boiling tubes L and D. Place living organisms in tube L and the equivalent number of dead organisms, or volume of inert material, in tube D. Put 5 g of soda lime into the tubes first, then the cotton wool, and then the organisms on top. Avoid inhaling any dust. (If you put the organisms at the bottom, carbon dioxide, which is heavier than air, may not be absorbed by the soda lime but accumulate at the bottom of the boiling tubes and kill the living organisms.)

Soda lime

3   Pour a coloured manometer fluid into the reservoir of one of the manometers. If air bubbles appear in the capillary tube of the manometer, use a pipette filler to blow air down the long arm of the manometer tube to remove them (care!).

Glassware

4   Gingerly, without creating air bubbles in the fluid, fit the long arm of the manometer tube into the rubber tubing attached to one of the rubber bungs. Fit the bung securely into one of the boiling tubes (care!).

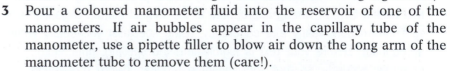

5 Repeat steps 3 and 4 with the other manometer tube and bung. Clamp the two boiling tubes vertically in the water bath, making sure that both spring clips are open. Your apparatus should now look like Figure 2.6.

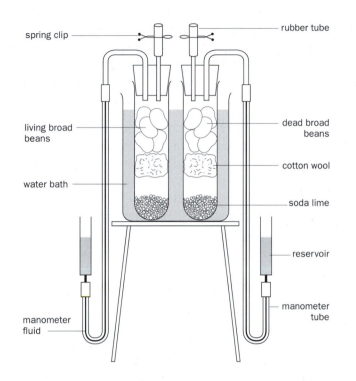

Figure 2.6 A respirometer, with control, for measuring the rate of oxygen uptake by small organisms, in this case broad beans.

Carrying out an experiment

1 Make sure both spring clips are open. Check that your water bath is at 20 °C. Mark the levels of the menisci of the coloured fluid in both manometer tubes. Close both the spring clips. Note the time.

2 Record the levels of the fluid in both manometers, for example after 3, 6 and 9 minutes. If the level of the manometer fluid attached to boiling tube L does not change, check carefully for leaks and start again.

3 Open both spring clips. If a constant-temperature water bath is not being used, gently heat the beaker with a Bunsen burner until the water temperature reaches 33 °C. Remove the Bunsen burner. Allow at least 5 minutes for the beans to reach this temperature and for the volume of the air in the boiling tubes to stabilise. By this time the water should have cooled to about 30 °C. Repeat steps 1 and 2 at this temperature.

4 Open both spring clips. Pour away the water at 30 °C and replace it with cold tap water. Add a few cubes of ice until the water reaches 8 °C. Allow 10 minutes for the beans to reach this temperature and for the volumes of air in the boiling tubes to stabilise. By this time the water in the beaker should have reached about 10 °C. Repeat steps 1 and 2 at this temperature.

Ideally, a thermostatically controlled
   water bath
Beaker
Bunsen burner, tripod, gauze, bench
   mat
Thermometer
Boiling tubes, ×2
Rubber bungs (each with two holes and
   two glass tubes with rubber
   attached), ×2
Cotton wool
Manometer tubes (capillaries), ×2
Pen for marking glass
Spring clips, ×2 *or* two-way taps
Clamp stand, two bosses and two
   clamps
Ice
Self-indicating soda lime
Manometer fluid
Mealworms, maggots *or* woodlice
Broadbean (*Vicia faba*) seeds (×6)
   soaked in cold water for 24 hours,
   and 6 beans, similarly treated but
   then boiled for 10 minutes

5 Plot your data on a graph which shows the volume of oxygen evolved against time for each of the three temperatures.

For consideration

1 How much faster is the respiration rate at 20°C than at 10°C? How much faster is the respiration rate at 30°C than at 20°C? In working out these values you are calculating two estimates of the Q_{10}. The Q_{10} indicates the extent to which the rate of reaction increases with a 10°C increase in temperature. The Q_{10} is slightly in excess of 2 for a large number of enzyme-controlled reactions. Do your results agree with this?

2 Explain, in terms of the behaviour of individual molecules, why the rate of an enzyme-controlled reaction doubles with a 10°C increase in temperature (there are two main reasons).

3 Suppose that the uptake of oxygen suddenly stops but the seeds remain alive. Suggest an explanation.

4 If you have been using soaked seeds, they may be respiring anaerobically as well as aerobically. How might this have affected your results, and why?

2.19 INVESTIGATION

Determination of the respiratory quotient

Using a modified respirometer (Practical Exercise 2.18 on p. 80), it is possible to determine the **respiratory quotient** (**RQ**) of organisms. This is the ratio of the volume of carbon dioxide produced to the volume of oxygen absorbed. Its value provides evidence as to the substrate being respired and the extent to which the tissue is respiring anaerobically.

Principle

If an organism is only respiring glucose **aerobically**, the volume of carbon dioxide produced equals the volume of oxygen absorbed, so the respiratory quotient should be 1.0.

If a tissue is respiring fats aerobically, the respiratory quotient should be about 0.7. Imagine, for example, that stearic (octodecanoic) acid is being respired:

$$C_{17}H_{35}COOH + 26O_2 \rightarrow 18CO_2 + 18H_2O$$

the respiratory quotient is $18/26 = 0.69$.

When **anaerobic respiration** to lactate is taking place, no carbon dioxide is produced. However, organisms respiring anaerobically to ethanol, such as yeast and plant tissue, produce carbon dioxide. Their respiratory quotient is very high.

In practice, many organisms carry out aerobic and anaerobic respiration simultaneously. The relative extents of aerobic and anaerobic respiration can then be estimated from the respiratory quotient. Imagine, for example, that seeds produce twice as much carbon dioxide as the oxygen they absorb (RQ = 2). The aerobic respiration of a gram of glucose produces three times the volume of carbon dioxide as anaerobic respiration, so this respiratory quotient might indicate that glucose was being broken down three times faster by anaerobic than by aerobic respiration. Think about it!

Guidance

Obtain batches of broad bean seeds which have been soaked in water (i) for 48 hours, (ii) for 42 hours and removed for 6 hours, (iii) for 36 hours and removed for 12 hours; these make ideal material.

The apparatus required is a pair of respirometer tubes in a water bath (Figure 2.6 on p. 81), but in this case one contains soda lime and the other does not. Avoid inhaling dusts. It is important that the volume of gas is identical in each tube, so that any temperature fluctuations will affect both equally. The tubes must both contain equal masses of the same species of respiring organisms, and the one without soda lime must contain an equivalent volume of an inert compound. Above all, the temperature of the water bath must not fluctuate during the experiment. You may wish to devise your own system of thermostatic control – a good opportunity to apply technology to biology.

As soda lime absorbs carbon dioxide, the tube containing it measures oxygen uptake. The other tube measures net gas exchange. The carbon dioxide output is the difference between these two readings. A decrease is negative and an increase is positive.

For consideration

1 Suppose that your germinating seeds appeared to have a net oxygen production. Suggest two possible reasons for this result.
2 Look up how fatty acids are respired in a cell. Why can't they be respired anaerobically?
3 Imagine that you obtained a respiratory quotient of 0.9. Discuss possible reasons.

Soda lime

Effect of temperature on the rate of anaerobic respiration of yeast[BM]

Many yeasts of the genus *Saccharomyces* can grow in the absence of oxygen; some do not even have mitochondria for aerobic respiration. Under these conditions, yeast respires anaerobically: glucose is converted to carbon dioxide and ethanol in the process of **fermentation**:

$$C_6H_{12}O_6 \rightarrow 2CO_2 + 2C_2H_5OH$$

The rate at which carbon dioxide is produced can be used to measure the rate of anaerobic respiration of yeast. In this experiment you will determine the effect of temperature on the rate of fermentation.

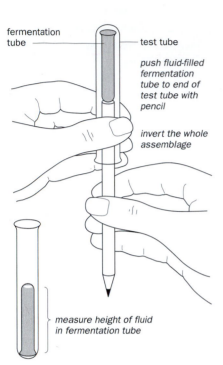

fermentation tube ——— test tube

push fluid-filled fermentation tube to end of test tube with pencil

invert the whole assemblage

measure height of fluid in fermentation tube

Figure 2.7 Assembling a fermentation tube.

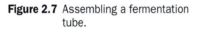

Requirements

Balance
Beaker (250 cm³)
Fermentation tubes, ×6
Graph paper
Dropping pipettes, ×3
Pipette *or* syringe (3 cm³), ×3
Ruler with millimetre scale
Spatula
Stopclock *or* stopwatch
Test tubes, ×6
Water bath (at 20 °C, 35 °C and 50 °C)
Test tube racks in water baths
Thermometers

Note: An hour before the practical starts, set up a culture of yeast in a beaker containing glucose (3 g), dried yeast (2 g), yeast extract (1 g) and water (100 cm³). Place this culture in an incubator or water bath at 35 °C for 1 hour to allow fermentation to begin.

Procedure

1 You are provided with a yeast culture set up an hour before. Using a pipette or syringe, transfer 10 cm³ of the culture to each of six test tubes.

2 Place two tubes in each of three water baths, at 20 °C, 35 °C and 50 °C. If thermostatically controlled water baths are not available, use three water-filled beakers, each containing a thermometer, supported on a tripod and gauze, over a Bunsen burner. Keep the temperature of the water as constant as possible by a judicious combination of heating and, when necessary, adding bits of ice.

3 Leave the tubes in the water baths for 5 minutes to allow the temperatures of their contents to reach the temperature of the water bath.

4 Now fill a fermentation tube and insert it upside down into an empty test tube. Carry out the following procedure for each of the six tubes:

   a Insert a teat pipette into the culture, suck up some of the culture, and fill the fermentation tube to the brim.

   b With a pencil, push the fermentation tube into an inverted test tube, then turn the whole assemblage the other way up, as shown in Figure 2.7.

   c If the fermentation tube collects a bubble during the procedure, remove it, refill it and try once more.

5 At intervals of 10 minutes, record the length of the carbon dioxide bubble within each fermentation tube. Work out the mean bubble length for each temperature at each time interval.

6 Draw a graph of mean bubble length (vertical axis) against time (horizontal axis). Plot three lines on it, one each for 20 °C, 35 °C and 50 °C. Estimate the rate of fermentation at each temperature by measuring the slope of each line.

For consideration

1 In what way does the rate of fermentation vary with temperature? Most enzyme-controlled processes approximately double in rate for each 10 °C increase in temperature. Do your results confirm this general rule, or not?

2 Carbon dioxide is very soluble in water. Why did it accumulate at the end of the tube, instead of dissolving in the water?

3 What lessons might brewers learn from the results of this experiment?

Brewing and bread-making are perhaps the earliest, and still the most economically important, examples of biotechnology. Both are eminently suitable for investigations in school, but brewing is usually longer-term and investigations may extend over several practical sessions. Here, we shall concentrate on bread-making, because this provides rapid results and several different procedures can be carried out by different individuals simultaneously.

Guidance

A good way of assessing dough production is to make it rise within a measuring cylinder, as follows. If you have been given dried yeast rather than fresh yeast, revitalise 1 g of it in 50 cm^3 of water, in a beaker, stirring with a glass rod. Add 75 g of flour and continue to mix well. It is difficult to put the dough into the measuring cylinder without it sticking to the sides – if you pour it into the measuring cylinder, be very careful. Standard techniques are to roll it into a sausage shape on kitchen-roll paper before dropping it down the middle of the cylinder, or to mix in a known mass of vegetable oil, which makes the dough much more slippery. Record the height of the dough at 2 minute intervals.

Plan an experiment to compare the rates at which different types of dough rise in two or more cylinders, setting them all up at about the same time. The following information about dough will enable you to decide what to vary:

- Yeast cells are trapped in water in the matrix of flour, which contains proteins (collectively known as **gluten**) which bind it together.
- Breakdown of starch in the dough occurs because amylases present in the flour convert the starch to sugars, which the yeast can respire.
- Meanwhile, proteases break the proteins down to peptides, which the yeast uses as a source of nitrogen.

You could test the effects of different types of yeast, different qualities of flour, or different quantities of additives, such as amylases, salt, vitamin C or potassium bromate:

Potassium bromate   Potassium bromate

- Amylases might increase the rate at which glucose is made available to the yeast.
- Salt might inhibit the protein-digesting enzymes and yeast growth.
- Vitamin C is meant to reduce the rate at which enzymes from the flour bind the gluten together.
- Potassium bromate should have the opposite effect, helping enzymes to bind together adjacent gluten proteins, making the dough more elastic.

Plot the volumes of dough against time, putting the results from all your treatments on the same graph. This will give you the rate of rising. To compare the rates statistically, by a t-test (see Statistical Analysis Appendix, p. 304), the class will need to pool their results for the rates at which dough rises in the same treatments.

For each part of the experiment:
    Measuring cylinder, 200 cm³
    Beaker, 250 cm³
    Glass rod
    Kitchen roll, paper *or* vegetable oil
    Balance, electrical
    Stopclock
    Graph paper
    Yeast, 1 g
    Water, 50 cm³
    Flour, strong, 75 g
Optional:
    Amylase (sold for wine-making) or
    amylase solution
    Vitamin C (ascorbic acid), e.g. 1 g per
    cylinder
    Salt
    Potassium bromate

Key skills

For consideration

1 Explain, in terms of the biochemistry of yeast cells, why dough rises.
2 Did the dough rise at a constant rate during the investigation? If not, why not?
3 Find out what biochemical processes occur within a seed as it germinates. Work out the similarities and differences between seed germination and what happens in dough as it rises. How are the two processes related?
4 Suggest some tests to compare the different qualities of the dough, such as elasticity, manifested in the various treatments.

Reference

National Centre for Biotechnology Education. *Practical Biotechnology – A Guide for Schools and Colleges*, 1993. National Centre for Biotechnology Education, School of Animal and Microbial Sciences, University of Reading, Whiteknights, Reading RG6 6AJ.

> **Note:** Beware of allergic reactions to amylase solution; avoid spills on the skin or rubbing eyes with contaminated fingers.

✓ **Application of number:** Calculate the growth rates of the dough, pool the class results and test the null hypothesis that the rate at which dough rises is the same in the various treatments.

✓ **Information technology:** Use books and/or the internet to search for information about possible factors to vary. Show that your selections are based on relevance (i.e. likely importance). Once you have obtained your results, bring them together in a consistent form, using automated routines to plot the data and draw lines of best fit through the points.

✓ **Working with others:** Before the experiment starts, you need to discuss with others which treatments you wish to apply, and ensure that at least four estimates are made of each treatment in the class, in order that the results may be tested statistically. At the end of the experiment, you need to pool class results – but analyse them independently.

2.22 TECHNIQUE

Dissection

The object of **dissection** is to reveal the anatomy, not to destroy it. Here are 10 golden rules of dissection, with particular reference to the dissection of a mammal:

1 Keep your dissecting instruments in good condition; always disinfect and dry them after use.
2 Pin the specimen to a dissecting board or to the bottom of a dissecting dish so that the body wall is stretched. Disinfect boards and dishes after use.
3 When appropriate, dissect the animal under water; the water supports the organs and will help you to separate the tissues.
4 If you are not dissecting in water, keep your dissection moist at all times. If you need to leave it for a while, cover it with a damp cloth.

Caution

In the interests of hygiene, wear a lab. coat while you are dissecting, and wash your hands thoroughly afterwards. When dissecting tissue such as bone or cartilage, wear eye protection to guard against flying splinters.

5 Before making a cut, consider what organ you are looking for and where it is likely to be. *Never cut or remove anything without knowing what it is.*

6 When dissecting such structures as nerves and blood vessels, work along – not across – their course.

7 When following nerves and blood vessels, avoid damaging them, by cutting upwards away from them rather than downwards towards them.

8 Remove only those structures which, if left in position, would obscure the structures you want to expose.

9 In the final stage of your dissection, make sure all the structures that you wish to show are clearly displayed.

10 In displaying your dissection, make judicious use of pins and thread to separate structures from each other.

> ***Note:* Dissection**
>
> You should not be required to dissect if you would prefer not to. Think carefully about whether you wish to dissect or not. Recent years have seen significant advances in alternatives to animal dissection. (See for example, M. Predavec, Evaluation of E-Rat, a computer-based rat dissection, in terms of student learning outcomes, *Journal of Biological Education*, **35**, 75–80, 2001.)

Dissection of the gaseous exchange system of the rat

2.23 PRACTICAL EXERCISE

The purpose of this dissection is to investigate the pathway by which air passes into and out of the lungs. This pathway, an essential part of the **gaseous exchange system**, can be seen by dissecting a rat.

Procedure

1 If it has not already been done, deflect the skin in the thoracic and neck regions of the rat and pin it back as explained in Practical Exercise 2.31 on p.100. The specimen should look like Figure 2.8.

2 Open up the thorax by cutting along the dotted lines shown in Figure 2.8. Tie a thread round the xiphoid cartilage and pull it back so as to pull the **diaphragm** down (Figure 2.9). Note the **muscles of the diaphragm** and the **intercostal muscles** between the ribs.

> **Caution**
>
> In the interests of hygiene, wear a lab. coat while you are dissecting, and wash your hands thoroughly afterwards. When dissecting tissue such as bone or cartilage, wear eye protection to guard against flying splinters. Disinfect equipment after use.

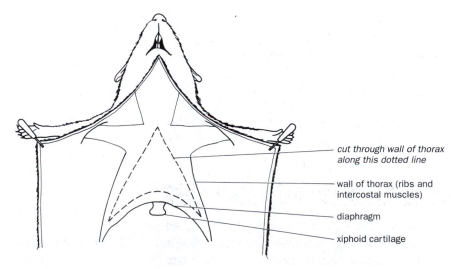

cut through wall of thorax along this dotted line

wall of thorax (ribs and intercostal muscles)

diaphragm

xiphoid cartilage

Figure 2.8 How to open up the thorax of a rat.

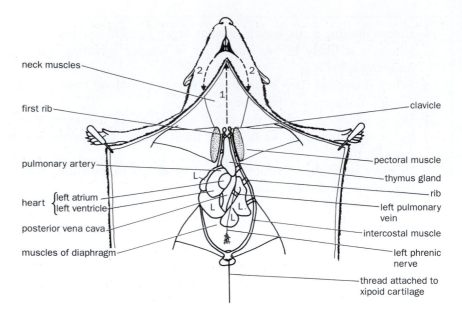

Figure 2.9 Stage in the dissection of the breathing apparatus of the rat. L, lobes of the lungs.

Scalpel

3 Remove the thymus gland from the surface of the heart. Be careful not to damage the heart and blood vessels, for you may want to explore them in a future dissection (p. 125). Note the **phrenic nerve**, which innervates the diaphragm.

4 With a scalpel cut along the centre of the neck muscles (arrow 1 in Figure 2.9). Deflect the muscles so as to see the **trachea** underneath.

5 Cut along the angle of the jaws on both sides of the head (arrow 2 in Figure 2.9).

6 Grasp the tongue with forceps and cut along the sides of the **pharynx** as far back as the **glottis**. This is the point where the breathing tract crosses the alimentary canal.

7 Pull back the tongue and floor of the pharynx and notice the **epiglottis** guarding the glottis (Figure 2.10). Insert a seeker into the glottis and confirm that it enters the **larynx** ('voice box') and trachea.

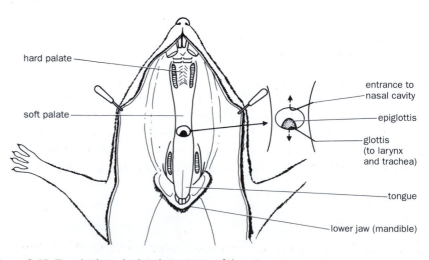

Figure 2.10 The glottis and related structures of the rat.

8 Under the trachea, as you look at your dissection, is the **oesophagus**. Insert a seeker into the entrance to the oesophagus. Wiggle the seeker from side to side and notice that it distends the wall of the oesophagus.

9 Now identify the soft palate. Beneath this, as you look at your dissection, is the **nasal cavity**. Insert a flexible bristle into the nasal cavity from the glottis and push it upwards. It should come out of one of the **nostrils**.

10 Insert the tip of an air-filled teat pipette into the glottis so that it points down the trachea. Squeeze the rubber bulb. This should have the effect of inflating the **lungs**.

11 Follow the trachea down to the thorax. It passes under the heart, as you look at your dissection, and divides into a pair of **bronchi**, one to each lung. Seeing the connection between the bronchi and the lungs necessitates removing the heart and major blood vessels. Don't do this now if you will be using this rat for dissecting the circulatory system later (Practical Exercise 2.47 on p. 125).

For consideration

1 Draw a diagram, *based on your dissection*, showing in side view how the breathing tract crosses the alimentary canal in the throat.

2 What are the possible advantages and disadvantages of the fact that the breathing tract crosses the alimentary canal in the throat?

3 Trace the path taken by a molecule of oxygen from the air just outside a person's nose to the lungs.

Reference

Rowett, H. G. Q. *Dissection Guides*, *III The Rat*. John Murray, London, 1951.

Requirements

Dissecting instruments
Dissecting board and pins
Teat pipette
Thread
Flexible bristle
Rat for dissection
Eye protection

Microscopic structure of the mammalian gaseous exchange system

2.24 PRACTICAL EXERCISE

Functionally, the gaseous exchange system consists of two components:

* The surface where gaseous exchange takes place: the **gaseous exchange surface**.
* The pathway through which air is moved to and from the gaseous exchange surface: the **breathing tract**.

In its microscopic structure, the gaseous exchange surface would be expected to show an intimate relationship between the inspired air and the bloodstream, while the breathing tract should keep the tubes permanently open and prevent anything other than air reaching the gaseous exchange surface. In this practical exercise you will examine the **trachea** and the **lungs** under the microscope and see if these predictions are correct.

Procedure

Trachea

The trachea is a permanently open tube which permits the unimpeded flow of clean air to and from the lungs.

1 Examine a transverse section of trachea under first low and then high power. Use Figure 2.11 to help you identify the various structures in the tracheal wall.

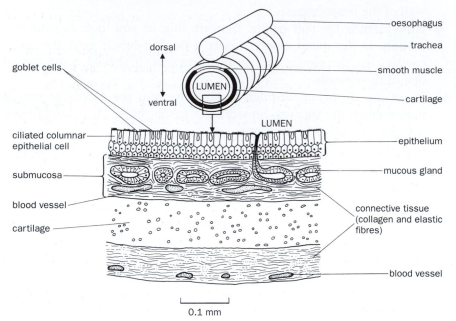

Figure 2.11 Diagram of a transverse section through the wall of the mammalian trachea.

2 Look carefully at the **ciliated epithelium** lining the inner surface of the wall. The ciliated cells are interspersed with mucus-secreting **goblet cells**. What are the functions of the cilia and mucus?

3 Look out for **mucous glands** in the submucosa immediately beneath the epithelium. If you are lucky, your section may show a duct leading to the surface from one of the glands. (Why do you need to be 'lucky' to see this?)

4 Notice the incomplete ring of **cartilage** embedded in the centre of the wall. What is the function of the cartilage, and why is the ring incomplete?

Lung

The lung consists of a tree-like system of branching tubes (bronchi and bronchioles) which lead, via cavities called **atria**, to numerous **alveoli**.

1 Examine a section of lung under low or medium power. Use Figure 2.12 to help you identify the structures visible in your section. Here are some tips to help you distinguish between the various structures:

- **Bronchi** are like smaller versions of the trachea: their inner epithelium is ciliated and their walls contain mucous glands and cartilage.
- **Bronchioles** are usually ciliated, but they are much smaller than bronchi and lack mucous glands and cartilage.
- **Atria** are relatively large cavities into which terminal bronchioles open; they have very thin walls of squamous epithelium (see p. 44).
- **Alveoli** are much smaller cavities leading from the atria; they too have very thin walls of squamous epithelium.
- **Blood vessels** can be distinguished from other cavities by the fact that they contain numerous red blood cells. **Arteries** can be

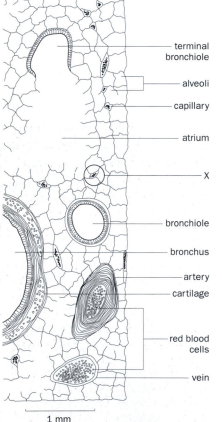

Figure 2.12 Semi-diagrammatic drawing of a section of mammalian lung. X identifies a region of intimate association between an alveolus and an adjacent blood capillary.

distinguished from veins by their thicker walls (see p. 131). **Blood capillaries** are very small and are lined with a single layer of squamous epithelium.

2 Notice how numerous the alveoli are in your section. Can you work out their approximate frequency?

3 Using high power, with oil immersion if available, explore the intimate association between an alveolus and an adjacent blood capillary. In Figure 2.12 this would be the region marked X, for example.

4 Carefully observe the barrier between the blood in a capillary and the air in an alveolus? What exactly does this barrier consist of? Is it uniformly thick or does it vary in thickness?

5 If you have an eyepiece graticule and stage micrometer, determine the minimum thickness in micrometres (μm) of the barrier between the blood in a capillary and the air in an alveolus.

6 Examine the electron micrograph of the barrier between the blood in a capillary and the air in an alveolus shown in Figure 2.13. Try to relate the micrograph to what you have seen under the light microscope. Identify the capillary and alveolar epithelial cells abutting against each other.

7 On the electron micrograph, measure the minimum thickness of the barrier between the blood in a capillary and the air in an alveolus and, from the known scale of the micrograph, calculate its thickness in micrometres.

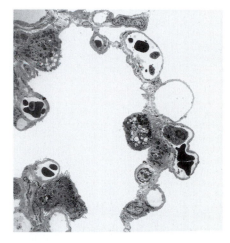

Figure 2.13 Electron micrograph showing the barrier between the blood in a capillary and the air in an alveolus.

For consideration

1 Did your two determinations of the minimum thickness of the barrier between the blood in a capillary and the air in an alveolus agree with each other? Suggest possible reasons for any discrepancy between them.

2 Review the ways in which the mammalian lung is adapted to perform its function of ensuring rapid gaseous exchange between inspired air and the blood.

Reference

Freeman, W. H. & Bracegirdle, B. *An Advanced Atlas of Histology*. Heinemann, Oxford, 1976.

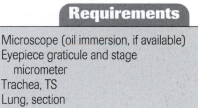

Requirements

Microscope (oil immersion, if available)
Eyepiece graticule and stage
    micrometer
Trachea, TS
Lung, section

How to use a spirometer

2.25 TECHNIQUE

A **spirometer** can be used for investigating a person's breathing movements and oxygen consumption.

A type of spirometer commonly used in schools and colleges is shown in the Illustration. It consists of a Perspex 'lid', hinged to a tank of water. The lid encloses a chamber which is connected to the subject by a rubber mouthpiece at the end of a flexible breathing tube. As the subject breathes in and out, the lid goes up and down in time with his or her breathing. An inlet tube at the side can be used for filling the chamber with oxygen. A canister of soda lime in the course of the breathing tube ensures that all the carbon dioxide in the subject's expired air is removed before the subject breathes in again.

Caution

Experiments involving breathing in and out of a spirometer should be carried out only under close supervision by a teacher/lecturer. *Either* use a disposable mouthpiece *or* be sure that the mouthpiece is disinfected and washed thoroughly before use. The flexible breathing tube should also be disinfected after use. Work in pairs, one of you acting as the subject, the other as the experimenter.

Soda lime

Make sure that all tubes are connected correctly so that the subject exhales, *not* inhales, through soda lime. Use soda lime that is not 'dusts' or that has been poured from container to container outdoors to blow away dust. Using a layer of aquarium filter material at the top and bottom of the canister helps prevent soda lime dust from entering the spirometer.

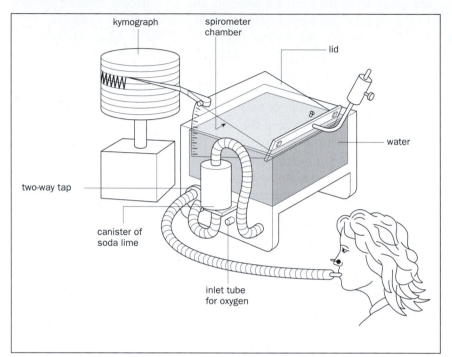

Illustration A recording spirometer in use. The horizontal lines on the kymograph represent 250 cm³ divisions.

A two-way tap controls the flow of air into and out of the chamber. By rotating this tap in the appropriate direction, the spirometer chamber can be opened to the atmosphere (or to a subject if the breathing tube is connected to the mouth) or closed.

The lid is counterbalanced by a moveable mass, the position of which should be set so that the lid falls very slowly when the spirometer chamber is open to the atmosphere. When the chamber is closed, the lid should remain stationary; if it falls there is a leak in the system.

Changes in the volume of oxygen in the spirometer chamber can be read off the scale attached to the side of the lid. Movements of the lid can be recorded by a pen writing on a **kymograph drum** or **chart recorder**. The recording paper should be calibrated for volume and time. To calibrate for volume, make a series of horizontal lines on the paper, separated by a distance corresponding to 20 cm³. To calibrate for time you need to know the speed at which the recording paper moves; ideally the speed should be approximately 20 mm per minute. Knowing the speed, you can make a series of vertical lines on the recording paper corresponding to 1 minute intervals.

Alternatively, the spirometer can be attached to a transducer and the data logged with a microcomputer programmed with appropriate software.

Using the spirometer

1   With the two-way tap closed, connect a cylinder of oxygen to the inlet tube. Fill the spirometer chamber with oxygen, then adjust the position of the recording pen so that the writing point is near the top of the paper.

2   Subject: remove the rubber mouthpiece from the antiseptic and rinse it in clean water. Then insert it into your mouth. Clip your nose. With the two-way tap closed, you are connected to the outside atmosphere and should remain so until you have got accustomed to breathing through the mouthpiece.

3   When you are ready to proceed, the experimenter should open the two-way tap so that the subject is connected to the spirometer chamber and breathes in and out of it. Breathe as naturally and as regularly as possible. If necessary, read a book or write out a sentence over and over again so as to take your mind off the procedure.

4   Record a few normal breaths. Then the experimenter closes the two-way tap so that the subject is disconnected from the spirometer and reconnected to the atmosphere.

5   Repeat steps 3 and 4 until you are familiar with the apparatus and can use it competently. At all times monitor the subject to ensure that they are breathing and behaving as normal.

Stethograph

As an alternative to the spirometer, a **stethograph** can be used to record human breathing movements. It consists of a corrugated tube round the chest. The tube can be linked via a tambour or electronic manometer to a kymograph, chart recorder, oscilloscope or microcomputer for recording expansion and contraction of the chest. (For details see R. Lock & C. Wood-Robinson, Equipment for recording human breathing, *Journal of Biological Education*, **17**, 88–92, 1983.) Stethographs can be purchased commercially, and come with instructions.

> ### Requirements
>
> Spirometer
> Kymograph *or* chart recorder
> Disposable mouthpiece *or*
>   mouthpiece in beaker of antiseptic
>   (see below)
> Nose clip
> Clean water, in beaker
> Oxygen cylinder
> Stethograph (alternative to
>   spirometer)
> Tambour *or* electronic manometer
> Oscilloscope *or* microcomputer

> **Note:** If disposable mouthpieces are not used, Milton is recommended as a suitable disinfectant – follow the instructions on the bottle.

Ventilation of the lungs in the human

2.26 PRACTICAL EXERCISE

How much of our lungs do we use when we breathe, in resting conditions and during exercise? We can answer this question by recording the breathing movements of a human subject with a **spirometer**. This kind of information is particularly relevant to athletes who wish to improve their performance and make best use of their breathing system.

> ### Caution
>
> Always work in pairs, and in the presence of a teacher/lecturer, when you use a spirometer.

Procedure

The spirometer is explained in Technique 2.25 on p. 91. Study the technique carefully and practise using the apparatus before you attempt the experiments outlined below. Work in pairs, one of you acting as subject, the other as experimenter.

Lung volumes at rest

1   Fill the spirometer with oxygen from a cylinder, then connect the subject to the spirometer. Don't forget the nose clip.

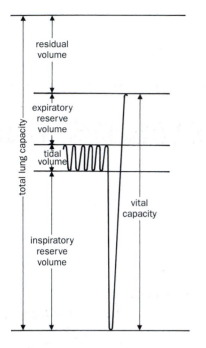

Figure 2.14 Spirometer recording showing the breathing movements of a typical human subject.

Key skills

2 Record about six normal resting breaths followed by a maximum inspiration and then a maximum expiration. The recordings should look like those in Figure 2.14.

3 From the horizontal lines on the recording paper, determine the **tidal volume**, **inspiratory reserve volume**, **expiratory reserve volume** and **vital capacity**. What percentage of your vital capacity do you use in normal resting breathing?

4 Compare your vital capacity with that of other members of your class. What do you think determines a person's vital capacity?

Effect of exercise on breathing

1 Record the subject's normal resting breaths for 1 minute, then continue to record for a further 3 minutes while the subject takes vigorous, but not excessive, exercise such as jogging on the spot or pedalling a stationary bicycle. Alternatively, if it is uncomfortable to exercise while attached to the spirometer, for instance because it has a narrow breathing tube, attach the subject to the spirometer immediately after the exercise.

2 Compare the volume of air inspired in a single breath at the beginning and end of the bout of exercise. Express each volume as a percentage of the vital capacity. Do the breaths during exercise extend into the inspiratory reserve volume, the expiratory reserve volume, or both?

3 The rate of gaseous exchange may be expressed as the total volume of air inspired per minute. This is the **ventilation rate**. Work out, by whatever means you think fit, the ventilation rate for each minute from the beginning to the end of your set of recordings . Express the ventilation rates in $dm^3 min^{-1}$.

4 Plot the change in the ventilation rate as a graph with time on the horizontal axis and ventilation rate on the vertical axis.

5 Compare your graph and your recordings with those of other members of your class. How do they differ?

For consideration

1 A person may increase his or her ventilation rate by breathing faster and/or more deeply. How do members of your class differ in which of these two alternatives they use? Suggest possible explanations for any differences observed.

2 Why do you think the inspiratory reserve volume is so much greater than the expiratory reserve volume?

3 How might the residual volume of the lungs be measured? What is the significance of this part of the lungs?

✓ **Application of number:** Carry out your calculations on the ventilation rate for each minute from the beginning to the end of your set of recordings to an appropriate level of accuracy, clearly showing your methods. Check your methods and results to help ensure any errors are found and corrected. Select appropriate methods of presentation and justify your choice. Present your findings effectively. Explain how the results of your calculations relate to the purpose of the practical exercise.

✓ **Improving own learning and performance:** Manage your time effectively to complete tasks, revising your working procedure as necessary. Seek and actively use feedback and support from relevant sources to help you achieve your aims. At the conclusion of the practical exercise, review the quality of your learning and performance. Exchange views with the partner you worked with to agree ways to improve your performance further.

Gaseous exchange in a fish

In fishes, gaseous exchange takes place between water that has been drawn into the body from the outside, and blood that is flowing through a series of gills. Here you are invited to investigate gaseous exchange in a teleost (bony) fish. Three approaches are suggested: observing a live fish, dissecting the pharynx and gills, and examining a prepared slide of a gill. Disinfect any dissection equipment after use.

Guidance

Figure 2.15 is a diagram of the gill region of a generalised teleost. It is intended to help you locate the various structures that you may encounter.

1   Observe a fish such as a carp in a small aquarium tank. You have probably read that water enters the buccal cavity and pharynx through the mouth and leaves through the opercular opening, but how do you *know* that water does not enter through the opercular openings and leave through the mouth? Devise, and carry out, a simple experiment to decide between these two possibilities. Your procedure, which should be discussed with your teacher/lecturer first, must not harm the fish.

2   Investigate the position and structure of the gills by dissecting the head of a mackerel or herring. First, pull one of the opercula towards you and look for the gills underneath. Then remove the operculum by cutting round it with scissors. How many gills are there and how are they held in position? Trace the course that water takes when it flows past the gills. How is food prevented from getting between the gills?

3   Does the structure of the buccal cavity and pharynx suggest how a flow of water is maintained over the gill surfaces? Look again at your live specimen for further clues on this.

4   Remove a single gill and observe it under a binocular microscope. What features of the gill would you expect to increase the efficiency of gaseous exchange?

5   Examine a prepared slide of a section through a gill. Decide whether the section has been cut horizontally or vertically. Identify blood spaces inside the gill filaments. (Hint: look for red blood cells.) What information about the gaseous exchange surface does the slide provide that you could not get by examining the gill under the binocular microscope?

For consideration

1   In a fish, the medium (water) flows into the body through one opening and out through another. In mammals the medium (air) flows in and out through the same opening. Propose an advantage of the mammalian system in air and the fish system in water.

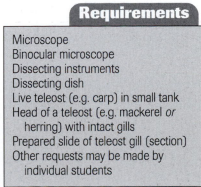

Figure 2.15 Horizontal hand section of the head of a generalised teleost, showing the gills and associated structures, looking towards the ventral side of the buccal cavity and pharynx.

Requirements

Microscope
Binocular microscope
Dissecting instruments
Dissecting dish
Live teleost (e.g. carp) in small tank
Head of a teleost (e.g. mackerel *or* herring) with intact gills
Prepared slide of teleost gill (section)
Other requests may be made by individual students

2 Some species of fish have supplementary gaseous exchange surfaces in such places as the buccal cavity, intestine and rectum. Suggest the benefits of these.

Gas analysis

Gas analysis, for biological purposes, involves determining what percentage of a sample of gas is carbon dioxide and what percentage is oxygen. The principle behind this is as follows. A sample of gas is drawn into a capillary tube and its volume noted. A reagent which absorbs carbon dioxide is then drawn into the tube, causing the sample of gas to decrease in volume. The new volume is noted. Then a reagent which absorbs oxygen is drawn into the tube, causing the remainder of the sample to decrease in volume once more. Again the new volume is noted.

Practical details

A type of gas analysis apparatus often used in colleges and schools is called a **J tube**. It consists of a bent capillary tube with a syringe at one end (see Illustration). The syringe is for drawing in the sample and reagents. The volume of the sample can conveniently be expressed as the length of capillary tube which it occupies. To improve accuracy, at least three samples of air should be analysed and the mean taken. It is important that the samples should be at constant temperature. For this reason, give each sample time to come to room temperature before its volume is measured.

1 Assemble four small beakers containing the following: A, water; B, potassium hydroxide solution (for absorbing carbon dioxide); C, pyrogallol (for absorbing oxygen); D, dilute hydrochloric acid (for cleaning the J tube when it becomes alkaline).

2 Push the plunger of the syringe to the far end of the barrel. Dip the open end of the J tube in the beaker of water, then pull the plunger back until a column of water approximately 5 cm long has been drawn into the tube.

3 Remove the tip of the tube from the water, then draw in approximately 10 cm of air. Then draw in water again until the column of air occupies the straight part of the J tube, as shown in the Illustration. Wait for at least 1 minute, and do not handle the straight part of the tube where the air is located (why?). Now measure the length of the air column with a ruler.

4 Expel all but about 1 cm of the water from the open end of the J tube (this forms a seal for the air column), then draw in **potassium hydroxide** solution. Keeping the tip of the tube in the hydroxide, carefully shuttle the potassium hydroxide backwards and forwards about six times so that the air sample comes into repeated contact with the glass lining of the tube which has been wetted with the hydroxide. The hydroxide will absorb carbon dioxide from the air sample. Wait for a further 1 minute, then re-measure the length of the air column.

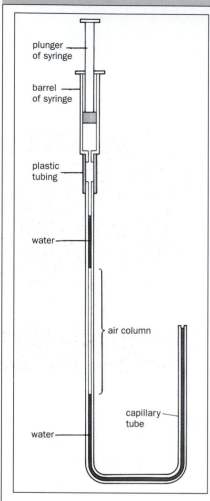

Illustration J tube for gas analysis. Commercial versions have a screw instead of a syringe.

Goggles must be worn

Potassium hydroxide

Pyrogallol

5 Now expel all but the last 5 cm or so of the hydroxide and draw in **pyrogallol**. Keeping the tip of the J tube in the pyrogallol, shuttle the pyrogallol backwards and forwards as before, but *don't* expel the hydroxide. The pyrogallol will react with the potassium hydroxide still in the tube, forming potassium pyrogallate (alkaline pyrogallol), which then absorbs oxygen from the air sample. Wait a further 1 minute, then measure the length of the air column again.

6 Wash out the J tube thoroughly, first with dilute hydrochloric acid, then with water.

7 Calculate the percentage of carbon dioxide and oxygen in the air sample:

$$\text{percentage of } CO_2 = \frac{a-b}{a} \times 100$$

$$\text{percentage of } O_2 = \frac{b-c}{c} \times 100$$

where
  a is the original length before potassium hydroxide was admitted
  b is the new length after potassium hydroxide was admitted
  c is the new length after pyrogallol was admitted.

Comparing the composition of exhaled air before and after exercise

2.29 PRACTICAL EXERCISE

The percentages of oxygen and carbon dioxide in inspired (i.e. atmospheric) and expired air can be determined by means of **gas analysis**, which involves using the **J tube** described in Technique 2.28 on p. 96. Here you can analyse samples of *exhaled* air before and after a bout of exercise. How would you expect them to differ and why?

Procedure

First be sure you are familiar with the J tube and how it works. Then proceed as follows:

1 Draw a sample of atmospheric air into the J tube. Draw water in first, then the air sample, then more water, as described in Technique 2.28 on p. 96. Then analyse the air for carbon dioxide and oxygen.

2 Wash out the J tube with dilute hydrochloric acid, followed by water, before continuing further.

3 Collect a sample of expired air in a large test tube by the method shown in Figure 2.16. *Be sure the bent tube has been washed in disinfectant, then rinsed in clean water, before you put it to your mouth.* The sample should come from as deep inside your lungs as possible; to ensure this, exhale through the bent tube but don't insert the tip into the test tube until the end of your exhalation.

4 After you have exhaled into the test tube, wait several minutes until your expired air cools down to room temperature.

5 Now draw a sample of expired air into the J tube as shown in Figure

Pyrogallol

Potassium hydroxide

Goggles must be worn

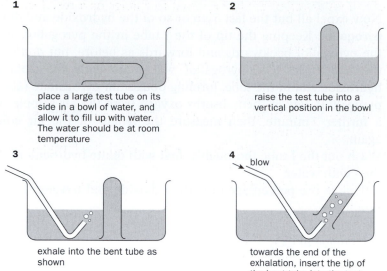

1 — place a large test tube on its side in a bowl of water, and allow it to fill up with water. The water should be at room temperature

2 — raise the test tube into a vertical position in the bowl

3 — exhale into the bent tube as shown

4 — blow — towards the end of the exhalation, insert the tip of the bent tube into the test tube and collect the last lot of expired air in the test tube

Figure 2.16 A method for collecting a sample of expired air in a test tube.

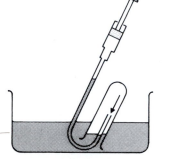

pull

Figure 2.17 Drawing a sample of expired air into a J tube.

2.17. Draw water in first, then the air sample, then more water in the usual way. Then analyse the air for carbon dioxide and oxygen. Wash out the J tube afterwards.

6 Perform a bout of vigorous exercise of your choice, then collect a sample of expired air and analyse it as before. Be sure it cools down to room temperature before you start your analysis, and don't forget to wash out the J tube afterwards.

7 Make a table comparing the percentages of carbon dioxide and oxygen in inspired air, expired air at rest and expired air after exercise.

For consideration

1 You will have found it difficult to measure the percentage of carbon dioxide in atmospheric air. Why? How might the J tube method be improved so as to achieve a more accurate result?

2 What sources of error might there be in the way you measured the percentage of oxygen in this experiment? How could you minimise the error?

3 What other gases besides carbon dioxide and oxygen are present in the air we breathe? What is their biological significance, if any?

4 In what circumstances might the percentage of carbon dioxide in atmospheric air be higher than usual?

2.30 INVESTIGATION

Effects of a training programme for humans

This investigation may extend over more than one practical session.

Exercise has both short-term and long-term consequences. Short-term consequences are those which take place during the exercise itself and during the minutes after the exercise has ended. Here we are concerned with the long-term consequences of a training programme for humans.

Each of the following might be expected to change as a result of a training programme:

- Resting heart rate
- Volume of blood pumped during each cardiac cycle
- Presence of fatty deposits in artery walls
- Vital capacity of the lungs
- Number of energy-producing mitochondria in muscle fibres
- Blood supply to muscles
- Synthesis of the oxygen-holding molecule myoglobin found in muscle
- Size of individual muscle fibres
- Muscle strength, endurance and resistance to fatigue
- Suppleness
- Feeling of well-being
- Skin condition and tone
- Tendons, ligament and bone strength

Guidance

First of all, for each of the above bullet points, predict whether you would expect a training programme of physical exercise to increase or decrease the factor in question. Secondly, identify three or four of these factors which you can realistically measure. For example, resting heart rate is straightforward to measure but the presence of fatty deposits in artery walls is not.

There are two ways in which you can investigate the effect of a training programme on fitness. One possibility is to measure the factors you are studying in a group of people who don't do much exercise *before* they undertake a training programme and then, perhaps 6 weeks later, *after* they have undertaken the training programme. The other possibility is to measure the factors in two *different* groups of people: one group of people who don't do much exercise, and one group of people who do. (Levels of exercise in each group should be appropriate for the fitness of the individuals concerned.)

Whichever of these two possibilities you choose, you will need to use safe, reliable methods for measuring those factors you are interested in. Try using the index of this book and consult books on physical fitness and Sports Science. Discuss your procedures with your teacher/lecturer before undertaking them. Think about how many people you need to study. You will need to explain to them what you intend to do and obtain their informed consent.

If you study the same group of people before and after they undertake a training programme, you will need to discuss with them what sort of training programme they will undertake. If you study two different groups of people, one group of whom doesn't do much exercise, the other group of whom does, you will need to match the people in the two groups as closely as possible for variables such as gender and age.

For consideration

1 Which, if any, of the factors you investigated seemed to change as a result of exercise?
2 Explain how any changes you observed are adaptive.
3 The Guidance above suggests two different possibilities for investigating the effects of a training programme. List the strengths and weaknesses of each of these possibilities.

Requirements

The requirements depend on the method adopted

- **Plan** your investigation. Ensure you have identified and defined a specific question that you are attempting to answer. Have you chosen safe procedures? You must show that you have explicitly considered ethical issues – for example, have subjects given their informed consent in writing?
- **Implement** your plan. Demonstrate that you have carried out your work in a methodical and organised way.
- **Analyse your evidence** and **draw conclusions**. Think carefully about the best way to communicate your findings. Use biological knowledge when drawing your conclusions. Assess the reliability of your data.
- **Evaluate** your investigation. Was your plan the best? Can you suggest improvements?

2.31 PRACTICAL EXERCISE

Dissection of the mammalian alimentary canal

Caution

In the interests of hygiene, wear a lab. coat while your are dissecting, and wash your hands thoroughly afterwards. Disinfect instruments after use.

The **alimentary canal**, or **gut**, is essentially a tube running from the **mouth** to the **anus**. Its function is to digest food physically and chemically, absorb the soluble products of digestion and get rid of indigestible waste. To this end it is specialised into a series of distinct regions, and various glands open into it.

Procedure

1 Pin the rat to a dissecting board, ventral surface upwards and head pointing away from you. Make a mid-ventral incision through the skin (but not through the underlying body wall) and cut forward as far as the lower jaw (mandible), and backwards to the anus. Cut either side of the urinogenital openings as shown in Figure 2.18.

2 Free the skin from the underlying body wall, using your fingers or the handle of a scalpel (Figure 2.19), then pin back the skin as shown in Figure 2.20.

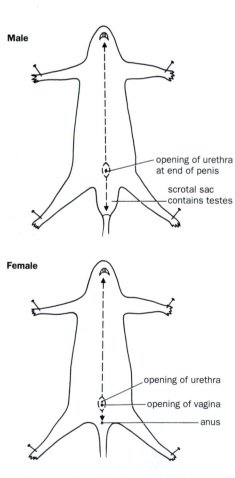

Male

— opening of urethra at end of penis

scrotal sac contains testes

Female

opening of urethra

opening of vagina

anus

Figure 2.18 Opening up the rat. Cut through the skin as indicated by the dotted line.

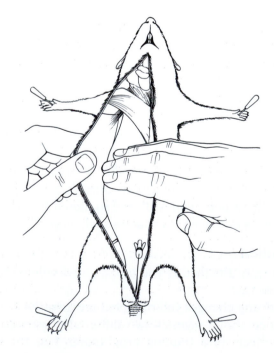

Figure 2.19 How to deflect the skin.

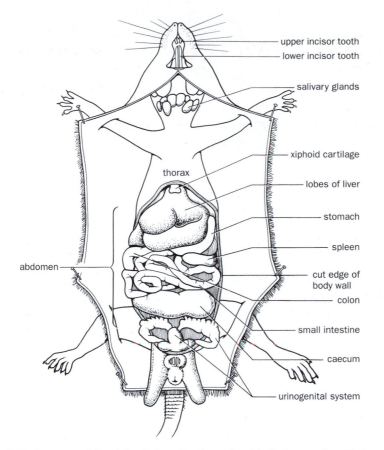

upper incisor tooth
lower incisor tooth
salivary glands
thorax
xiphoid cartilage
lobes of liver
stomach
spleen
abdomen
cut edge of body wall
colon
small intestine
caecum
urinogenital system

Figure 2.20 Contents of the abdominal cavity of a male rat in their normal positions.

3 With scissors, cut through the body wall so as to expose the contents of the abdomen (Figure 2.20). Identify the structures shown in Figure 2.20.

4 Wet your fingers under a tap so that they slide easily between the organs. Look between the **stomach** and **liver** and find the lower end of the **oesophagus** where it joins the top of the stomach. Using your fingers to move the organs this way and that, and *without cutting the mesentery by which the gut is suspended in the abdominal cavity*, follow the alimentary canal all the way back to the rectum.

5 Still without breaking the mesentery, push the liver forward and spread out the small intestine to your left as shown in Figure 2.21. Identify its two main parts: **duodenum** and **ileum**. Notice the **pancreas** in the loop of the duodenum and identify the **bile duct** and **pancreatic ducts**. Finally, observe the numerous branches of the hepatic portal vein and follow them back to where they unite to form the main trunk of the hepatic portal vein to the liver.

6 With the liver still pushed forward, deflect the whole of the stomach and intestine to your left and stretch the mesentery. Running in the mesentery are three arteries to the gut (Figure 2.22): **coeliac, anterior mesenteric** and **posterior mesenteric arteries**. All three are branches of the dorsal aorta, the first two arising at about the level of the left kidney, the last where the aorta splits into the iliac arteries to the legs.

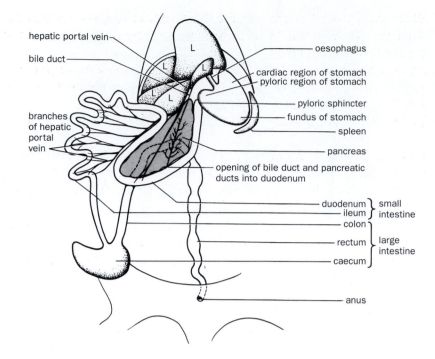

Figure 2.21 Alimentary canal of the rat, as seen with the duodenum deflected downwards, the stomach pushed to the observer's right, and the ileum spread out to the observer's left. The branches of the hepatic portal vein may not be visible from above because they are covered by lymph nodes; however, they are usually visible from beneath. L, lobes of the liver.

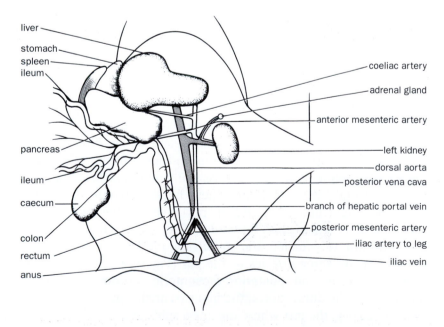

Figure 2.22 Arteries supplying the alimentary canal and associated structures of the rat.

7 Pluck away the fat clinging to the three arteries to show their origin from the dorsal aorta. Then trace them to their destinations. What organs do they supply?

8 Arrange the contents of the abdomen so as to display *in one view* as much as possible of the gut and its blood supply. This will require some ingenuity, as various organs lie on top of each other.

9 Either draw your dissection and label it, or flag-label it and take a photograph.

10 Remove the gut as follows. Ligature the main trunk of the **hepatic portal vein**, cut through the oesophagus where it enters the stomach, and cut through the rectum where it disappears under the urinogenital organs. Cut through the mesentery so as to lift out the whole of the gut, spleen and pancreas (keep a piece of ileum for Practical Exercise 2.32 (below)). Be careful not to cut any major blood vessels beneath the gut. Leave the liver. The rat can now be used again later for dissecting other systems.

For consideration

1 The veins serving most organs take blood straight to the heart. However, the vein serving the gut (the hepatic portal vein) takes blood to the liver, from which it then flows to the heart. Why is there this difference between the venous supplies of the gut and other organs?

2 In what ways is the gut, as you have observed it in your dissection, adapted to carry out its functions?

References

Rowett, H. G. Q. *Dissection Guides, III The Rat.* John Murray, London, 1951.

Institute of Biology in conjunction with the TV Centre of the University of Portsmouth. Video of a rat dissection. Available from the Institute of Biology, 20–22 Queensberry Place, London SW7 2DZ.

Requirements

Dissecting instruments
Dissecting board
Dissecting pins
Camera (optional)
Rat for dissection

Note: Embalmed rats with blood vessels triple-injected (arteries red, veins blue, hepatic portal vein yellow) can be purchased.

2.32 PRACTICAL EXERCISE   **Microscopic structure of the mammalian gut wall**

Although the gut is differentiated into regions, its wall always consists of the layers shown in Figure 2.23:

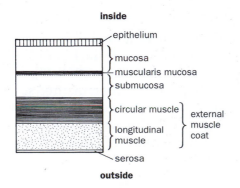

Figure 2.23 The principal layers in the wall of the mammalian alimentary canal, shown diagrammatically.

- **Epithelium.** Inner layer of cells showing various degrees of folding; its functions are protective, secretory and/or absorptive.
- **Mucosa.** Connective tissue, blood vessels, etc.
- **Muscularis mucosa.** Two thin layers of smooth muscle – an inner circular layer and an outer longitudinal layer.
- **Submucosa.** More connective tissue, blood vessels, etc., like the mucosa.
- **External muscle coat.** Smooth muscle differentiated into an inner circular layer and an outer longitudinal layer.
- **Serosa.** Connective tissue continuous with the mesentery by which the gut is attached to the body wall.

The aim of this practical exercise is to identify these layers in certain regions of the gut, and to relate their detailed structure to their functions.

Procedure

Small intestine

1 Examine a section of the **ileum** under low power. Without getting immersed in the details, identify the different layers of the wall using Figure 2.23 to help you. In what ways does your section depart from the simple diagrammatic pattern shown in Figure 2.23?

2 Now look at your section in detail, still under low power, and identify the parts shown on the left hand side of Figure 2.24. Notice in particular the **villi** and **crypts of Lieberkuhn**.

3 Go over to high power and carefully examine the individual parts shown in Figure 2.24. Try to answer these questions:
 a What sort of cells occur in the epithelium lining the villi and crypts of Lieberkuhn and what are their functions?
 b In what ways is the epithelium adapted to carry out its functions?
 c What functions are performed by the muscle tissue visible in your section? What type of muscle is it?

4 Examine a section of the wall of the **duodenum**. Identify its parts, using the right-hand side of Figure 2.24 to help you. How does the wall of the duodenum differ from that of the ileum?

5 Open up a short length of the ileum of a dissected rat. Pin it, inner surface uppermost, to a piece of cork and wash it thoroughly under a tap. Examine it with a binocular microscope. Can you see the villi? Disinfect instruments after use.

6 Look at the electron micrograph in Figure 2.25. This is a section through an individual epithelial cell lining a villus. Notice the numerous **microvilli** projecting from the free surface of the cell. Did you see these microvilli in the sections of the small intestine which you examined under the light microscope? They may have shown up as a **brush border**. If necessary, re-examine the sections to see if you can detect a brush border.

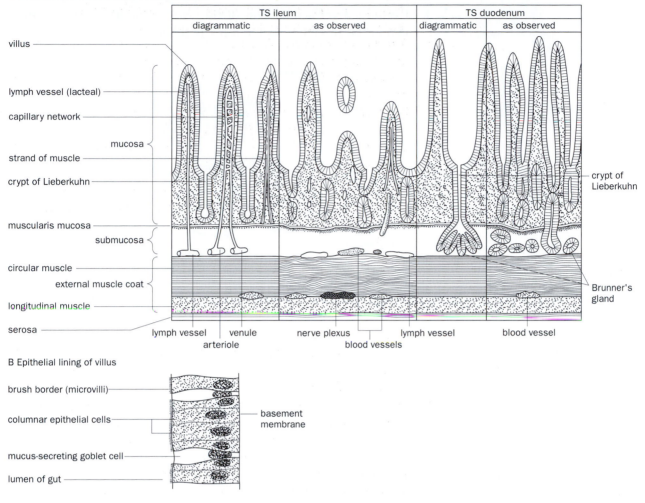

	TS ileum		TS duodenum	
	diagrammatic	as observed	diagrammatic	as observed

villus

lymph vessel (lacteal)

capillary network

mucosa

strand of muscle

crypt of Lieberkuhn

crypt of Lieberkuhn

muscularis mucosa

submucosa

circular muscle

external muscle coat

Brunner's gland

longitudinal muscle

serosa

lymph vessel   venule   nerve plexus   lymph vessel   blood vessel

arteriole   blood vessels

B Epithelial lining of villus

brush border (microvilli)

columnar epithelial cells

basement membrane

mucus-secreting goblet cell

lumen of gut

Figure 2.24 Microscopic structure of the wall of the mammalian small intestine.

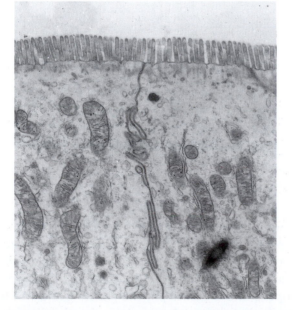

Figure 2.25 Electron micrograph of a section through an epithelial cell lining a villus in the wall of the small intestine.

Stomach

1 Examine a vertical section of the wall of the **stomach**. Identify the various layers of the wall and relate them to Figure 2.26.

A Vertical section of stomach wall

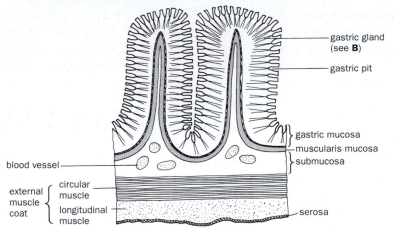

B Gastric glands in mucosa of stomach wall

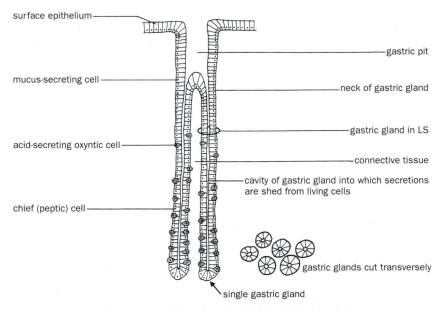

C Lining of gastric gland in detail

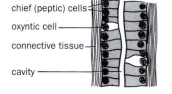

Figure 2.26 Microscopic structure of the wall of the mammalian stomach. LS, longitudinal section.

2 Identify the detailed parts of the stomach wall as shown in Figure 2.26A. In particular, notice the numerous **gastric glands**.

3 Examine a gastric gland in detail and identify the different types of cells in its epithelial lining (Figure 2.26B). Towards the surface where it opens into a gastric pit, the gastric gland will have been cut longitudinally, but deeper down where the gland twists and turns it will have been cut transversely and obliquely.

4   Using high power, examine an individual **mucus-secreting (goblet) cell**, **oxyntic cell** and **chief (peptic) cell**. What are the functions of these three types of cell?

Other regions of the gut

Obtain sections or photomicrographs of the tongue, oesophagus, colon, rectum and recto-anal junction. Before examining them, think what each of these parts of the gut has to do and from this *predict* the kinds of cells and tissues which you would expect to find in it. Then examine the sections and see if your predictions are correct. Here are some notes to help you:

1   **Tongue.** Look out for taste buds (flask-shaped bundles of sensory and supporting cells) and for striated muscle. Why should the tongue contain *striated* muscle?
2   **Oesophagus.** The external muscle coat consists mainly of circular muscle in which striated fibres are present, particularly in the upper part of the oesophagus. Why is this?
3   **Colon.** One of its functions is to reabsorb water. Can you detect any obvious adaptations for this?
4   **Rectum.** Faeces are stored here before being expelled through the anus. Numerous goblet cells secrete mucus to lubricate the passage of the faeces. Can you see any other adaptations?
5   **Recto-anal junction.** Here the rectal tissue gradually gives way to the thicker, more muscular anal tissue. Examining a section through this region provides an excellent opportunity to identify tissues and relate structure to function.

Reference

Newman, M. Inside the intestine. *School Science Review*, **70** (252), 70–72, 1989. (Describes the technique for viewing the intestinal villi under a binocular microscope.)

Digestion of starch   2.33 PRACTICAL EXERCISE

Normally when we ask you to carry out a practical exercise we make its aims clear. This practical exercise is different. Here you will be presented with a set of instructions for investigating the action of the enzyme **amylase** on starch. The aims will be considered afterwards.

Samples of starch will be mixed with the enzyme under various conditions, and after a given time the mixture will be tested for starch with iodine solution and for reducing sugar with Benedict's solution. Details of these tests are given in Technique 1.2 on p. 19.

Procedure

1   Obtain 20 cm³ of amylase solution. Transfer $\frac{1}{4}$ of the amylase to a test tube and place this in a boiling water bath for 15 minutes. Transfer a further $\frac{1}{4}$ of the amylase solution to another test tube and add four drops of hydrochloric acid, mix well and leave for at least 15 minutes. Keep the rest of the amylase solution untreated at room temperature.

Amylase solution Hydrochloric acid

Eye protection must be worn

2 Set up six pairs of test tubes as follows. Label each test tube with its code number: A1, A2, etc.:

Pair A			Pair D		
1	4 cm³ reducing sugar		7	4 cm³ starch plus 2 cm³ untreated amylase	
2	4 cm³ reducing sugar		8	4 cm³ starch plus 2 cm³ untreated amylase	
Pair B			Pair E		
3	4 cm³ starch		9	4 cm³ starch plus 2 cm³ preheated amylase	
4	4 cm³ starch		10	4 cm³ starch plus 2 cm³ preheated amylase	
Pair C			Pair F		
5	4 cm³ untreated amylase		11	4 cm³ starch plus 2 cm³ acidified amylase	
6	4 cm³ untreated amylase		12	4 cm³ starch plus 2 cm³ acidified amylase	

3 Place the test tubes in a rack in numerical order and leave them for at least 10 minutes.

4 Test the contents of each pair of test tubes (a) for starch by adding two drops of iodine solution, and (b) for reducing sugar by adding $\frac{1}{8}$ of a test tube of Benedict's solution and heating in a water bath (Technique 1.2 on p. 19). Do the starch test on the first of each pair of test tubes, and the sugar test on the second.

5 Record your results in a table, indicating which test tubes give a positive and which ones a negative result for starch and reducing sugar. It is possible that some may give a result in between; if so, say so.

For consideration

1 Three different, but related, hypotheses are tested by this experiment. What are they?

2 Are the hypotheses supported by your results? Would you say they were proved?

3 What were the controls in this experiment?

4 Identify the dependent and independent variables in the experiment. The independent variables are discrete (i.e. non-continuous). How would the experiment have to be altered to make the independent variables continuous?

5 Can you suggest any ways of improving the instructions given for this practical exercise?

Requirements

Eye protection
Test tubes, ×12
Test tube rack
Pipettes *or* syringes (5 cm³)
Measuring cylinder (20 cm³)
Water bath (250 cm³ beaker)
Bunsen burner, tripod and gauze
Wax pencil *or* marker pen
Amylase solution (see below)
Starch suspension
Reducing sugar, e.g. glucose (dextrose)
Iodine solution
Benedict's solution

Note: Amylase solution, suitable for enzyme work, is available from biological suppliers. Its activity depends on age, but a 0.1% solution is likely to be suitable.

Beware of allergic reactions to amylase solution; avoid spills on the skin or rubbing eyes with contaminated fingers.

2.34 INVESTIGATION

This investigation requires more than one practical session.

Pepsin solution
Trypsin solution

Digestion of protein

In the gut, proteins are hydrolysed by two main enzymes, **pepsin** and **trypsin**. Pepsin is present in the stomach where conditions are markedly acidic; trypsin is present in the small intestine where conditions are usually more neutral or even slightly alkaline. We may predict that these two enzymes work optimally at acidic and alkaline pH respectively. In this investigation you will test this hypothesis.

Guidance

Set up a series of large test tubes each containing a sample of protein together with a solution of the enzyme at the required pH. Then find out whether or not the enzyme succeeds in hydrolysing the protein. Use a solid protein such as boiled egg white: approximately $1 \, cm^3$ is sufficient. You can tell if it has been hydrolysed by seeing if it dissolves in the enzyme solution.

Make sure that in each test tube the egg white is completely covered by the enzyme solution and that the pH is appropriate. It is suggested that for acidic conditions the pH should be 2.0, and for alkaline conditions 9.0. The pH can be adjusted by adding acid or alkali to the enzyme solution, and tested by means of pH indicator paper. Don't forget to include any necessary controls. Do you need replicates?

When you have set up the test tubes, incubate the protein–enzyme mixtures at 37 °C for at least 24 hours before assessing the results.

For consideration

1 Do your results support the hypothesis that pepsin and trypsin work optimally in acid and alkaline conditions respectively?
2 What controls did you set up, and why?
3 How could you make this investigation more rigorous?
4 Suppose you were to use a *soluble* protein for this experiment. How would you assess whether or not the protein had been hydrolysed?
5 How could you determine the exact pH at which each of these enzymes works optimally?

Requirements

Large test tubes, ×4 (or more as required)
Test tube rack
Pipettes *or* syringes (for measuring $10 \, cm^3$ quantities), ×2
Pipettes *or* syringes (for measuring $1.0 \, cm^3$ quantities), ×2
Wax pencil or marker pen
pH indicator paper (universal indicator paper)
Incubator (at 37 °C)
Pepsin solution ($20 \, cm^3$, 1.0%)
Trypsin solution ($20 \, cm^3$, 1.0%)
Hydrochloric acid ($2 \, cm^3$, $0.1 \, mol \, dm^{-3}$)
Sodium carbonate solution ($2 \, cm^3$, $0.2 \, mol \, dm^{-3}$)
Egg white, coagulated by boiling

Note: Beware of allergic reactions to pepsin and trypsin solutions; avoid spills on the skin or rubbing eyes with contaminated fingers.

Digestion of fat

2.35 INVESTIGATION

In the human gut fats are acted upon by **bile salts** from the liver and by **lipase** from the pancreas. The aim of this investigation is to explore the action of these two agents and assess their roles in digestion.

Guidance

When fats are hydrolysed, glycerol and fatty acids are released. The presence of acid, creating a relatively low pH, may therefore be used as an indication that hydrolysis has occurred. You can demonstrate the formation of acid in a previously alkaline solution by using the pH indicator phenolphthalein: at a pH above 10, phenolphthalein is pink, but below pH 8.4 it is colourless. If phenolphthalein is added to a test tube in which an alkaline solution of fat is being hydrolysed, the colour of the contents should change gradually from pink to colourless as fatty acids accumulate. Sodium carbonate may be added to the mixture beforehand to ensure that the pH is above 10 to begin with.

Procedure

With phenolphthalein as your pH indicator, design and carry out experiments to test some or all of the following hypotheses:

1 Lipase can hydrolyse fat.
2 Bile salts can hydrolyse fat.
3 Lipase is more effective if the fat has been acted on by bile salts beforehand.
4 Lipase is inactivated by excessive heat.

You are provided with the basic requirements for testing these hypotheses, but if you need any other items you should ask for them.

Phenolphthalein

Phenolphthalein

Requirements

Water bath
Stopclock
Test tubes
Pipette (for delivering up to $5 \, cm^3$ quantities)
Beaker (for washing pipette)
Bile salts (5%)
Lipase solution (5%, fresh)
Phenolphthalein
Sodium carbonate solution ($0.2 \, mol \, dm^{-3}$)
Fat (e.g. butter)
Other items may be requested by individual students

Lipase solution

Note: Beware of allergic reactions to lipase solution; avoid spills on the skin or rubbing eyes with contaminated fingers.

Procedure

1 Place some pond or aquarium water (*not* tap water) into a watch glass. Place the watch glass near the vessel containing tadpoles.
2 Using a dessert spoon, scoop up a wriggling tadpole and transfer it to the watch glass. Watch it for 30 seconds.
3 As soon as the tadpole's movements slow down, place the watch glass under a dissection microscope with as high a magnification as you can obtain. Notice the movement of red blood cells.
4 Look both at the capillaries in the tail and at the beating heart, and try to work out the pattern of blood flow to and from the tail.
5 As soon as you have finished, transfer the tadpole back into its source vessel.

For consideration

1 Work out, in relation to the upper (dorsal) and the lower (ventral) surface of the tadpole, how the tail receives its blood and how the blood returns to the heart.
2 Examine and explain the relative speeds of blood flow in the various vessels which you can see.
3 How many ventricles and atria has the tadpole heart? Look up the anatomy of an amphibian heart and relate it to what you have seen.

Requirements

Watch glass
Dessert spoon
Teat pipette
Dissection microscope (high power)
Tadpoles of frog (*Rana temporaria*) *or* toad (*Xenopus laevis*)

2.44 PRACTICAL EXERCISE

Looking at red blood cells

Red blood cells (**erythrocytes**) are amongst the simplest of cells. They lack a nucleus and their cytoplasm appears to be less elaborate than that of other cells. Yet at the chemical level they perform the specialised job of taking up oxygen in the lungs and transporting it to the tissues. They are also involved in the transport of carbon dioxide from the tissues to the lungs. Bear these functions in mind as you examine red blood cells.

Procedure

1 You will be provided with a specimen tube containing a sample of mammalian blood. With a dropping pipette, place a drop of the blood towards one end of a slide. Then smear the blood over the slide using the technique shown in Figure 2.32.
2 Let the blood smear dry, then examine it under the microscope, low power first then high power. You will see large numbers of erythrocytes. What colour are they, and why?
3 Examine a single red blood cell in as much detail as possible. Can you get any clues as to its shape from its appearance under the microscope? What can you say about its internal structure?
4 Using a stage micrometer (see p. 42), measure the diameter of a red blood cell. How does this compare with the width of most animal cells? What limits the size of red blood cells?

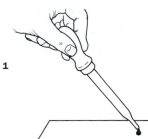
1 place the drop of blood at one end of a microscope slide

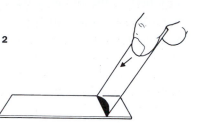
2 bring another slide into contact with the drop of blood

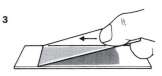
3 spread the blood over the surface of the slide so it forms a smear

Figure 2.32 How to make a blood smear for examination under the microscope.

5 Examine a prepared slide of frog's blood under the microscope. How do the red blood cells differ from those of a mammal? Which do you think might be more efficient at carrying oxygen, and why?

6 Examine a scanning electron micrograph of human red blood cells (Figure 2.33). What information does it provide about the shape of the cells?

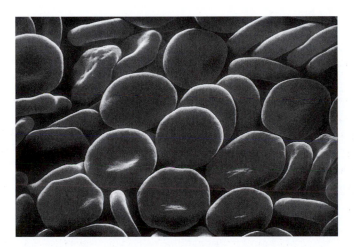

Figure 2.33 Scanning electron micrograph of human red blood cells.

7 Examine a transmission electron micrograph of a mammalian red blood cell in section (Figure 2.34). What does it tell you about its internal structure?

For consideration

1 A human red blood cell has a life span of approximately 120 days. What do you think limits its life span, and how are new red blood cells formed?

2 It has been said that a mammalian red blood cell is the ideal shape for performing its function of carrying oxygen. Comment.

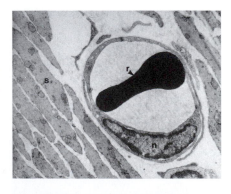

Figure 2.34 Transmission electron micrograph of a mammalian red blood cell in TS capillary.

Microscope
Eyepiece graticule and stage
  micrometer (see Technique 1.17 on
  p. 42)
Slides, ×2
Teat pipette
Mammalian blood in specimen tube
Prepared slide of frog's blood

3 Suppose you wanted to calculate the number of oxygen molecules supplied to the tissues each day. List all the information you would require and the assumptions you would need to make. (If you have access to the necessary information, carry out this calculation.)

> **Note:** Mammalian blood, treated to prevent clotting, is available from biological suppliers. It can be stored for up to a week in a refrigerator. Autoclave blood-contaminated items after use.

2.45 TECHNIQUE

How to use a haemocytometer^{BM}

A **haemocytometer** is principally designed for sampling blood cells, but can be used for sampling any cells that are uniformly distributed on the surface of the slide. For example, yeast cells can be sampled in this way (see Investigation 7.19 on p. 292).

The haemocytometer consists of a special slide with a ruled area in the centre, together with a coverslip (Illustration).

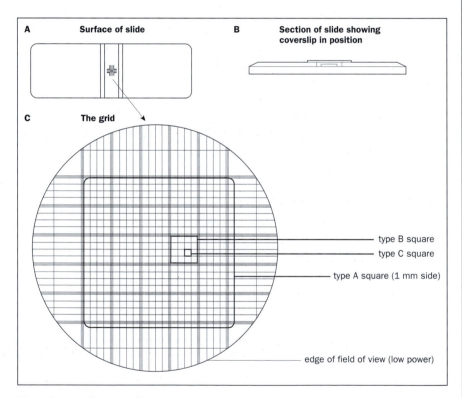

Illustration A Neubauer haemocytometer slide.

The haemocytometer slide

Examine the slide under the low power of the microscope and locate the ruled area in the centre. The middle of the ruled area consists of a grid with an area of $1\,mm^2$ – that is, its sides are 1 mm long. We shall call this the Type A square. If you use the ×10 objective and ×10 eye piece, the Type A square should just about fill the field of view.

Notice that the Type A square is subdivided by triple lines into 25 Type B squares, each of which has an area $1/25\,mm^2$. Each Type B square is further subdivided by single lines into 16 Type C squares, each of which has an area of $1/400\,mm^2$.

Now observe the two deep grooves that cross the slide on either side of the grid. The surface of the slide between these two grooves is 0.1 mm lower than the rest of the slide beyond the grooves. So when the coverslip is put on, its lower surface clears the ruled surface of the slide by 0.1 mm. The volume represented by the Type A square is therefore $0.1\,mm^3$, the volume represented by a Type B square is $0.004\,mm^3$, and the volume represented by a Type C square is $0.00025\,mm^3$.

To do a blood count, you place a sample of diluted blood under the coverslip. You then count the cells in, say, 96 Type C squares and work out the mean. Knowing the volume represented by a Type C square, and the degree to which the blood has been diluted, you can calculate the number of cells per mm^3.

Diluting the blood

If you looked at normal undiluted blood on a haemocytometer slide, the red blood cells would be far too close together for you to be able to count them satisfactorily. So the blood has to be diluted. A known volume of blood is mixed with a known volume of isotonic sodium chloride solution (saline), and a drop of the mixture is then pipetted onto the haemocytometer slide.

The blood is diluted either by mixing small samples of the blood and saline in a special pipette supplied with the haemocytometer, or by measuring out samples of the blood and saline with standard pipettes and mixing them in a beaker.

Cleaning the haemocytometer slide and coverslip

The haemocytometer slide is a delicate piece of equipment. Be careful not to scratch it. Ensure that both the slide and coverslip are cleaned after use. Wash them with distilled water followed by propanone. When the propanone has evaporated, rub them with lens paper.

Requirements

Microscope
Haemocytometer (slide and
  coverslip)
Lens paper
Distilled water
Propanone

Propanone   Propanone

How many red blood cells do you have?   2.46 PRACTICAL EXERCISE

It is obviously impossible to count individually all the blood cells present in a circulatory system, so we resort to *sampling* – that is, we count the cells in a representative volume.

A device for sampling cells is the **haemocytometer**. A measured volume of blood is diluted a known number of times. The red blood cells are then counted in a known volume of the diluted blood, from which the number of cells per mm^3 of undiluted blood can be calculated.

Procedure

1 First examine the haemocytometer and understand how it works (see Technique 2.45 on p. 122).

2 You will be provided with a specimen tube containing a sample of diluted mammalian blood. The blood has been diluted 100-fold with 0.75% sodium chloride solution, so the concentration of the blood is 1 in 100.

3 Place the coverslip in the centre of the haemocytometer slide. Using a teat pipette, place one drop of the diluted blood onto the slide, alongside the coverslip, in the area between the two deep grooves. The blood should be drawn under the coverslip. If the blood flows into the grooves, clean the slide and coverslip and start again.

4 Place the slide under the microscope and adjust the illumination so that the grid and the red blood cells can be clearly seen. If the cells are very unevenly distributed, clean the slide and coverslip and start again.

5 Count the red blood cells in 96 of the smallest (i.e. Type C) squares. (The number of 96 is convenient because the small squares are in blocks of 16, and 96 is 6×16.) Record your results by ruling out a grid and writing the number of cells in each square.
Note: In each square, count all the cells which lie entirely within it, plus those which touch or overlap the top and left hand sides. Do not include those which touch or overlap the bottom and right hand sides.

6 Clean the slide and coverslip when you have finished counting.

7 Calculate the mean number of red blood cells in a Type C square. Knowing the volume of a Type C square, and the dilution factor, calculate the number of cells per mm^3 of blood.

For consideration

1 A typical human red blood cell count might be 5 million per mm^3. Assuming that your total volume of blood is 5 litres, calculate the number of red blood cells you have.

2 Suggest under what circumstances a person's red blood cell count (the number of red blood cells per mm^3 of blood) might be (a) unusually high; (b) unusually low.

Propanone   Propanone

Key skills

✓ **Application of number:** Carry out your calculations to determine the number of cells per mm^3 of mammalian blood. Show your methods clearly, checking your calculations to identify and correct any mistakes. Which is likely to be more accurate and why: your calculation of the number of red blood cells per mm^3 of the mammalian blood with which you were presented or your calculation of the total number of red blood cells you have (in 'For consideration' 1)?

✓ **Improving own learning and performance:** Plan how you will effectively manage your time. Identify ways of overcoming possible difficulties (e.g. a shortage of haemocytometers in the group). Manage your time effectively to complete tasks, revising your plan (e.g. the number of Type C squares you sample) as necessary. Identify targets you have met, seeking information from relevant sources to establish evidence of your achievements (within what range should your answers lie?).

This practical exercise has two aims:

- To dissect the rat so as to show the heart and the arteries and veins that are attached to it.
- To trace the arteries and veins to their destinations.

Procedure

Use a rat which you may already have used for dissecting the alimentary canal. The alimentary canal should have been removed, the thorax opened up and the thymus gland removed (see Practical Exercise 2.31 on p. 100).

Observing the heart and vessels attached to it

1   Observe the **heart** and pluck away the fat from around the vessels that are attached to it. Be careful not to damage the **ductus arteriosus**, a slender strand linking the **pulmonary artery** and **aorta**. It is a relic of a vessel that was present in the fetus.

2   Push the heart to your left and identify the structures shown in Figure 2.35.

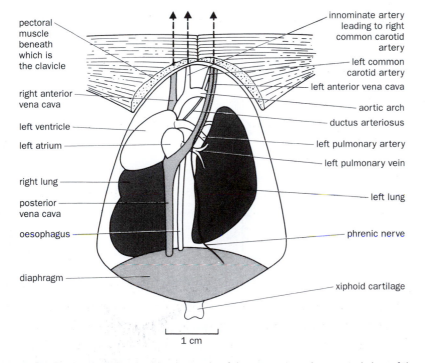

Figure 2.35 The heart and major blood vessels of the rat, as seen in a ventral view of the thorax, with the heart deflected to your left.

3   Push the heart to your right and identify the point where the **venae cavae** enter the right atrium (Figure 2.36).

4   Mentally reconstruct the flow of blood into, through, and out of the heart, identifying all the blood vessels along which it flows *en route*.

Tracing the vessels to their destinations

Do not use a dissection guide for this part of the dissection. Try to follow the arteries and veins to their destinations in a truly exploratory

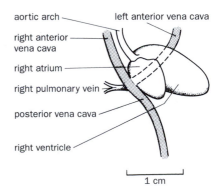

Figure 2.36 The heart and major blood vessels of the rat, as seen in a ventral view of the thorax, with the heart deflected to your right.

way. Bear in mind that William Harvey, who did much of the early work on the circulation, did not have a dissection guide.

1　Carefully trace the **anterior venae cavae** and the branches of the **aortic arch** from the thorax into the neck (the dotted arrows in Figure 2.35). This will necessitate removing the **pectoral muscle** and **clavicle** ('collar bone'). Be careful in the armpit region when you remove the clavicle, because the anterior venae cavae are immediately underneath and, because of their thin walls, are easily broken.

2　Continue tracing the veins and arteries forward towards the jaws, cutting away the neck muscles as necessary. Watch out for the branches of the arteries and veins. What structures are served by the various vessels?

3　Now trace the **posterior vena cava** and **aorta** from the thorax into the abdomen. What structures are served by these vessels?

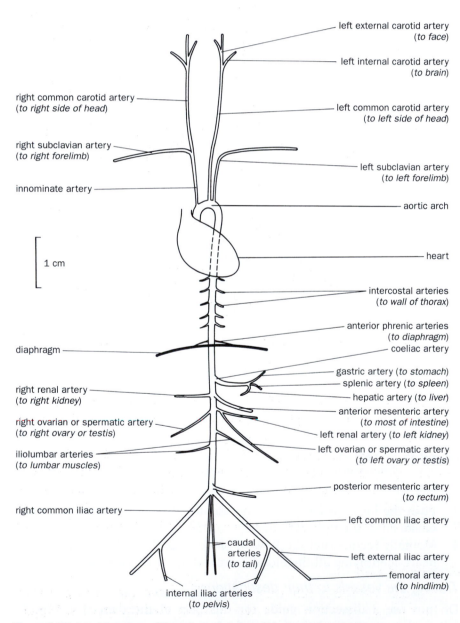

Figure 2.37 Arterial system of the rat, ventral view. Only the major arteries are shown.

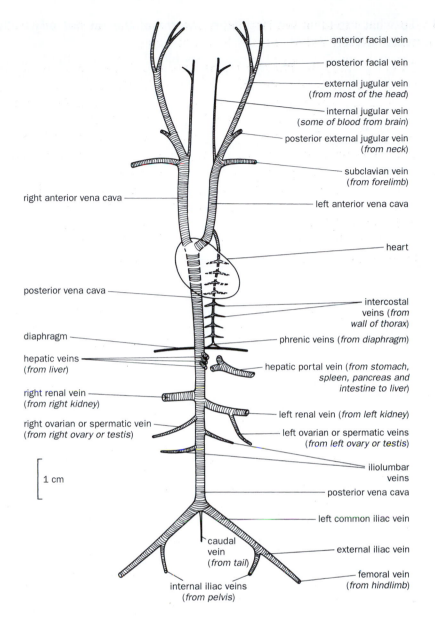

anterior facial vein

posterior facial vein

external jugular vein
(*from most of the head*)

internal jugular vein
(*some of blood from brain*)

posterior external jugular vein
(*from neck*)

subclavian vein
(*from forelimb*)

right anterior vena cava

left anterior vena cava

heart

posterior vena cava

intercostal
veins (*from
wall of thorax*)

phrenic veins (*from diaphragm*)

diaphragm

hepatic veins
(*from liver*)

hepatic portal vein (*from stomach,
spleen, pancreas and
intestine to liver*)

right renal vein
(*from right kidney*)

left renal vein (*from left kidney*)

right ovarian or spermatic vein
(*from right ovary or testis*)

left ovarian or spermatic veins
(*from left ovary or testis*)

iliolumbar
veins

1 cm

posterior vena cava

left common iliac vein

caudal
vein
(*from tail*)

external iliac vein

femoral vein
(*from hindlimb*)

internal iliac veins
(*from pelvis*)

Figure 2.38 Venous system of the rat, ventral view. Only the major veins are shown.

4 Towards the posterior end of the abdomen, the aorta and posterior vena cava split into vessels which go to the hind legs. Follow these vessels into the legs, noting their branches.

5 Check your dissection against Figures 2.37 and 2.38. Can you identify all the vessels shown in these diagrams? To what extent, if any, do the blood vessels in your rat differ from those in the diagram?

6 Draw and label your dissection, showing the arteries and veins in the same view.

For consideration

1 In your dissection you will have noticed that the veins generally have a wider diameter and a darker colour than the arteries. Explain the reason for the difference.

Requirements

Dissecting instruments
Dissecting board
Dissecting pins
Rubber gloves
Rat for dissection

Note: Double injected rats (arteries red, veins blue) can be purchased.

2 To what extent is the circulatory system of the rat *not* bilaterally symmetrical?
3 Through which series of vessels does blood flow from the heart to (a) the brain, (b) the right forelimb, (c) the liver, (d) the left kidney, (e) the left hindlimb?
4 Through which series of vessels does blood flow to the heart from (a) the side of the head, (b) the left forelimb, (c) the lungs, (d) the intercostal muscles, (e) the small intestine?

Reference

Rowett, H. G. Q. *Dissection Guides, III The Rat*. John Murray, London, 1970.

2.48 PRACTICAL EXERCISE

Structure and action of the mammalian heart

Caution

In the interests of hygiene, wear a lab. coat while you are dissecting, and wash your hands thoroughly afterwards. Disinfect equipment after use.

The purpose of this practical exercise is to study the anatomy of the heart and to relate this to its job of pumping blood round the body. You will be given detailed instructions on how to proceed, but first draw up a plan of your own based on the following preliminary considerations.

Preliminary considerations

First recall your theoretical knowledge of the heart, using Figure 2.39 to help you. Notice the direction in which blood flows through the heart, as indicated by the arrows.

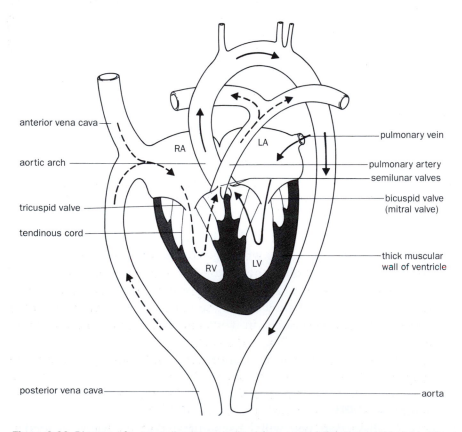

Figure 2.39 Diagram of a generalised mammalian heart, ventral (front) view. RA, right atrium; LA, left atrium; RV, right ventricle; LV, left ventricle. Deoxygenated blood, broken arrows; oxygenated blood, solid arrows.

One of the most interesting questions about the heart is: *how does it keep blood flowing in one direction and prevent it flowing backwards?* In this the **valves** play a crucial part, and one aim of this practical is to see how the valves work.

With this in mind, draw up a detailed plan of how you might investigate the heart. Then read through the following procedure and see to what extent your plan coincides with the instructions given here.

Procedure

You will be provided with the heart of a sheep or pig.

1 Distinguish between the ventral (front) and dorsal (back) sides of the heart. The ventral side is the more rounded (convex) side, and the thick-walled arteries arise from this side. The veins open into the heart on the more concave dorsal side.

2 Identify the parts of the heart shown in Figure 2.40. Observe the **coronary vessels** ramifying over the surface of the heart. Can you distinguish between the main coronary artery and coronary vein? What are their functions? Observe the pattern of their branching.

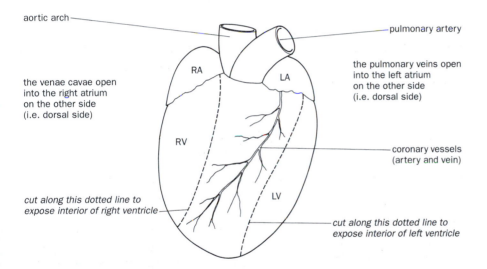

aortic arch

pulmonary artery

RA

LA

the pulmonary veins open into the left atrium on the other side (i.e. dorsal side)

the venae cavae open into the right atrium on the other side (i.e. dorsal side)

RV

coronary vessels (artery and vein)

cut along this dotted line to expose interior of right ventricle

LV

cut along this dotted line to expose interior of left ventricle

Figure 2.40 Ventral aspect of the mammalian heart, showing the attachment of the aorta and pulmonary artery to the ventricles. The veins are on the other side. RA, right atrium; LA, left atrium; RV, right ventricle; LV, left ventricle.

3 Attach a rubber tube to a water tap and insert the other end into the **anterior vena cava**. Clamp the **posterior vena cava**. Run water into the anterior vena cava and note its flow through the heart. From which blood vessel does the water emerge? This is the **pulmonary artery**. Now run water into the **pulmonary vein** and note the vessel from which it emerges. This is the **aorta**.

4 Expose the interior of the left and right **ventricles** by making two longitudinal cuts on the ventral side of the heart along the course of the broken lines in Figure 2.40. Notice how thick the walls of the ventricles are. What is the significance of this?

5 Peer into the **right ventricle**. Notice the valve between the atrium and ventricle. It consists of three flaps, for which reason it is called the **tricuspid valve**. Examine the entrance to the pulmonary artery

and notice that it is guarded by **semilunar valves**. Why are they described as *semilunar*?

6 Now peer into the **left ventricle**. In this case the valve between the atrium and ventricle consists of *two* flaps, for which reason it is called the **bicuspid valve**. It is also called the **mitral valve**, because of its resemblance to a bishop's mitre. To help his students remember which side of the heart has the mitral valve, T. H. Huxley (a well-known agnostic) used to say: 'The mitre's on the left because bishops are never right'!

7 Notice the semilunar valves guarding the entrance to the aorta. They are similar to the valves at the entrance to the pulmonary artery on the other side of the heart.

8 Observe the **tendinous cords** by which the flaps of the bicuspid and tricuspid valves are attached to the walls of the ventricles. What sort of tissue do you think they are made of?

9 Turn the heart the other way up and run water into the ventricles through the slits that you have cut. What happens to the bicuspid and tricuspid valves? What is the function of these valves, and what part do the tendinous cords play?

10 Now turn the heart back the way it was. Run water into the cut ends of the pulmonary artery and aorta and notice the action of the semilunar valves. What is the function of these valves? They are also called *pocket valves* – why?

11 Cut into the atria and examine the bicuspid and tricuspid valves from above. Notice the opening of the coronary vein on the left-hand side of the right atrium (the right-hand side as you view it from the ventral side).

12 Cut into the pulmonary artery and/or aorta and examine the semilunar valves from above. Notice the opening into the coronary artery from the aorta just above the semilunar valves.

13 Examine the openings of the venae cavae and pulmonary veins into their respective atria. Are there any valves guarding these openings? If there are, what do they achieve? If there are not, how does the heart manage without them?

14 Finally, notice the relative sizes of the four chambers of the heart and the relative thickness of their walls. Which is the largest chamber, and which one has the thickest wall? Explain the reasons for any differences observed.

For consideration

1 In what ways might the valves of the heart show malfunctions, and what would the consequences be?

2 What would be the result of a blockage in the coronary artery or one of its branches? How might such a blockage arise? If you were a heart surgeon what would you need to do to rectify the condition?

3 Can you suggest a functional reason why the tricuspid valve has three flaps but the bicuspid valve has only two?

4 Looking back over this practical, how might the instructions given above be improved?

Reference

Rouan, C. The heart – a different approach. *Journal of Biological Education*, **15**, 189–190, 1981.

Requirements

Dissecting instruments
Access to water tap
Rubber tubing
Clamp for sealing blood vessel
Heart of sheep *or* pig

Note: Preserved sheep and/or pig hearts are available from biological suppliers. Fresh hearts can be obtained from an abattoir or butcher, though the atria and/or ventricles are usually damaged.

Pumped by the heart, blood is propelled round the body in tubular **blood vessels**. The blood vessels include **arteries** and **veins**. The arteries carry blood from the heart to the tissues, and the veins carry the blood back to the heart. Knowing their functions, can you *predict* the physical properties of the walls of the arteries and veins, and the kinds of tissues which each is likely to possess? The purpose of this investigation is to test your predictions.

Guidance

Properties of the vessels

You will be provided with a short length of an artery and a vein, each in the form of a ring. Using the apparatus provided, compare the elastic properties of the artery and vein rings. Figure 2.41 shows one way of carrying out the experiment, but you may be able to devise a better way. Make your investigation quantitative. The data you obtain should provide information on the stretchability of the artery and vein and their ability to return to their original length after being stretched.

Consider carefully how to express your results. For example, should you express a change in length of the artery or vein in absolute terms or as a percentage of the initial length?

Structure of the vessels

From the results of your experiment on the artery and vein, try to predict the kinds of tissues which each is likely to possess in its wall.

After you have made your predictions, examine a transverse section of an artery and vein under the microscope. How do they differ in the thickness of their walls and the tissues in the walls? Both contain elastic fibres, collagen fibres and smooth muscle, but these three types of tissue differ in their relative amounts and distribution.

Try to relate differences in the structure of the artery and vein to their elastic properties.

For consideration

1　How do the elastic properties and microscopic structure of the artery and vein relate to the stresses and strains which these vessels are likely to experience in life?
2　Find out as much as you can about varicose veins. Can you relate this condition to the structure and properties of veins?
3　In an experiment, masses were hung on blood vessel rings until they broke. Here are the results for three specific vessels: dorsal aorta 5000 g; pulmonary artery 3500 g; vena cava 800 g. Comment.
4　Why do veins not transmit a pulse?

Reference

Freeman, W. H. & Bracegirdle, B. *An Advanced Atlas of Histology.* Heinemann, Oxford, 1976. (For the microscopic structure of arteries and veins.)

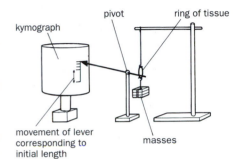

Figure 2.41 Technique for recording and measuring changes in length of a ring of tissue with increasing load. The lever amplifies the changes in length, which can be recorded on a kymograph.

Requirements

Kymograph
Stands and clamps, ×2
Recording lever
Cotton thread
Hooks, ×2
Masses, 10 g
Ring of large artery
Ring of large vein

- **Plan** your investigation. Demonstrate that you have developed a strategy which is well structured, logical and linked coherently to underlying scientific knowledge and understanding.

- **Implement** your plan. Practise your approach until you can demonstrate skilful and proficient use of all techniques and equipment.

- **Analyse your evidence** and **draw conclusions**. Relate your findings from the different parts of the investigation.

- **Evaluate** your investigation. Discuss any inconsistencies in your data that have arisen. How could an extension of this investigation generate new, relevant data?

2.50 PRACTICAL EXERCISE

Effect of fitness on the pulse rate and blood pressure

Your **pulse rate** tells you the number of times your heart beats per minute – that is, your **cardiac frequency**. Your **blood pressure** tells you how hard your heart is working to pump your blood round the body. The purpose of this practical is to measure your resting blood pressure and then to measure your pulse rate under different conditions and, from these, assess your physical fitness.

How to measure blood pressure

Blood pressure is traditionally measured using a **mercury sphygmo-manometer**. A mercury sphygmomanometer consists of a cuff, a small rubber pump with a regulation valve, and a mercury column. The cuff is fitted around the subject's upper arm and inflated, using the pump, to a pressure at which the pulse disappears.

A **stethoscope** is then placed on the artery, and as the cuff is deflated a sound is heard at a point corresponding to the **systolic pressure**. As the cuff is further deflated, this sound disappears when the pressure decreases to the **diastolic pressure**. The level of the mercury at these two points provides the readings for the two blood pressure values.

Operating a mercury sphygmomanometer is not easy. If you do use one, your teacher/lecturer must be present. In recent years a range of monitors have become available which do not rely on a person listening to changes in sounds. These monitors automatically record both the systolic and the diastolic pressure.

How to measure pulse rate

You can feel your pulse by placing a finger immediately over the radial artery on the lateral side of the wrist (Figure 2.42). Practise taking your pulse rate by counting the number of throbs in a 30 second period and doubling this figure.

To measure changes in the pulse rate continuously over a short period, count the number of pulses every 10 seconds and convert to pulses per minute.

Nowadays there are also various automatic methods which allow pulse rates to be recorded and displayed.

Sphygmomanometer

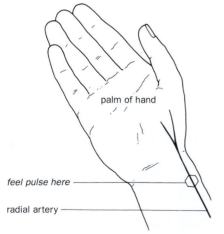
palm of hand

feel pulse here

radial artery

Figure 2.42 One way of feeling your pulse.

Procedure

Blood pressure

First, sit down, relax for 2 minutes and then determine your systolic and diastolic blood pressure.

Pulse rate

You can use the modified version of the **Harvard Step Test** given below. This involves finding the effect of posture and exercise on the pulse rate. Throughout, measure pulse rates in pulses (beats) per minute.

Effect of posture

1 Lie down quietly for 2 minutes, then measure your pulse rate over 30 seconds.
2 Stand up for 2 minutes, then measure your pulse rate over 30 seconds.
3 Calculate the increase in your pulse rate on standing.

Effect of exercise

1 Engage in a standard bout of exercise by stepping onto a stool 45 cm high and then down again, once every 3 seconds. Do this five times, thus taking 15 seconds in all.
2 Immediately after the 15 seconds exercise, measure your pulse rate at 10 second intervals until it returns to the normal *standing* rate. Record how long this takes in seconds.
3 Calculate the increase in the pulse rate immediately after the 15 seconds exercise compared with your standing rate.

Interpretation of results

Table 2.3 shows the World Health Organisation classification of adult resting blood pressure. Note that high blood pressure can result from anxiety when the readings were taken! So don't jump to any conclusions about whether you are suffering from hypotension or hypertension. However, around 15% of adults in Britain are thought to suffer from hypertension. Its causes include being very overweight, smoking, excessive saturated fat intake accompanied by insufficient exercise, certain kidney diseases, stress, high salt intake and being pregnant. People with high blood pressure are more likely to suffer a stroke or heart attack.

Table 2.3 World Health Organisation classification of adult resting blood pressures. 'Hypertension' is high blood pressure; 'hypotension' low.

Blood pressure condition	Systolic (mmHg)	Diastolic (mmHg)
Hypotension	less than 100	less than 60
Normal	100–139	60–89
Borderline	140–159	90–94
Hypertension	more than 159	more than 94

To convert your pulse rate findings into a fitness score, use Table 2.4 parts A, B, C, D and E to determine a single value from each table. Add these five values and determine your fitness using Table 2.5.

Table 2.4 Stages in the determination of fitness using a modified Harvard Step Test

A Pulse rate lying down ('reclining pulse')

Rate	Points
50–60	3
61–70	3
71–80	2
81–90	1

B Pulse rate standing up ('standing pulse')

Rate	Points
60–70	3
71–80	3
81–90	2
91–100	1
101–110	1

C Increase in pulse rate on standing

Reclining pulse rate (A)	Increase in pulse rate on standing		
	0–10 beats	11–18 beats	19–26 beats
50–60	3	3	2
61–70	3	2	1
71–80	3	2	0
81–90	2	1	−1

D Time taken for pulse to return to standing rate after exercise

Seconds	Points
0–30	4
31–60	3
61–90	2
91–120	1

E Increase in pulse rate immediately after exercise compared with standing rate

Standing pulse rate (B)	Increase in pulse rate immediately after exercise		
	0–10 beats	11–20 beats	21–30 beats
60–70	3	3	2
71–80	3	2	1
81–90	3	2	1
91–100	2	1	0
101–110	1	0	−1

Table 2.5 Classification of fitness in terms of points scored on a modified Harvard Step Test

Point score	Fitness
<8	Poor
8–11	Fair
12–15	Good
16	Excellent

For consideration

1 To what extent might these measures of physical fitness be influenced by your life style? For example, do you take regular exercise, smoke, etc.?

Reference

Reiss, M. Monitoring human blood pressure and pulse rate. *Journal of Biological Education*, **23**, 80–82, 1989.

Requirements

Stool (45 cm high)
Mercury sphygmomanometer *or* blood pressure monitor
Pulse monitor *or* sensor (if available)

Note: If you use a sphygmomanometer, do not leave the cuff inflated for longer than the instructions state.

Primary structure of stems

2.51 PRACTICAL EXERCISE

The **primary tissues** of the stem are formed from the dividing cells at the apex of the growing shoot. The three main functions of the stem are to lift the leaves and flowers into an elevated position, to convey water and mineral salts from roots to leaves and to transport synthesised food materials from the leaves to other parts of the plant. The stem needs strengthening tissues to support the aerial parts and to resist the sideways forces of the wind, and it requires conducting tissues for transport.

The aim of this practical exercise is to examine the structure of the various primary tissues inside stems, and to relate their positions to their functions.

Procedure

1 Investigate the internal structure of the stem of a dicotyledonous plant such as sunflower (Figure 2.43) by cutting thin transverse and longitudinal sections and staining in acidified phloroglucinol, iodine solution or Schultze's solution (see Technique 1.20 on p. 49).

2 Using Figure 2.43 to help you, look at prepared slides of transverse and longitudinal sections of a dicotyledonous stem (*Helianthus* or *Cucurbita*) and identify the following tissues, arranged here roughly from outside to inside:

- **Epidermis.** Single layer of cuboidal cells covering the surface of the stem.
- **Collenchyma.** See Practical Exercise 1.19 on p. 47; several layers of living thick-walled cells immediately beneath epidermis, cells vertically elongated and cellulose walls thickened at the corners; constitutes outer part of cortex.
- **Parenchyma.** See Practical Exercise 1.19 on p. 47; living thin-walled packing and storage cells, usually more or less circular in cross section, making up the bulk of the cortex, pith and medullary rays.

Razor blade

Acidified phloroglucinol

Acidified phloroglucinol Schultze's solution

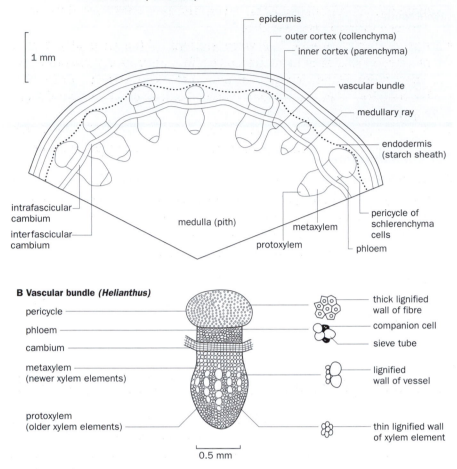

A Transverse section of stem (Helianthus)

1 mm

epidermis
outer cortex (collenchyma)
inner cortex (parenchyma)
vascular bundle
medullary ray
endodermis (starch sheath)

intrafascicular cambium
interfascicular cambium

medulla (pith)

metaxylem
protoxylem

pericycle of schlerenchyma cells
phloem

B Vascular bundle (Helianthus)

pericycle
phloem
cambium
metaxylem (newer xylem elements)

protoxylem (older xylem elements)

thick lignified wall of fibre
companion cell
sieve tube

lignified wall of vessel

thin lignified wall of xylem element

0.5 mm

Figure 2.43 Structure of the stem of a dicotyledon, based mainly on the sunflower, *Helianthus*. This particular plant is unusual in having an endodermis (starch sheath) in its stem.

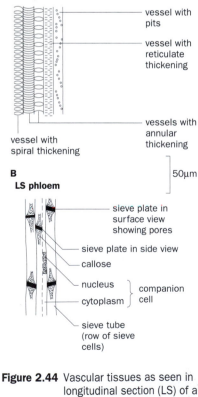

A
LS xylem

vessel with pits
vessel with reticulate thickening
vessels with annular thickening
vessel with spiral thickening

50μm

B
LS phloem

sieve plate in surface view showing pores
sieve plate in side view
callose
nucleus ⎤
cytoplasm ⎦ companion cell
sieve tube (row of sieve cells)

Figure 2.44 Vascular tissues as seen in longitudinal section (LS) of a dicotyledonous stem, based on *Cucurbita*.

- **Sclerenchyma.** See Practical Exercise 1.19 on p. 47; dead, empty, thick-walled, vertically elongated fibres on the immediate outside of each vascular bundle, which together, in a large group, constitute the **pericycle**.
- **Phloem.** Vertically elongated **sieve tubes**, **companion cells** and parenchyma, on the immediate inside of the pericycle; sieve tube elements are living but lack nuclei (Figure 2.44B) and have sieve plates with pores; each sieve tube element is associated with a smaller nucleated companion cell.
- **Cambium.** Several layers of small living rectangular cells wedged between xylem and phloem in each vascular bundle; cambium tissue continuous (in *Helianthus*) between vascular bundles (**interfascicular cambium**). Cambium cells can divide to produce **secondary tissues** such as the annual rings of woody plant stems.
- **Xylem.** Mainly composed of dead, vertically elongated, empty, lignified tube-like cells which make up **vessels** (Figure 2.44A) or **tracheids**; small cells in inner parts of vascular bundle, formed first, constitute the **protoxylem**; larger cells nearer cambium, formed later, constitute the **metaxylem**.

3 Now examine macerated tissue (see Practical Exercise 1.19 on p. 47) mounted in safranin and fast green and see if you can distinguish between the various types of cells.

4 Cut, stain and mount transverse sections of the stem of a typical monocotyledon such as maize, iris or lily. Alternatively, examine prepared slides. Under low power, note that the arrangement of vascular bundles differs from that in the dicotyledon. How would you explain the difference?

5 Examine under high power an individual vascular bundle of a monocotyledonous stem. Identify phloem and xylem; cambium is absent.

For consideration

1 List the functions of each of the visible tissues in the cross section.

2 What advantages might there be to a dicotyledon in having the vascular bundles arranged in a ring towards the outside of the stem, instead of in a central cylinder, as in the root?

Reference

Clegg, C. J. & Cox, G. *Anatomy and Activities of Plants*, John Murray, London, 1978.

Requirements

Microscope
Microscope slides
Coverslips
Dish for sections
Fine brush
Razor blade
Iodine solution
Acidified phloroglucinol
Safranin
Fast green
Schultze's solution
Dilute glycerol (25%, aqueous, for mounting)
Prepared microscope slides of TS and LS *Helianthus* or *Cucurbita* stems, and TS monocotyledon stem
Stems of sunflower (*Helianthus*) *or* marrow (*Cucurbita*), fresh *or* in 70% alcohol
Stem of monocotyledon e.g. maize, *Iris*
Macerated stem tissue (see Practical Exercise 1.19 on p. 47)

Structure of roots
2.52 PRACTICAL EXERCISE

Roots absorb water and mineral salts from the soil, and transport these to the stem. They expose to the soil a large surface area for absorption and contain xylem and phloem – vascular tissues that link up with those in the stem. Roots also store food reserves and anchor the plant in the soil. As you examine each tissue, ask yourself how it contributes to these functions.

The tissues are derived from cell divisions in the root apex (see Practical Exercise 5.1 on p. 207 to find out how the mature tissues develop).

Procedure

External structure

1 Examine the **radicle** of a seedling such as mustard, cress or pea. Notice that the **root hairs** (functions?) are confined to a particular zone just behind the apex. The radicle develops into the taproot, or main root, from which lateral roots sprout. Are any lateral roots visible in your seedling?

2 Compare your seedling with that of a grass such as maize or wheat. Notice that, instead of one main root, grasses produce several fibrous roots of equal importance.

3 Mount a radicle in iodine solution without crushing it. Examine it under the microscope. Note that each root hair is a single cell.

Internal structure

4 Cut cross sections of a young primary root, such as broad bean or buttercup. Insert the root into a vertical slit in a piece of moistened elder pith or carrot tap root (see Technique 1.20 on p. 47), and cut thin sections with a safety razor blade into a dish of water.

Razor blade

Acidified
phloroglucinol

Acidified
phloroglucinol

5 Using a brush, transfer two or three of the thinnest sections to a microscope slide. Add a drop of iodine solution and examine your sections under the microscope. To highlight the vascular tissue, stain with acidified phloroglucinol, which stains lignin red.

6 Using Figure 2.45 as a guide, and supplementing your observations with the use of prepared slides of transverse sections of roots, identify the following tissues:

• **Outer cell layer.** In the younger parts of the root, this is the epidermis (in the root hair zone known as the **piliferous layer**). This

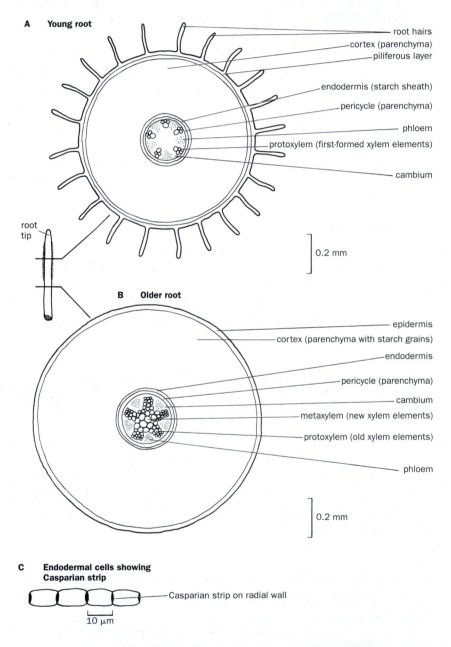

Figure 2.45 Transverse sections of a dicotyledonous root, based on buttercup (*Ranunculus*). **A** Young part of the root in the root hair zone just behind the tip. **B** Older part of the root, just behind the tip. **C** Endodermal cells from above, showing suberised thickening (Casparian strips) on the radial walls. In a monocotyledonous root (e.g. *Iris*) there are more (up to 20) points on the xylem star.

is one cell wide and is sloughed off in the older part of the root. There, the outer layer of cortex cells may become suberised (corky), constituting the **exodermis**.

- **Cortex.** An extensive volume of parenchyma cells which present a massive area to soil water (which saturates their cell walls) for water and mineral ion uptake; also stores starch. Can you see the grains, which stain blue-black with iodine solution?
- **Endodermis.** Single layer of prominent cuboidal cells (inner layer of cortex). Notice the suberised radial walls, containing **Casparian strips** (Figure 2.45C). What is the function of these?
- **Pericycle.** An indistinct layer of parenchyma cells immediately inside endodermis; may become lignified in older roots. Lateral roots originate here.
- **Vascular tissues.** Within the endodermis and pericycle, the water-conducting xylem tissue is generally star-shaped in older roots, with sucrose-conducting phloem between the spokes of the star (Figure 2.45B). Xylem (protoxylem) first forms at the points of the star (Figure 2.45A). The xylem elements in the centre of the star (metaxylem) develop later.
- **Cambium.** Small cells are wedged between xylem and phloem and divide in older roots to produce secondary xylem and phloem.

For consideration

1 List the ways in which each of the tissues in the root cross section contributes to the uptake and transport of water from the soil.
2 Why do roots have an endodermis?
3 Stems are generally stiff and erect, but roots are flexible. Explain this difference in terms of their internal structure.

Tracing the supply of water to the leaves of broad bean	2.53 PRACTICAL EXERCISE

The water which evaporates from the leaves of a plant is replaced by uptake from the vascular bundles of the **petioles** (leaf stalks). The vascular bundles in the stem must branch to provide bundles which run up the petioles of the leaves to the leaf blades. The pattern of bundles can be investigated by dissecting part of a leafy stem after its vascular bundles have taken up a stain.

Procedure

1 Fill a beaker with water. Select two healthy shoots of broad bean. Cut them off at soil level and immediately plunge the cut ends into the water.
2 Pour eosin and rose Bengal stain into two separate test tubes, until each is filled to about 2 cm from the rim. Place them in a rack.
3 Cut the lower end of each stem under water, obliquely, about 5 cm from the base of the lowest expanded leaf. Immediately transfer each shoot to a test tube containing stain and make sure that the cut surface is fully immersed.

Eosin

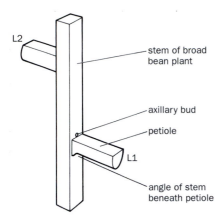

Figure 2.46 Diagram of part of a stem of broad bean (*Vicia faba*), showing the distance over which vascular bundles should be dissected. L1, fully expanded leaf; L2, top leaf.

L2

L1

stem of broad bean plant

axillary bud

petiole

angle of stem beneath petiole

Requirements

Test tubes, ×2
Test tube rack
Beaker
Dissecting instruments (including a blunt scalpel *or* razor blade)
White tile
Lens
Plain paper
Stain (75 cm³; a mixture of equal volumes of 0.1% eosin and 0.1% aqueous rose Bengal)
Turgid transpiring shoots of broad bean (*Vicia faba*), at least 4 weeks old, growing in soil, ×2

4 Leave the shoots in the stain in a light and well-ventilated place for at least 30 minutes. The stain will stain the xylem tissue in the vascular bundles.

5 Remove one of the shoots from its test tube. The other plant is an emergency reserve.

6 Cut a cross section of the shoot near the base and examine with a lens the pattern of stained bundles. Immortalise the pattern in a labelled diagram.

7 Examine and draw in a similar manner a cross section across a leaf petiole.

8 Using a fairly blunt scalpel or razor blade, begin to scrape gently on one of the angles of the stem just below a fully expanded leaf (Figure 2.46). The stained xylem of a major vascular bundle should soon become visible.

9 Now use further scraping and dissection to investigate the arrangement of the stained xylem. Begin your investigation about 1 cm below a fully expanded leaf (L1 in Figure 2.46) and complete it 1 cm above the top leaf (L2), which will be on the opposite side of the stem from L1. Aim to find the courses of all the stained bundles in the stem between the start and finish points. Pay particular attention to the junctions of bundles.

10 Follow vascular bundles as far as you can along the petiole and into the leaf.

For consideration

1 If water is continually taken up by the cells between the vascular bundles, why is the dye restricted to the vascular bundles in your sections?

2 Speculate on the internal factors which determine the pattern of vascular bundles in the leaf petiole and the stem during leaf and shoot development.

2.54 TECHNIQUE	**How to use a microbalance**

A **microbalance** is a sensitive device which can be used to measure small changes in mass, such as when water is lost from a transpiring leaf. A home-made microbalance is shown in the Illustration.

Procedure

Determining the mass of a leaf

1 Suspend the leaf from the S-shaped hook. Alter the shape of the plasticine and, if necessary, the position of the fulcrum, until the balance beam is more or less horizontal.

2 Record the position of the leaf by marking a line on the paper behind the tip of the knitting needle. Then *remove* the leaf, making sure that the plasticine at the other end does not change in shape or position.

3 Slide a wire rider up and down the beam until the tip of the beam

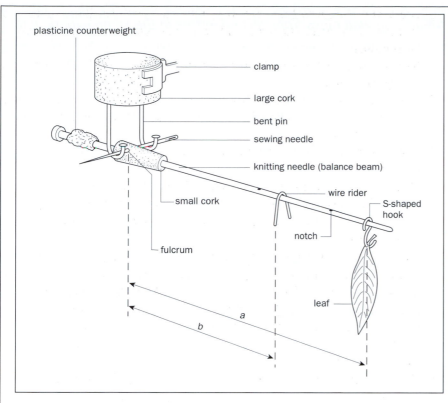

plasticine counterweight

clamp

large cork

bent pin

sewing needle

knitting needle (balance beam)

wire rider

S-shaped hook

small cork

notch

fulcrum

leaf

a

b

Illustration Using a microbalance to measure the mass of a leaf. Graph paper is clamped behind the apparatus. The microbalance is set up away from air currents, as these can seriously upset its equilibrium. Distances *a* (of leaf from fulcrum) and *b* (of rider from fulcrum) are used in the calculation of leaf mass.

reaches the same horizontal position as before. Then measure the distances *a* and *b* from the fulcrum (see Illustration). By moments, $ax = by$, where

a = distance of leaf from the fulcrum
b = distance of the rider from the fulcrum (sewing needle)
x = mass of the leaf (as yet unknown)
y = known mass of rider

Since $ax = by$, $x = by/a$. If the rider is measured in grams, the units of *x* will also be grams.

Measuring water loss from a transpiring leaf

4   Attach the leaf to the tip of the horizontal balance beam using the S-shaped hook and mark the position of the tip of the knitting needle on the graph paper behind. Allow the leaf to lose water whilst still suspended from the balance. The tip of the balance beam will rise.

5   After a known time, slide a rider up and down the notched beam until its tip returns to its previous position. Measure the distance (*b*) of the rider from the fulcrum at equilibrium. The mass of water lost $= by/a$, as explained above.

Microbalance (Illustration)
Weighed riders of 10, 20 and 50 mg
    made from fuse wire
Plasticine
Clamp stands, bosses and clamps
Graph paper
String
Ruler
Large sheets of cardboard to shelter
    the microbalance from draughts

Measuring water loss from several leaves in the same experiment

6 Make the plasticine counterweight concave on top. Arrange it in such a position that, when you add a leaf to the other end of the knitting needle, it can be counterbalanced exactly by an additional tiny ball of plasticine placed on top of the counterweight. When you hang the leaf up to dry, carefully save its appropriate plasticine ball.

7 Now place other leaves or leaf bundles on the microbalance, and save a balancing plasticine ball for each of them.

8 When you come to re-weigh a particular leaf, you must place its appropriate plasticine ball on the counterweight.

2.55 TECHNIQUE

How to use a potometer

A **potometer** is a device for measuring the rate of water uptake by an isolated leafy shoot. The water in the xylem elements in the shoot is continuous with the water filling a capillary tube attached to its cut end. The rate at which a bubble of air moves along the capillary indicates the rate of water uptake.

The major influence on the rate at which water is taken up by a detached shoot is the rate at which water evaporates into the atmosphere from the leaves and stem in **transpiration**. You can alter the conditions around the leaves and assess their influence on water uptake.

Look at the three different types of potometer depicted in the Illustration. It is important, whilst setting up the apparatus, to minimise contact between the air and the cut end of the stem, to exclude air bubbles and to seal potentially leaky joints with vaseline or silicone grease.

Setting up a potometer

Using secateurs, cut a leafy shoot of, for example, holly or sycamore, and plunge its base into a bowl, bucket or beaker of water straight away, to prevent air bubbles from being trapped in the xylem. Bear in mind when you select the shoot that the base of the shoot will have to fit snugly into the rubber tubing or stopper of the potometer, and that shoots with few leaves often yield inadequate results.

In the laboratory, rapidly transfer your shoot to a large sink or bowl of water so that its stem base (but not any leaves) are immersed. Using a razor blade (secateurs might crush the xylem), cut off the bottom 1 cm of the stem obliquely *under water*.

Razor blade

Immerse the potometer in the water and move it around to remove all the air bubbles. Carefully, under water, insert the cut end of the stalk into the rubber tubing or bung, keeping the leaves out of the water as much as possible. Make sure that any reservoir taps are closed before you remove the apparatus. As you take it out of the water, grease the joint between the stem and the potometer with vaseline or silicone grease.

Set up the apparatus with the end of the capillary tube in a beaker of water. Check it for leaks and expel any air bubbles. Set up a millimetre scale along the capillary tube.

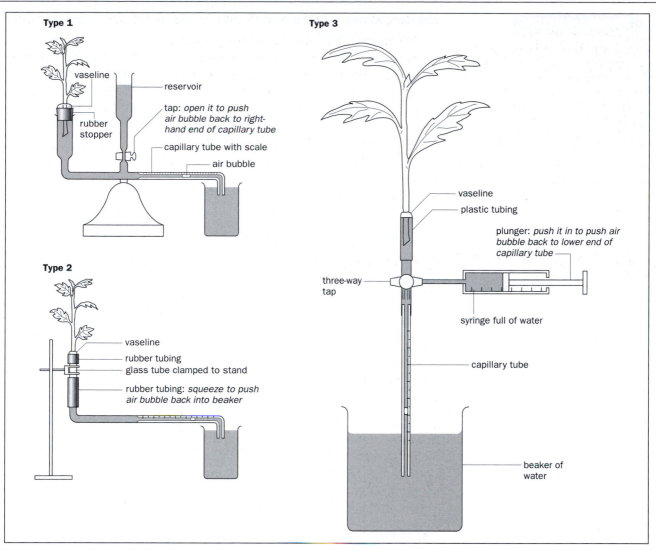

Illustration Three types of potometer.

Obtaining data with a potometer

Perform a trial run with the plant in normal room conditions. Remove the capillary tube from the beaker for a few seconds to allow a bubble of air to enter it. Measure the distance moved by the air bubble in a certain interval of time.

Return the bubble to its original position in the capillary tube, as indicated in the Illustration. Take at least three readings with the plant in each experimental condition and average the results. Allow the plant 3 minutes to settle down in a new condition before you begin to take readings.

Calculation of results

Your initial measurements will be in terms of distance moved by the air bubble in a certain time interval, e.g. in millimetres per minute. You can convert these results to the volume of water taken up per unit time (e.g. $mm^3 min^{-1}$) if you can estimate the radius, r, of the

Potometer (Illustration)
Secateurs
Razor blade
Vaseline or silicone grease
Graph paper
Ruler (in millimetres)
Bowl, bucket *or* beaker of water
Leafy shoots of, e.g., holly and
    sycamore

capillary tubing (volume $= \pi r^2 h$, where h is the distance travelled by the bubble and $\pi = 3.142$).

The best way to compare water loss in different shoots (e.g. of different species) is on the basis of unit leaf area. After the experiment, remove the leaves and lay them on graph paper. Draw outlines of the leaves on the graph paper and count the squares to determine their area. Then you can express water loss in terms of volume per unit area per unit time (e.g. mm^3 per m^2 per hour).

2.56 INVESTIGATION

Comparing the rates of water loss from leaves

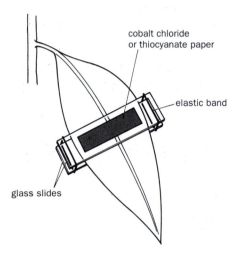

cobalt chloride
or thiocyanate paper

elastic band

glass slides

Figure 2.47 The attachment of cobalt chloride or thiocyanate paper to a leaf, to compare the rate of water loss from its upper and lower surfaces.

Cobalt paper

Clamp stands
String
Cotton thread
Fuse wire
Electrical top-pan balance
Microbalance (Technique 2.54) and
    accessories, such as weights, wire
    riders and S-shaped hooks
Convector heater, fan *or* hair dryer
Microscope
Microscope slides
Coverslips
Elastic bands *or* paper clips
Pin
Forceps
Marking pen   ⇨

The rate at which leaves **transpire** depends both on the structural characteristics of the leaves and on the environment to which they are exposed. One might expect the number and distribution of stomata, for example, to influence the evaporation rate. The aim of this investigation is to compare water loss from the leaves of different species, or from the upper and lower surfaces of leaves, and relate it to **stomatal frequency**.

Guidance

Water loss can be measured by weighing groups of detached leaves at intervals. Bundles of leaves can be strung together with thread and hung between readings from 'washing lines' consisting of string between clamp stands. They can be treated in different ways. For example, some bundles can be subjected to turbulent air from a fan, hair dryer or convector heater. Others can have their upper or lower surfaces covered with a thin layer of vaseline or silicone grease. Weigh each bundle at intervals and plot water loss on a graph.

Water loss from individual leaves is best compared with a **microbalance** (see Technique 2.54 on p. 140) or **cobalt paper**. Anhydrous cobalt paper is blue, but in the hydrated state it is pink. Attach strips of anhydrous cobalt chloride or cobalt thiocyanate paper to both surfaces of leaves (Figure 2.47) and compare the time taken for the paper to change colour on the upper and lower surfaces. Handle the papers as little as possible and wash your hands immediately afterwards.

The results can be related to stomatal frequency as follows. Place a drop of polystyrene cement or nail varnish on the surface of a leaf and spread it out with a pin. When it is dry, peel it off with forceps, place it on a microscope slide under a drop of water, add a coverslip and count the numbers of stomata in the field of view. Do at least four counts at different places and take the mean.

To express the results on a unit area basis, estimate the diameter of the field of view with either a transparent ruler or an eyepiece graticule with a micrometer slide (Technique 1.15 on p. 39). To express the results on a unit leaf basis, trace the outlines of the leaves on graph paper and count squares.

For consideration

1 On the basis of your results, to what extent does stomatal frequency influence the rate of transpiration?

2 What other structural features of leaves, apart from the density of stomata, may influence the rate of transpiration?

3 In what sorts of environment would you expect to find (a) plants with a large number of stomata per unit leaf area and (b) plants with relatively few stomata?

Requirements

Transparent ruler/scale *or* micrometer eyepiece graticule and micrometer slide
Vaseline *or* silicone grease
Anhydrous cobalt chloride *or* cobalt thiocyanate paper
Polystyrene cement *or* nail varnish
Leaves, e.g. of cherry laurel (*Prunus laurocerasus*) or *Rhododendron*

Assessment

- **Plan** your investigation. Can you provide a reasoned explanation for the procedures selected?

- **Implement** your plan. Ensure that you work in a methodical way and record your results to an appropriate degree of accuracy (what is meant by 'appropriate'?).

- **Analyse your evidence** and **draw conclusions**. Use

appropriate scientific terminology to provide a full report of the data obtained. Analyse patterns and draw conclusions supported both by your own evidence and by generally accepted scientific knowledge.

- **Evaluate** your investigation. How valid are your various measurements – e.g. of stomatal frequency?

Factors affecting the rate of transpiration
2.57 INVESTIGATION

The aim of this investigation is to investigate the influence of various environmental factors on **transpiration**. This can be determined experimentally with a cut shoot attached to a **potometer** (Technique 2.55 p. 142). Remember that when you investigate the effect of one condition, it is generally most effective to keep all other conditions constant if this is possible.

Razor blade

Procedure

Attempt some or all of the following investigations:

1 Place the plant in a current of air created by, for example, an electric fan – does a hot or a cold airstream make any difference?

2 Put the plant in a humid environment – for example by covering the shoot with a large polythene bag. See whether it makes any difference if the bag is black or transparent. (Why might this make a difference? Think about the effect of this on temperature and on the behaviour of stomata.)

3 Increase the temperature (measure it!) by putting the plant close to a heat source such as a radiator.

4 Smear the upper surfaces of the leaves with vaseline or silicone grease. Measure the rate of water uptake. Then compare the effect of smearing the lower surfaces too.

For consideration

1 What effect might the removal of the roots have had on the flow of water through the plant?

2 How and why might the rate of water uptake be affected by (a) wetting the leaves whilst attaching the shoot to the apparatus and

Requirements

Potometer with beaker (see Technique 2.55, p. 142)
Secateurs
Bucket of water
Bowl *or* sink of water
Razor blade
Clamp stand, boss and clamp
Millimetre scale
Electric fan
Polythene bags, transparent and black
Heat source
Squared paper
Vaseline *or* silicone grease
Leafy shoot, e.g. sycamore (*Acer pseudoplatanus*) or holly (*Ilex aquifolium*)

(b) allowing the end of the stem to be exposed to the air for a long time before attaching it to the potometer?

3 Under what circumstances might the rate of water uptake differ from the rate of water loss?

Rate of translocation of sucrose in a stolon of potato

The products of photosynthesis are transported away from the leaves to the rest of the plant in the phloem sieve tubes. In a potato plant (*Solanum tuberosum*), much of the sucrose is transported along **stolons** – narrow tube-like underground outgrowths from the base of the main stem – and is stored as starch in **tubers** ('potatoes') at the ends. As all the dry matter in a tuber has entered through its stolon, you can estimate the rate of phloem transport if you measure certain things and make a few assumptions.

In particular, you need to know (i) the volume of sucrose solution which enters the tuber in a given period of time and (ii) the cross sectional area occupied by sieve tubes in the stolon. As volume = length × area, length = volume/area. To calculate the length of phloem sieve tube which empties per hour, divide the volume of sucrose solution that enters the tuber per hour by the cross sectional area through which it has travelled. This is the *rate* at which sucrose solution is translocated in the stolon.

Guidance

To estimate the *volume of sucrose* that enters the tuber each hour, you need to know the fresh mass of a clean potato, which has probably taken 30 days to form. You can assume that 80% of its mass is water and the rest is derived from sucrose transported into it down the stolon. (How could you determine the dry mass of the potato more accurately?) This will allow you to calculate the mass of sucrose entering the tuber each hour. You may wish to increase this figure by 25%, to allow for the sucrose which has been used in cellular respiration to keep the potato cells alive.

If you assume that the sieve tube contents are a 2% sucrose solution, you can calculate the volume of sucrose solution which must have passed down to the tuber each hour.

Razor blade

To determine the *cross sectional area occupied by sieve tubes* in the stolon, cut several thin cross sections of a stolon and stain with acidified phloroglucinol. Examine under a microscope with an eyepiece graticule which has been calibrated with a stage micrometer (see Technique 1.17 on p. 42), and estimate the cross sectional area of the phloem in a single vascular bundle (see Figure 2.43 on p. 136 for the structure of a stem). Assume that one-fifth of this area consists of the conducting area of the sieve tube elements. Multiply by the number of vascular bundles in the cross section to obtain the total cross sectional area of the sieve tubes.

Acidified phloroglucinol

Acidified phloroglucinol

Divide the volume of sucrose by the cross sectional area of the sieve tubes to estimate the rate of translocation (be careful with your units!).

For consideration

1 What assumptions are made in this investigation? List them.
2 Compare your estimate of the rate of translocation with those in Table 2.6. If it is not within the same range, evaluate the accuracy of each of the assumptions, alter the figures accordingly, and recalculate the result.

Table 2.6 Some measured rates of phloem transport in plant organs. The values in the table are calculated on the basis that the solutes in the sieve tubes make up to 2% of the mass of the translocated solution.

Plant and organ	Translocation rate (cm h^{-1})	Experimenters
Potato tuber stem	225	Dixon & Ball
Potato tuber stem	105	Crafts
Yam tuber stem	220	Mason & Lewin
Bear (*Phaseolus*) petiole	28	Birch-Hirschfield

3 Outline the various factors which might determine the rate at which a tuber fills up with starch, and its ultimate size.

Projects

Before starting a project, assess the risks inherent in your intended procedure and discuss your intended procedure with your teacher/lecturer.

1 Compare the water potentials of the innermost and outermost tissues of a potato tuber. After investigating the structure and permeability of the outermost layers of the potato, suggest how water moves within, and out of, a tuber – that is, from cell to cell and also across the 'skin'. Relate water movement across the skin to the structure of the skin.

2 Compare the water potentials of potato tubers with those of the submerged stems or roots of aquatic plants (e.g. Canadian pondweed, *Elodea canadensis*), and/or with those of salt marsh plants (e.g. samphire, *Salicornia* spp. and sea lavender, *Limonium* sp.) and/or seaweeds. Relate the differences to the habitats, water relations and tissue structures of the plants. If you have to remove parts of a plant from the wild, keep damage to the bare minimum, and under no circumstances uproot any complete plants.

3 Investigate the effect of water potential on adventitious root production. Use various sucrose concentrations ranging from 0 to 1 mol dm^{-3}. (See M. R. Negus, Experiments with willow cuttings – two suggestions for projects on root growth, *School Science Review*, **77** (281), 71–73, 1996.)

4 Determine the solute potential of red blood cells in blood from an abattoir or HIV-free heat-treated human blood from a hospital. Investigate the effects on red blood cells of altering the water potential of the surrounding solution. Compare with plant cells.

5 Use the catalase apparatus (Practical Exercise 2.9, p.67) to investigate in more detail the effect of temperature, enzyme concentration and substrate concentration on the reaction rate.

(For an alternative way of measuring the volume of oxygen released from the breakdown of hydrogen peroxide by catalase, see D.-Y. Yip, A simple and accurate method for measuring enzyme activity, *School Science Review*, **78** (285), 97–99, 1997.)

6 Proteases are available in the form of trypsin or pepsin extracts of mammalian tissues from laboratory suppliers, from commercial products such as meat tenderisers, biological washing powders or contact lens cleaners, and from certain fruits such as pineapple, kiwi or papaya. Obtain proteases from a variety of such sources and investigate their biological activity. Suitable alternative substrates are provided by exposed and developed colour photographic film (which releases its pigment granules) and gelatine (which goes runny). (See D. Y. Yip, Investigations with protease, *Journal of Biological Education*, **31**, 249–252, 1997, and P. Ridd & C. Cork, Activity of a protease on a protein, *School Science Review*, **80** (292), 111–113, 1999.)[BM]

7 Investigate the distribution pattern of the enzymes nitrate reductase and nitrite reductase in leaves, stem and roots of seedlings of dwarf French bean (*Phaseolus vulgaris*). Incubate mashed-up tissues in water and use reagent strips to assess the rate of appearance of nitrite and ammonia. (See P.W. Freeland, *Problems in Practical Advanced Level Biology*, Hodder & Stoughton, London, 1985.)

8 Investigate the properties of the protein-digesting enzyme 'stem bromelain'. Derived from pineapple fruit and stems, this enzyme is commercially available and can be purchased as a meat tenderiser. It can be used to break down the protein, gelatin. (See S. R. Dickson & G. F. Bickerstaff, Pineapple bromelain and protein hydrolysis, *Journal of Biological Education*, **25**, 164–166, 1991.)[BM]

9 Study the distribution of acid phosphatase enzymes in the seeds of various legumes – such as kidney beans (*Phaseolus vulgaris*) and mung beans (*Phaseolus aureus*). Phenolphthalein disphosphate is a convenient artificial substrate. (See B. Meatyard, Phosphatase enzymes from plants: a versatile resource for post-16 courses, *Journal of Biological Education*, **33**, 109–112, 1999.)

10 Investigate the properties of the enzyme rennin, which is cheaply available from food stores as rennet. It acts on the soluble protein caseinogen in milk to produce insoluble casein. As it acts in the stomach, its optimum pH might be expected to be on the acidic side.**BM**

11 Investigate the properties of the enzyme lipase, using pH sensors and data-logging equipment (see Investigation 2.35, p. 109). The hydrolysis of lipids (triacylglycerols) produces fatty acids and glycerol. As the fatty acids are released, the pH of the solution decreases. Using a calibrated pH probe connected to the analog port of a microcomputer, the reduction in pH can be logged over a period of 30 minutes or so. The effects of different treatments (initial pH, temperature, enzyme concentration, substrate concentration) on the rate of enzyme activity can be assessed.**BM**

12 Investigate the specificity of urease (Practical Exercise 2.12, p. 72) by comparing its effects on urea and thiourea, and its sensitivity to inhibition by sodium fluoride. (See D. Hawcroft, Simple studies on an immobilized enzyme, *School Science Review*, **77** (280), 65–68, 1996.)**BM**

13 Tears contain an enzyme known as lysozyme (see Practical Exercise 3.13, p. 167), which kills bacteria by breaking down the polysaccharides in their cell walls (lysis). Investigate the lytic activity of human tears. You can induce tears with a freshly cut onion. Devise a suitable, *safe* way of collecting the tears. Add drops of serially diluted tears to populations of *Staphylococcus aureus* or *Escherichia coli* growing on agar plates. Be sure to use suitable sterile techniques.**BM**

14 Compare the effects of different antibiotics on the growth of bacteria (see Practical Exercise 3.17, p. 172). One way of doing this is to grow colonies of bacteria (e.g. *Bacillus subtilis, Janthinobacterium lividum, Staphylococcus aureus* or *Escherichia coli*) on agar plates on the surfaces of which are placed discs of filter paper impregnated with the antibiotics. In a similar way, you could compare the efficiency in killing microbes of various toothpastes, antiseptics, deodorants or disinfectants.**BM**

15 Compare the abilities of different 'biological' washing powders to break down starch and proteins. A possible technique is to use a cork borer to cut wells in starch—iodine agar and milk nutrient agar. Solutions of the detergents can be placed in the wells, and their efficiency compared by measuring the area of the clear zones which appear around each well.**BM**

16 Assess the value of the enzyme pectinase for manufacturing fruit juice from certain fruits. Pectinase is released from certain fungi when they rot fruit, but is widely available from shops and suppliers for home brewing.**BM**

17 Using a respirometer, compare the respiratory quotients of germinating seeds which store fats (e.g. castor oil bean, sunflower) with those which store carbohydrates (e.g. wheat, maize) (see Investigation 2.19, p. 82).

18 Determine the respiration rates per gram of plant material (e.g. germinating broad bean seeds) and animal material (e.g. blowfly maggots) at the same temperature. List as many reasons as you can to explain the difference.

19 Test the hypothesis that a given part of the gut of an animal contains an enzyme which hydrolyses a particular substrate. You will need to extract the contents of different parts of the gut (or gut wall) of the animal that you choose to investigate, and test them for enzymatic activity. Animals suitable for examination include the locust (*Locusta*), cockroach (*Periplaneta*), earthworm (*Lumbricus*) and garden snail (*Helix*). (See H. Tat-keung & T. T. Sau-mei, Digestive enzymes in the grasshopper, *School Science Review*, **70** (253), 63–65, 1989, and G. S. Preece, To demonstrate the distribution of invertase in the gut system of *Periplaneta americana*, *School Science Review*, **69**, 744–745, 1988.)

20 Test the hypothesis that pepsin and/or trypsin act only on protein and have no effect on other substrates such as starch and fat, whatever the conditions.

21 Investigate the enzymatic efficiency of trypsin at a series of different pHs. At what pH does trypsin work optimally? How does this relate to the normal range of pH found in the small intestine of a mammal?

22 Investigate the action of human saliva. There are several things you might do here. For example, you could find out how long a sample of starch has to remain in the mouth (with and without chewing) for salivary amylase to hydrolyse the starch to sugar. This would enable you to assess how effective *in practice* your salivary amylase is in the normal digestion of starchy foods.

23 It has been suggested that the saliva produced just before a meal is more potent than the saliva produced after a meal. Test the truth of this suggestion. N.B. *Experiments on saliva should be done on your own saliva, not on anyone else's. Clean all glassware thoroughly afterwards, using sodium hypochlorite disinfectant.*

24 Investigate how the garden snail (*Helix aspersa*) feeds. With the animal on a sheet of glass, observe the mouth from underneath. How is food drawn in and eaten? Examine prepared sections of the head under the microscope and find out as much as you can about the feeding apparatus. Relate the structures observed to the animal's feeding behaviour.

25 Use the data-logging apparatus in Practical Exercise 2.41 (p. 117) to compare the light compensation points of a species habitually found growing in shade (e.g. bluebell (*Hyacinthoides non-scripta*) or wood anemone (*Anemone nemorosa*)) with one characteristically found in full sunlight.

26 Compare the leaves of an individual plant with leaves growing both in sun (at the top of the leaf mosaic) and in shade (at the bottom of the leaf mosaic). Suggest how the differences between them might allow the plant to photosynthesise more efficiently. Compare the leaves with regard to area, thickness,

number of palisade layers, chloroplast number, pigment concentration, cuticle thickness, stomatal frequency and, if possible, photosynthetic rate.

27 An alternative design for a photosynthometer is shown in Figure 2.48. Adapt this to investigate the effect of limiting factors such as temperature, light intensity and hydrogen carbonate concentration on photosynthesis. Can you design an alternative apparatus and compare its efficiencies with others? (See P. W. Freeland, *Problems in Practical Advanced Level Biology*, Hodder & Stoughton, London, 1985.)

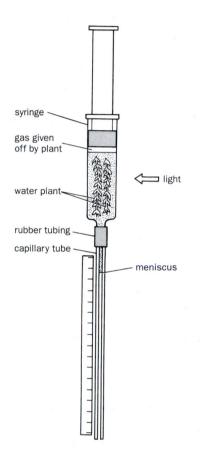

Figure 2.48 Apparatus for investigating the effect of limiting factors on the rate of photosynthesis of a water plant such as *Elodea*. Gas given off by the plant accumulates under the plunger in the barrel of the syringe and forces the water down the capillary tube. The rate of photosynthesis is estimated by measuring the rate of movement of the meniscus.

28 If you are keen on dissection, compare the circulatory systems of different vertebrates – for example fish, frog or toad, lizard, snake and bird. Concentrate on specific aspects, such as the number of atria and ventricles, the way the aorta arises from the heart, whether or not structures other than the lungs receive blood from the pulmonary arteries, and the presence of portal veins other than the hepatic portal. (A portal vein is one which, instead of returning blood to the heart, sends it to another organ first.) Any animals you plan to dissect must be obtained through your teacher/lecturer.

29 Top athletes generally eat a high-carbohydrate diet for three to four days before prolonged exercise, such as running a marathon. Does such 'carbo-loading' work? You will need at least 10 volunteers. All of them must be fit and capable of running half-marathons! (See C. Williams, Does carbo-loading work?, *Biological Sciences Review*, **12** (2), 22–24, 1999.)

30 Investigate the effect of posture and/or exercise on blood pressure. Blood pressure may be measured using a sphygmomanometer or digital blood pressure monitor (Practical Exercise 2.50, p. 132). Quantify the exercise and present your results as a graph, with exercise as a continuous variable.

31 Test the hypothesis that people's blood pressure and/or pulse rate increase when they tell lies. You could also investigate other mental factors that might increase the blood pressure and/or pulse rate, such as reading an exciting book or receiving a sudden fright. However, be sure that any volunteers you use are not subjected to undue stress.

32 Carry out a fitness test (e.g. the Harvard Step Test – see Practical Exercise 2.50. p. 132) on a wide range of volunteers and ask them to complete a questionnaire on their smoking habits, amount of sleep, exercise regime, etc. Using appropriate statistical techniques (see Appendix, p. 304), test the hypothesis that there is no relationship between fitness and any of these variables.

33 An effective way to determine whether someone is underweight or overweight is to calculate their **body mass index** (**BMI**). This equals their body mass in kilograms divided by the square of their height in metres – i.e. $BMI = mass/height^2$ and has the units of $kg\,m^{-2}$. When BMI is less that $20\,kg\,m^{-2}$, the person is generally considered underweight. When BMI is greater than $25\,kg\,m^{-2}$, the person is generally considered overweight. Obtain this value for both males and females of a range of ages and apparent sizes. What factors seem to correlate with BMI? Is there a relationship between BMI and body fat as measured using callipers (Technique 2.37, p. 111)? (See K. Frayn, Obesity: a weight problem, *Biological Sciences Review*, **10** (1), 17–20, 1997.)

34 Use a stethograph (see Technique 2.25, p. 91) to investigate the effect on a person's pattern of breathing of any or all of the following: talking, laughing, yawning, gasping, sighing, crying, sobbing, coughing and sneezing. From your recordings, assess the relative importance of inspiration and expiration in these actions.

35 Test the hypothesis that, during exercise, fit people breathe more deeply and at a lower frequency than unfit people. Use a spirometer or stethograph, with a kymograph, chart recorder or computer, for recording breathing movements and, if available, a bicycle ergometer for taking measured amounts of exercise. In selecting volunteers, you will need to consider what constitutes a 'fit' as contrasted with an 'unfit' person. You must also consider how to test your results statistically.

36 Investigate the composition of the expired air of people engaged in different types of muscular exertion – for example

sprinting, long-distance running, walking, etc. You will need to collect samples of expired air *during* the exercise period. If one is available, use a Douglas bag. This is an expandable bag fitted with valves which enable you to inhale fresh air from outside but exhale into the bag. A short side tube allows samples of the expired air to be collected and analysed. Alternatively, devise your own way of collecting the air.

37 Is there a correlation between the mass of water lost from different species of flowering plants, and the stomatal frequency or distribution (see Investigation 2.56, p. 144)?

38 Using Technique 2.54 (p. 140), compare the rate of water loss per unit leaf area from the leaves of a mesophyte (a species habitually found in habitats where the water supply is average) and a xerophyte (a species habitually growing where water is scarce).

39 Investigate the effect of hair points on the water relations of mosses. Hair points are prolongations of the midrib vein beyond the leaf blade in some species (e.g. *Tortula muralis, Bryum capillare*). Expose saturated clumps of mosses to dry environments created by silica gel in closed containers and plot decline in mass, first with intact leaves and then with hair points removed with a razor blade (care).

40 When you bend stems, some bend but others snap. Investigate the possible reasons why stems behave in this way. Cut sections to correlate the presence and distribution of different types of mechanical and strengthening tissue with the properties of the stem. Does the age of the stem matter?

41 It has been suggested that, in the locust, air is drawn into the tracheal system through the first four pairs of spiracles and leaves via the remaining spiracles. Devise a method to test this hypothesis experimentally. If it turns out to be true, suggest a hypothesis to explain the mechanism that ensures this unidirectional flow of air. Then make predictions from your hypothesis and gather as much information as you can to test the predictions.

42 Grow some radishes (*Raphanus sativus*) in normal sunlight and some in weak light. This simulates 'sun' and 'shade' leaves. Then investigate such features as leaf morphology, chlorophyll concentration and leaf area index (= total leaf area of a plant divided by the surface area of the plant when viewed vertically from above). (See J. D. B. Weyers, H.-O. Höglund & B. McEwen, Teaching botany on the sunny side of the tree: promoting investigative studies of plant ecophysiology through observations and experiments on sun and shade leaves, *Journal of Biological Education*, **32**, 181–190, 1998.)

43 Investigate stomatal physiology and behaviour under varying environmental conditions using isolated epidermal strips from *Commelina communis*. (See J. D. B. Weyers, Investigating stomatal physiology with epidermal strips from *Commelina communis* L. (Dayflower), *Journal of Biological Education*, **28**, 255–259, 1994.)

The pancreas has two distinct functions:

- It secretes **digestive enzymes** (which ones?) into the pancreatic ducts, down which they flow to the duodenum. In this capacity the pancreas functions as a ducted exocrine gland.
- It secretes the hormones **insulin** and **glucagon** into the bloodstream. In this capacity the pancreas functions as a ductless endocrine gland.

The pancreas is thus both an **exocrine** and an **endocrine** gland. Knowing this, can you make any predictions about its microscopic structure?

Procedure

1 Examine a transverse section of mammalian pancreas under low power. The bulk of it is made up of groups of enzyme-secreting cells called **acini** (singular: **acinus**). Here and there, amongst the acini, are **islets of Langerhans** which secrete the hormones. A typical section might include about six islets. Use Figure 3.1A to help you locate the acini and islets.

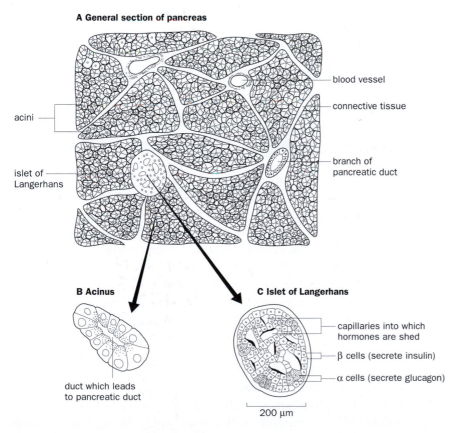

A General section of pancreas

acini

islet of Langerhans

blood vessel

connective tissue

branch of pancreatic duct

B Acinus

duct which leads to pancreatic duct

C Islet of Langerhans

capillaries into which hormones are shed

β cells (secrete insulin)

α cells (secrete glucagon)

200 μm

Figure 3.1 Microscopic structure of the pancreas.

2 Go over to high power and examine an acinus in detail (Figure 3.1B). The term acinus can he applied to any exocrine gland: an acinus is simply a group of secretory cells associated with a branch of a duct, in this case the pancreatic duct. Do the acini in your section fit this description?

3 Now look at an islet of Langerhans in detail (Figure 3.1C). How does the arrangement of the cells differ from that of an acinus? Notice the intimate association between the islet cells and the capillaries. Why is this important?

4 Within the islet of Langerhans, can you distinguish between the **beta (β) cells** which secrete **insulin** and the **alpha (α) cells** which secrete **glucagon**? How do these cells differ in their appearance and position within the islet?

5 Use an eyepiece graticule and stage micrometer to compare the sizes of an acinus and an islet of Langerhans.

For consideration

1 Imagine you are a teacher and you wish to explain to your students how to find the islets of Langerhans in a section of the pancreas. Write precise instructions to guide the students.

2 How does the structure of the pancreas suit it for its functions?

3 If you were to examine a section through an islet of Langerhans in the transmission electron microscope, what special features might you expect to see?

4 What sort of experiments could have led scientists to conclude that insulin is secreted by the β cells and glucagon by the α cells?

3.2 INVESTIGATION

Detecting the presence of glucose in a solution

Doctors and diabetic persons require a rapid test to detect the presence of **glucose** in the urine of those who may be suffering from **diabetes**. Humans with the capacity to regulate their blood sugar levels do not excrete glucose, but if the concentration of glucose in the blood exceeds $180\,mg$ per $100\,cm^3$, glucose can be detected in the urine.

Guidance

You are provided with Clinistix reagent strips. Read the accompanying instructions carefully and notice the colour changes to be expected as the concentration of glucose in the medium increases.

Following the instructions, use the reagent strips to estimate the concentrations of glucose in the five liquids A–E; afterwards, check the results with your teacher or lecturer.

If further reagent strips are available, you may wish to test the glucose concentrations in, for example, soft drinks, aphid honeydew or nectar from flowers.

For consideration

1. Draw a flow diagram summarising the chain of events that leads to the appearance of glucose in a person's urine, starting with the inactivation of some of the β cells in the islets of Langerhans in the pancreas.
2. Speculate on the effects that extra glucose in the bloodstream might have in the short term and the long term.
3. Try to determine how the reagent strip works. Why is it so specific to glucose? Did the sucrose solution give a positive test? If so, explain.

Requirements

Specimen tubes
The following five solutions should be labelled A–E but only the teacher knows which solution is which:
Distilled water
Glucose solution, $0.1\,g\,dm^{-3}$ of water
Glucose solution, $0.3\,g\,dm^{-3}$ of water
Glucose solution, $0.5\,g\,dm^{-3}$ of water
Sucrose solution, $0.5\,g\,dm^{-3}$ of water
Clinistix reagent strips

Microscopic structure of the liver

3.3 PRACTICAL EXERCISE

The liver has many functions. Here are three of the main ones:

- It secretes **bile** into the **bile duct,** down which the bile flows, via a **gall bladder**, to the duodenum.
- It regulates the amounts of blood sugar, lipids and amino acids by removing them from the bloodstream or adding them to it, as appropriate.
- It detoxifies the blood.

Recall that the liver receives blood from two sources: oxygenated blood is taken to it via the **hepatic artery**; blood rich in food substances arrives via the **hepatic portal vein** (see p. 153). Blood is removed from the liver via the **hepatic vein**.

Knowing these facts about the liver, can you make any predictions about its microscopic structure?

Procedure

1. Examine a transverse section of mammalian liver under low power. It consists of numerous closely packed **lobules**, each approximately 1.0 mm in diameter. Locate the lobules and other structures shown in Figure 3.2A.
2. Look at the edges of the lobules and locate branches of the **hepatic portal vein**, **hepatic artery** and **bile duct** (Figure 3.2B). They can be distinguished by their relative sizes and the structure of their walls.
3. Now examine the centre of a lobule (Figure 3.2C). Observe the branch of the **hepatic vein** in the centre. **Sinusoids** (blood capillaries) radiate out from this vein. Between the sinusoids are rows of **liver cells (hepatocytes)** and very narrow **bile channels (canaliculi)**.
4. Examine an electron micrograph of a section through a liver cell. Using Figure 3.3 to help you, identify the various structures in the cell, particularly the **glycogen granules**. If a canaliculus is visible, examine it carefully. What can you say about its lining? From the magnification of the micrograph, work out the widest diameter of the canaliculus.

For consideration

1. How does the microscopic structure of the liver, as seen under the light microscope, suit it for its functions?

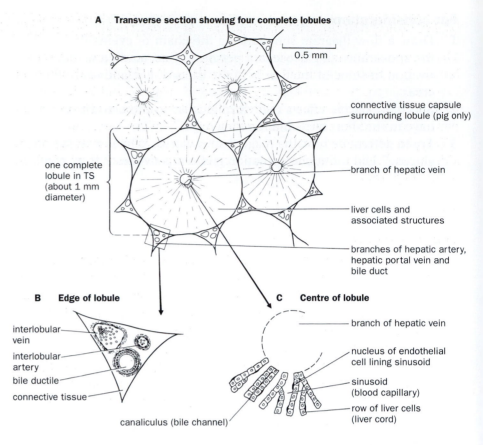

A   Transverse section showing four complete lobules

0.5 mm

connective tissue capsule surrounding lobule (pig only)

one complete lobule in TS (about 1 mm diameter)

branch of hepatic vein

liver cells and associated structures

branches of hepatic artery, hepatic portal vein and bile duct

B   Edge of lobule

interlobular vein

interlobular artery

bile ductile

connective tissue

canaliculus (bile channel)

C   Centre of lobule

branch of hepatic vein

nucleus of endothelial cell lining sinusoid

sinusoid (blood capillary)

row of liver cells (liver cord)

Figure 3.2 Microscopic structure of the liver. TS, transverse section.

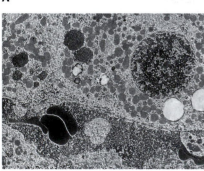

A

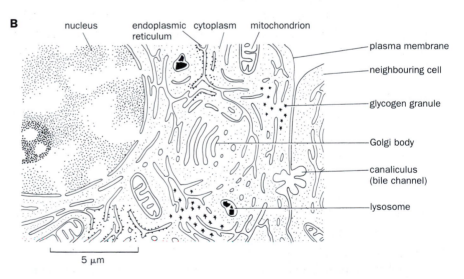

B

nucleus   endoplasmic cytoplasm mitochondrion
            reticulum

plasma membrane

neighbouring cell

glycogen granule

Golgi body

canaliculus (bile channel)

lysosome

5 μm

Figure 3.3 Liver cells as seen in section with the electron microscope. **A** Low power electron micrograph. **B** Diagram of a high power electron micrograph.

2   Under what circumstances would you expect liver cells to contain fewer glycogen granules than usual?

3   Liver cells are unremarkable in structure but remarkable in function. Explain.

4   Recall the meaning of the term 'acinus' as applied to the pancreas (see p. 152). Now apply it to the liver. What comprises an acinus in the liver?

The kidney is the mammal's principal organ of **excretion** and **osmoregulation**: it extracts unwanted substances from the blood, adjusting the blood's composition so that it has the correct osmotic and ionic concentration. The basic functional unit of the kidney is the **nephron**. In the human each kidney contains approximately 1.5 million nephrons.

The aim of this practical is to look first at the coarse anatomy of the kidney, and then at its microscopic structure, concentrating particularly on the nephrons.

Procedure

Coarse anatomy of the kidney

1   You will be provided with a fresh sheep's or pig's kidney, still surrounded by fat. Remove the fat so as to expose the **ureter**, **renal artery** and **renal vein** (Figure 3.4). Be careful not to damage these structures.
2   Gently massage the kidney in warm saline (1% solution of sodium chloride) so as to empty the vessels of their contents.
3   Using separate 5 cm³ syringes, inject
    a   the **ureter** with warm yellow latex, then tie a thread round it,
    b   the **renal artery** with warm red latex, then tie a thread round it,
    c   the **renal vein** with warm blue latex, then tie a thread round it.

    Allow the latex to cool for 10 minutes. As it does so it will harden like rubber.
4   Slice your injected kidney longitudinally with a sharp razor. Ensure that your cut passes as closely as possible through the centre. Distinguish between the light-coloured **cortex** towards the outside and the darker **medulla** towards the inside. Which structures, if any, are shown up by the latex?

Microscopic structure of the kidney

Figure 3.5 shows how the nephrons and blood vessels are orientated in

(Instructions for dissecting the mammalian urinary system are given on p. 226.)

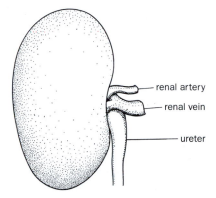

Figure 3.4 Mammalian kidney, showing its attachment to the renal artery, renal vein and ureter.

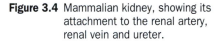

Razor blade

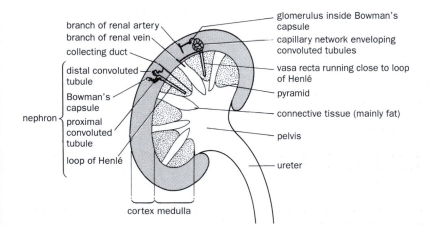

Figure 3.5 Mammalian kidney sectioned to show the position of the nephrons and their blood supply. For clarity, the nephron and blood vessels are shown separately; in reality they are intimately associated. A Bowman's capsule and its associated glomerulus together constitute a Malpighian body. Note how the nephron and its blood supply are orientated relative to the kidney as a whole, and also which parts of the nephron are in the cortex and which ones in the medulla.

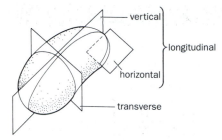

Figure 3.6 The different planes in which a kidney may be sectioned.

relation to the kidney as a whole. Use this diagram to predict what you should see in sections of the kidney cut in different planes (Figure 3.6).

1   Examine prepared longitudinal and vertical sections of a kidney under low power. Note the demarcation between the cortex and medulla.

2   Examine the cortex under low power. It contains **Malpighian bodies** which should be quite easy to see. Choose a good one and examine it in detail, using Figure 3.7 to help you.

3   The cortex also contains **proximal** and **distal convoluted tubules**, **collecting ducts** and **blood capillaries**. Try to distinguish between them, using Figure 3.8 to help you.

4   Examine the medulla under low power. This contains **loops of Henlé** (descending and ascending limbs), collecting ducts and capillaries (vasa recta). Try to distinguish between them, using Figure 3.9 to help you.

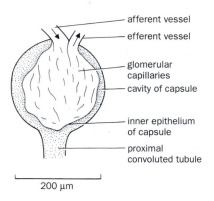

Figure 3.7 A Malpighian body as it may appear in a mciroscopic section of the kidney. This drawing is idealised; rarely would a section pass through the afferent vessels, the efferent vessels and the proximal tubule.

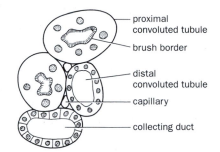

Figure 3.8 Tubules, collecting duct and capillaries as they appear in a microscopic section of the cortex of the kidney. Plasma membranes are not usually visible between adjacent cells in the walls of the tubules, hence their absence from this drawing. Red blood cells are sometimes present in the blood capillaries.

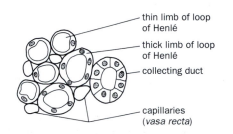

Figure 3.9 The loop of Henlé, collecting duct and capillaries as they appear in a microscopic section of the medulla of the kidney. The thin limb is the top two-thirds of the descending limb of the loop of Henlé; the thick limb is the rest of the descending limb plus the whole of the ascending limb. Plasma membranes are not usually visible between adjacent cells in the walls of the loop of Henlé, hence their absence from this drawing.

Requirements

Microscope
Enamel dish
Razor
Syringes, 5 cm³, ×3
Thread
Sodium chloride solution, 1.0%
Warm latex solutions, yellow, red and blue
Kidney, fresh (pig or sheep)
Kidney, TS and LS

For consideration

1   The kidney adjusts the composition of the blood partly by a process of ultrafiltration. Whereabouts in Figure 3.7 does ultrafiltration occur, and what does this process achieve?

2   You will have noticed in the prepared sections of the kidney that the blood capillaries are very close to the tubules. How does this help the kidney to carry out its function of adjusting the composition of the blood?

3   The proximal and distal convoluted tubules are coiled, whereas the loops of Henlé are straight. What might be the functional significance of this?

The **contractile vacuole**, found in freshwater unicellular organisms, is a comparatively simple osmoregulatory device. As quickly as water enters by osmosis, it is collected into the vacuole, which expands and, when full, discharges its contents through a temporary pore in the plasma membrane.

If the function of the contractile vacuole is to eliminate excess water from the cell as fast as it enters, we may predict that increasing the solute concentration of the medium should decrease the activity of the contractile vacuole. In this investigation we shall test this prediction.

The organism

It is best to use a sessile organism – that is, one that is attached to the substratum and therefore does not move around. A suitable organism is *Podophrya* (Figure 3.10). It has two contractile vacuoles which discharge relatively frequently while the organism, being sessile, will remain steady under the microscope. The organism has already been cultured for you and specimens will be provided attached to fine pieces of silk thread.

Guidance

Your task is to estimate the rate at which one of the contractile vacuoles discharges, first in pure water and then in a series of solutions of gradually increasing solute concentrations.

To see the contractile vacuole, you should mount the organism on a slide and view it under the microscope. There's no problem with that. The problem is changing the medium without disturbing the organism.

Think of possible ways of doing this. One method, which has been tried and tested, is illustrated in Figure 3.11. The organism is mounted between two pieces of filter paper saturated with the mounting fluid. To change the mounting fluid, you simply add the new fluid to one of the two pieces of filter paper with a pipette and withdraw the old fluid from the other piece of filter paper with dry filter paper. This must be done for sufficiently long to ensure that the mounting fluid is completely changed.

Make sure that, as far as possible, the only environmental factor that alters is the concentration of the medium; other factors should be kept constant. Arrange the illumination in such a way that the temperature of the organism does not increase. Avoid using a microscope with a built-in lamp.

Feel free to improve this method, or to use a different method if you prefer. Once you have decided what to do, proceed with the experiment.

When you have completed the experiment, make an approximate estimate of the diameter of the whole organism and of a fully inflated contractile vacuole (see Technique 1.17, p. 42).

For consideration

1 How does the frequency of discharge of the contractile vacuole compare in the different media? Interpret your results.
2 Why is it important to ensure that all environmental factors apart from the concentration of the medium are kept constant?

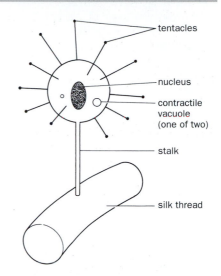

Figure 3.10 *Podophrya,* a unicellular sessile organism. The tentacles are used for catching and feeding on *Paramecium.* The two contractile vacuoles are easily seen from their glistening appearance.

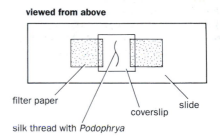

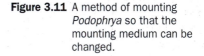

Figure 3.11 A method of mounting *Podophrya* so that the mounting medium can be changed.

Microscope (*without* built-in lamp)
Eyepeice graticule and stage
  micrometer
Slide and coverslip
Fine pipette
Small forceps
Filter paper
Scissors
Distilled water
Sucrose solutions: 0.05, 0.1 and
  $0.5\,mol\,dm^{-3}$
Podophrya on silk thread in culture
  solution

How to prepare Podophrya

Tease out short fine fibres from a small
piece of undyed silk fabric and float
them on the surface of a *Paramecium*
culture (about $200\,cm^3$) in a crystallising
dish. Add culture of *Podophrya*. In two
or three days, larvae of *Podophrya* settle
on the threads and grow rapidly. After a
further week, fully grown adults should
be ready for observation. Maintain the
culture by feeding with *Paramecium*
every 2–3 days.

3 Assuming that the organism and its contractile vacuole are both
spherical, estimate the volume of fluid discharged per unit time in
pure water. How long would it take for a contractile vacuole to discharge a volume of fluid equal to the volume of the organism's
body?

Key skills

✓ **Application of number:** Under 'For consideration' 3, above, you are
expected to calculate the volume of fluid discharged per unit time, and the
time taken for the organism to discharge a volume of fluid equal to the
volume of the organism's body.

✓ **Problem solving:** This technique is difficult and you will have to use your
imagination to make minor adjustments to the technique in order to
collect worthwhile results.

3.6 INVESTIGATION

Comparison of water loss from arthropods in dry and humid air

Animal species differ markedly in their abilities to conserve water, and
their distribution patterns can often be related to this.

In this investigation the water-retaining ability of the woodlouse
(*Armadillidium*), a terrestrial crustacean, is compared with that of an
insect such as the flour beetle (*Tribolium*) or the mealworm (*Tenebrio*).
Water loss will be estimated by measuring changes in mass.

Guidance

Devise a small receptacle which will hold the animals in a humane way
and from which water can evaporate freely. You will need two such
receptacles, one for the woodlice, the other for the insects. It must be
possible to place the receptacles (with the animals in them) in a dry
atmosphere, and to weigh them at frequent intervals The animals themselves should be handled and/or disturbed as little as possible.

You need to decide how many animals to place in each receptacle,
how often to carry out weighings and the period of time over which
changes in mass should be measured. Avoid continuing the experiment
for so long that the animals become stressed.

You should also decide how best to express the results. For example,
should you express them as absolute changes in mass or as percentage
changes? Would it be helpful to draw graphs?

When you have decided exactly what to do and have assembled all the things you require, carry out the experiment.

For consideration

1 Which species appears to be better at controlling water loss? What structural and/or physiological features might explain its better water-conserving powers?
2 In this investigation we have assumed that the animals' loss in mass is equal to their water loss. Is this assumption justified? Can you think of a way of measuring an animal's water-conserving ability without making this assumption?
3 Can your results be related to the habitats of the two species? Speculate freely, but beware of concluding more than is justified.

✓ **Problem solving:** This technique is a little tricky and several decisions and minor adjustments have to be made along the way.
✓ **Application of number:** Express the masses of the arthropods in appropriate fashion. Calculate the changes in mass and plot graphs showing the changes.
✓ **Information technology:** Use a computer to plot a graph of your results.

Materials for making animal receptacles, as requested by students
Balance
Anhydrous calcium chloride (drying agent)
Woodlice (*Armadillidium*)
Flour beetles (*Tribolium*) *or* mealworm larvae (*Tenebrio*)
Other items may be requested by individual students

Key skills

Adaptations of xerophytes

3.7 INVESTIGATION

Plants adapted to very dry conditions are called **xerophytes**. The purpose of this investigation is to examine some possible adaptations of xerophytes.

Guidance

First, make a list of possible adaptations that you might expect xerophytes to exhibit. Think, for instance, about such features as leaf surface area, leaf thickness, stomatal density, cuticle thickness and root length. Include life cycle adaptations as well as those involving plant structure and plant physiology.

The next step is to obtain suitable plants. It may be that you are provided with some plants from an appropriate habitat, such as a sand dune, or you may have access to suitable plants growing on a window-ledge or in a greenhouse.

Now examine the plants. Make slides where appropriate and/or examine prepared slides. To what extent have your predictions been confirmed or refuted?

For consideration

1 What would be a suitable 'control' for your study?
2 How can you be sure that what you think is an adaptation for water conservation actually is? Give examples of where there might be some doubt.
3 To what extent are the water conservation devices of plants comparable to those of animals?

Reference

Marjot, C. Water loss from model leaves. *School Science Review*, **75** (272), 61, 1994. (For a simple but effective way of modelling some structural adaptations of xerophytes.)

Requirements

Microscope
Graticule
Hand lens
Whole specimens of xerophytes and/or access to xerophytes in the field, and/or microscope slides of parts of xerophytes

Note: Do not dig up any plants from the <u>wild</u>; this is illegal!

Microscopic structure of mammalian skin

As the outermost part of the body, the mammalian skin is important in protection against, and adjustment to, changing external conditions. The purpose of this practical is to examine the microscopic structure of mammalian skin and relate it to this overall role.

Procedure

Make a list of all the specific functions of skin that you can think of. From your list predict what structures you would expect to see in a section of skin.

1 Examine a vertical section of mammalian skin under low power. Use Figure 3.12 to help you to distinguish between the **epidermis**, **dermis** and **subcutaneous** tissue.

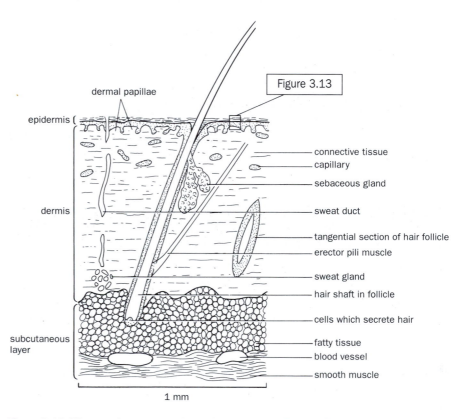

Figure 3.12 Microscopic structure of human skin (scalp). Few sections will be as complete as this. Seldom will a hair follicle be cut throughout its length; usually it will be incomplete, as shown on the right-hand side of the drawing. The same applies to the sweat glands and their ducts.

2 Examine the epidermis in detail under high power. Use Figure 3.13 to help you identify the different layers. New cells are constantly formed by division of the cells in the **Malpighian layer**. Once formed, the cells get pushed upwards, flattening as they do so. Finally, the cells die and become converted into scales of keratin which flake off. The cells of the Malpighian layer may contain the pigment **melanin** towards their outer surface. Function?

3 Now move to the dermis and examine it in detail. Note the structures shown in Figure 3.12, but bear in mind that your section is unlikely to be as complete as our drawing. The organisation of the dermis must therefore be pieced together bit by bit by searching the entire section for clues and, if necessary, looking at other sections.

4 Examine the subcutaneous layer in detail. It is composed mainly of adipose (fatty) tissue. What are its functions?

5 The skin contains numerous **receptors**. What kind of receptors would you expect to find in a section of human skin? Can you see anything in your section that might conceivably be a receptor? Most of the receptors require special staining techniques to show them up. If you can obtain a specially stained slide, see what you can discover about the skin receptors.

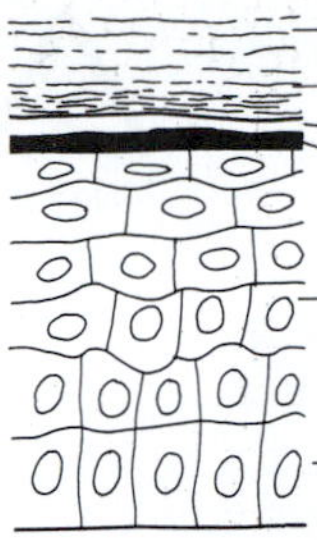

For consideration

1 Which areas of human skin would you expect to have:
   a no hair follicles
   b particularly abundant subcutaneous fat
   c little or no subcutaneous fat
   d a particularly thick cornified layer
   e numerous receptors sensitive to touch?

2 Why is it a good thing for sunlight (in moderation) to fall on the skin? Why can excessive exposure to bright sunlight be dangerous?

3 A man may have a luxuriant beard but a bald head. Speculate as to the biological cause of this apparent paradox.

Figure 3.13 The epidermis of human skin in detail. In the Malpighian layer, new cells are constantly being formed by cell division. The spiny layer is composed of cells that may show a prickly (spiny) appearance. The cells of the granular layer have granules in their cytoplasm, and those of the clear layer have a clear cytoplasm; those of the cornified layer are keratinised and hard, and the cells of the disjunctive layer flake off.

Requirements

Microscope
Mammalian skin, VS
Mammalian skin, section stained to
   show receptors, if available

Heat energy loss from an insulated and a non-insulated hand

3.9 INVESTIGATION

Birds and mammals maintain their body temperature by generating heat energy within their bodies, so insulation would appear to be of prime importance. How effective is their insulation, though? In this investigation you will compare the heat energy loss from an insulated and a non-insulated human hand.

Procedure

Work in pairs, one of you acting as the subject, the other as experimenter.

1 Place two digital thermometers, with probes, in identical conditions and ensure that they both give the same reading to ±0.2 °C.

2 With masking tape, attach the thermometer probes to the subject's hands, one to each hand.

3 Check that the skin temperature is the same for each hand. If the temperatures differ, check that the subject's clothing (shirt, sweater) comes to the same point on each arm.

4 Insulate one hand thoroughly with duvet filling, making sure that the insulation is of even thickness all round the hand. Tape the insulation to the hand, making sure that you can still read the thermometer.

5 Make sure that both hands and arms are in exactly the same

Infection

Caution

To avoid any risk of infection when recording the core temperature, a different clinical thermometer should be used for each subject. The thermometer should be immersed in disinfectant beforehand and replaced in the disinfectant immediately after use.

Requirements

Digital thermometers with probes, ×2
Clinical thermometer, in disinfectant
Duvet filling
Masking tape

conditions except for the presence of the duvet filling round the insulated hand. Allow time for equilibration.

6 Record the skin temperatures of both hands. Also record the subject's core temperature using a clinical thermometer placed under the tongue, and the environmental temperature.

7 Repeat step 6 at different environmental temperatures. Record your results in a table.

8 Present your results in a graph that best illustrates the effectiveness of the duvet material in insulating the hand. (You will have to decide what to plot against what.)

For consideration

1 What conclusions can you draw from your results about the effectiveness of human skin as an insulator?

2 Did you find that the skin temperatures of the two hands differed even when both were uninsulated and in the same conditions? If so, suggest an explanation.

3 Do the results of this experiment allow you to suggest a possible function for the thermoreceptors in the skin? How might your suggestion be tested?

4 How could you measure the rate at which heat energy is lost from the human body?

We are indebted to Dr J. M. Gregory, late of Winchester College, for providing information on this experiment.

Assessment

- **Plan** your investigation. Do you have a testable hypothesis?
- **Implement** your plan.
- **Analyse your evidence** and **draw conclusions**. Take care over the calculations. If possible, use a t-test to test your hypothesis by pooling class results (see Statistical Analysis Appendix, p. 304).
- **Evaluate** your investigation. List limitations of the technique used and discuss the influence of these on your results.

3.10 PRACTICAL EXERCISE **Effect of temperature on the heartbeat of *Daphnia***

Daphnia, the water flea, is a small freshwater crustacean which lacks physiological methods of maintaining a constant body temperature. This means that, if the environmental temperature changes, its body temperature does so too, and its metabolic rate will be expected to increase or decrease accordingly.

In this practical exercise we shall test the hypothesis that as the environmental temperature increases, the metabolic rate increases too. We shall use the rate at which the heart beats (cardiac frequency) as a measure of the metabolic rate. Fortunately, *Daphnia* is relatively transparent and its heart can be seen quite easily under the low power of the microscope.

Procedure

Setting up the experiment

1 Select a large specimen and, with a pipette, transfer it to the centre of a small, dry Petri dish. With filter paper, remove excess water from around the specimen, so that it is completely stranded.

2 With a seeker, place a small blob of silicone grease onto the floor of the Petri dish. Then wipe the needle clean and use it to push the posterior end of the animal gently into the grease so that it is firmly anchored. Now fill the Petri dish with water at room temperature.

3 Place the Petri dish on the stage of a microscope and observe the animal under low power. Figure 3.14 shows the position of the heart. Watch it beating. Don't confuse the beating of the heart with the flapping of the legs. If you cannot see the beating of the heart clearly, you can use instead the rate at which the legs beat.

4 Surround the animal with a circular heating coil and fix it in position as shown in Figure 3.15. Also clamp a small mercury thermometer, or the temperature probe of a digital thermometer, into position. If you have no coil, you can use instead water at say, 5°C, 15°C and 25°C.

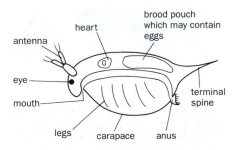

Figure 3.14 Diagrammatic side view of *Daphnia* as seen under low power, to show the position of the heart.

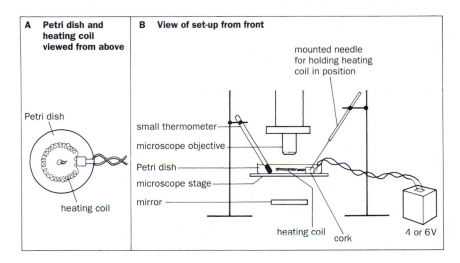

Figure 3.15 An experimental set-up for studying the effect of temperature on the heartbeat of *Daphnia*.

Estimating the cardiac frequency

A convenient way of doing this is to time how long it takes for the heart to beat 50 times. If it is beating too frequently for every beat to be counted, make a mark on a piece of paper every 10th beat. Do several practice runs to get used to the technique. When you feel ready, proceed as follows:

5 Replace the room-temperature water in the Petri dish with water at 10°C. Estimate the cardiac frequency and note the temperature.

6 Switch on the heater so that the water gradually warms up. Estimate the cardiac frequency at 5°C intervals from 10°C to 30°C, noting the temperature each time. If the temperature of the water increases too rapidly, switch off the heater and, if necessary, add a few ice chippings.

7 Present your results in a table and, if you have sufficient readings, draw a graph of the cardiac frequency as a function of the temperature.

Small Petri dish
Mounted needle
Heating coil
Small thermometer or temperature
    probe (see Figure 3.15)
Stands and clamps, ×2
Power supply, 5 V with switch
Insulated wire
Seeker
Filter paper
Stopwatch
Teat pipette, 10 cm³
Teat pipette, 25 cm³
Water and ice
Silicone grease
Water fleas, *Daphnia*

For consideration

1 What conclusions would you draw from your results? Do you think *Daphnia* has no means of controlling its body temperature? Explain your answer.

2 What criticisms can you make of the experimental technique? How might it be improved?

3 How could the same investigation be carried out in a human subject? In what respects would you expect the results to differ from those obtained with *Daphnia*?

Reference

Pyatt, F. B. & Storey, D. M. Toxicity testing using *Daphnia magna* in student assessments of water pollution. *Journal of Biological Education*, **33**, 164–170, 1999. (*Daphnia* heartbeat can also be used as an indication of the toxicity of water. This paper discusses *Daphnia*'s response to aluminium, zinc, lead and pH.)

Key skills

✓ **Information technology:** If you need to plot a graph, it should be plotted on a computer.

3.11 PRACTICAL EXERCISE

Different types of white cells in human blood

Blood is the major fluid transport medium of many animal groups, including annelids, arthropods, molluscs and chordates. In mammals, blood consists of **red blood cells**, **white blood cells** and **platelets** suspended in a fluid medium, **plasma**. No staining is required to see the red blood cells (see p. 120), but staining is necessary to distinguish the platelets and various types of white blood cells.

In this practical exercise, prepared slides of human blood are examined, and the various types of cells identified. Such slides are usually stained with either **Leishman's stain** or **Wright's stain**. Both contain eosin and methylene blue.

Procedure

1 Focus on a slide at medium power and notice the abundance of red blood cells, which lack nuclei. White blood cells possess nuclei, but can at first be difficult to find, both because they are rare, relative to red blood cells, and because they stand out less obviously.

2 Focus on your slide at high power and find a group of platelets.

3 Still at high power, find a white blood cell. Identify it by referring to Figure 3.16. Lymphocytes and monocytes are quite easy to identify, as are basophils. However, neutrophils and eosinophils can be difficult to distinguish.

4 Find at least 20 more white blood cells and identify them as far as you are able.

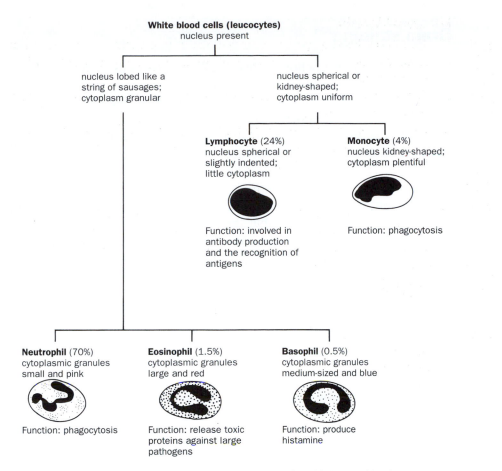

Figure 3.16 Key to the different types of white blood cell found in human blood as seen under the light microscope after staining. The figure in brackets after the name of each type indicates the typical percentage of white blood cells belonging to that type. Basophil nuclei are frequently indistinct.

For consideration

1 Which were the most numerous types of white blood cell you saw? Does this agree with the figures for frequency given in Figure 3.16?

2 Were there any types of white blood cell that you failed to see? If so, can you suggest why?

3 Leishman's stain and Wright's stain each contain acidic eosin (red) and alkaline methylene blue (blue). Can you suggest why eosinophils, neutrophils and basophils stain differently with these stains, and why they are given their respective names? (Hint: *philos* is the Greek for loving.)

4 Which types of white blood cell are capable of leaving capillaries by passing through the endothelial walls of the capillaries? Can you relate this to the structure of the cells?

5 Can you suggest circumstances which might cause one or more of these types of white blood cells to be produced by the body in greater numbers?

Requirements

Microscope
Prepared slides of human blood stained with Leishman's or Wright's stain

Gram staining[BM]

One of the major distinctions between different types of bacteria is the ability, or otherwise, of their cell walls to stain with a dye called **Gram stain**, devised by C. Gram in 1884. Those bacteria which pick up the stain are known as **Gram-positive**, and those which do not are **Gram-negative**. The distinction is of medical importance, because this is the first step in identification of a disease-causing bacterium, and because Gram-positive and Gram-negative bacteria differ in their responses to antibiotics. This Technique describes how to perform the test.

We suggest that you should try it on both a Gram-positive and a Gram-negative bacterium, so that the difference is obvious. The principle is that the Gram-positive bacteria firmly take up a dye called crystal violet and retain it, even when washed with propanone (acetone). Gram-negative bacteria, however, lose the violet dye in propanone, but counterstain with safranin.

Throughout this procedure, bear in mind the need for safety precautions, which is emphasised in Technique 3.16, Basic Techniques of Microbiology, p. 171.

Hazard

Procedure

Work in pairs. Ideally, each pair should have access to a sink. The members of a pair should each carry out the procedure on a different bacterium.

1 Sterilise a wire inoculating loop by flaming it until it is red hot.
2 Using the loop, place a drop of tap water in the middle of a clean glass slide. Do not touch the surface of the slide with your fingers.
3 Resterilise the loop and allow it to cool for a few seconds.
4 With the tip of the loop, remove a small amount of growth from the surface of the bacterial culture. Immediately after you have withdrawn the loop, flame the neck of the test tube or screw-cap bottle and close it with cotton wool, to maintain sterile conditions.
5 Mix the bacterial cells on the tip of the inoculating loop with the drop of water on the slide and, using a circular motion, spread out the bacteria over the slide surface. Now let the water evaporate so that the smear dries.
6 Immediately afterwards, hold the inoculating loop above the flame to dry it (if you put it into the flame straight away you may spray bacteria all over the place). Then flame the loop and put it well away where it cannot be touched accidentally.
7 Hold one end of the slide with forceps and 'heat fix' the smear by passing the slide quickly, film side up, through the hottest part of the Bunsen flame, just above the blue cone. Only do this once. If, afterwards, the slide is too hot to handle, you have heated it too much, and the preparation will be ruined.
8 Switch off the Bunsen burner.

The remaining steps are best carried out over a sink. If a sink is not available, it helps if the chemicals are added with the microscope slide resting on a small Petri dish within a larger one.

9 Flood the dry smear with crystal violet solution from a teat pipette. Leave it for *exactly 1 minute*.

10 Pour off excess stain and gently wash the slide with distilled water from a squirt bottle, but do not allow the bottle to touch the smear.

11 Flood the slide with Gram's iodine *for just over 1 minute*.

12 Tilt the slide to remove excess stain and *gently* wash with a few drops of water from a squirt bottle.

13 This step is critical; do not overdo it. Tilt the slide and add drops of propanone (6–8 drops altogether) *for 2–3 seconds* until no violet colour appears in the liquid that runs off.

14 *Quickly* wash with drops of water from a squirt bottle or tap.

15 Pour off the water and add safranin *for 15 seconds*. Then pour off the stain, wash with water from a squirt bottle, pour off the drops of water and allow the preparation to dry naturally.

16 Whilst the slide is drying, prepare your microscope. Ideally, you should place a drop of immersion oil directly onto the preparation, and view it at high magnification under oil immersion (Technique 1.16, p. 41). You will have to ask your teacher or lecturer for assistance at this stage.

17 Relate what you see to the technique you have used.

Reference

Reed, R. H. Holmes, D., Weyer, J. and others. *Practical Skills in the Biomolecular Sciences*. Addison Wesley Longman, Harlow, 1998.

Propanone

Requirements

Access to sink and tap water, or else Petri dishes (two sizes)
Bunsen burner
Matches
Wire inoculating loops
Microscope slides, glass
Forceps
Pasteur (teat) pipettes
Squirt (wash) bottle
Paper towel
Microscope
Immersion oil
Propanone (ethanol (70%) is an alternative; in that case step 13 takes 10–15 seconds)
Crystal violet (Note 1)
Gram's iodine (Note 2)
Safranin (Note 3)
Agar-slant cultures of two bacteria, one Gram-positive (e.g. *Bacillus subtilis*, *B. megatherium* or *Micrococcus luteus*), and the other Gram-negative (e.g. *E. coli* strain K_{12})

Notes: Preparation of stains

1 Crystal violet: Create a solution of 20% ethanol in water. To 100 cm³ of this solution, add 2 g of crystal violet and mix thoroughly.

2 Gram's iodine: First add 2 g of potassium iodide, and then 1 g of iodine, to 300 cm³ of water, and mix thoroughly.

3 Safranin: Mix 95 cm³ of ethanol with 100 cm³ of water. To the mixture, add 2.5 g of safranin and mix thoroughly.

Presence and action of lysozyme[BM]

3.13 PRACTICAL EXERCISE

Lysozyme is an enzyme which kills bacteria and is present in certain body fluids. It was discovered by Alexander Fleming. The enzyme hydrolyses the main structural component of bacterial cell walls.

Gram-positive bacteria (see Technique 3.12, p. 166) are very sensitive to this enzyme. The yellow bacterium *Micrococcus luteus* is especially sensitive to lysozyme, and so provides a convenient assay for it. The yellow culture rapidly becomes less turbid as the cells are broken open by the enzyme.

In this practical you can determine whether or not lysozyme is present in various sources, and its concentration in them.

Procedure

1   Collect the following fluids using the methods suggested.

Glass

- Egg white: break open a fresh egg and pour the white into a test-tube.
- Sweat: run up and down the stairs a few times, and collect some sweat from the surface of your skin with a pipette, taking especial care if the pipette is made of glass.
- Tears: expose one of your eyes to a polythene bag containing half a chopped onion, and allow your tears to drop into a test tube. Do not put the tube too near your eye.
- Saliva: dribble into a test-tube.

2   Produce a standard curve for the action of lysozyme on *Micrococcus luteus* as follows:

   a   Pipette 9 cm³ of phosphate buffer solution into a colorimeter tube, or a test tube that fits into your colorimeter. Pipette 0.3 cm³ of *M. luteus* suspension into the buffer sample. Cap and shake the mixture.

   b   Place the tube in the colorimeter, and write the colorimeter reading on your recording sheet. You will be taking a reading every 20 seconds, so have a stopwatch ready.

   c   Pipette 0.3 cm³ of the lysozyme solution (1 mg cm⁻³) into the colorimeter tube and start the stopwatch. Record a colorimeter reading every 20 seconds for 3 minutes, and then at 1 minute intervals for a further 2 minutes.

   d   Plot a graph of the colorimeter readings against time.

   e   Repeat in turn steps 2(a) to 2(d), first with 0.3 cm³ of lysozyme solution diluted to half its original strength (0.5 mg cm⁻³), and then with 0.3 cm³ of lysozyme solution diluted to a quarter of the original strength (0.25 mg cm⁻³). The three curves, plotted on the same axes, constitute your standard curves.

3   Now test one of the fluids you obtained in step 1. First dilute it to one-fifth of its strength with distilled water, using a pipette. Follow the same procedures as outlined in steps 2(a) to 2(e), and then plot a graph of the colorimeter readings against time.

4   Compare your graph with the standard curves you drew earlier (step 2(e)). From the comparison, calculate the lysozyme concentration of the fluid you tested.

For consideration

1   A cup of egg white left on a kitchen shelf may take months to go bad. Hard-boiled eggs, on the other hand, go mouldy within days. Why the difference?

2   Were the concentrations of lysozyme in tears and saliva different? If they were, how would you account for the difference?

3   Do different people have different concentrations of lysozyme in their saliva? If so, can you suggest why?

4   Besides the ones you have tested, which other body fluids might you expect to contain lysozyme?

Key skills

✓   **Information technology:** The graphs will look more elegant if they are plotted by using an appropriate computer program.

A questionnaire must be designed as a tool to help you investigate a particular problem. For example, suppose your questionnaire is meant to help you study the extent to which people of different ages enjoy different leisure activities. Clearly, your questionnaire will need to ask questions about age and preferred leisure activities.

Procedure

1   Before starting your questionnaire, think carefully about the following points:
    - What sort of people will be completing it?
    - Will they complete the questionnaire on their own, or will you interview them and record their answers?
    - Should the questionnaire be anonymous?
    - How will you distribute and collect your questionnaires so that as many as possible are completed and returned?
2   Devise a suitable sampling strategy. Are you going to give your questionnaire to everyone in a small group, or to, say, every 10th person in a large group?
3   Think carefully about how precise you want the answers to be. If you are asking questions about age, do you want the answers to be in 10 year units (i.e. 0–9 years, 10–19 years, 20–29 years, etc.) or to the nearest year, or to the nearest month? There is no single correct answer to this question. It will depend on the range of ages of people answering the question, and on the reason you have for asking the question. For example, if the whole of your sample lies within the range 17–18 years, you may need to know each person's age to the nearest month.
4   Ensure your questions are unambiguous and easy to understand.
5   Decide approximately how long you want the questionnaire to be. Too short and you may end up wishing you had asked more questions; too long and people may be put off completing it and you will also waste time analysing answers to unimportant questions.
6   Consider how you are going to analyse the results you obtain before you finalise your questions (see pp. 304–316). Appropriate statistical analysis will probably mean that you need a minimum of 50 returned questionnaires.
7   Take care with the design and layout of your questionnaire. If it looks boring or is poorly designed, fewer people will complete it.
8   Produce a first draft of your questionnaire and try it out on a few friends to identify any problems.
9   Finally, before you run off copies of your questionnaire, discuss it with your teacher or lecturer.

Key skills

✓   **Working with others:** This exercise addresses skills such as agreeing realistic objectives, exchanging information, carrying out tasks, exchanging accurate information on progress, assessing the success of the survey and suggesting improvements.

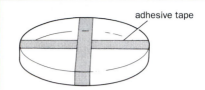
adhesive tape

Illustration 2 Petri dishes should be sealed, but not completely (all the way round), as this might allow anaerobic microorganisms to grow, and some of these are harmful.

Microorganisms

Preparing Petri dishes for the growth of microorganisms

In schools and colleges, the following rules should be observed when using Petri dishes for the growth of microorganisms:

1 Use sterile techniques (see above) when transferring microorganisms to a Petri dish.

2 Ensure your name and other relevant information (date, microorganisms used) are on the underside of the Petri dish.

3 Never attempt to culture microorganisms from food (whether cooked or uncooked), faeces, vomit, places that have been in contact with these (such as under the rim of a toilet) or any human body fluids.

4 Once microorganisms have been transferred to a Petri dish, always close it with an adhesive tape as shown in Illustration 2, unless you have clearly been instructed otherwise by your teacher.

5 After use, dispose of Petri dishes and their contents with care. The best procedure is to put them in autoclavable plastic bags obtained from laboratory suppliers. Glass Petri dishes (and any other non-disposable items such as McCartney bottles) are placed in one bag, and disposable materials (including plastic Petri dishes) into another. This is done without removing the contents or adhesive tape. The two bags should each be lightly closed with a wire tie and then autoclaved (i.e. heated to 120°C for 15 minutes in a container filled with steam under pressure). After autoclaving, the plastic bag with disposable materials can be placed in a normal dustbin. The bag with non-disposable items can be opened and its contents cleaned in the normal way.

6 Wash your hands thoroughly with soap and water after all micro-biology work.

References

Department of Education and Science. *Microbiology: An HMI Guide for Schools and Non-Advanced Further Education.* Her Majesty's Stationery Office, London, 1985.

Advice and information about all aspects of biotechnology and microbiology can be obtained from the National Centre for Biotechnology, School of Animal and Microbial Sciences, University of Reading, Whiteknights, Reading RG6 6AJ (www.ncbe.reading.ac.uk)

3.17 PRACTICAL EXERCISE

This exercise extends over more than one practical session.

Antibiotics and bacteria[BM]

Antibiotics are compounds, produced by certain microorganisms, which harm other microorganisms, including bacteria. Such substances, which include the well-known antibiotic penicillin, are of great medical and economic importance. This practical demonstrates the anti-bacterial action of certain antibiotics.

Procedure

1 Obtain a stoppered bottle or test tube containing 15 cm³ of sterile nutrient agar. Melt the agar by placing the bottle in a water bath at 80–100°C.

2 Remove the bottle and cool to about 45 °C. (At this temperature the agar will still be liquid, but will be cool enough to hold against your cheek. Most agars solidify at about 42 °C.)

3 Obtain a test tube containing a culture of non-pathogenic bacteria on an agar slope (see list of requirements). The tube should be kept plugged with sterile cotton wool.

4 Transfer a sample of bacteria from the agar slope to the liquid agar in the bottle (see Technique 3.16, p. 171).

5 Without delay, pour the liquid agar containing the bacteria into a warm, sterilised Petri dish (Figure 3.17). (Warming the Petri dish prevents water condensing beneath the lid as you pour in the agar.)

6 After replacing the lid, ensure an even distribution of the agar by gently moving the Petri dish from side to side on a flat surface.

7 After the agar has solidified, use sterile forceps to place on the surface of the agar a small disc of filter paper impregnated with an

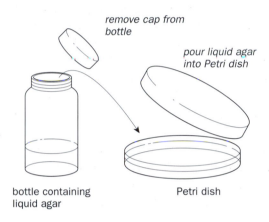

remove cap from bottle

pour liquid agar into Petri dish

bottle containing liquid agar

Petri dish

Figure 3.17 Procedure for transferring bacteria from a liquid culture to a Petri dish.

Microorganisms

antibiotic. As a control, place another disc of the same size (previously soaked in sterile water and allowed to dry) on a different part of the agar. Make sure you can distinguish these two discs.

8 As an alternative to step 7, use a '**mast ring**'. This consists of a central control disc – without antibiotic – surrounded by side-arms leading to small discs, each impregnated with a different antibiotic.

9 Tape and label the Petri dish in the usual way (see the section on 'Preparing Petri dishes for the growth of microorganisms', Technique 3.16 on p. 171).

10 Incubate at 30 °C and examine at daily intervals over the next week for signs of bacterial growth.

For consideration

1 Why is it necessary to ensure sterile conditions in this practical?

2 How do the areas where growth of bacteria has occurred relate to the positions of the antibiotic and control discs?

3 Antibiotics have been extracted from various species of fungi and other soil microorganisms. What functions might antibiotics have in such organisms?

Requirements

Hand lens or binocular microscope
Water bath at 80–100 °C
Incubator at 30 °C
Bunsen burner or spirit lamp
Petri dish
Inoculation loop
Small forceps
Sterile nutrient agar (15 cm³, in stoppered bottle)
Sterile cotton wool
Antibiotic discs (e.g. penicillin, streptomycin or aureomycin) or 'mast ring'
Disinfectant for cleaning bench
Pure culture of non-pathogenic containment level 1 bacteria on agar slope in test-tube. (Suitable bacteria are listed in suppliers' catalogues.)
Sterile water

Before starting a project, as on p. 57 assess the risks inherent in your intended procedure discuss your intended procedure with your teacher/lecturer.

1 Investigate the abilities of invertebrates from the sea and estuaries to regulate their water contents when transferred to diluted salt solutions. Failure to control their water contents (osmoregulate) results in water being retained in the body, causing an increase in mass. Increase in mass can therefore be used as an indication of whether or not osmoregulation has been taking place. If possible, relate your findings to the environments these species encounter in the habitats in which they are found. Suitable animals for investigation include molluscs and species of polychaete worms which live in burrows. Treat the animals with respect and do not subject them to undue stress.

2 Extend the investigation on the water-conserving powers of woodlice, beetles or mealworms (Investigation 3.6 p. 158) to other animal species. Relate their different water-conserving powers to their anatomy, physiology, behaviour and/or habitats.

3 The water-conserving ability of insects is said to be due to the presence of a thin layer of wax on the surface of the cuticle. Test this hypothesis. The cockroach would be a suitable insect for this investigation. First, you would have to find out if it really does have a layer of wax on its cuticle. Then you would need to devise a humane way of removing the wax. Using a very sensitive balance, you could then compare loss of mass of normal and de-waxed specimens.

4 Select a species of moss growing in a moist situation (e.g. in or close to water) and a species growing in a dry place (e.g. on top of a wall). Compare the rates at which known masses of each species dry out when exposed to the same environmental conditions. Relate your results to the structure of the two species and their ability to trap and retain water (see Investigation 7.6, p. 273).

5 Sacrifice a cactus, cutting sections using the methods in Technique 1.20, p. 49. How is it adapted to living in a dry habitat?

6 Compare the effectiveness of different materials for insulating the human hand. Include natural materials such as hair and feathers, as well as artificial materials.

7 It is claimed that one function of water loss from plant leaves (transpiration) is to cool them. Test this hypothesis by recording the temperatures of a leaf (or leaves) transpiring at different rates. You will have to decide how to induce different rates of water loss in isolated leaves. Leaf temperatures can be measured with a thermistor (see Technique 7.15, p. 287).

8 Investigate the effect on the heartbeat of *Daphnia* of other factors besides temperature. For example, you might investigate the effect of drugs such as alcohol, caffeine and nicotine, and of natural transmitter substances such as adrenaline and acetylcholine. The following article describes how *Daphnia* can be kept: C. D. Whittaker, Keeping *Daphnia* in the laboratory over a long time period, *School Science Review*, **70** (250), 66, 1988.

9 Investigate the factors which affect lysozyme activity (e.g. pH, length of time since sample was obtained, temperature). Or test the effectiveness of lysozyme against different bacteria. (See, e.g. I. A. Benathen, & L. S. McKenzie, Differential sensitivity of *Staphylococcus epidermidis* and *Escherichia coli* to lysozyme, *Journal of Biological Education*, **33**, 49–51, 1998.)

10 Investigate the effectiveness of different antibiotics against a non-pathogenic bacterium. Your teacher will provide you with a culture of a suitable bacterium and with a range of different antibiotics (see Practical Exercise 3.17, p. 172). Alternatively, you could assess whether the anti-bacterial claims for garlic have any foundation (see C. Maidment, Z. Dembny, & P. King, Investigations into the anti-bacterial properties of garlic using the disc assay method, *Journal of Biological Education*, **32**, 162–165, 1998), or whether wine or other beverages are toxic to bacteria, such as *E. coli* strain B (see M. Harding & C. Maidment, An investigation into the anti-bacterial effects of wine and other beverages, *Journal of Biological Education*, **30**, 237–239, 1996).**BM**

11 Most toothpastes contain about 2% by mass of an anti-bacterial agent. Test the hypothesis that different toothpastes are equally effective against the growth of bacteria or other microorganisms, for example by adding them to wells in agar in which *Micrococcus luteus* is embedded. (See M. Thornton & J. Terry, Now rinse please: investigating the antimicrobial activity of mouthwashes, *Journal of Biological Education*, **28**, 181–184, 1994.)**BM**

12 Compare the effect of different (dilutions of) household disinfectants on the growth of microorganisms.**BM**

Response and coordination

Microscopic structure of the spinal cord and brain   4.1 PRACTICAL EXERCISE

The spinal cord and brain make up the **central nervous system** (**CNS**). Put simply, their job is to coordinate nervous information so that the right impulses are sent to the right place at the right time.

The purpose of this practical exercise is to examine sections of the spinal cord and brain and relate their microscopic structure to their overall function of coordination.

Procedure

Spinal cord

Before you look at the spinal cord under the microscope, it is helpful to have the picture of a generalised **reflex arc** in your mind (see left-hand side of Figure 4.1A). You will then know what to expect to find inside different regions of the cord.

1   Examine a prepared transverse section of spinal cord under low or medium power. Identify the structures shown on the right-hand side of Figure 4.1A. Distinguish between the central **grey matter** and the more peripheral **white matter**. The grey matter contains the **cell bodies** of numerous neurones; the white matter contains slender

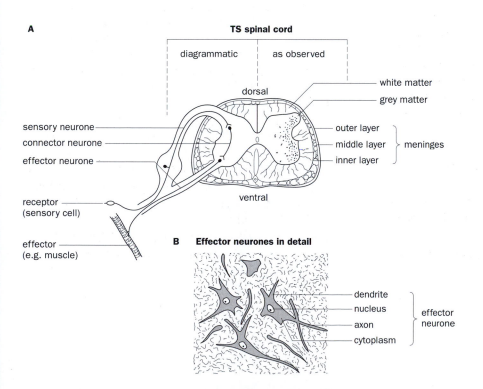

Figure 4.1 Microscopic structure of spinal cord, based on cat. There are variations in the shape and relative proportions of white matter and grey matter according to the part of the cord (neck, thorax, etc.). TS, Transverse section.

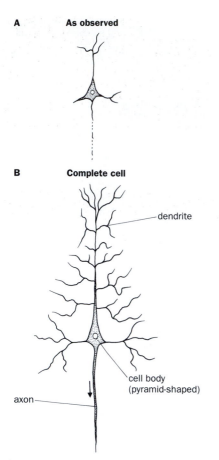

A As observed

B Complete cell

dendrite

cell body
(pyramid-shaped)

axon

Figure 4.2 Pyramidal cell from the motor area of the cerebral cortex. The arrow shows the direction in which impulses are transmitted.

axons which transmit impulses into and out of the spinal cord and axons which transmit impulses up and down the cord to and from the brain.

2 Note the **meninges** surrounding and protecting the spinal cord: the outer and inner layers are separated by a delicate vascular middle layer.

3 Locate the cell body of an **effector neurone** in the ventral part of the grey matter (Figure 4.1B). Examine it under high power. Note in particular its slender branches (**dendrites**). These connect with other neurones. Look for a particularly long branch which may be the **axon**.

4 Extend your study of the motor neurone by examining neurones in a prepared smear of spinal cord.

Brain

1 Examine a vertical section of the **cerebral cortex** and notice numerous **pyramidal cells**, so called because they are shaped like little pyramids (Figure 4.2). Examine one of them in detail under high power. Numerous dendrites connect with other neurones, and the axon transmits impulses to the spinal cord and thence, via reflex arcs, to the muscles.

2 Examine a vertical section of the **cerebellum**. Observe **Purkinje cells** (Figure 4.3). How do the Purkinje cells differ in appearance from the pyramidal cells in the cerebral cortex? The cerebellum controls fine movements by sending impulses down the axons of the Purkinje cells.

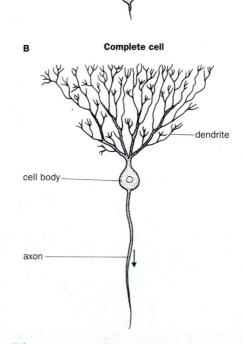

A As observed

B Complete cell

dendrite

cell body

axon

Figure 4.3 Purkinje cell from the cortex of the cerebellum. The arrow shows the direction in which impulses are transmitted.

For consideration

1 Figures 4.2B and 4.3B show entire brain cells. However, when you look at sections of the brain under the microscope you can only see fragments of these cells. How, then, are we justified in making such complete drawings?

2 This investigation has been entirely about the microscopic *structure* of the CNS. To what extent can such structural studies help us to understand how the CNS carries out its function of coordination?

Requirements

Microscope
Spinal cord, TS
Spinal cord, smear
Cerebral cortex, VS
Cerebellum, VS

Microscopic structure of a nerve

4.2 PRACTICAL EXERCISE

Nerves transmit impulses from receptors to the CNS and from the CNS to effectors. In this investigation we shall examine the microscopic structure of a nerve and relate this to its function of transmitting impulses to and from the CNS.

Procedure

First appreciate that a whole nerve consists of numerous **axons** arranged in bundles as shown in Figure 4.4A. Try to imagine what a longitudinal section, and a transverse section, of a whole nerve might look like.

1 Examine a longitudinal section of a myelinated nerve, concentrating on the way the axons are arranged rather than on their detailed structure. Use Figure 4.4B to help you.

2 Examine a transverse section of a myelinated nerve, using Figure 4.4C to help you interpret it.

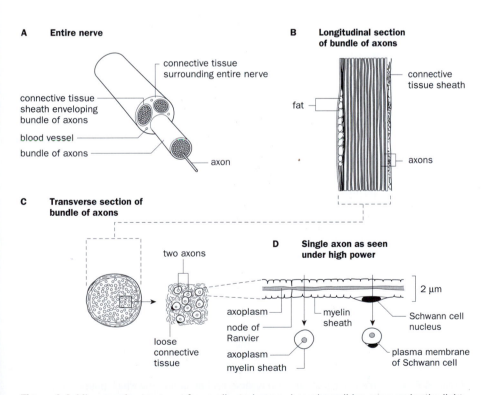

Figure 4.4 Microscopic structure of a myelinated nerve, based on slides seen under the light microscope.

3   Now examine a longitudinal section of a myelinated nerve which has been specially stained to show the **myelin sheath** and associated structures. Use Figure 4.4D to help you identify the myelin sheath, **nodes of Ranvier** and nuclei of **Schwann cells**.

4   Examine an electron micrograph of a transverse section of an axon which passes through a Schwann cell (Figure 4.5A). Look at the myelin sheath very closely and notice that it consists of an extension of the plasma membrane of the Schwann cell which is wrapped tightly round the axon. As the plasma membrane contains a substantial amount of lipid, the myelin sheath also contains much lipid. Figure 4.5B, which shows a standard textbook interpretation of an electron micrograph of a transverse section through an axon at the level of a Schwann cell, should help you in your observations.

A

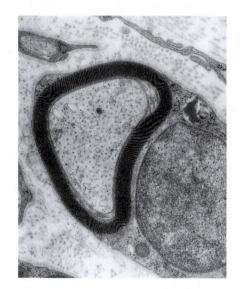

B

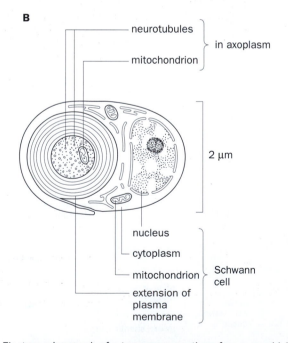

Figure 4.5 A Electron micrograph of a transverse section of an axon which passes through a Schwann cell. **B** Standard, textbook interpretation of an electron micrograph of a generalised transverse section through an axon at the level of a Schwann cell.

5 Now examine the inside of the axon (the **axoplasm**) in Figure 4.5A. Can you see any **neurotubules**? These longitudinally oriented microtubules are thought to assist the transport of materials from the nerve cell body to the far end of the axon.

6 Certain axons innervate skeletal muscles. Examine a slide of skeletal muscle which shows **effector nerve endings** (Figure 4.6). Each ending makes synaptic contact with a muscle fibre at a **neuromuscular junction**.

7 Examine an electron micrograph of a section through a **nerve–nerve synapse**. What you will see depends on the plane in which the section has been cut (Figure 4.7A). Use Figure 4.7B to help you interpret your particular section.

For consideration

1 Here are two well known observations about the human nervous system. (a) In a typical nerve, impulses can travel in two directions: towards the CNS and away from the CNS. (b) The muscles in the human leg are innervated by branches of a single nerve (the sciatic

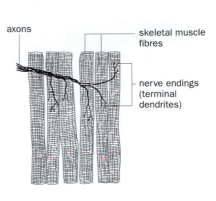

Figure 4.6 Representation of a longitudinal section of skeletal muscle fibres, showing nerve endings as viewed under the light microscope. The nerve endings terminate at neuromuscular junctions.

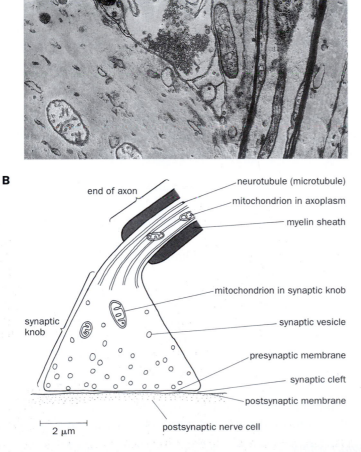

Figure 4.7 A Electron micrograph of a section through a nerve–nerve synapse. **B** Standard, textbook interpretation of such an electron micrograph.

Microscope
Myelinated nerve, LS
Myelinated nerve, TS
Motor nerve endings in skeletal muscle
Electron micrograph of myelinated axon, TS
Electron micrograph of synapse, LS

nerve), yet the muscles do not all contract at the same time. Which features of a myelinated nerve, as observed by you in this practical exercise, help to explain these two observations? Explain your answer.

2 The function of the myelin sheath is to *insulate* the axon. What exactly does this mean and why is it important?

3 Look carefully at Figures 4.5A and 4.5B. How does the standard interpretation (Figure 4.5B) of an electron micrograph of a transverse section through an axon at the level of a Schwann cell compare with an actual electron micrograph (Figure 4.5A)?

4.3 INVESTIGATION — Investigating some human reflexes

A **reflex** is a rapid, unconscious, stereotyped response to a stimulus. Most reflexes involve the brain, but some use only the spinal cord. Either way, reflexes can give us important information about the functioning of the nervous system, and abnormalities in our reflex responses can help doctors to diagnose certain disorders of the nervous system.

The purpose of this investigation is to look at some human reflexes and draw conclusions about the way the nervous system functions. Work in pairs, one of you acting as subject, the other as experimenter.

Procedure

Knee jerk

1 The subject should sit on a table with his or her legs hanging loosely over the edge. With a small **tendon hammer**, the experimenter should tap the tendon just below the knee cap. *There is no need to tap hard*! If the tap is applied correctly, the extensor muscle in the front of the thigh contracts and the leg gives a little kick.

2 Practise eliciting the knee jerk until you get it right every time. Try varying the intensity and location of the stimulus. Note that a response is elicited only by applying a sudden tap in just the right place.

Danger

3 Draw a diagram of the nervous pathways responsible for the knee jerk. Bear in mind that when an extensor muscle contracts its **antagonist** (the flexor) should relax, and that when the leg gives a kick more than one extensor muscle may be involved.

4 Compare your diagram with Figure 4.8. How many nervous pathways, if any, have you left out?

Ankle jerk

1 The subject should kneel on a chair with his or her feet hanging loosely over the edge. The experimenter should now tap the tendon at the back of the foot, just above the heel. Describe the response. Reconstruct the reflex arc involved, using your experience with the knee jerk to help you.

2 Repeat tapping the tendon at approximately two taps per second. Does the response decline, get larger or stay the same? Explain.

Swallowing reflex

1 Swallow the saliva in your mouth cavity, and immediately afterwards

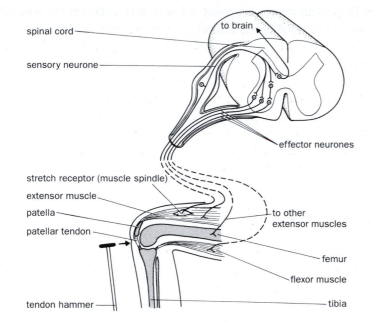

Figure 4.8 Nervous pathways involved in the knee jerk reflex.

try to swallow again – and again. You will probably find it difficult to swallow the second time, and even more difficult the third time. Why do you think this is?

2 Now drink a glass of water and note that you have no difficulty swallowing several times in rapid succession. Propose an explanation for the difference.

Pupil reflex

1 Point a torch or bench light at your partner's eye in a darkened room with the torch/bench light switched off. Watch his/her pupil.

2 Switch on the torch/bench light. Observe the pupil constricting. How is this achieved?

For consideration

1 What general conclusions about the working of the nervous system can be drawn from your observations of human reflexes?

2 The reflexes which you have looked at are simple, discrete responses. However, reflex actions may also form the basis of more complex activities such as locomotion. What part may reflex action play in locomotion?

3 In Figure 4.8, four of the synapses shown in the spinal cord are excitatory and one is inhibitory. Which one is likely to be the inhibitory one, and why?

Requirements

Tendon hammer
Glass of drinking water
Torch *or* bench light

Reaction times in humans

4.4 INVESTIGATION

An organism's **reaction time** to a particular stimulus is the time interval between the moment the stimulus is applied and the moment when the response commences. Measuring reaction times can give us some indication of the speed at which impulses are transmitted in the nervous system. That is the main purpose of this investigation. Work in pairs, one of you acting as subject, the other as experimenter.

Procedure

Various devices can be used to measure reaction times, but they all work on the same principle. There are two switches, one operated by the experimenter (switch E), the other by the subject (switch S). A recording device monitors the time interval between the operation of the two switches. It is important that the experimenter should avoid giving the subject any clue that he or she is about to press the E switch.

Reaction time to sight

1   With the subject watching, the experimenter presses switch E. As soon as the subject *sees* the experimenter pressing switch E, the subject presses switch S. The reaction time is then measured. Repeat at least 10 times and calculate the average reaction time.

2   Test the hypothesis that the subject's visual reaction time decreases with practice.

Reaction time to touch

1   The subject should close his or her eyes, and the experimenter should rest his or her foot lightly on the subject's foot. The experimenter presses switch E and simultaneously treads on the subject's foot. Subject: as soon as you feel the pressure on your foot, press switch S. Measure the reaction time as before.

2   Assess whether the reaction time to touching the foot is slower than the visual reaction time. Identify possible sources of error and try to overcome them. For example, errors may arise if the subject improves with practice and if all the instances of one type of reaction time are determined before all the instances of the other. If necessary, use a statistical test to see if any difference is significant. Use the **t-test** (see p. 307).

Reaction time to coloured lights

Switch E should be connected to two coloured lights, one red, the other green. Find out if a person reacts at the same speed to a red light as to a green light of the same intensity. Take precautions to avoid sources of error, as before. Use the t-test to see if any difference between the reaction times is significant. Do your results support the use of red as a warning colour?

Reaction time to sound

Switch E should be connected to a sound generator and headphones, which should be worn by the subject. Test the hypothesis that a subject reacts more quickly to a loud sound than to a quiet sound. Take precautions to avoid sources of error, and apply the t-test as before.

Estimating transmission speed

With a ruler, measure the length of the nervous pathway between the point where the stimulus is received (foot, eye, ear, as the case may be) and the part of the body which responds (the finger with which the subject presses the S switch). If available, use a text book of human anatomy to confirm the pathways. From your measurements, calculate the speed in metres per second at which impulses are transmitted in the nervous system.

Variation in reaction times

What sort of variation is there in the reaction times of different people? Choose one of the reaction times you have measured (sight, touch, red light, green light or sound) and compare your results with those of other members of your class. Present the data as a histogram.

For consideration

1 What are the possible causes of delay between the application of a stimulus and the onset of the response?
2 Reaction times give only an approximate idea of how quickly nerve impulses are transmitted in the nervous system. Why only approximate? Suggest other, more accurate, ways of measuring transmission speeds in the human nervous system.

References

Buck, M. A non-invasive method for finding the speed of conduction of a nerve using a human subject. *Journal of Biological Education*, **21**, 81–84, 1987. (A method for measuring the delay between the stimulus and response in the knee jerk by means of a simple electrical circuit and voltmeter.)

Spurgin, B. Reaction times in athletics. *School Science Review*, **76** (274), 35–43, 1994. (Other ways of measuring reaction times, and problems that may occur.)

Requirements

Reaction time recorder
Lights, red and green
Sound generator with volume control
Headphones
Ruler
Textbook of human anatomy, if available

Note: Suitable systems for recording reaction times include a pair of switches linked to a triggered cathode-ray oscilloscope, microcomputer, chart recorder or stimulus marker writing on a kymograph. Reaction times can also be measured by timing how long it takes for the subject to catch a falling ruler. The distance the ruler falls, d (in metres), can be converted to the time taken, t (in seconds), using the equation of motion: $d = 1/2at^2$, where a is the ruler's acceleration due to gravity, namely $9.8\,\mathrm{ms^{-2}}$. Rearranging, we have.

$$t = \sqrt{\frac{d}{4.9}}$$

Assessment

- **Plan** your investigation. Provide a justification for the method you use. Show that you have undertaken a thorough risk assessment for hazardous procedures and have given appropriate consideration to ethical implications.

- **Implement** your plan. How can you demonstrate that your manipulative techniques have been used with a high degree of skill? Ensure you pay sufficient attention to detail when it comes to making and recording measurements.

- **Analyse your evidence** and **draw conclusions**. Tabulate and present collected data clearly. How can you display your findings clearly? Ensure that you have described and, where possible, explained any anomalies and inconsistencies. What statistical tests can you use?

- **Evaluate** your investigation. Provide coherent, logical and comprehensive explanations of your results using appropriate biological knowledge and terminology. Discuss limitations of the experimental techniques you used.

Analysis of human skin as a receptor   4.5 INVESTIGATION

The efficiency of the skin in monitoring changes at the surface of the body depends on:

- The **range of stimuli** to which the receptor cells respond.
- The **sensitivity** of the receptor cells.
- The ability of the receptor cells to distinguish between two identical stimuli applied simultaneously (**two-point touch discrimination**).
- The rapidity with which the receptor cells adapt when stimulated repeatedly (**sensory adaptation**).

The purpose of this investigation is to explore these four aspects of the skin as a receptor. You will need to work in pairs.

Guidance

The range of stimuli to which the skin responds

Danger

With a fine ball-point pen, rule a grid of not less than 25 squares, each with an area of 4 mm², on the back of your partner's hand. Then explore each square in turn for its sensitivity to touch, heat, cold and pain. Devise your own method of applying each type of stimulus, ensuring that there is no confusion between one type and another. *Be sure that the skin is not damaged or your partner hurt in this or any of the subsequent experiments.*

Sensitivity

Assess the sensitivity of different parts of the skin to touch. The difficulty in assessing sensitivity, if you apply the stimuli by hand, is quantifying the stimulus – that is, knowing how strong it is. Overcome this difficulty as best you can.

Two-point touch discrimination

The aim here is to find the minimum distance which must exist between two simultaneously applied identical stimuli for the stimuli to be detected as two separate stimuli rather than as a single stimulus. Use a pair of cocktail sticks pushed into a ball of plasticine to apply two simultaneous tactile stimuli to your partner's arm. Repeat, varying the distance between the two points of the dividers, until you find the minimum distance for discrimination. Repeat the experiment in different parts of the body, including the thigh and fingertips.

Adaptation

With a cocktail stick, wiggle one of the hairs on the back of your partner's hand until he or she ceases to feel it. In this way, determine how long it takes for the receptors at the base of the hair to adapt to repeated stimulation.

For consideration

1 Make a list of all the difficulties you experienced in carrying out these experiments, and in drawing conclusions.
2 What are the roles of touch, temperature and pain receptors in the normal functioning of the human body?
3 Is the skin sensitive to any other types of stimulus besides the ones which you have investigated in this practical? What might be the function(s) of such sensitivity?
4 Which part of your skin is most efficient at two-point touch discrimination? How would you explain this in terms of the receptors in the skin? What are its practical applications?

Requirements

Fine ball-point pen
Ruler
Cocktail sticks
Plasticine
Items requested by individual students

4.6 INVESTIGATION

Structure of the mammalian eye

Caution

In the interests of hygiene, wear a lab. coat while you are dissecting, and wash your hands thoroughly afterwards. Disinfect equipment after use.

You have probably seen a diagram of the **mammalian eye** like the one in Figure 4.9, but what is the inside of the eye really like? In this investigation you will dissect the eye of a large mammal such as a sheep or pig and examine prepared sections of the eye under the microscope. You will then appreciate how a combination of dissection and microscope work has enabled scientists to build up an understanding of the structure of the eye.

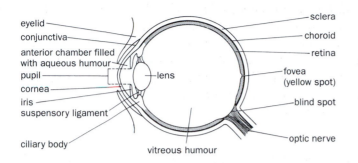
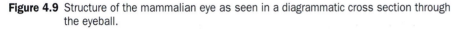

Figure 4.9 Structure of the mammalian eye as seen in a diagrammatic cross section through the eyeball.

Guidance

Dissection of the eye

1   The posterior part of the eyeball will probably have fat clinging to it. Remove the fat so as to expose the **optic nerve** and **eye muscles**. Investigate the eye muscles and reflect (no pun intended) upon their functions.

2   To see the inside of the eye you need to cut into the eyeball. The main objectives are to see how the **lens** is attached to the **ciliary body** and how the **optic nerve** is attached to the **retina**. Consider how best to cut into the eye so as to achieve these objectives with minimum destruction. You may find it helpful to examine a model of the eye first. This will help you to see where the various internal structures are in relation to each other, so you can decide where best to make your cuts.

3   Now look at Figure 4.10. This explains one way of cutting into the

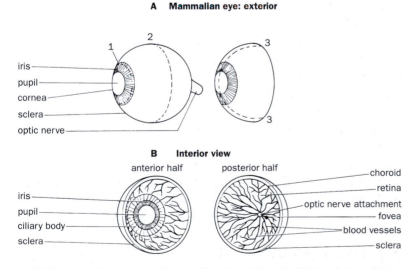

Figure 4.10 One way of opening up the eye. The dotted lines in diagram **A** show three different cuts that should be made in succession. Cut 1 is an *almost* complete circular cut, enabling the cornea to be deflected, rather like opening a book. Cut 2 is a complete circular cut, dividing the eyeball into anterior and posterior halves; this enables you to see inside, as shown in diagram **B**. Cut 3 is a vertical cut through the anterior half of the eye; cut to one side of the lens so that it remains attached to the wall of the eye.

eye. However, it is not the only way; you may have thought of a perfectly suitable alternative.

4 After you have cut into the eye, remove the gelatinous **vitreous humour** from inside the eyeball. What is the function of the vitreous humour?

5 Which features of the eye shown in Figure 4.9 can you see in your dissected eye? Use a hand lens or binocular microscope as necessary.

Sections of the eye

Examine microscope slides of the anterior and posterior portions of the eye. The anterior portion will give you details of the **conjunctiva**, **cornea**, **iris**, **ciliary body** and **lens**. The posterior portion will give you details of the **sclera**, **choroid**, **optic nerve** and **retina**. Use whatever magnification is necessary to see the parts of the eye shown in Figure 4.9.

Further analysis of the eye

Find out, if you do not already know, the functions of the iris and ciliary body. Predict what structures should be present inside the iris and ciliary body to enable them to carry out these functions. Then examine the iris and ciliary body under high power to see if your predictions are correct.

For consideration

1 Which features of the eye shown in Figure 4.9 can be seen in your dissected eye, and which ones are visible only in the microscope slides?

2 Assess the relative importance of dissection and microscopic studies in establishing the structure of a complex organ such as the eye.

Requirements

Microscope
Binocular microscope
Hand lens
Dissecting instruments
Dissecting dish
Eye protection
Model of mammalian eye
Eye of sheep or pig
Eye, anterior portion, VS
Eye, posterior portion, VS

4.7 PRACTICAL EXERCISE

Microscopic structure of the retina

The **retina** of the eye contains **photoreceptor cells** sensitive to light. Collectively, these cells enable an accurate image of the environment to be registered and transmitted to the brain. In this practical we shall look in detail at the microscopic structure of the retina.

Procedure

1 Examine a vertical section of the retina which has been stained with a silver stain to show up the neurones and photoreceptor cells. Distinguish between the various layers, using Figure 4.11 to help you interpret them. Notice the position of the nerve fibres that lead to the optic nerve relative to the layer of photoreceptor cells. Light rays that have entered the eye have to pass through these fibres, and the layer of bipolar neurones, before they reach the photoreceptor cells. This feature derives from the way the eye develops, and is found in all vertebrates.

2 Observe the **choroid** and **sclera** outside the retina. The choroid is vascular and its epithelial lining is pigmented. The sclera is composed of tough connective tissue – mainly collagen fibres with some elastic fibres. What are the functions of the choroid and sclera?

3 Examine the photoreceptor cells in detail under high power, preferably using oil immersion. Can you identify both **rods** and **cones**?

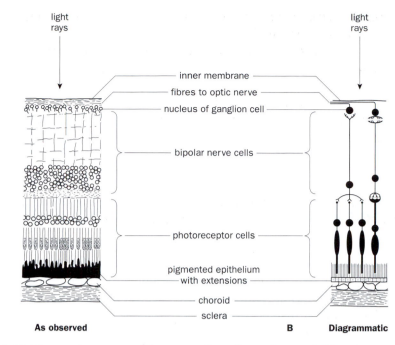

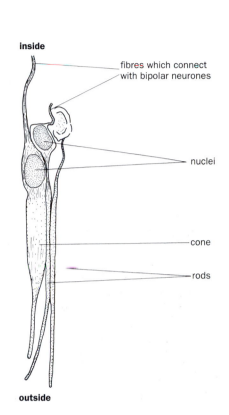

Figure 4.11 Microscopic structure of the mammalian retina and associated layers.

Whether or not you can will depend on which part of the retina your section passes through and how the section has been stained. The centre of the **fovea** contains nothing but densely packed cones. Further out, the cones are fatter and rods are present as well (Figure 4.12). As one moves further away from the fovea, the number of cones decreases until, at the extreme edge of the retina, only rods are present.

4 If you have a well-stained section which passes through the fovea, use an eyepiece graticule and stage micrometer to estimate the relative frequencies of rods and cones at different distances from the fovea. Present your results as a graph.

5 Figure 4.13 is an electron micrograph of a vertical section through a group of rods and cones. Suggest two features which may tell us how these work.

Figure 4.12 A cone and two rods lying side by side, as drawn from a section of the retina seen under the light microscope.

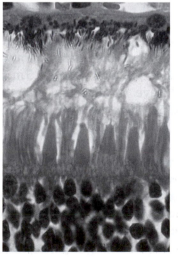

Figure 4.13 Electron micrograph of part of a group of rods and cones.

Procedure

1 Investigate the effect of different light intensities on the diameter of the pupil.

2 Investigate the effect of viewing near and far objects on the diameter of the pupil.

3 Test the hypothesis that, for judging distances, two eyes are needed (**binocular vision**).

4 Under what circumstances do you see double images?

5 Test the hypothesis that the central part of your retina (i.e. the foveal region) can distinguish between different colours, but that the peripheral part can not.

6 Test the hypothesis that, under conditions of low illumination, the peripheral part of your retina is more sensitive than the central part.

7 Investigate the ability of the eye to distinguish between colours in conditions of low illumination.

8 Investigate the effect of subjecting the eyes to a bright light on subsequent vision in dim conditions (**dark adaptation**).

9 Look at Figure 4.15 from a distance of at least 40 cm. Close your left eye and focus on A with your right eye. Now slowly move the book towards you. What happens to B as you do this? Repeat the process, but this time focus on B and see what happens to A. This is a way of demonstrating the **blind spot** (see Figure 4.9 on p. 185).

Figure 4.15 Chart for demonstrating the blind spot.

10 If you wear glasses or contact lenses, remove them. Look at Figure 4.16 through one eye from a distance of at least 30 cm. Do some of the radii appear darker and clearer than others? Repeat with the other eye. This is used as a test for **astigmatism**. What causes astigmatism?

11 Use colour vision test cards to find out if you, and/or others in your class, are **red–green colour blind**. Follow the instructions provided with the cards. Try to find out what red and green look like to a colour-blind person.

Interpret the results of each of the above investigations and tests in the light of what you know about the structure and functioning of the eye.

For consideration

Which of these investigations and tests

- have a practical medical value
- tell us something about how the eye works
- provide information on the structure of the eye?

Explain your answers.

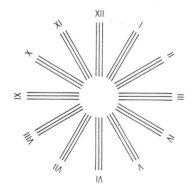

Figure 4.16 Chart for diagnosing astigmatism.

References

Ward, A. *Experimenting with Light and Illusions.* Batsford/Dryad, London, 1985.

Ward, A. 'Magic' in your eyes. *School Science Review*, **71** (256), 120–121, 1990. (Some fascinating practical phenomena are described.)

Requirements

Colour vision test cards
Torch *or* bench light
Other requirements as requested by individual students

Key skills

✓ **Communication:** Produce a report written for the general public – *not* your teacher/lecturer. Organise your information clearly and coherently. Use specialist vocabulary when appropriate, but explain it clearly. Think about the variety of images you might include (e.g. photographs, sketches, annotated drawings, graphs). Decide whether an A4 format is best for your report or whether it would be more accessible if produced in a different format, for example as a folded leaflet.

✓ **Working with others:** Ensure that you and your partner agree realistic objectives and arrangements for working together. Did you find that working with someone else provided benefits beyond simply having someone on whom to carry out the investigation? Could you improve your ways of working with others in the future? If so, how?

Action of skeletal muscle

4.10 PRACTICAL EXERCISE

Some of the physiological properties of **skeletal muscle** can be investigated by recording the contractions of the flexor muscle of your index finger on a kymograph or chart recorder. That is what you will be trying to do in this practical. Work in pairs, one of you acting as the subject, the other as experimenter. The following instructions assume that a kymograph is being used.

Procedure

Tie one end of a length of thread to the subject's index finger as shown in Figure 4.17. Place the hand in a harness which immobilises the whole of the hand except the distal joint of the index finger. With a small piece of Blu-Tack, attach the other end of the thread to a lever fitted with a writing point. Bring the writing point into contact with the recording paper so that it will record accurately the movements of the finger on the rotating drum of the kymograph. Practise to get used to recording the finger movements.

Maximum speed of contraction

With the kymograph set at about 10 mm per second, record a single very quick flexion of the finger – that is, make the muscle contract as quickly as possible. Knowing the speed at which the kymograph drum is rotating, calculate the maximum speed of contraction of the flexor muscle. Think about how best to express the speed. Is the contraction produced by a single impulse in the nerve that supplies the muscle, or by more than one impulse? Explain your answer.

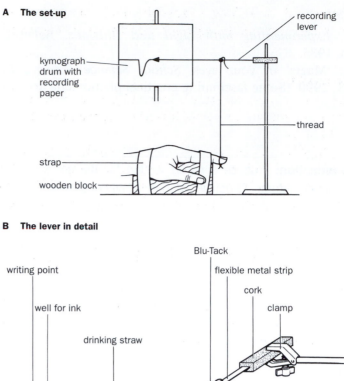

A   The set-up

recording lever

kymograph drum with recording paper

thread

strap

wooden block

B   The lever in detail

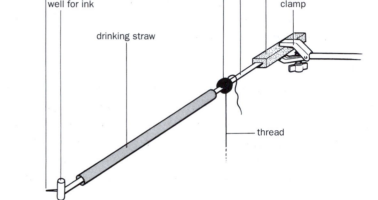

Blu-Tack

writing point

flexible metal strip

cork

well for ink

clamp

drinking straw

thread

Figure 4.17 Set-up for recording movements of the index finger. A chart recorder can be used instead of a kymograph.

Minimum speed of contraction

Repeat the previous experiment, but this time flex the finger as slowly as possible. Calculate the minimum speed of contraction of the flexor muscle.

Size of contraction

Record the smallest and largest flexions of the finger that you can produce, again as quickly as possible. What determines the size of the contraction undergone by the muscle?

Sustained contraction

With the kymograph set at a slower speed (about 1 mm per second), flex the finger slowly then keep it as still as possible in the flexed position for at least 5 seconds. Does the finger fluctuate – that is, 'wobble'? If it does, suggest an explanation for the fluctuations. Relate your observations to the way posture is maintained.

Fatigue

With the kymograph still set at a slow speed, repeatedly flex your finger at maximum speed for as long as possible. Study the pattern of recordings as the muscle gradually fatigues. Suggest possible causes of muscle fatigue.

For consideration

1 Outline any sources of error and ambiguity in this investigation. Suggest a more accurate way of investigating the physiological properties of muscle.
2 One of the points to emerge from this investigation is how varied the speed, size and duration of a muscle's contractions can be. What part is played by the nervous system in producing such *graded* contractions, and why is this important in the normal functioning of the body?

Requirements

Kymograph or chart recorder with recording paper
Harness for hand
Recording lever
Thread
Ink for writing point of lever
Blu-Tack

Determining the effect of ATP on muscle fibres

4.11 PRACTICAL EXERCISE

Despite the fact that skeletal muscle is a living tissue, skeletal muscle removed from a freshly killed animal *sometimes* (!) retains sufficient of its properties to demonstrate the involvement of ATP (adenosine triphosphate) in muscular contraction.

Caution

In the interests of hygiene, wear a lab. coat while you are dissecting, and wash your hands thoroughly afterwards. Disinfect equipment after use.

Procedure

1 Take a piece of fresh skeletal muscle and, using a blunt seeker, scalpel and dissection tile, carefully and under Ringer's solution, dissect out six longitudinal strands, each about 1 mm in width and 15–30 mm in length. Each strand may consist of one or more muscle fibres.
2 Transfer three of these strands to one microscope slide and the other three to another slide. Each strand should be parallel to, but not touching, its neighbours.
3 Measure the length of each strand to the nearest millimetre, noting which strand is which.
4 Counting the number of drops you use, add a few drops of Ringer's solution to the strands on one of the slides, sufficient to wet each of them. Wait 1 minute and then measure the length of each strand to the nearest millimetre.
5 Add the same number of drops of ATP in Ringer's solution to the strands on the other slide. Wait 1 minute and then measure the length of each strand to the nearest millimetre.
6 Compare the percentage shortening of the strands on the two slides.

Requirements

Dissection instruments
Dissection tile
Teat pipette
Ringer's solution
ATP in Ringer's solution, 0.2%
Skeletal muscle, approx.
   5 cm × 1 cm × 0.5 cm

For consideration

1 Why were you told to add Ringer's solution to one of the microscope slides?
2 By looking at electron micrographs of contracted and relaxed muscle in a textbook, or by making deductions from Figure 4.21 on p. 195, calculate by what percentage skeletal muscle can contract. How does the percentage contraction you observed compare with this figure?
3 How might you expect your findings to differ if you added glucose-1-phosphate to the ATP in Ringer's solution? Why?
4 In the light of your findings, comment on the fact that human hearts obtained from people who have died can sometimes be successfully used in transplants.

Note: The muscle (meat) must be obtained from an animal which has been recently killed and not frozen. A helpful butcher or abattoir is invaluable. After purchase, store the meat in Ringer's solution at about 4 °C (a refrigerator) and use as soon as possible. Different students in a group could try different meats – for example pork, chicken, beef.

Structure of skeletal muscle

Examining the structure of skeletal muscle is a useful exercise for three reasons:

- It provides an excellent opportunity to relate structure to function.
- It illustrates the limitations of the light microscope.
- It shows how the electron microscope can be used to predict how a biological structure works.

Procedure

1 Dissect out a whole muscle from the leg of the rat which you have dissected on previous occasions. Alternatively, use shin meat provided by a butcher. Cut the **tendons** by which the muscle is attached to the bones.

2 The muscle is enclosed within a connective tissue **sheath**. Refer to Figure 4.18 to see how the **muscle fibres** are arranged within the sheath. With needles, break through the sheath and tease out a few fibres on a slide. Crush some of them with a glass rod, add a drop of sodium chloride solution (0.75%) and put on a coverslip. Examine under the microscope. Can you see **striations** running across the fibres? Irrigating with ethanoic acid may help you to see nuclei.

3 Examine a prepared longitudinal section of skeletal muscle under low power. You will now see the muscle fibres more clearly. Striations and nuclei should be plainly visible (Figure 4.19A).

4 Now turn over to high power and examine a single fibre in detail. In a good section, well stained and illuminated, you should be able to see very fine **myofibrils** inside the fibre, and some detail of the striations (Figure 4.19B).

5 Examine a low magnification electron micrograph of skeletal muscle (Figure 4.20A). The myofibrils are now sufficiently magnified to enable you to see them in detail. Try to relate the pattern of striations in the electron micrograph to your section under the light microscope. Use Figure 4.20B to help you.

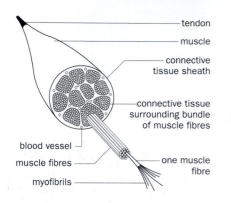

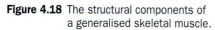

Figure 4.18 The structural components of a generalised skeletal muscle.

Ethanoic acid

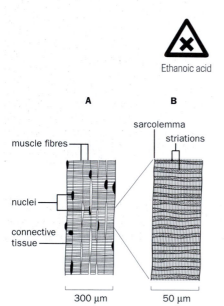
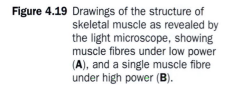

Figure 4.19 Drawings of the structure of skeletal muscle as revealed by the light microscope, showing muscle fibres under low power (**A**), and a single muscle fibre under high power (**B**).

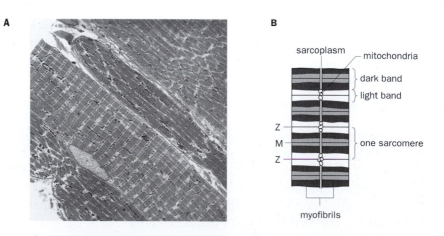

Figure 4.20 **A** Low magnification transmission electron micrograph of a section through skeletal muscle. **B** Standard, textbook interpretation of part of such an electron micrograph.

6 Now examine a high magnification electron micrograph of a single myofibril (Figure 4.21A). Notice how the myofibril is composed of **filaments**. Distinguish between the thick (**myosin**) and thin (**actin**) filaments. Does their arrangement agree with the diagrammatic representation in Figure 4.21B?

A

B

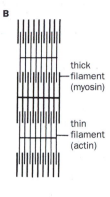

thick filament (myosin)

thin filament (actin)

Figure 4.21 A High magnification transmission electron micrograph of a section through skeletal muscle. **B** Standard, textbook interpretation of part of such an electron micrograph.

For consideration

1 Compare the information about the structure of skeletal muscle provided by the light microscope and electron microscope.

2 What contribution has the electron microscope made to our understanding of how skeletal muscle contracts?

3 What would you expect Figure 4.21B to look like if the muscle was fully contracted?

Requirements

Microscope
Rat for dissection
Dissecting board and pins
Dissecting instruments
Slide and coverslip
Glass rod
Mounted needles, ×2
Sodium chloride solution, 0.75%
Ethanoic acid, 2 mol dm⁻³
Eye protection
Skeletal (striated) muscle, LS
Electron micrograph of skeletal muscle, LS, low magnification
Electron micrograph of skeletal muscle, LS, high magnification

---

Comparison of smooth, cardiac and skeletal muscle

4.13 INVESTIGATION

Vertebrate muscle is classified into **smooth muscle**, **cardiac muscle** (heart muscle) and **skeletal muscle** (striated muscle). The purpose of this investigation is to compare the structures of these three vertebrate muscle types.

Guidance

Examine prepared slides of smooth, cardiac and skeletal muscle. Make drawings of all three types as they appear under the light microscope in the best possible conditions. Pay particular attention to the **muscle fibres**. Resist the temptation to include features which you think should be there but which you cannot actually see!

For each type of muscle try to answer these questions:

1 Are the muscle fibres separate or interconnected?

2 Is each muscle fibre composed of separate cells or are the cells combined into a **syncytium**? (Hint: locate the nuclei and see if they are separated from each other by 'partitions' running across the fibre.)

3 Can **myofibrils** be seen inside the fibres?

4 Are **striations** visible inside the fibres?

Make a table comparing the three types of muscle. The table should provide answers to the above questions.

For consideration

1 Knowing where these three types of muscle occur in the body, predict the functional properties of each type.

2 For each type of muscle, relate one structural feature, visible under the light microscope, to the functional properties of the muscle.

3 In the electron microscope, two of the three types of muscle appear very similar but the other one is quite different. Which two do you think look alike? How do you arrive at your answer?

4.14 PRACTICAL EXERCISE — The vertebrate skeleton: a comparative study

As the solid framework to which the muscles are attached, the skeleton is one of the most important parts of the body. The skeleton of all land-living vertebrates is essentially the same, but the detailed structure of the component parts varies according to the method of locomotion and other features of the animal's life history.

In this practical exercise you will compare the skeletons of different vertebrates, relating the differences to their respective methods of locomotion.

Procedure

1 Start by examining the skeleton of a **rabbit** or **rat**. Of the animal skeletons you will study, these have the most 'conventional' ('ancestral' to an evolutionary biologist) method of locomotion – walking on all fours. Identify the parts of the skeleton, using Figure 4.22 to help you. Observe the **articulating surfaces** where one bone moves against another, and various **processes** (projections) for the attachment of ligaments and tendons. Such processes are sometimes flattened to allow the attachment of particularly large muscles.

2 Examine the skeleton of a **frog**. Compare it with the rabbit or rat skeleton, particularly with respect to the sacral vertebrae, pelvic girdle and hindlimbs. How is the structure of the frog's skeleton related to its method of locomotion?

3 Examine the skeleton of a bird, for example **pigeon**. Compare it with the rabbit or rat skeleton, particularly with respect to the pectoral girdle and forelimbs. Notice that the sternum is drawn out into a deep **keel**. This is for the attachment of the flight muscles. There are two flight muscles on each side of the body. One of them pulls the wing down, and the other one pulls it up. How do you think the flight muscles are arranged in order to achieve these actions?

4 Examine a **human skeleton**, or a model of one. Compare it with the rabbit or rat skeleton, particularly with respect to the structure of the pelvis and vertebral column. To what extent is the structure of the human skeleton related to the fact that we are **bipedal**?

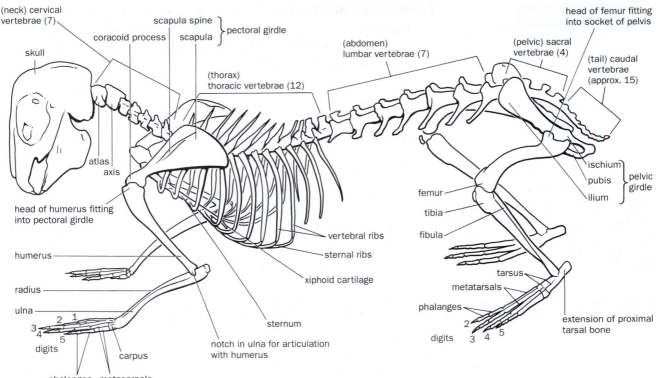

Figure 4.22 Skeleton of a rabbit. The rat is similar.

Other things you can do

1 Compare an individual **lumbar vertebra** of the rabbit or rat with that of the human. Identify the parts of the rabbit or rat vertebra, using Figure 4.23 to help you. Find the equivalent parts in the human vertebra. Try to explain the differences in functional terms.

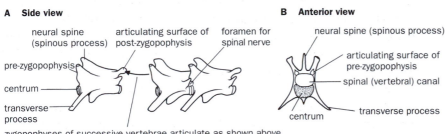

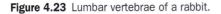

Figure 4.23 Lumbar vertebrae of a rabbit.

2 Study individual vertebrae from different regions of the vertebral column of the rabbit or rat and human. Relate any regional differences to the functions of the vertebrae in different parts of the body.

3 Examine the skeletons of other vertebrates, as available. If possible include a **bony fish** (**teleost**), **lizard** and **snake**. Try to relate the structure of their skeletons to their different methods of locomotion.

Mounted skeletons of rabbit or rat, frog,
    bird (e.g. pigeon) and human (or
    model)
Vertebrae of rabbit or rat
Vertebrae of human
Mounted skeletons of bony fish
    (teleost), lizard and snake, as
    available

For consideration

1   The skeleton of a mammal that walks on all fours has been likened to a bridge. In what sense is the skeleton a bridge, and what sort of bridge do you think it is?

2   To what extent does the human skeleton depart from a bridge construction? Can you think of a more appropriate metaphor for the human skeleton?

4.15 PRACTICAL EXERCISE

Microscopic structure of bone

Think about the stresses and strains to which a bone such as the human femur is subjected. What sort of properties will it need to possess? How can a bone be formed, during a mammal's growth, so that it finishes up with these properties? Bear these questions in mind as you look at the microscopic structure of **bone tissue**.

Bone tissue varies in its microscopic structure according to where it occurs. Here we shall look at **compact bone**, a very dense and hard kind of bone tissue which occurs in the shaft of limb bones such as the femur.

Procedure

Bone tissue consists of a non-living **matrix** (an organic material impregnated with mineral salts) and the cells which give rise to it (**osteoblasts**). In compact bone tissue these two components are arranged in a characteristic pattern.

1   Examine a transverse section of compact bone. It consists of numerous **Haversian canals** each surrounded by a series of concentric rings of bone matrix (Figure 4.24A).

2   Examine an individual Haversian system in detail (Figure 4.24B). Notice that the central Haversian canal contains blood vessels. The concentric layers of bone matrix are called **lamellae**. Observe **lacunae** and **canaliculi** which house the bone-forming osteoblasts and their fine processes.

3   Focus on an individual lacuna and the canaliculi extending from it. Reconstruct the shape of a single osteoblast (Figure 4.24C).

4   To gain a three-dimensional picture of compact bone, examine a longitudinal section as well as a transverse section. Make a three-dimensional plasticine model of a sample of compact bone tissue, based on your observations.

For consideration

1   Suggest as many functions as you can think of for the blood vessels in the Haversian canals.

2   The canaliculi are important during the development of bone tissue. Explain.

3   Suppose you were employed by a construction firm as a consultant to suggest a building technique based on compact bone tissue. What might you suggest and what would be the scientific basis for your suggestion?

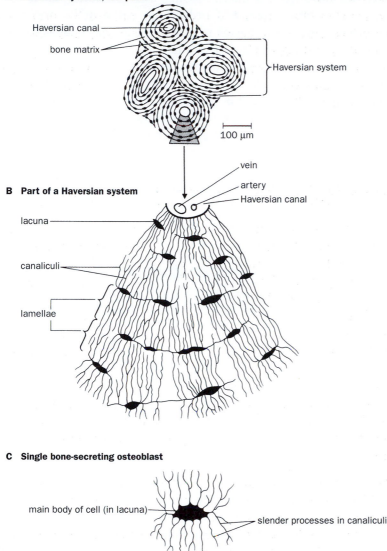

A Haversian systems, low power

Haversian canal

bone matrix

Haversian system

100 μm

B Part of a Haversian system

vein

artery

Haversian canal

lacuna

canaliculi

lamellae

C Single bone-secreting osteoblast

main body of cell (in lacuna)

slender processes in canaliculi

Figure 4.24 Microscopic structure of compact bone tissue, based on transverse sections
viewed under the light microscope.

Analysis of the muscles in the leg of a mammal

4.16 INVESTIGATION

The purpose of this investigation is to study the muscles in the hind leg
of a mammal. There are various ways of carrying out such an analysis.
We shall adopt a functional approach, the muscles being described in
terms of the actions they produce.

Caution

In the interests of hygiene, wear a lab.
coat while you are dissecting, and wash
your hands thoroughly afterwards.
Disinfect equipment after use.

Guidance

The analysis can be carried out on the leg of a rat or on a pig's trotter.

Systematically dissect all the muscles of the leg, starting with the superfi-
cial ones and then proceeding to the ones underneath. Free each muscle
from its neighbours by cutting away the connective tissue in between.
Follow the muscle upwards to its **origin** and downwards to its **insertion**.
The origin and insertion are usually on bones, but in some cases they may
be on the connective tissue sheath surrounding other muscles.

When you have freed a muscle from its neighbours, pull it so as to determine its action. Then, and only then, cut it at its origin and/or insertion and either deflect it or remove it. This will enable you to see, and dissect, the deeper muscles beneath.

At appropriate stages of your investigation, make diagrams of the leg, showing the various muscles. Classify the muscles according to their action on the leg (**protractor**, **retractor**, **abductor**, **adductor**, **flexor**, **extensor**, **rotator**). Make clear which joints the muscles act on, and which muscles are antagonistic to each other.

For consideration

1 How many muscles have you accounted for in the leg? Are there any which you expected to find but have not?
2 How many muscles belong to each of the functional groups mentioned above?
3 Which muscles do you consider to be the most important in moving the body forward during normal locomotion?
4 Numerous muscles are responsible for operating the leg, yet only one nerve leads to the leg (the sciatic nerve). How can one nerve coordinate the actions of so many muscles?

Requirements

Dissecting instruments
Dissecting board and pins
Rat's leg or pig's trotter for dissection

4.17 INVESTIGATION

Orientation response of blowfly larvae to light

Blowflies (also known as bluebottles and greenbottles) lay their eggs in a variety of habitats. In some species the larvae feed on decaying meat; in others they live in dung. A few species are parasites. *Lucilia*, for example, often lays its eggs in sores or cuts on sheep. The eggs hatch and the larvae bury into the sheep's flesh. In this investigation you can study the response of blowfly larvae to light and relate this to their way of life.

Guidance

You will need to devise a way of observing the response of blowfly larvae to light. It will probably be necessary to work in a darkened room and to use one or two laboratory lamps which can be switched on or off. You can vary the intensity of the light and its direction. Look carefully at how the larvae move and see what happens if a light is switched on and off at different frequencies. After making preliminary observations, suggest some hypotheses and test them rigorously. Can you separate the larvae's response to light and their response to gravity?

For consideration

1 Relate your findings to the life style of blowfly larvae in their natural habitat.
2 Find out as much as you can about the larva's sense organs and nervous system. Put forward a hypothesis to explain the mechanism by which the larva detects and responds to light.

Requirements

Lamps, ×2
Sheet of white paper (at least 25 cm square)
Pencil
Blunt forceps (for moving larvae)
Stopwatch
Beaker of damp sawdust or bran
Blowfly larvae (ideally 8–10)

- **Plan** your investigation. Identify and define the nature of a question using available information and knowledge of biology. Consider ethical implications in the choice and treatment of the organisms you intend using.

- **Implement** your plan. Make and record detailed observations in a suitable way. Can you use IT to collect, store, analyse or model your data? Ensure you work in a methodical way, with appropriate consideration for the well-being of living organisms.

- **Analyse your evidence** and **draw conclusions**. Think about how you can communicate your findings in an appropriate way. Ensure you assess the reliability and precision of your data.

- **Evaluate** your investigation. How appropriate was your plan? How adequate was your methodology? What additional apparatus would you like to have to further your investigation – why?

Taxes and kineses

4.18 INVESTIGATION

A **taxis** is a movement that is oriented in relation to the *direction* of a stimulus. For example, earthworms move away from light and are therefore **negatively phototactic**. A **kinesis** is a behaviour pattern in which an animal responds to an *alteration in stimulus intensity* by changing its activity level.

In this investigation you will use woodlice (*Porcellio scaber* or a related species) to see whether they respond to light showing a taxis or a kinesis. Work in pairs.

Procedure

1   Use a Petri dish, its lid and some card to devise an arena in which a woodlouse can move freely, yet which is half in dark and half in light. Position a light so that there is a gradient of light intensity along the light half – shine a light from the side rather than above. This is an example of a **choice chamber**.
2   Introduce a woodlouse into the middle of the half of the Petri dish that is in light and replace the lid of the dish.
3   Get a partner to say 'now' once a second. Each 1 second, indicate the position of the woodlouse by using a felt-tip pen on the Petri dish lid to record the position of the woodlouse below. Every now and again, draw arrows to show the direction of movement. Continue for 2 minutes or until the animal disappears into the dark half of the Petri dish.
4   Remove the woodlouse and repeat with four other woodlice.

For consideration

1   Did your woodlice show a taxis or a kinesis? Explain your answer.
2   What would you predict would happen if you repeated your study in dim light?
3   Woodlice are said to show **thigmokinesis**, that is, to be attracted to solid stimuli. Did you find any evidence for this? How might you investigate this possibility further?

References

Cheverton, J. Animals in action. *Biological Sciences Review*, **7** (2), 31–35, 1994.

Requirements

Petri dish and lid
Card
Felt-tip pen
Scissors
Bench lamp
Blunt forceps (for moving woodlice)
Stopclock
Five woodlice (preferably *Porcellio scaber*)

Morris, M. C. Using woodlice (Isopoda, Oniscoidea) to demonstrate orientation behaviour. *Journal of Biological Education*, **33**, 215–216, 1999. (For further studies on woodlouse orientation.)

Learning in rats or gerbils

A number of animals, from several phyla, can learn to find their way through mazes of varying degrees of complexity, particularly if encouraged by a reward. This practical involves training rats or gerbils to master a comparatively simple maze.

starting point

food area

Figure 4.25 Plan of maze suitable for use with rats and gerbils. The maze should be at least 10 cm in height and have sides approximately 50 cm long.

Danger

Requirements

Maze of the type shown in Figure 4.25 (or the means of making one)
Stopwatch
Gloves
Camcorder (if available)
Non-odorous rat or gerbil food (e.g. solid food pellet)
Rat or gerbil, not overfed and with no experience of mazes

Procedure

1   Use a maze of the type shown in Figure 4.25. Such a maze can be constructed from a cardboard or wooden box fitted with hardboard or polystyrene partitions. At one end there is a 'starting point'. At the other end there is a 'food area'. The whole maze should have a transparent cover.

2   Place a gerbil or rat at the starting point *without* there being any food in the food area. For obvious reasons, the animal should not have had any previous experience of mazes nor should it have eaten large amounts of food immediately before the exercise. *However, the animal must not be unduly deprived of food for the purposes of the exercise.*

3   Now run a **trial**. This consists of letting the animal find its way to the food area. Time how long this takes *and* score the number of **errors** it makes in doing so. You must decide what constitutes an error: for example, does the animal have to insert all of its body, or only part of it, into a wrong turning to make an error? A camcorder would be valuable, if you have access to one. If not, ensure you have decided what constitutes an error *before* you carry out the first run.

4   When the animal reaches the food area, reward it with a small item of food. Once it has eaten it, transfer the animal to the starting point and run another trial. As before, record the time taken to complete the maze and the number of errors made *en route*.

5   Repeat the procedure, ideally until the animal can complete the maze several times in succession without making any errors. Wash your hands if you have chosen not to wear gloves.

6   Plot two graphs: (a) the time taken to complete the maze (vertical axis) against the number of trials; (b) the number of errors made in each trial (vertical axis) against the number of trials.

For consideration

1   What conclusions can you draw regarding the ability of rats or gerbils to learn?

2   What bearing do your results have on the behaviour of these animals in their natural habitats?

3   Can you suggest any factors that might speed up the rate at which these animals learn to master the maze?

✓ **Improving own learning and performance:** Agree targets (the two graphs you need to plot) and plan how these will be met. Manage your time effectively to complete tasks, revising your plan as necessary (working with children and animals can be more problematic than one thinks). Seek and actively use feedback and support from relevant sources (? your teacher/lecturer) to help you meet your targets. Review your progress by providing information on the quality of your learning and performance and by identifying targets you have met. Exchange views with appropriate people (these could be your peers) to agree ways to improve your performance still further.

Learning in humans

4.20 PRACTICAL EXERCISE

Memory is one of the most important human attributes and is the basis of much of our behaviour. In this practical you will construct a **trial and error** graph illustrating your ability to recall a list of words, and then consider some of its implications.

Procedure

1 A list of 20 words will be read to you (e.g. by a teacher/lecturer). Listen carefully, and then, once the entire list has been read out, write down as many of the words as you can. They need not be in the right order. Head your list *Trial 1* and fold the paper so that you cannot see what you have written.

2 The list will then be read out again. As before, wait until the entire list has been read out and then write down as many of the words as you can. Head the list *Trial 2* and fold the paper as before.

3 Repeat the above procedure until you can remember all 20 words. Head your lists *Trial 3*, *Trial 4*, etc.

4 You will now be given a copy of the list of words. Score the result of each trial as the number of errors. An error is a word left out or a wrong one included. (Don't count simple misspellings as errors.)

5 Make a trial and error graph of your results. Plot the number of errors (vertical axis) against the number of the trial (horizontal axis).

6 Now look again at the master list of the 20 words. Divide them up into five groups as follows: *Group A* consists of the first four words, *Group B* the second four, *Group C* the third four, *Group D* the fourth four, and *Group E* the fifth and last four.

7 Look at your *Trial 1* list and score how many words in each of the five groups you included in your list. It doesn't matter where in your list the words occur, as long as they occur somewhere. Write the five scores at the end of your list.

8 Plot the results of step 7 as a bar chart, putting the number of correct words in each group on the vertical axis and the letters designating the groups on the horizontal axis (Figure 4.26).

9 Repeat steps 7 and 8 for the rest of your trials.

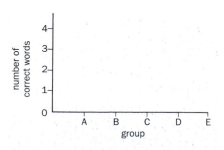
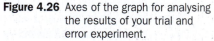

Figure 4.26 Axes of the graph for analysing the results of your trial and error experiment.

For consideration

1 Which features of *your* trial and error graph (step 5) are also seen in the graphs of any others who have carried out this practical with you? Are there any features peculiar to *you*?

2 What factors might cause you to learn the list of words more slowly? How could you investigate such factors?

3 It has been suggested that, when you try to learn a list of words, you tend to remember the ones at the *beginning* and the *end* of the list more quickly than the ones in the middle. These phenomena are known to psychologists as **primacy** and **recency**. Do your results support this suggestion? Of what value might primacy and recency be in everyday life?

4 It could be argued that the test carried out in this investigation is a measure of concentration and intelligence as well as of memory. How might the test be modified to eliminate the influence of these alternative factors?

Projects

Before starting a project, as on p. 57 assess the risks inherent in your intended procedure and discuss your intended procedure with your teacher/lecturer.

1 Devise a method for recording on a kymograph or chart recorder a person's knee jerk or ankle jerk. Then investigate factors that affect the size of the response: for example, where precisely the stimulus is applied, the intensity of the stimulus, and which leg or foot (left or right) is tested. Can the subject consciously suppress the reflex? Is the size of the response larger if the subject is reading a book aloud while the test is carried out?

2 Construct your own reaction-time recorder. Ideally this should be compact, easy to use and provide as many stimulus options as possible – for example touch, sight and sound.

3 Investigate the effect of different factors on a person's reaction time. Possible factors might include time of day (e.g. early morning and late at night) and drinking – for example coffee or a measured amount of an energy drink such as lucozade.

4 Test the hypothesis that people who are good at fast ball games – for example tennis, squash and cricket – have quicker reaction times than other people. Be sure you obtain sufficient data from enough people, and evaluate them statistically.

5 Investigate the effect on a person's reaction time of combining different stimuli. For example, the subject might be asked to respond only when a certain type of light stimulus is combined with a certain type of sound stimulus. Is there any evidence that the subject improves with practice or that certain combinations of stimuli evoke quicker responses than others? Which properties of the nervous system are being demonstrated by such tests, and what use might be made of them in preparing people for different kinds of occupation?

6 Investigate the effect of caffeine on the heart rate of *Daphnia* (water flea). It is recommended that the maximum concentration you use is 0.02%. (See R. Foster, A stroboscopic method to investigate the effect of caffeine on *Daphnia* heart rate, *Journal of Biological Education*, **31**, 253–255, 1997, and A. Dickson, Caffeine – our daily drink, *Biological Sciences Review*, **7** (5), 19–21, 1995.)

7 Blind people can 'read' with their fingertips by using Braille. Investigate people's ability to recognise shapes and/or the positions of dots with their fingertips. You might use Braille itself and/or the alternative system Moon, both of which are available from the Royal National Institute for the Blind. Alternatively you might devise 'touch tests' of your own.

8 Use a Snellen chart to estimate the visual acuity, without wearing glasses, of different people of approximately the same age. Does the variation between people show a normal distribution (see p. 310)?

9 Test the hypothesis that the maximum distance from the eye at which letters of a certain size can be seen clearly decreases with age.

10 Look at the face in Figure 4.27. Whose is it? What features of this computerised image enable you to identify the person? Use this as the jumping-off point for investigating the minimum amount of visual information required by people to recognise an object. You might, for example, present volunteers with progressively more detailed pictures of a well-known person and find out at what point they recognise him or her. Try to devise a way of quantifying the amount of information in the pictures. Assess which particular features (eyes, shape of mouth, etc.) are most important in enabling recognition, and relate these to the drawings of well-known people made by cartoonists.

Figure 4.27 Computer representation of . . . whom?

11 Devise an optical illusion in which a picture or model can be seen as two different objects. You may want to use one of M. C. Escher's etchings. Use it to test the hypothesis that, once a person 'sees' one of the two alternatives, it is difficult for him or her to see the other one.

12 Investigate the ability of different people to discriminate between sounds of slightly different pitch. Test the hypothesis that musicians are better at pitch discrimination than non-musicians.

13 The violinist in Figure 4.28 is moving the bow backwards and forwards with the right hand while simultaneously performing a vibrato wrist action with the left hand and pressing the appropriate strings (in the correct places) with the fingers. This may look easy, but in fact it is remarkably difficult if you're not a string player (try it yourself). Devise a test which assesses a person's ability to perform different actions with his or her right and left hands simultaneously. Test the hypothesis that, although most people can learn to do this with practice, some are innately better at it than others.

Figure 4.28 The violinist Nigel Kennedy in action. The left and right hands perform different actions simultaneously.

14 Compare the maximum load which can comfortably be carried by various muscles (arm and/or leg) of human subjects. See if you can correlate the results with the different sports and recreational activities engaged in by the subjects (tennis, gymnastics, weight-lifting, etc.). Obtain volunteers from a wide range of sports, and include some subjects who do no sports at all. Is there any evidence that a limb which is used a lot (e.g. the right arm of a right-handed tennis player) has better developed muscles and/or skeleton?

15 Investigate how stick insects walk. Insects have six legs and the way these are coordinated makes a fascinating study. Stick insects have the advantage that they move slowly and are easy to observe. They can be kept in the laboratory without difficulty and they readily shed their legs by a natural spontaneous process called autotomy. In any colony of stick insects there will always be some specimens that lack one or more legs. The effect of this on locomotion can therefore be studied without deliberately harming the animals. Observe the order in which the legs are raised in different conditions and consider how balance is maintained. (See P. Bragg, The use of stick insects in schools, *School Science Review*, **73** (264), 49–58, 1992.)

16 Test the hypothesis that, for an insect to fly, the tarsi (i.e. the terminal part of the legs) must *not* be in contact with a solid object. Possible insects to use include housefly, bluebottle and locust. The insect can be suspended in mid-air by attaching its dorsal side to the end of a match stick with wax or glue. Don't do anything that is likely to hurt the animal. For how long will an insect beat its wings when suspended? Do the wings stop beating when contact of the tarsi with a solid object is restored?

17 Devise a method of estimating the frequency of an insect's wing-beat. If available, use a stroboscope or high-speed cinematography. (Avoid equipment that operates at frequencies of 7–15 Hz, as these have been known to trigger epileptic fits. Take special care with 'safer' stroboscopes in the presence of anyone who has epilepsy.) Alternatively, suspend the insect in mid-air as in the previous project and allow one of its wings to beat against a rapidly revolving kymograph drum fitted with sooted paper. From the positions of the marks and the known speed of the drum, the wing frequency can be estimated. Once you have perfected a method, find the effect of various external factors, for example temperature, on the wing frequency.

18 Study the method of locomotion of the garden snail *Helix*. It appears to glide along the surface of the ground. What is happening on the underside of its foot that allows this to happen? Are cilia involved, or is propulsion achieved only by muscular contractions? If muscular contractions do take place, what sort are they and how do they propel the body forward? Snails leave a trail of slime (mucus) behind them. Where does the mucus come from, and does it play a part in locomotion?

19 The earthworm is an ideal animal on which to carry out simple experiments on response and coordination. Take its escape response, for example. This consists of a rapid shortening of the body in response to a stimulus at one end. What sort of stimuli evoke the escape response? What part do the chaetae (bristles) play in the response? Try to think of simple, clear-cut hypotheses which you can test. What is the role of the escape response in the normal life of the animal? Go out into a garden on a warm wet night and observe earthworms lying on the surface of the ground. Assess the effectiveness of their escape response in these natural conditions.

20 Observe the walk, trot, canter and gallop of horses. Take still photographs and/or make slow-motion films. How do the gaits differ? In what order are the legs raised? How many legs are in contact with the ground at any one moment? At what speed does the horse change from one gait to another? Similar studies can be carried out on many other animals – for example dogs and cats.

21 Investigate the effect of partial and complete decalcification on the mechanical properties of a limb bone. Progressive decalcification can be achieved by immersing bones in a 3% solution of hydrochloric acid for different periods of time. Consider how you might assess the amount of decalcification that has taken place. The mechanical properties may be investigated by measuring the bending when masses are hung on the bone placed horizontally.

22 Study the movement of snails in a pond or aquarium. Is their movement random or related to stimuli? Is an individual's movement affected by the presence of other individuals? Is movement more usual at certain times of the day?

23 Devise and carry out experiments to compare the maze-learning abilities of two different species (e.g. gerbil and laboratory rat or cockroach and locust).

24 Investigate the responses of earthworms to different stimuli (e.g. light, sound, vibrations). What sorts of learning do earthworms show (e.g. habituation, trial and error learning, conditioned reflexes)?

25 Study the foraging behaviour of garden snails. Combine observations in the field with experiments in the laboratory designed to test hypotheses you have generated.

26 Carry out a project on the courtship behaviour of aquarium fish (e.g. guppies) or garden birds (e.g. blackbirds or house sparrows).

27 Investigate territorial behaviour in humans by studying seating arrangements in a library. After initial observations, try placing piles of books on tables or jackets over the backs of chairs to manipulate conditions.

28 Study the ability of small mammals (in the laboratory) or birds (at a bird table) to select one type of food in preference to another. (See A. J. Churchill, Food selection by zebra finches – a starting point for further investigation, *School Science Review*, **75** (273), 72–73, 1994.)

29 Identify the factors that affect the length of time that kestrels spend hovering and the success rate of their dives (e.g. weather, time of year, sex of bird).

30 Birds at a bird feeder are potentially at risk from predators such as domestic cats and even sparrowhawks. They show vigilance behaviour by stopping feeding at intervals and scanning their surroundings. Study how this vigilance behaviour is affected by such things as the distance of a feeder from cover in which a predator could hide. (See J. Cheverton, Four investigations of animal behaviour, *School Science Review*, **78** (285), 39–43, 1997, and M. Kaszap, A scientific approach to a bird-feeder problem, *School Science Review*, **78** (283), 105–107, 1996.)

31 Study the movement of *Tenebrio* (mealworm) larvae. Do they show taxes or kineses? See X. Espadaler, Stimulus integration in *Tenebrio* larvae: an easy laboratory study (or how to show Euclidean larvae), *Journal of Biological Education*, **28**, 130–134, 1994.)

32 Study the ability of female seed beetles (*Callosobruchus maculatus*) to discriminate between different types of bean when laying their eggs. (See M. Dockery, *Callosobruchus maculatus* – a seed beetle with a future in schools, *Journal of Biological Education*, **31**, 262–268, 1997; in addition to explaining how this animal can easily be kept in captivity, this paper describes several investigations on its behaviour and gives details of how to obtain it.)

33 Keep Dwarf Russian hamsters (*Phodopus sungorus*) or golden hamsters (*Mesocricetus auratus*) in continuous dim red light and use an 'event' mode data-logging system to see whether they maintain a perfect 24 hour activity cycle or 'slip' by taking slightly shorter or longer than this. Simulate a flight to the other side of the world by resetting light and dark by 24 hours. How long does it take the animals to adjust? (See J. Cheverton, & F. Ebling, Datalogging hamster activity rhythms, *Journal of Biological Education*, **31**, 11–16, 1997, E. Morgan, Measuring time with a biological clock, *Biological Sciences Review*, **7** (4), 2–5, 1995 and C. D. Antinuchi, F. Luna, & C. Busch, Automatic data recording of circadian rhythms, *Journal of Biological Education*, **33**, 220–223, 1999.)

34 Record the mating calls of male stoneflies or cockroaches and see what effect playing back these calls has on (a) the male that produced it; (b) other adult males; (c) adult females. (See M. Vidal, E. Alvarez, & P. Membiela, Bio-acoustical experience with insects: the mating calls of stoneflies, *Journal of Biological Education*, **31**, 17–19, 1997.)

Observation of stages of mitosis in a growing root   5.1 PRACTICAL EXERCISE

In most tissues, new cells are formed as a result of mitosis. If the chromosomes of such cells are selectively stained with a dye such as acetic (ethanoic) orcein, stages in mitosis can be observed. An example of a tissue in which mitosis occurs is the **meristematic tissue** located in the **zone of cell division** in the apical meristem near the tip of a growing root. In this practical, you can try to prepare your own microscope slides. Skill and luck are required to obtain good results.

Procedure

1 Carefully cut the apical 5 mm from the tip of a growing lateral root of, for example, broad bean.
2 Place the root tip in a watch glass containing orcein ethanoic stain and $1.0\,mol\,dm^{-3}$ of hydrochloric acid in the approximate proportions of 10 parts of stain to 1 part of acid.
3 Warm, but do not boil, for 5 minutes on a hotplate, or by passing repeatedly through a low Bunsen flame.
4 Place the fixed root tip on a microscope slide and add 2 drops of orcein ethanoic.
5 Without interfering too much with the arrangement of the cells, break the root tip up with a mounted needle so as to spread it out as thinly as possible.
6 Put a coverslip over it, cover it with filter paper and squash gently by pressing down on the coverslip. Take care to avoid any lateral movement and don't break the coverslip.
7 Warm the slide on a hotplate for about 10 seconds, or quickly pass it through a Bunsen burner a few times. (This helps to intensify the staining. The slide should be hot, but not too hot to touch.)
8 Carefully examine the slide and identify any stages of mitosis. It may help to make annotated sketches showing the arrangement of the chromosomes.
9 Supplement the information obtained from your own slide by observing a prepared slide showing mitosis in a plant root tip (e.g. *Allium*) or an animal (e.g. *Ascaris*).
10 If possible, watch a film or video recording of mitosis. Notice in particular that it is a dynamic and continuous process. Dividing it up into a series of discrete stages is a helpful but arbitrary convention.

Orcein acetic

Hydrochloric acid

Eye protection must be worn

Requirements

Microscope
Slide and coverslip
Hotplate or Bunsen burner
Filter paper
Mounted needle
Razor blade or fine scissors
Watch glass
Orcein ethanoic stain
Hydrochloric acid $(1.0\,mol\,dm^{-3})$
Lateral root of, e.g. broad bean
Slide of LS through a plant root tip (e.g. *Allium*)
Slide of an animal (e.g. *Ascaris*) showing mitosis

For consideration

1 The acid added in step 2 above helps to soften the tissue. Why is this desirable?
2 How many chromosomes do there seem to be in each cell? Is this the haploid or diploid number?
3 Sometimes, search as one may, no dividing cells are visible in a root squash. Suggest possible reasons for this. (The authors hope that you have not been so unlucky!)

Note: Broad bean seeds should be germinated in blotting paper 10 days before the laboratory session. When the radicle is approximately 12 mm long, cut off its tip to stimulate growth of lateral roots. Suitable alternatives to broad bean include sunflower, hyacinth and garlic. Roots growing out from bulbs often give good results.

Reference

Martin, M. & James, C. Looking at chromosomes: a review of cytological methods. *Journal of Biological Education*, **27**, 171–172, 1993. (For other methods of examining mitoses in root tips.)

Preparation of a karyotype from a print of chromosomes

The diagnosis of chromosomal and genetic disorders during pregnancy is undertaken as part of **amniocentesis** and **chorionic villus sampling**. At present, little if anything can be done to treat chromosomal and genetic disorders revealed by these procedures. If the condition is severe, the mother is simply offered the option of a termination of pregnancy (abortion). In the future, though, it may become possible to treat some such disorders.

Chromosomal disorders are typically revealed by means of a **karyotype**. A karyotype is a conventional way of illustrating the chromosomes of a cell, as explained below.

Procedure

1   Figure 5.1 shows the chromosomes in a particular cell, photographed at metaphase of mitosis. Make a good quality photocopy of Figure 5.1, taking care to adjust the photocopying machine to maximise the contrast between the dark and light bands of the chromosomes. If possible, adjust the photocopier so that it doubles the size of the image.

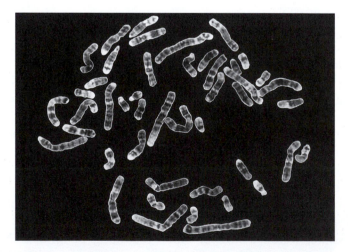

Figure 5.1 A set of human chromosomes stained to indicate banding structure, at metaphase of mitosis.

2   Carefully cut round all the chromosomes.
3   Count the number of chromosomes. What does the number suggest to you?
4   Assemble the chromosomes in pairs, taking care to match the chromosomes by length, centromere position and bands.
5   Arrange the chromosome pairs in order, starting with the largest and going down to the smallest. Place the sex chromosomes after the smallest autosomal chromosomes.

Requirements

Access to good photocopier
Scissors
Hand lens

For consideration

1 Does your karyotype show the chromosomes of a boy or a girl?
2 Does your karyotype confirm or refute your suggestion in step 3 above?

The cell cycle in the tip of a growing root

In a cell dividing by mitosis, the cell cycle is the series of events from a particular stage in a mother cell (e.g. interphase) to the same stage in the two daughter cells. In this practical you will be able to work out the relative amounts of time spent in interphase and the various stages of mitosis, by examining a prepared slide.

Procedure

1 Place a prepared slide of a longitudinal section through a root tip under a light microscope and focus at medium power.
2 Find the zone of cell division just behind the root cap. (Too near to the tip and you will focus on the protective root cap where little cell division occurs; too far from the root tip and you will be in the zone of cell differentiation.)
3 Ensure that you can identify the various stages of mitosis – **prophase**, **metaphase**, **anaphase** and **telophase**, as well as **interphase** (the stage between mitotic divisions). If necessary, refer to photographs or annotated diagrams in a text book.
4 Count a representative number of cells (50–100) and classify each of them into its stage.
5 Pool your results with others and work out the percentage of time spent in each of the five stages.
6 On the assumption that the cell cycle lasts approximately 8 hours in the cells in the zone of cell division, work out the duration of each of the five stages.

For consideration

1 Which stage lasts the longest and which the shortest?
2 Can you account for the differences in the lengths of the stages?
3 Explain how looking at a prepared slide enabled you to work out the relative lengths of the stages of mitosis.
4 Suggest how your results might have differed if you had been looking at a tissue in which the cells divide much more slowly.

Requirements

Microscope
Photographs or diagrams of stages of mitosis
Slide of LS through a plant root tip (e.g. *Allium*)

The stages of meiosis

The stages of meiosis can most easily be seen in immature anthers that are still enclosed inside the flower bud. Within such anthers, diploid **pollen mother cells** may be found dividing meiotically to form haploid pollen grains. In this investigation it is suggested that you examine prepared slides showing the stages of meiosis in a lily or other flowering plant and relate what you see to your knowledge of the movement of the chromosomes during these stages.

Guidance

1 Focus on your slide at high power.

2 Identify the various stages of meiosis – **prophase I**, **metaphase I**, **anaphase I**, **telophase I**, **prophase II**, **metaphase II**, **anaphase II** and **telophase II**, as well as **interphase I** and **interphase II**. If necessary, refer to photographs or annotated diagrams in a textbook.

3 Concentrate on cells in prophase I. Can you observe **chiasmata**? If possible, use oil immersion.

4 If chiasmata are visible, distinguish between **bivalents** with one chiasma, bivalents with two chiasmata and, if present, bivalents with three chiasmata. Use Figure 5.2 to help you.

5 Try to determine the diploid number of chromosomes in the species you are observing.

6 Compare your results with those obtained by observing a prepared slide of an animal testis.

For consideration

1 Why can meiosis more easily be observed in immature anthers than in mature anthers?

2 Were there any stages of meiosis you failed to see? If so, why do you think this was?

A Photomicrograph

B Interpretive drawing

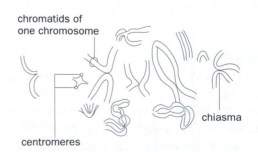

chromatids of one chromosome

centromeres

chiasma

Figure 5.2 Chromosomes at late prophase I in a meiotically dividing cell from the testis of a locust. Note the pairing of homologous chromosomes.

3   Why does the number of chiasmata in a bivalent in prophase I affect the appearance of the chromosomes?
4   What differences are there between meiosis in an anther and meiosis in an animal testis?

Observation of stages of meiosis in insect testis squash

A convenient place where the stages of meiosis can be seen is in the testes of a locust.

Procedure
1   Pin out a freshly killed male locust, dorsal side uppermost, under water in a dish. Pin out the wings on either side.
2   Open up the abdomen by a mid-dorsal longitudinal cut. Pin back the body wall.
3   Using a hand lens or binocular microscope, identify the testes. Together with fat, these make up an oval body lying above the gut in abdominal segments 5 and 6 (Figure 5.3). Transfer the testes to a microscope slide.

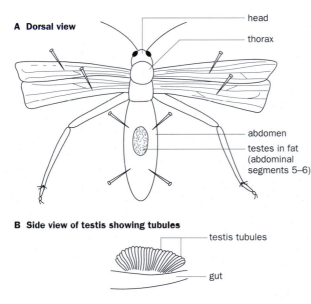

A Dorsal view
— head
— thorax
— abdomen
— testes in fat (abdominal segments 5–6)

B Side view of testis showing tubules
— testis tubules
— gut

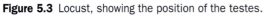

Figure 5.3 Locust, showing the position of the testes.

Requirements
Microscope
Hand lens or binocular microscope
Hotplate
Slide and coverslip
Small dissecting dish
Dissecting instruments
Glass rod
Filter paper
Orcein acetic stain
Locust (freshly killed)

Note: Use an adult male within 7–14 days of its last moult or a fifth instar male which is almost ready to moult into adulthood. Testes are easier to dissect from the desert locust (*Schistocerca gregaria*) than from the migratory locust (*Locusta migratoria*), as the desert locust has less fat.

4   Remove as much of the fat (yellow material) as you can, leaving the white tubules of the testis.
5   Gently squash the tubules with a glass rod so as to spread out the tissue. Remove excess water from the slide with filter paper.
6   Add several drops of orcein acetic stain and put on a coverslip. Cover with filter paper and squash gently, tapping the protected coverslip with the wooden handle of a blunt seeker (this helps to spread the chromosomes).

Orcein acetic

7 Warm the slide on a hotplate for about 10 seconds. This intensifies the staining. The slide should be very warm but not too hot to touch.

8 Examine the stages of meiosis.

For consideration

Which stages of meiosis (if any!) are most visible? Why do you think that this is?

Evidence relating smoking to lung cancer

This exercise extends over more than one session.

You will know that cigarette smoking is almost universally said to be bad for your health. But how sure are we of this?

Guidance

1 Obtain literature from one or more organisations opposed to cigarette smoking, and from one or more that are in favour of it. To get you going, try ASH (Action on Smoking and Health), 102 Clifton Street, London EC2A 4HW (tel: 020-7739-5902) and FOREST (Freedom Organisation for the Right to Enjoy Smoking Tobacco), 13 Palace Street, London SW1E 5HX (tel: 020-7233-6144). Your local hospital, general practitioner (GP) surgery or health clinic may have relevant leaflets too.

2 Carry out an internet search. You might try 'cigarette' and 'health' (together, not separately!)

3 Obtain some information from the longitudinal study – began in 1951 – of the cohort of British doctors whose smoking habits and health have been regularly monitored. Contact the Clinical Trials Service Unit and the Epidemiological Studies Unit, Radcliffe Infirmary, Oxford OX2 6HE.

4 What conclusions can you draw? How sure are you of these conclusions? Is there a consensus on the subject, or is the relationship between cigarette smoking and health controversial?

Requirements

Internet access

Note: It would be silly and inconsiderate for everyone in a group of students to write to the same people. Use common sense and organise your working to maximise the range and quality of the information you are likely to obtain.

For consideration

1 What does this investigation tell you about the nature of science?

2 What sorts of people might you expect (a) strongly to argue that smoking is bad for health; (b) strongly to argue that smoking is not bad for health?

Key skills

✓ **Information technology:** You will need to carry out internet searches to ferret out the relevant facts, frequently combining and exchanging information.

✓ **Working with others:** Organise the harvesting of this information with others; continually discuss progress, and what to search next, so that you do not duplicate effort.

Many herbaceous plants survive the winter by means of a **perennating organ** which lies dormant in soil over the winter and develops into one or more new plants the following year.

The perennating organ may be a modified stem, root, bud or leaves, depending on the species in question, but from whatever structure the perennating organ develops, the fundamental cycle of events is the same: food materials are translocated from the leaves of the plant to the developing organ, and the following year these food reserves are mobilised and moved to the growing regions of the new plant.

Perennation is often associated with **vegetative reproduction** (a form of asexual reproduction). In this investigation we shall look at some of the methods by which perennation and vegetative reproduction take place.

Guidance

Stem tuber

A **stem tuber** is a swollen underground stem which stores food, survives the winter, and gives rise to new plants from axillary buds the following year (Figure 5.4A).

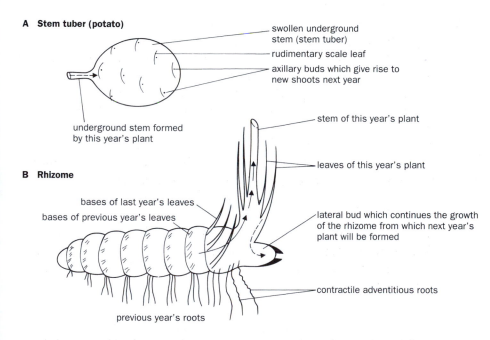

A **Stem tuber (potato)**
- swollen underground stem (stem tuber)
- rudimentary scale leaf
- axillary buds which give rise to new shoots next year
- underground stem formed by this year's plant

B **Rhizome**
- stem of this year's plant
- leaves of this year's plant
- bases of last year's leaves
- bases of previous year's leaves
- lateral bud which continues the growth of the rhizome from which next year's plant will be formed
- contractile adventitious roots
- previous year's roots

Figure 5.4 Two types of perennating organs formed from stems. Solid arrows indicate movement of food materials from the perennating organ to the new plant or new perennating organ. Broken arrows indicate movement of food materials from the foliage leaves into the perennating organ.

Examine a potato plant showing new tubers and, if possible, the remains of the old tuber. Now look at a single tuber. Being a stem, albeit a modified one, it possesses axillary buds and leaves in much the usual way. These are the so-called 'eyes' of a potato. Can you distinguish the leaves and the buds? You will probably know that the bulk of a potato tuber contains starch, but try testing different parts of a tuber for protein.

Rhizome

A **rhizome** is a horizontally growing underground stem which continues to live for many years (Figure 5.4B). Each year the terminal bud at the end of the stem turns up and produces leaves and flowers above the ground. At the same time, contractile adventitious roots are formed below ground. The lateral bud closest to the terminal bud continues the growth of the rhizome, food materials for this being supplied by the aerial shoot. In some species the rhizome is short and thick and grows slowly. In others it is long and thin and grows quickly. Which type do you think is shown in Figure 5.4B?

Examples of the short, thick type of rhizome include iris (*Iris*), water-lily (*Nymphaea*) and Solomon's seal (*Polygonatum*). Examples of the long, thin type include bracken (*Pteridium aquilinum*), couch grass (*Elymus repens*), marram grass (*Ammophila arenaria*) and ground-elder (*Aegopodium podagraria*).

Examine both types and test for food reserves. Cut transverse sections. Wear eye protection and stain in acidified phloroglucinol. What do you conclude?

Bulb

A **bulb** consists of a short vertical stem bearing adventitious roots, thick fleshy leaves (or leaf bases) and a variable number of axillary buds (Figure 5.5). In the centre is the terminal bud, which develops into a

Razor blade

Acidified phloroglucinol

Eye protection must be worn

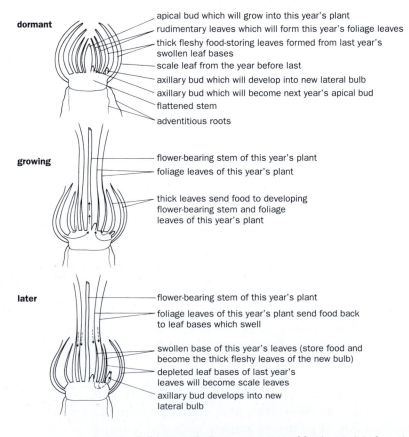

dormant
- apical bud which will grow into this year's plant
- rudimentary leaves which will form this year's foliage leaves
- thick fleshy food-storing leaves formed from last year's swollen leaf bases
- scale leaf from the year before last
- axillary bud which will develop into new lateral bulb
- axillary bud which will become next year's apical bud
- flattened stem
- adventitious roots

growing
- flower-bearing stem of this year's plant
- foliage leaves of this year's plant
- thick leaves send food to developing flower-bearing stem and foliage leaves of this year's plant

later
- flower-bearing stem of this year's plant
- foliage leaves of this year's plant send food back to leaf bases which swell
- swollen base of this year's leaves (store food and become the thick fleshy leaves of the new bulb)
- depleted leaf bases of last year's leaves will become scale leaves
- axillary bud develops into new lateral bulb

Figure 5.5 Diagram of a bulb. Solid arrows indicate movement of food materials from the perennating organ to the new plant or new perennating organ. Broken arrows indicate movement of food materials from the foliage leaves into the perennating organ.

new plant after the winter is over. The axillary buds develop into new bulbs.

Examine a bulb (e.g. an onion or a daffodil). Cut it vertically in half. Identify the various features, particularly the terminal bud and the fleshy leaves. Is each fleshy structure a complete leaf or just a leaf base? How do the outermost leaves differ from those further in, and what is their function? Test a leaf for food reserves.

Runner

Vegetative reproduction does not necessarily involve the formation of a perennating organ. Some plants reproduce vegetatively by sending out side-branches which develop into new plants. Such is the case with **runners** (Figure 5.6).

A runner is a horizontally growing, above-ground stem which grows from one of the lower axillary buds on the main stem. At intervals along the length of the runner are small axillary buds which give rise to new plants. Once the new plants are self-supporting, the internodal sections of the runner may wither away.

In the field, find some creeping buttercups (*Ranunculus repens*) with several runners and note the above features. Do the runners appear to be sent out randomly, or are they concentrated in one direction?

For consideration

1   Which structure or structures mentioned in this investigation involve:

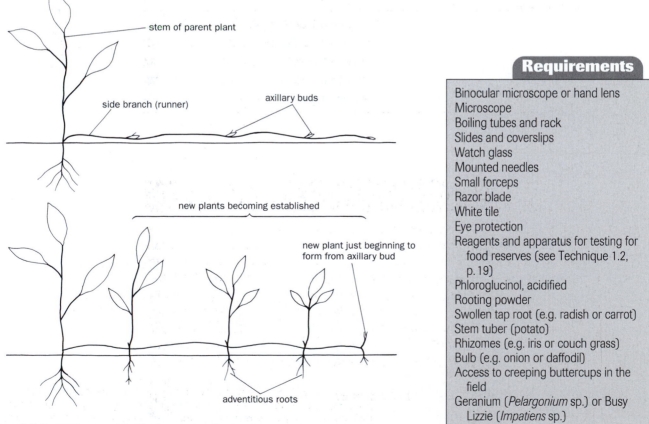

Figure 5.6 Vegetative reproduction by means of a runner.

Requirements

Binocular microscope or hand lens
Microscope
Boiling tubes and rack
Slides and coverslips
Watch glass
Mounted needles
Small forceps
Razor blade
White tile
Eye protection
Reagents and apparatus for testing for food reserves (see Technique 1.2, p. 19)
Phloroglucinol, acidified
Rooting powder
Swollen tap root (e.g. radish or carrot)
Stem tuber (potato)
Rhizomes (e.g. iris or couch grass)
Bulb (e.g. onion or daffodil)
Access to creeping buttercups in the field
Geranium (*Pelargonium* sp.) or Busy Lizzie (*Impatiens* sp.)

    a perennation and reproduction
    b perennation without reproduction
    c reproduction without perennation?

2 The products of asexual propagation of an individual are genetically identical. Why might it be useful for gardeners or farmers to grow genetically identical plants? What problems might be encountered as a result of this practice?

3 How could you test the hypothesis that creeping buttercups send out more runners in poorer soil?

5.8 INVESTIGATION   **The life cycle of 'fast plants'**

'Fast plants' or 'rapid cycling brassicas' (*Brassica campestris*, Figure 5.7) are closely related to the turnip and the Chinese cabbage. They were selected in Wisconsin, USA from cultivated ancestors for small size, short life cycle, uniform flower maturation, high fertility and absence of seed dormancy; they flower after 2 weeks and the life cycle lasts only 35 days (Figure 5.8). In order to grow and develop so rapidly, they must

Figure 5.7 'Fast plants' growing beneath a bank of high-intensity lights.

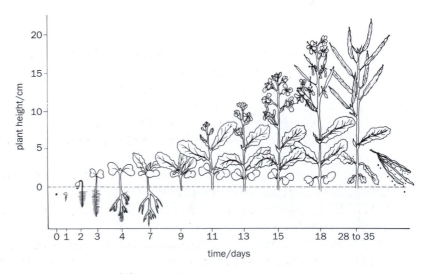

Figure 5.8 The life cycle of 'fast plants'.

be reared in peat/vermiculite in small containers under high-intensity lights. The aim of this practical is to demonstrate all the stages in the life cycle of a flowering plant in a very brief period of time.

Guidance

Sow three seeds of fast *Brassica* at least 2 cm apart about 5 mm below the surface of a 1:1 mixture of sieved peat and vermiculite and place the pot on the capillary mat in the light cabinet provided.

Examine and water the plants every 3 days, taking notes and drawing sketches to show the development of the organs. Many of the practicals and investigations over the next few pages can be performed on fast plants.

For consideration

Fast plants only retain their short life cycles if individuals that appear to have longer life cycles are persistently eliminated. A population of fast plants, left alone to reproduce, gradually reverts to a longer average life cycle. Explain in detail why this happens.

References

Price, R. Perfect plants for projects. *Biological Sciences Review*, **4** (1), 32–36, 1991.

Tomkins, S. P. & Williams, P. H. Fast plants for finer science – an introduction to the biology of rapid-cycling *Brassica campestris* (*rapa*) L. *Journal of Biological Education*, **24**, 239–250, 1990.

The Science and Plants for Schools (SAPS) website is at http://www-saps.plantsci.cam.ac.uk

Requirements

Equipment for growing fast plants, including light bank, capillary mat, small polystyrene containers such as test tube caps, nutrient pellets, water with 30 ppm copper(II) sulphate and mixture of 1:1 sieved peat and vermiculite. Details from SAPS, Homerton College, Cambridge CB2 2PH.

Note: 'Fast plants' (rapid-cycling *B. campestris*) and kits for growing them are available from MacIntyre Mottingham, Mottingham Lane, London SW12 9AW.

Microscopic structure of anthers and ovules

5.9 PRACTICAL EXERCISE

The internal structure of stamens and carpels can be seen most clearly in cross sections of unopened flower buds. The stamens produce **pollen grains** (the male spores) in **pollen sacs** in the **anthers**. The carpels ultimately contain **egg cells** (the female gametes) produced inside the **ovules** within the **ovaries**.

Procedure

1   Examine, under low power, a cross section of a flower bud of lily (Figure 5.9A) and identify the anthers.

2   Examine an anther under high power (Figure 5.9B). Notice the four pollen sacs and examine their contents.

3   The contents depend on the state of maturity of the anther:

   a   If immature, the pollen sacs will be full of closely packed **pollen mother cells**.

   b   If more mature, they will contain pairs or tetrads of cells (**pollen tetrads**) which result from meiotic division of the pollen mother cells. Chromosomes may be visible within the cells, revealing the stage of meiosis at which the cells were fixed.

   c   If completely mature, the anthers will contain separate pollen grains, each with a sculptured wall and one or two haploid nuclei (Figure 5.9C).

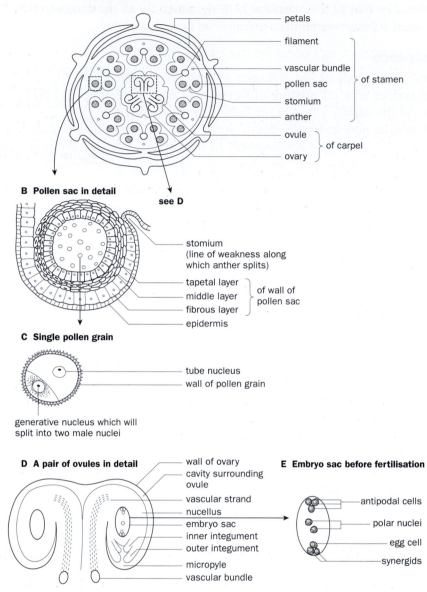

A Transverse section of flower bud

petals

filament

vascular bundle ⎫
pollen sac ⎪
stomium ⎬ of stamen
anther ⎭

ovule ⎫
ovary ⎬ of carpel

B Pollen sac in detail

see D

stomium
(line of weakness along
which anther splits)

tapetal layer ⎫
middle layer ⎬ of wall of
fibrous layer ⎭ pollen sac
epidermis

C Single pollen grain

tube nucleus
wall of pollen grain

generative nucleus which will
split into two male nuclei

D A pair of ovules in detail

wall of ovary
cavity surrounding
ovule
vascular strand
nucellus
embryo sac
inner integument
outer integument
micropyle
vascular bundle

E Embryo sac before fertilisation

antipodal cells

polar nuclei

egg cell

synergids

Figure 5.9 The microscopic structure of the flower bud of a lily (*Lilium* sp.).

4 Notice the **tapetum**, the layer of closely packed columnar cells which immediately surrounds each pollen sac and nourishes the developing pollen grains.

5 Look at the wall of the pollen sac and identify the middle and fibrous layers. When cells in the fibrous layer dry out, the tension causes the anther to split open at the stomium, a line of weakness that runs from the top to the bottom of each side of the anther, and the pollen grains are released.

6 Return to low power and identify the ovary in the centre of the flower bud (Figure 5.9A). Make sure that you can find the six ovules within it.

7 Examine an ovule under high power, and observe the structures labelled in Figure 5.9D.

8 Focus on the **embryo sac** in the centre of the ovule. How many nuclei can you see inside it? This depends on its state of maturity and on the level of the section:

The embryo sac starts by having a single haploid nucleus which is formed by meiosis from an embryo sac (**megaspore**) mother cell. The haploid nucleus of the megaspore then undergoes successive mitotic divisions to give a total of eight haploid nuclei, three at each end of the embryo sac and two in the centre (the **polar nuclei**). The nuclei at the ends of the embryo sac become surrounded by membranes to give the cells shown in Figure 5.9E. One of them is the female gamete (**egg cell**).

In the act of fertilisation, the female gamete fuses with one male nucleus (from a pollen tube) to give the **zygote**, which ultimately produces the embryo and the next generation. The two polar nuclei fuse with the other male nucleus to form a triploid nucleus which gives rise to the endosperm tissue. This envelops and nourishes the embryo.

After fertilisation, an ovule develops into a **seed** and the ovary wall becomes the fruit wall or **pericarp**.

For consideration

1 When and where does meiosis take place in a flowering plant?
2 In terms of the 'alternation of generations', the pollen grains represent the male spores and the germinated pollen grains represent the male gametophytes. What structures on the female side represent the equivalent female spores and female gametophytes in the life cycle of a flowering plant?
3 Compare the gametes, and the way in which they develop, in a flowering plant and a mammal.

Requirements

Microscope
TS of flower bud of lily (*Lilium* sp.)

Determination of seed viability   5.10 INVESTIGATION

A *viable* seed is one which is capable of germinating. **Germination** is regarded as the moment when the embryonic root (radicle), has protruded through the seed coat by a millimetre. Seeds in storage, or dormant underground, gradually lose their ability to germinate; in other words, they become *inviable*. It is necessary for seedspeople, farmers or gardeners to know the proportion of viable seeds in a batch, because this influences the sowing density, and hence the numbers of seeds required, and the overall cost.

Living seeds respire, and electrons produced in mitochondria reduce oxygen to water. Most of the methods to estimate seed viability depend on dyes that change colour when they are reduced. Several suitable compounds are available: for example, tetrazolium chloride, resazurin, and phenolphthalein diphosphate. (Phenolphthalein diphosphate is hydrolysed by starch phosphorylase to red phenolphthalein, and hence is only suitable for use with seeds which store starch.)

The metabolism of dormant seeds is slow but, after soaking, the respiration rate may increase a thousand-fold, and enzymes which break down starch begin to be made.

Guidance

Slice six soaked seeds in half. Try to identify how much of the inside of the seed is endosperm (that is, food store), and how much is embryo (that is, the next plant generation).

Dip the tip of a paint brush in the solution of the dye and spread it onto the cut surfaces of six seeds, making sure that you cover the embryo particularly thoroughly. Do not expect an immediate colour change. Wait for 5 minutes, watching the surfaces of the seeds to see where the colour change occurs first. How many seeds are viable?

Repeat the test on a sample of seeds which has been stored in the laboratory for some years.

For consideration

1 Where on the seed surface did the colour first appear, and what does this tell you about the localisation of either respiration or starch breakdown in the seed?

2 List possible reasons why seeds might lose their capacity to germinate over the years.

3 Suggest the advantages and disadvantages to a species of having long-lived seeds.

Razor blade

5.11 PRACTICAL EXERCISE

Structure and dispersal of fruits and seeds

A **fruit**, in the strict sense of the word, is formed from the **ovary.** The ovary expands once the ovules in it have been fertilised and begin to develop into **seeds**. The wall of the fruit, known as the **pericarp**, is derived from the ovary wall. It encloses and protects the seeds and frequently promotes their dispersal.

In practice, a number of other floral structures besides the ovary may contribute to the formation and distribution of the fruits. These include the **style**, **receptacle**, **sepals** and **bracts** (Figure 5.10). Constantly refer to this diagram as you investigate various fruits.

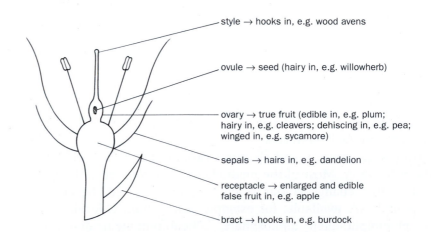

style → hooks in, e.g. wood avens

ovule → seed (hairy in, e.g. willowherb)

ovary → true fruit (edible in, e.g. plum; hairy in, e.g. cleavers; dehiscing in, e.g. pea; winged in, e.g. sycamore)

sepals → hairs in, e.g. dandelion

receptacle → enlarged and edible false fruit in, e.g. apple

bract → hooks in, e.g. burdock

Figure 5.10 Schematic diagram summarising examples of the contribution made to fruit formation and dispersal by floral structures other than the ovary. In most cases the ovary is situated above the receptacle as shown here (*superior ovary*); in other cases the ovary is sunk down into the receptacle (*inferior ovary*). There may, of course, be more than one carpel present, and in some cases the whole inflorescence may enter into the formation of the fruit.

Procedure

1 To set the scene, examine a **pod** of pea or bean. The pod is a fruit formed from a single carpel, the leathery pericarp of which splits along one or both sides. It used to be the ovary of a flower. The peas or beans inside it are seeds which began life as unfertilised ovules. The wild ancestors of our domesticated species probably released the seeds explosively, flinging them some distance, as in gorse (*Ulex* sp.) or broom (*Cytisus scoparius*) today.

2 Examine a fruit of buttercup or one of its close relatives, such as *Clematis* or *Anemone*. Notice that the fruit is little more than an expanded carpel containing a single seed (Figure 5.11A). Such fruits are known as **achenes**. How might they be dispersed?

3 Look at a fruit of wood avens. This is an achene too, but in this case the style becomes woody and its tip is hooked. It may cling to the fur of animals. Test its ability to cling to your clothes.

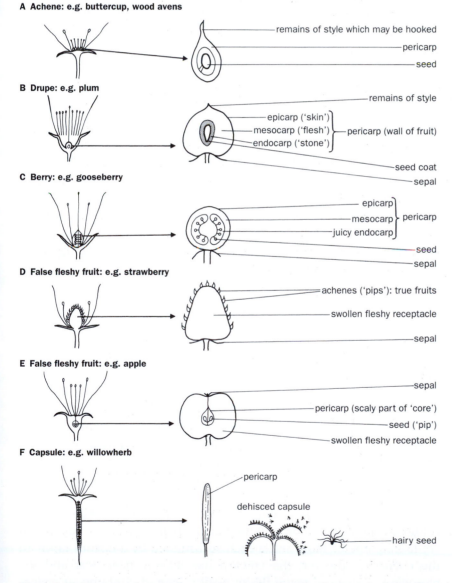

A Achene: e.g. buttercup, wood avens
- remains of style which may be hooked
- pericarp
- seed

B Drupe: e.g. plum
- remains of style
- epicarp ('skin')
- mesocarp ('flesh') } pericarp (wall of fruit)
- endocarp ('stone')
- seed coat
- sepal

C Berry: e.g. gooseberry
- epicarp
- mesocarp } pericarp
- juicy endocarp
- seed
- sepal

D False fleshy fruit: e.g. strawberry
- achenes ('pips'): true fruits
- swollen fleshy receptacle
- sepal

E False fleshy fruit: e.g. apple
- sepal
- pericarp (scaly part of 'core')
- seed ('pip')
- swollen fleshy receptacle

F Capsule: e.g. willowherb
- pericarp
- dehisced capsule
- hairy seed

Figure 5.11 Diagrams of a selection of fruits showing how, in all cases, the fruit is formed from the ovary and the seeds from the ovules.

4 Examine a fruit of goose grass. Notice the hooked hairs on the pericarp. It is another animal-dispersed species.

5 Members of the daisy family (Asteraceae, formerly known as Compositae) have flowers aggregated into heads known as **capitula**. A group of florets is situated on a platform and surrounded by modified leaves (bracts). Each floret produces a single fruit. In some species, the whole capitulum is dispersed as a unit after fertilisation, and the seeds fall out one by one.

6 Look at a bur of burdock, test its ability to cling to your clothes, and look for the single-seeded fruits inside.

7 Cut open a plum or cherry and examine its contents. This fleshy, succulent fruit, called a **drupe**, develops from a single carpel containing a single seed (Figure 5.11B). The pericarp is three-layered. A thin outer **epicarp** surrounds a fleshy and tasty **mesocarp**. Inside this the **endocarp** (the 'stone') protects the seed (against what?). How are these seeds dispersed?

8 Cut a tomato in half vertically, and another one horizontally. This kind of fruit (a **berry**) consists of several multiseeded carpels fused together (Figure 5.11C). Suggest other examples of this kind of fruit. Count the number of carpels in your cross section.

Razor blade

In a tomato the epicarp is thin and red, and the mesocarp and endocarp are soft, fleshy and juicy. The seeds have hard protective seed coats. How are they dispersed?

9 Examine the external features of a strawberry. In this case the red, edible part of the 'fruit' is formed from a swollen receptacle to form a **false fleshy fruit** (Figure 5.11D). Embedded in its surface are the numerous small dry fruits (**achenes**), each containing a single seed. Cut the strawberry vertically and notice the relationship between these achenes and the receptacle.

Razor blade

10 The apple is another example of a false fleshy fruit (Figure 5.11E). The sweet-tasting swollen receptacle surrounds the 'core', which represents the true fruit. In the centre, the pericarp surrounds the seeds ('pips'). The pear is similar. Cut an apple or pear vertically and horizontally through the centre. How many carpels are there, and how many seeds in each carpel?

Razor blade

11 Examine the fruit of rosebay willowherb. It is a **capsule**, formed from several carpels fused together. Determine the number of carpels by cutting the capsule transversely, which should also allow you to examine the hairy seeds (Figure 5.11F).

Investigate the mechanism by which the seeds of rosebay willowherb are released. Place the unopened capsule on a hotplate and observe the dispersal mechanism in action. What happens if you breathe onto the open capsule, or place it in a drop of water?

Razor blade

12 Examine the fruit of a sycamore tree. The wall of the carpel is expanded to form two (or in some species three) **wings**. Notice the twirling parachute effect when the fruit is thrown into the air.

13 Relatively few fruits are habitually dispersed by water. The coconut is an exception. Examine a half-coconut. It is a drupe, a fleshy fruit containing one or more seeds each surrounded by a fibrous layer. In the coconut, however, the epicarp has usually been lost and the mesocarp, instead of being fleshy, is fibrous and contains air spaces to aid flotation.

For consideration

1 Some seeds are dispersed on animals' coats and others are dispersed in animals' guts. Discuss the advantages and disadvantages of these methods.

2 Lines of hawthorn seedlings are sometimes seen to sprout up along fences or beneath telephone wires, and seedlings of many exotic plant species (e.g. tomatoes) are found on sewage sludge. Suggest explanations.

3 What type of fruit is a raspberry or blackberry, and what sort of flower gives rise to it?

Requirements

Binocular microscope or hand lens
Fine forceps
Razor blade
Ceramic tile
Hotplate
Fruits of pea (*Pisum sativum*) or bean (*Vicia faba*), buttercup (*Ranunculus* sp.), wood avens (*Geum urbanum*), goose grass (cleavers: *Galium aparine*), burdock (*Arctium* sp.), plum (*Prunus* sp.), cherry (*Prunus avium*), tomato (*Lycopersicon esculentum*), strawberry (*Fragaria × ananassa*), apple (*Malus pumila*) or pear (*Pyrus communis*), rosebay willowherb (*Chamanerion angustifolium*), sycamore (*Acer* sp.), and coconut (*Cocos nucifera*).

Structure and germination of pollen

5.12 INVESTIGATION

By using evidence from a variety of sources – scanning electron micrographs, microscopic examination and pollen germination – we can gain a comprehensive understanding of the role of pollen in the life cycles of flowering plants.

Acetocarmine
Methyl green in acetic acid

Methylene blue

Chloral hydrate
Phenol

Eye protection must be worn

Guidance

Collect pollen grains from the anthers of the plants provided, mount them in water and examine under medium power. Can you deduce from the structure of its pollen grains whether a species is insect- or wind-pollinated?

Look at pollen grains under high power. Clear some in chloral hydrate, and mount in iodine solution, or methyl green in acetic acid. Can you see the two-layered wall (functions?) and the two nuclei?

Next try to germinate some pollen grains. Transfer the grains of a mixture of species with a paint brush into a drop of sucrose solution (0.4 mol dm^{-3}) in the depression of a cavity slide. Put your slide in a dark place at 20–30°C and examine at intervals for 1–2 hours. Once you can see pollen tubes add a coverslip, irrigate with acetocarmine or neutral red, and look for nuclei. What normally happens to the two male nuclei in a pollen grain at germination?

Examine prepared longitudinal sections of pollinated gynoecia. Make sketches to illustrate the growth of the pollen tube into the stigma and down the style into the ovary.

Alternatively, squash the ripe stigmas of 'fast plants' (see Investigation 5.8, p.216), or a member of the daisy family, beneath a coverslip on a microscope slide. Irrigate with methylene blue and examine under medium power. You should be able to see germinated pollen grains with pollen tubes protruding from them.

Examine scanning electron micrographs of the pollen grains of different species. What can you infer from your observations?

Requirements

Microscope
Microscope slides and coverslips
Cavity slide
Paint brush
Sucrose solution (0.4 mol dm^{-3})
Chloral hydrate
Iodine solution
Methyl green in acetic acid
Acetocarmine or Neutral red
Methylene blue
Flowers of a variety of wind- and insect-pollinated plants (with ripe stamens)
Flowers of nasturtium (*Tropaeolum majus*), deadnettle (*Lamium* sp.), chickweed (*Stellaria* sp.) or grasses (with ripe stamens)
Prepared slides of LS of pollinated gynoecia
Scanning electron micrographs of pollen grains

For consideration

1 How could your pollen germination experiment be extended to investigate the effect of temperature?

2 It is said that, when a pollen grain lands on a suitable stigma, the latter produces a 2–4% sugar solution, which holds the pollen grains and facilitates their germination. How would you test the claim that the sugary secretion facilitates pollen germination? How would you determine the optimum concentration of the solution?

5.13 INVESTIGATION

Value of appendages in fruit dispersal

Many fruits and seeds have various appendages, such as the hairy 'pappuses' on dandelion fruits or the 'rotor blades' of sycamore, which are frequently interpreted as aiding wind dispersal. How much do they help? In this investigation you will assess the distances to which seeds fall with and without such dispersal structures normally attached to them, in both windy and still conditions.

Guidance

Look at the wild species with wind-dispersed fruits that are accessible to you, and the range of fruits available to you in the laboratory. Concentrate on two or three species. Collect the fruits if necessary.

If you have selected a tree, you can assess the efficiency of its fruit dispersal by (i) making careful observations and notes about the distances to which fruits fall around fruiting trees, and (ii) laying quadrats at measured distances from the trunk and counting the numbers of fruits per unit area.

In the laboratory, evaluate the roles of the appendages by dropping a sample of fruits from the same position onto large sheets of paper and recording the places where they land or come to rest. Measure and record the distances from the origin. Try this also in air blown from a hair dryer. Then cut off the appendages and repeat the experiments. Use a t-test (see Statistical Analysis Appendix, p.307) to test the hypothesis that there is no difference in the distance travelled by the fruits as a result of each treatment.

You could also find the dry mass of an appendage as a percentage of the fruit's mass. Then calculate the total annual investment by a parent plant in the appendages on its seeds or fruits, in terms of either mass or energy (appendages contain about $22\,\mathrm{kJ\,g^{-1}}$ dry mass). Is this investment by the parent plant worthwhile?

For consideration

1 Is the only role of the appendages you have investigated to help wind dispersal? Might they (i) reduce the numbers of seeds eaten by animals, (ii) aid water uptake for germination, (iii) facilitate burial when the seed reaches the ground, or (iv) place the embryo the right way up when the seed germinates? Evaluate each alternative.

Razor blade

Requirements

Quadrats
Measuring tape
Clip-board and recording paper
Large sheet of paper
Pencils
Metre rule
Hair dryer
Safety razor blade
Balance
Fruits or seed of species which appear to be wind-dispersed

Key skills

✓ **Application of number:** You will need to calculate the average distances travelled by the seeds with and without the appendages, and to estimate with a t-test whether or not these are significantly different. Then, calculate the average dry mass of appendages of each species from the measurements which you have made. Work out from this the annual energy invested in appendages.

It was discovered in the 1950s that whole plants could be grown from single cells. Unspecialised plant cells are **totipotent**: that is, they retain the potential to generate the whole range of specialised tissues which occur in an adult plant. The production of new plants from tissue fragments (**explants**) or from individual cells in sterile solution culture or on nutrient agar has become routine in agriculture and horticulture. It enables hundreds of individuals to be produced from a single plant. This is very useful if the parent plant is of a rare species, has a unique genotype, or is a virus-free individual.

The investigation has a considerable success rate with the 3 mm tip of an eye of a potato, the mini-florets from the florets of a cauliflower head, or a segment of a carrot tap root treated with the plant growth regulator 2,4-dichlorophenoxyacetic acid (2,4-D). In all such cases, it is essential to use sterile apparatus and technique. It is also just about possible to isolate single plant cells, and (we hope) watch them grow into new plants on sterile nutrient agar or nutrient solution, but this technique is much more 'hit or miss'.

Guidance

When setting up this experiment, take care to avoid contamination at all stages. Close windows and doors, swab your bench with 70% ethanol, wash your hands in 70% ethanol, and use sterilised instruments and glassware.

Ethanol

Cut off several fragments of the appropriate tissue and sterilise them in bleach solution for 10 minutes. Then, using sterile forceps, transfer the fragments through four separate washes of sterilised distilled water before placing them, widely spaced and gently pressed into the agar, in sterilised Petri dishes. As each culture is prepared, seal the lid with insulating tape and loosely surround the whole Petri dish with clingfilm. Transfer it to the growth cabinet at 20–28 °C in the light.

Clumps of cells, known as **calluses** and resulting from cell division, should develop over the next few weeks, and new plantlets will then develop from buds on their surfaces. Examine from time to time under a microscope, write detailed notes and keep a photographic record if possible.

For consideration

1. Similar procedures have been used for a long time in industry and horticulture. What has been their commercial value? A web search might help you to find out.
2. Individual plants can now be grown from pollen grains. What is unusual about such plants?

References

Fuller, M. P. & Fuller, F. M. Plant tissue culture using *Brassica* seedlings. *Journal of Biological Education*, **29**, 53–59, 1995. (For an alternative methodology.)

Steinitz, B. An exercise in the formation of potato microtubers in tissue culture. *Journal of Biological Education*, **31**, 119–124, 1997. (For potato tissue cultures, on which the influence of various compounds can be tested.)

> ## Requirements
>
> Beakers
> Microscope
> Sterilised forceps
> Sterilised Petri dishes
> Illuminated growth cabinet at 25 °C
> Insulating tape
> Clingfilm
> Sterilised distilled water (500 cm³)
> Ethanol, 70%
> Bleach solution (250 cm³ of 1% sodium chlorate(I) solution with 2 cm³ of teepol)
> Nutrient agar containing mineral salts, sucrose, vitamins, 0.1 mg dm⁻³ of 2,4-D and 2.5 mg dm⁻³ of kinetin, a cytokinin growth regulator.
> Floral meristems of cauliflower, tap root of carrot, or tuber of potato

5 Plot your results on linear (arithmetical) graph paper, with the number of cells per centimetre cubed on the vertical axis against time on the horizontal axis.

6 Plot a second graph of the results with, as before, time on the horizontal axis, but with the logarithm of the number of cells per centimetre cubed on the vertical axis. The easiest way of doing this is to use semi-logarithmic graph paper. On this kind of graph paper, the marks on the vertical axis have already been calibrated on a logarithmic scale.

7 Compare your two graphs. Forgetting about any differences in scale, are there any differences between the two plots? If there are, suggest reasons for these differences. What is the purpose of the semi-logarithmic plot?

For consideration

1 Describe the shape of your plot on linear graph paper. Explain the reasons for each phase of the curve.

2 From your semi-logarithmic plot, determine the length of time it takes for population size to double (the **doubling time**) during the exponential phase.

3 Below are estimates for the world human population since the year 1800:

Year	Population size
1800	8.1×10^8
1850	1.1×10^9
1900	1.7×10^9
1950	2.5×10^9
1960	3.0×10^9
1970	3.7×10^9
1980	4.5×10^9
2000	6.0×10^9

Plot these data on semi-logarithmic graph paper, putting population size on the vertical (semi-logarithmic) axis and the year on the horizontal (linear) axis. How does the plot compare with the semi-logarithmic plot for yeast? What factors may affect the world human population in future?

Reference

Monger, G. (Ed.). *Nuffield Advanced Science Revised Biology, Practical Guide 7: Ecology.* Longman, Harlow, 1986. (For assessment of the population growth of unicellular algae (e.g. *Chlorella*) by colorimetric methods.)

Requirements

Microscope
Haemocytometer
Graduated cylinder (50 or 100 cm³)
Conical flask (250 cm³)
Cotton wool
Pipette
Linear (usual, arithmetical) graph paper
Semi-logarithmic graph paper
Nutrient medium for yeast (e.g. cider, 2% sucrose solution or malt broth)
Suspension of brewer's yeast

Key skills

✓ **Application of number:** There are three graphs to draw, two on semi-logarithmic graph paper.

✓ **Information technology:** You should be able to work out a method of drawing these graphs by using a suitable computer program.

Development of shepherd's purse embryos

In a flowering plant the following changes take place after fertilisation: the zygote develops into the embryo; the endosperm nucleus divides to form a mass of tissue, known as the endosperm, which surrounds and nourishes the embryo; the ovule develops into the seed, the integuments forming the seed coat (testa); and the ovary forms the fruit (pericarp).

These developmental changes can conveniently be seen in *Capsella bursa-pastoris*, shepherd's purse.

Procedure

1   Examine a whole plant of shepherd's purse. The youngest part of the plant is at the apex, where unopened flower buds may be seen; further back open flowers should be visible; further back still, heart-shaped fruits should be seen. Trace the developmental sequence from apex to base. Two stages are illustrated in Figure 5.17.

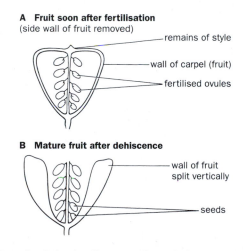

Figure 5.17 Fruit and seeds of shepherd's purse, *Capsella bursa-pastoris*.

2   Open one of the youngest fruits and note the two rows of ovules (Figure 5.17A). Remove a few of the ovules and mount in chloral hydrate or acetocarmine. Identify the structures shown in Figure 5.18A.

3   Mount ovules of different ages in chloral hydrate. Start with ovules from fruits towards the apex of the plant, and then work your way down the stem towards the base. In each case observe intact ovules first, then gently press the coverslip with a needle so as to burst the ovule and release its embryo. If the embryo is too transparent, try mounting another one in acetocarmine.

4   Using Figure 5.18 to help you, reconstruct the sequence of stages in the development of the embryo and the formation of the seed. What happens to the endosperm and suspensor as development proceeds?

5   Supplement the investigation by examining a prepared longitudinal section of the fruit of shepherd's purse.

For consideration

1   What is the function of the suspensor?

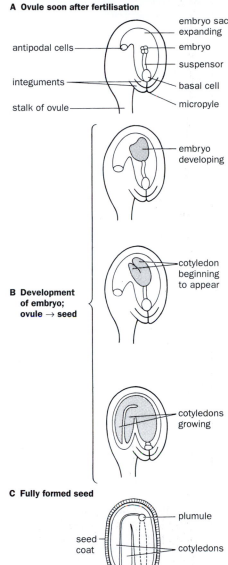

Figure 5.18 Diagrams illustrating development of the embryo and associated structures in shepherd's purse, *Capsella bursa-pastoris*. The diagrams are not all drawn to the same scale: the carpel and its contents grow steadily longer after fertilisation.

Acetocarmine   Chloral hydrate   Eye protection must be worn

2 During development the embryo bends over so the cotyledons point downwards. What are the consequences of this?

3 The final event in the formation of the seed is the loss of water, with the result that the water content is reduced from approximately 80% to 10%. What is the purpose of this? Suggest how it might be achieved.

5.19 PRACTICAL EXERCISE

Seed structure

In most seeds the embryo is surrounded by **endosperm tissue** which serves as a food supply during germination. In other seeds there is little or no endosperm, food being supplied by the enlarged **cotyledons**. Flowering plants are divided into **monocotyledons**, the seeds of which have only one cotyledon, and **dicotyledons**, the seeds of which have two cotyledons.

Whatever other factors are required for germination, one essential factor is water: the first clearly observable event in germination is the **imbibition** of water. As a result of this, the embryonic tissues swell and rupture the seed coat.

In this practical you will examine seeds and identify the ways in which they carry their food reserves.

A End-on view

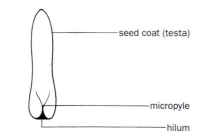

seed coat (testa)

micropyle

hilum

B Cut open

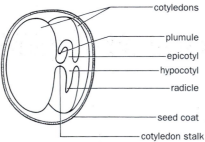

cotyledons

plumule

epicotyl

hypocotyl

radicle

seed coat

cotyledon stalk

Figure 5.19 Structure of broad bean seed.

Castor oil seed   Razor blade

Procedure

1 Examine dry and soaked seeds of the following plants: broad bean, castor oil plant and wheat. Determine the approximate percentage increase in mass after soaking.

2 Slice longitudinally through the soaked seeds and identify the structures you observe, using Figures 5.19, 5.20 and 5.21 to help you.

3 Determine whether each seed is endospermic or non-endospermic and monocotyledonous or dicotyledonous.

4 Carry out food tests on different parts of the seeds of each species (see p.19). It may help to present your results in the form of a table.

For consideration

1 Does the percentage increase in mass on soaking represent the percentage increase in water content? Explain your answer.

2 Were there substantial differences in the food reserves of different parts of the various seeds?

3 What are the advantages of seeds being in a dried-out state while they are lying in the soil?

4 Why is it necessary for a seed to absorb water before it can germinate?

5 How, and by what route, do you think these seeds take up water? How might your ideas be tested?

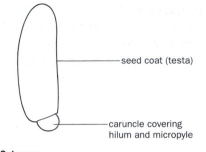

A End-on view

seed coat (testa)

caruncle covering
hilum and micropyle

B Cut open

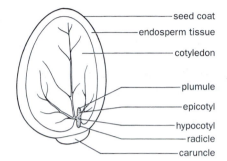

seed coat
endosperm tissue
cotyledon
plumule
epicotyl
hypocotyl
radicle
caruncle

Figure 5.20 Structure of the seed of the
castor oil plant, *Ricinus
communis*. Caruncles in most
species are adaptations for
dispersal by animals.

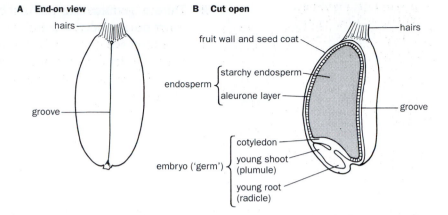

A End-on view

hairs

groove

B Cut open

hairs
fruit wall and seed coat
endosperm { starchy endosperm
aleurone layer }
groove
embryo ('germ') { cotyledon
young shoot (plumule)
young root (radicle) }

Figure 5.21 Structure of a wheat grain. A wheat grain is in fact a fruit, the seed itself being
inside.

Primary growth in flowering plants

5.20 PRACTICAL EXERCISE

Primary growth in flowering plants takes place at the apex of the stem
and root. It involves division of primary meristematic cells in apical
meristems. To examine primary growth it is necessary to study sections
and/or cleared whole mounts of young root and shoot apices. Clearing
is a process in which a chemical such as chloral hydrate is added to
make the section more transparent, and thus easier to see through.

Procedure

Root apex

1 Obtain a germinating seed of maize or some other grass (Figure
   5.22). Instead of having the main root found in many plants, most
   grasses, including maize, develop a bundle of **adventitious roots**.
2 Cut one of the roots about 1.5 cm from the tip and mount in chloral
   hydrate.
3 Examine under medium power, reducing the illumination as much
   as possible. Start with the extreme tip and work back to the older
   parts of the root. Note successively:
   a **Root cap cells** (protective)
   b **Zone of cell division** (cells cube-shaped, dividing mitotically)
   c **Zone of cell expansion** (cells progressively more elongated
      further back along the root)
   d **Zone of differentiation** (cells acquire features characteristic of
      specific tissues – xylem vessels with annular or spiral thickening
      should be evident).

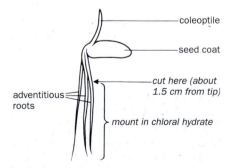

coleoptile
seed coat
cut here (about 1.5 cm from tip)
adventitious roots
mount in chloral hydrate

Figure 5.22 Preparation of young maize
roots for viewing under the
microscope.

Chloral hydrate

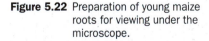

Razor blade

4   Take a germinating pea or bean with a radicle 1–2 cm long and examine it under a hand lens or binocular microscope. Describe what you see.

5   With a sharp razor blade, cut thin longitudinal sections and mount them in water or dilute glycerol. Examine under a microscope. Note the zones of cell division, expansion and differentiation. How do these relate to the root hair zone?

6   Examine a prepared longitudinal section of the root tip of onion (*Allium* sp.) under low and high powers (Figure 5.23). Start at the tip and work back noting, in particular, cells undergoing mitosis. Where are such cells most often found?

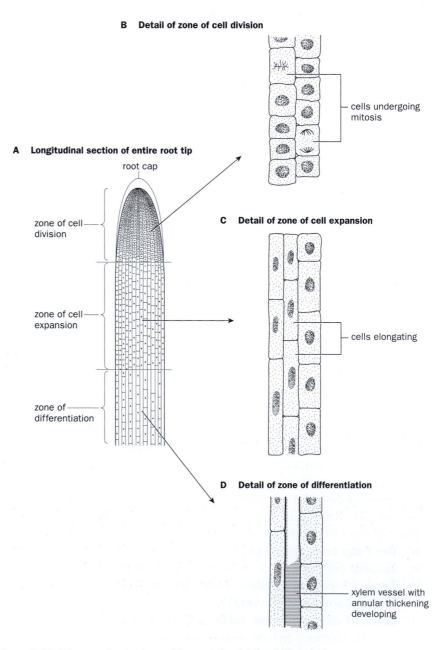

Figure 5.23 Microscopic structure of the root tip of onion (*Allium* sp.).

Shoot apex

1 Remove the tip of the plumule of a germinating broad bean, and cut it close to its attachment to the seed.
2 Holding the isolated shoot in a piece of moistened pith (see Technique 1.20 p. 49), cut transverse sections at levels **a**, **b** and **c** in Figure 5.24 and place them in water in separate labelled watch glasses.
3 Stain a thin section from each watch glass in acidified phloroglucinol, then mount in dilute glycerine.
4 Compare your sections. What conclusions can you draw regarding the development of primary tissues in the shoot?
5 Examine a longitudinal section through the shoot apex of, for example, lilac (Figure 5.25). Start at the tip and work back. How does the section compare with that of the root apex? In addition to the zones of cell division, expansion and differentiation, note the developing vascular strands, leaf primordia with vascular tissue going to them, and axillary buds.

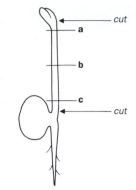

Figure 5.24 Young seedling of broad bean. Cut the shoot at the two points indicated. Section at levels **a**, **b** and **c**.

Acidified phoroglucinol

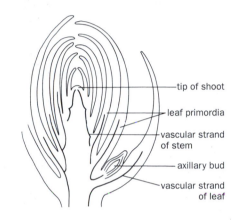

tip of shoot

leaf primordia

vascular strand of stem

axillary bud

vascular strand of leaf

Figure 5.25 Longitudinal section of the stem apex of lilac (*Syringa* sp.).

For consideration

1 Compare the development of a primary shoot and root. Explain the differences between them in terms of the functions that these two parts of the plant have to carry out.
2 In the apical meristem of a root or shoot, the cell divisions do not all occur in the same plane. Describe the planes in which they occur, and explain the contribution each makes to the developing organ.

Key skills

✓ **Problem solving:** Under 'For consideration' 2, you should consider the pattern of the cells in the various sections of the root tip, and work out the planes in which the divisions must occur – in other words, the directions in which new cell walls are formed – in order to allow the root to extend whilst maintaining the dividing tissues in essentially the same place. Repeat the prediction for the shoot tip.

Measurement of tropic responses of coleoptiles and roots

It is well known that stems usually grow towards light – that is, they are **positively phototropic**. In this experiment the rapid phototropic response of a coleoptile is observed and measured. The same technique can be used to measure the responses of coleoptiles and radicles to other stimuli (see Projects 15 and 16, p.247). For this experiment you require a microscope in which eyepiece has been fitted with a micrometer scale (see Technique 1.17, p.42).

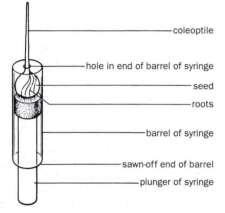

Figure 5.26 Moist chamber, constructed from a plastic syringe, for mounting a germinating seed for observations on phototropism (or other plant responses).

Procedure

1 Bend the microscope downwards towards you, so that the tube is horizontal and the stage vertical. Darken the room and arrange for the light to strike the microscope stage from one side.

2 Select a germinating seed with a straight coleoptile. Mount it in a moist chamber constructed from a plastic syringe (Figure 5.26), with the coleoptile protruding.

3 Attach the moist chamber horizontally to a microscope slide with an elastic band. Clip the slide to the microscope stage so that the horizontal coleoptile is pointing directly towards the top of the field of view. Position it so that the tip of the coleoptile, when viewed down the microscope, corresponds exactly with the midpoint of the micrometer scale. Illuminate it from one side and observe the tip of the coleoptile for 5–15 minutes until it starts moving in a definite direction.

4 Loosen the elastic band, and rotate the moist chamber through 180° on the slide so that the other side of the coleoptile now receives the strongest illumination. Adjust the position of the moist chamber so that the coleoptile tip points toward the midpoint of the micrometer scale, as before.

5 Take readings of the position of the coleoptile tip on the micrometer at regular intervals for up to half an hour.

6 Plot the positions of the coleoptile tip against time. What conclusions can you draw?

For consideration

1 State two reasons why the coleoptile was rotated through 180° at step 4 of the experiment.

2 What is the relevance of your results to the normal life of the plant?

3 Try to explain anything unexpected which happened during the experiment, or any anomalous results.

The tips of seedling shoots exhibit growth bending towards a light source. How do they detect the direction from which the light is shining?

Procedure

1 You are provided with four photographic film containers with coloured filters in the walls. For each container, cut out two circles of filter paper of sufficient size to fit into the base, insert them and add drops of water from a dropping pipette until the paper is moist.

2 Place onto the centre of the filter paper three germinating cereal grains or seeds of 'fast plants' (see Investigation 5.8, p. 216). Put the top on the container. Carefully place it where it will not be disturbed but will be equally illuminated from all sides.

3 Examine the seedlings at daily intervals, but never leave the top off the containers for long. Record the directions in which the coleoptiles or hypocotyls (shoots) bend, their lengths and colours. In the case of dicotyledonous fast plants, note the degree of unfolding of the cotyledons in each case.

4 Interpret your results with reference to the wavelengths of light transmitted through each filter.

For consideration

1 The containers were equally illuminated from all sides, but did the seedlings necessarily receive an equal intensity of light from all sides through the filters?

2 On the basis of the absorption spectra of various pigments in the plant, suggest which pigment(s) might be absorbing the light to which the shoots are responding.

3 In direction finding for a shoot emerging from the soil, why might it be advantageous for the shoot to respond to some wavelengths of light rather than others?

Requirements

Four photographic film containers, in the sides of each of which three 'windows' have been cut and filters stuck. One container should have a blue, a red and a green filter. The other three containers should each have the same colour of filter stuck over all the windows – blue for one container, red for a second and green for a third.
Filter paper
Scissors
Dropping pipette
Measuring scales, thin, graduated in millimetres
Seeds of wheat or 'fast plants' (*Brassica campestris* (*rapa*) L.) which have germinated to a point where the shoots are about 10 mm long.

Deciduous trees in the northern hemisphere lose their leaves in autumn. This is called **abscission**, and it seems to be a response to the increasing night length as the days shorten. The changes in night length, monitored by the pigment **phytochrome**, probably trigger abscission by altering the concentrations of plant growth substances in the leaves. This in turn causes a layer of cells, the **abcission layer**, to develop across the base of the petiole. Once this layer is in place, the leaf falls off.

One hypothesis is that the growth substance auxin, produced in the tip of a leaf, diffuses down the leaf stalk (petiole) during the summer and prevents the leaf from being shed. Leaves only fall off when the inhibition of leaf abscission ceases. In this experiment we test this idea on geraniums (*Pelargonium* sp.).

This practical exercise extends over more than one practical session.

Procedure

1 Select a mature *Pelargonium* plant with at least 12 leaves, and count the exact number of leaves.

2 By drawing numbers out of a hat, assign each leaf on the plant randomly to one of three treatments:
   - Treatment 1 (the control): the leaves receive no special treatment.
   - Treatment 2: the leaf blades (laminas) are carefully removed but the stalks (petioles) are left intact.
   - Treatment 3: the leaves are treated in the same way as treatment two – the blades are removed but the petioles are left – but in addition, a blob of lanolin containing 1% auxin is placed on the end of each petiole.

3 Set up the treatments, and as you do so, attach a numbered string tag to each petiole indicating the treatment which it has been given.

4 Keep the plant well watered in a light place. Examine it after 3 weeks, and again after 6 weeks. Record on each occasion exactly what has happened to each leaf. Are your results consistent with the hypothesis?

For consideration

1 How could you test experimentally whether an increase in night length triggers leaf abscission?

2 If a herbivore eats a leaf blade, what happens to the petiole?

3 What are the functions of the abscission layer?

4 Which other plant growth substances, besides auxin, are involved in leaf abscission and in what way?

5 Suggest four possible advantages to deciduous trees of losing their leaves in winter.

Requirements

String tags
Indoleacetic acid (IAA) in lanolin (1%) (see below)
Healthy leafy plant of geranium (*Pelargonium* sp.)

Note: IAA is an auxin; dissolve it in a little ethanol before mixing it into the lanolin. The pure auxin may be toxic, but a 1% solution carries no risk.

5.24 PRACTICAL EXERCISE

Gibberellic acid and the production of amylase in germinating barley grains

When a cereal grain germinates, the insoluble storage compounds in the endosperm, such as starch, are broken down to soluble sugars, such as maltose, which are absorbed by the growing embryo. What triggers the digestion of the starch in the endosperm by enzymes? One hypothesis suggests that the stimulus is provided by the growth substance **gibberellic acid** released from the embryo. The aim of this practical exercise is to determine whether or not gibberellic acid is necessary for germinating barley grains to release the starch-digesting enzyme, amylase.

Procedure

1 You are provided with eight Petri dishes containing blue starch–iodine agar. If amylase enzymes are released into this agar, they will digest the starch and the blue colour will disappear.

2 Four of your Petri dishes have had gibberellic acid incorporated into the agar and four have not. Label the bases of the dishes which have received gibberellic acid with G END L, G EMB L, G END D and G EMB D respectively. Mark the remaining dishes END L, EMB L, END D and EMB D. In this code, G stands for gibberellic acid, END for the endosperm end of the grain, EMB for the embryo end of the grain, L for living and D for dead.

3 Place 20 barley grains in a beaker of boiling water for 10 minutes. Then lift them out carefully with forceps and place them on a white tile.

4 Using a razor blade, cut each boiled grain transversely about halfway down (Figure 5.27). Make sure that you can distinguish between the

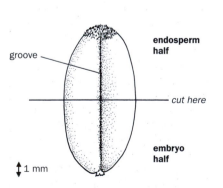

Figure 5.27 Diagram of barley grain to show where to make the transverse cut to separate the embryo and endosperm halves.

Razor blade

endosperm half and the embryo half. After each grain has been cut, transfer its endosperm and embryo halves to the appropriate D Petri dishes, with the cut side of the grain exposed to the agar. The two END D dishes should each receive 10 boiled endosperm halves, and the two EMB D dishes should each receive 10 boiled embryo halves. Place the grains on the agar as far apart from one another as you can.

5 Repeat step 4 with 20 unboiled grains. In this case the two END L dishes will each receive 10 unboiled endosperm halves, and the two EMB L dishes will each gain 10 unboiled embryo halves.

6 Place the Petri dishes in an incubator for 36 hours at 30 °C.

7 When incubation is complete, examine the dishes. For each grain in each treatment, record the diameter (in millimetres) of any clear region in the agar beneath the grain.

8 Examine the insides of the grains themselves. In which grains have the contents been liquified? Test the contents of the grains for reducing sugars with Benedict's reagent, or for glucose with Clinistix (Practical Exercise 1.4, p. 22). Record your results.

9 Calculate the area of the clear region surrounding each grain (area of a circle $= \pi r^2$). Work out the average area of the clear region in each treatment and tabulate the results. If you consider it appropriate, carry out a t-test to determine whether the grains in each treatment produced significantly different quantities of amylase (see Statistical Analysis Appendix, p. 307).

For consideration

1 Does gibberellic acid affect the production of amylase by barley grains?

2 Suggest a reason for the difference in amylase production between the boiled and unboiled grains.

3 Did your embryo halves produce some amylase? If so, how?

4 Gibberellic acid might cause the release by the aleurone layer of enzymes stored there. Alternatively, it might trigger the synthesis of enzymes as well as their release. Suggest two experiments which would distinguish between these hypotheses.

5 The brewing of beer begins with the production of maltose inside barley seeds. Suggest how this process could be speeded up.

References

Black, M. *Control Processes in Germination and Dormancy. Oxford Biology Reader 20*. Oxford University Press, Oxford, 1972.

Coppage, J. & Hill, T. A. Further experiments of gibberellin-stimulated amylase production in cereal grains. *Journal of Biological Education*, **7**, 11–18, 1973.

Freeland, P. W. Gibberellic acid enhanced α-amylase synthesis in halved grains of barley (*Hordeum vulgare*): a simple laboratory demonstration. *Journal of Biological Education*, **6**, 369–375, 1972.

Requirements

Marking pen
Bunsen burner, tripod, gauze
Beaker, 250 cm³
Forceps
Razor blade
White tile
Incubator at 30 °C
Refrigerator
Clinistix strip
Benedict's reagent
Petri dishes containing starch–iodine agar, ×8 (four containing gibberellic acid and four not; see below)
Barley grains, ×40 (soaked in water for 6 hours before the experiment)

Note: Prepare Petri dishes as follows:

Dissolve 200 mg of soluble starch in a little water and make up to 100 cm³. Heat until boiling and then add 1.5 g of Oxoid no. 1 agar powder. Stir vigorously until the agar is dissolved. Then split the hot agar into two halves. To one half add 0.5 cm³ of 100 ppm (0.01%) gibberellic acid in ethanol and stir. To the other half of the agar, add 0.5 cm³ of ethanol as the control.

When the agar cools to 60 °C, pour 10 cm³ into each of the eight Petri dishes, having distinguished the four control dishes from the four impregnated with gibberellic acid. Immediately add 2 drops of iodine solution to each dish. Stir vigorously, distributing the iodine to form a uniformly coloured gel. Store in fridge at 4 °C until required.

✓ **Application of number:** You should work out the average areas of the clear regions in each treatment, and then carry out a t-test to determine whether or not the grains produced significantly different quantities of amylase in each treatment.

✓ **Information technology:** Use the internet to find out about the role of gibberellic acid in the brewing industry.

5.25 PRACTICAL EXERCISE

Localisation and activity of enzymes at various stages of maize grain germination

First, familiarise yourself with the structure of a grain of maize (*Zea mays*) (Figure 5.28). On the outside, the seed and fruit walls are fused. Within the large seed, a small plate-like embryo, the potential new plant, is embedded in a large starchy endosperm, a food store.

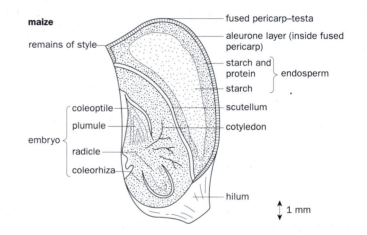

Figure 5.28 Vertical section through grain (fruit) of maize (*Zea mays*) – the old inflorescence, covered with such fruits, is sweetcorn or corn on the cob.

When a cereal grain germinates, its starch reserves are broken down. One of the enzymes involved is **starch phosphorylase**, which yields glucose.

Stages in this process can be followed in maize by using stains to detect starch, starch phosphorylase and glucose.

The procedure below describes how to stain seedlings of the same age. If, however, seeds at different stages of germination are available, the events that occur during germination can be followed in sequence.

Procedure

Eye protection must be worn

Gloves should be worn

Fungicide

Silver nitrate

1   Select two maize seedlings at the same germination stage. Cut each one carefully down its longitudinal axis to produce a total of four half-seedlings.

2   Using forceps, place a single half-seedling into each of the three solutions provided so that the cut surface is immersed in the liquid. The three solutions contain iodine, silver nitrate and phenolphthalein diphosphate respectively. Do not get silver nitrate on your fingers, as it is corrosive and it stains.

3   Leave your half-seedlings in the solutions for at least half an hour.

4   Remove the half-seedling from the iodine solution. This stains starch a blue colour. Draw a diagram to show the distribution and intensity of the blue staining on the cut surface of the seedling. Ignore the brown colour of the iodine itself.

5   Remove the half-seedling from the silver nitrate solution. This stains reducing sugars (such as glucose) black. Draw a diagram to show the distribution and intensity of the black staining.

6   Remove the half-seedling from the phenolphthalein diphosphate solution. In the presence of starch phosphorylase enzymes, the solution is hydrolysed to phenolphthalein, which gives a red colour in alkaline solution. Place the half-seedling in the 'alkali' solution for 2 minutes. Examine it and draw a diagram showing the distribution and intensity of the red colour.

For consideration

1   Account for the distribution and intensity of colours in terms of the biochemistry of seed germination. Assume that the starch phosphorylase activity is proportional to the metabolic rate of the tissues.

2   Which parts of the embryo are most metabolically active, and why?

3   Of what use will glucose be to the embryo?

Notes: Preparation of solutions and maize seedlings

1   Iodine: Dissolve 4 g of potassium iodide in 600 cm³ of distilled water, add 2.5 g of iodine crystals and make up to 1 dm³.

2   Silver nitrate: Make up a small volume with 1.7 g per 100 cm³ of distilled water.

3   Phenolphthalein diphosphate: Dissolve 0.5 g of the calcium salt in 100 cm³ of distilled water. Store in a refrigerator until needed and filter before use.

4   'Alkali': 0.1 mol dm⁻³ sodium hydroxide.

5   Maize seedlings: Use a large-seeded variety which has been treated with a fungicide. Sow in cool, well-lit conditions about 2 weeks before the practical session. The maize should have germinated to the point where the radicles have emerged but not started branching, and the plumules have emerged but have not broken through the coleoptiles. Before use, wash the seedlings thoroughly to remove soil. After handling the seedlings, wash your hands thoroughly to remove any fungicide.

Effect of an impermeable testa on seed germination

5.26 INVESTIGATION

The seeds of many species remain dormant for some time because the seed coat is impermeable to water and oxygen. Germination occurs sporadically when the seed coats are damaged. Seeds in this category include those of rock rose (*Helianthemum* sp.) and many members of the family Leguminosae (Fabaceae) – gorse (*Ulex* sp.), broom (*Cytisus scoparius*), vetches (*Vicia* sp.), etc.

Design and carry out an experiment to test the hypothesis that seeds of a particular species will only germinate if the testa is damaged.

Guidance

Seeds can be held in forceps and chipped with a mounted needle. They can be germinated on two layers of moistened filter paper in Petri dishes.

For consideration

1　Why do you think that undamaged seeds do not germinate? Suggest an experiment to test your hypothesis.
2　Suggest ways in which the testa of a seed in the soil might be broken down under natural conditions.
3　What effect will an impermeable testa have on the timing of germination under natural conditions? In what circumstances might this be favourable to the species?

Key skills

✓　**Application of number:** Provided that you have replicated your Petri dishes, carry out a suitable statistical test of the hypothesis that the number of seeds germinating in the chipped and unchipped treatments is the same.

5.27 INVESTIGATION

Effect of gibberellic acid on hypocotyl elongation in seedlings[BM]

This investigation extends over more than one practical session.

In Gregor Mendel's peas, those which had one or two alleles for 'tallness' grew to a height of nearly 2 m, whereas 'short' plants lacked this allele and reached a height of only about 0.5 m. Mendel himself had no idea *why* this happened, but today we are in a position to speculate about it. One hypothesis explaining how the alleles influence height is that the tall plants produce enough of the plant growth substance, gibberellic acid, to elongate rapidly, whereas the short plants do not produce enough growth substance to achieve this.

Gibberellic acid is effective in very small quantities (around $10^{-9}\,mol\,dm^{-3}$) and its concentration in plant tissues is difficult to measure. It is possible, however, to test the hypothesis that the absence of gibberellic acid causes tall plants to be short. All you have to do is to add gibberellic acid (in lanolin) to short plants and see if they turn into tall ones.

Guidance

Fungicide

This investigation takes several weeks. Design it carefully. Pea plants (*Pisum sativum*) or rapid-cycling brassicas can be used. Germinate the seeds of tall and dwarf varieties at equivalent densities in pots but, when planting, allow for seeds which do not germinate or which become infected.

You will need to try various ways of adding the gibberellic acid in lanolin to the short plants without damaging their shoot meristems and hence their capacity to grow. An obvious way is to place a dollop of lanolin containing $10^{-6}\,mol\,dm^{-3}$ of gibberellic acid on the shoot apex of each short plant, amongst the terminal leaves, when it is 8 cm tall. As this may supply too much gibberellic acid to the tissue, it may be wise to incorporate in the experiment some lanolin at $10^{-8}\,mol\,dm^{-3}$ of gibberellic acid.

Measure the heights of all the plants at frequent intervals. Make sure that each treatment is applied to several plants. Then you can ultimately perform t-tests (see Statistical Analysis Appendix, p. 307) to determine whether or not there is a significant difference in mean growth rate between the plants which have received extra gibberellic acid and those which have not.

For consideration

1 On the basis of your results, is the absence of gibberellic acid sufficient on its own to account for the difference in height between the short and tall phenotypes?
2 What does the dominant allele for tallness code for?
3 Does gibberellic acid increase the rate of cell division or cause each cell to grow longer, or both. How would you investigate this?

Ethanol

✓ **Application of number:** Once you have determined the average growth rates in the various treatments, you can perform t-tests (see Statistical Analysis Appendix, p. 304) to determine whether or not there is a significant difference in mean growth rate between the plants which have received extra gibberellic acid and those which have not.

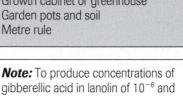

Requirements

Seeds of tall and dwarf plants of the same species (e.g. pea, *Pisum sativum*, or rapid-cycling brassicas – see Investigation 5.8, p. 216) from biological suppliers
Gibberellic acid in lanolin (see below)
Growth cabinet or greenhouse
Garden pots and soil
Metre rule

Note: To produce concentrations of gibberellic acid in lanolin of 10^{-6} and 10^{-8} mol per litre, dissolve measured masses of the plant growth substance into small quantities of ethanol before stirring into the lanolin.

Key skills

Effects of rooting powders and weed killers[BM]

5.28 INVESTIGATION

Some plant growth regulators, either natural or synthetic, are useful in gardening and farming. You can devise your own investigation to assess their effects and their efficiency.

There are three possibilities:

- Rooting powders, rubbed onto the base of cut stems, are meant to stimulate the rapid formation of roots (strictly, these should be called adventitious roots, because they do not arise from the usual place in the usual way).
- Some synthetic compounds not only disrupt the growth of plants and kill them, but are **selective**: when applied to a mixture of plant species at the right concentration, they kill the broad-leaved species (the dicotyledonous weeds) whilst allowing the crop grasses, such as wheat, barley, rice or maize, to survive. In this investigation we suggest that you use a commercial preparation of an auxin analogue, such as 2,4-dichlorophenoxyacetic acid or 2,4,5-trichlorophenoxyacetic acid.
- Maleic hydrazide is used to slow down the growth of patches of vegetation, such as the plants on a roadside verge.

Guidance

Decide exactly what you want to investigate. Discuss with your fellow students the principles of designing your investigation. In the case of the rooting powder investigation, you will be supplied with young plants from which you can take cuttings, and in the case of the weedkiller

This investigation extends over more than one practical session and should be carried out by the whole class working as a group.

Razor blade

Potentially toxic plant growth regulators

Caution

Although the concentration of growth regulator that you will use is low, safety is important. Look at the instructions on the outside of the container and obey them. In particular, wash your hands thoroughly if they come into contact with the preparation, and do not breathe in droplets of the fluid.

experiment, with mixtures of a cereal and a broad-leaved weedy species grown in pots.

You will need to decide:

- What 'controls' do you need?
- How many 'replicates' do you require? At least four repeats of each treatment are recommended.
- How will the treatments be applied, paying due regard to safety?
- What apparatus will be needed?
- What measurements will be collected to assess the efficacy of the treatments, and how often? The measurements must be numerical, so that the data can be analysed statistically.
- Who will keep an eye on the plants and who is responsible for collecting the results, and when?

After the data have been collected, it is important that each individual should write up the class results, and carry out, for experience, his or her own statistical analysis.

For consideration

1 What are the pros and cons of using the terms 'growth regulators' and 'plant hormones' to refer to compounds such as those you have used in your experiment?
2 If you have shown that the growth regulator has a significant effect on plant growth, speculate on how it might work to affect growth at the level of cells, genes and enzymes.

Requirements

Greenhouse or laboratory bench where the experiment can be undisturbed for 2–3 weeks if necessary
Marker pens
For rooting powder experiment:
  Trays or pots of suitable plants from a garden shop
  Beakers
  Muslin or gauze
  Elastic bands
  Razor blades or scalpels
  Nutrient solution in distilled water
  Rooting powder
For experiments with selective herbicides or growth retardants:
  Mixtures of a cereal grass (e.g. wheat) and a broad-leaved herb (e.g. lettuce) grown up in seed trays or pots (×10 at least)
  Watering can or spray bottle
  Selective herbicide or growth retardant

Key skills

✓ **Application of number:** Select and carry out an appropriate statistical test from the Statistical Analysis Appendix (p. 304).
✓ **Working with others:** Work out what to do in discussion with your classmates; you will also have to organise the collection of data amongst yourselves over several days.

► Projects

Before starting a project, as on p. 57 assess the risks inherent in your intended procedure and discuss your intended procedure with your teacher/lecturer.

1 Use the technique suggested on p. 209 (for staining cells dividing by meiosis) to stain cells obtained from immature anthers in the dormant inflorescence of a hyacinth bulb. Vary your approach (e.g. maturity of anther, length of time acetic orcein applied) to obtain the best results.
2 Grow onions or daffodils and examine the bulbs at different stages of development.
3 Compare the success of different commercial rooting powders at rooting cuttings.
4 Compare the reproduction and growth of different species of

mammal, for example rabbit and cat. You will need to make accurate observations of things such as number of offspring in a litter, their weight gain and their development. Supplement your findings with information from secondary sources (e.g. on age at first reproduction and gestation length).

5 Compare the urinogenital system of a rat with that of a mouse or a rabbit. Dissect the urinogenital system of a mouse or a rabbit and compare your findings with those in Practical Exercise 5.15, p. 226.

6 The 'pollen count' is the number of pollen grains caught on a sticky microscope slide exposed to the air for 24 hours. Devise a brief questionnaire which can be rapidly completed each day by classmates who suffer from hay fever to record their

degree of suffering. Then correlate your pollen count with a 'suffering index'. Do some types of pollen grain contribute more to suffering than others?

7 Investigate the pollinators or pollination mechanism of any species which interests you – for example, Lords and Ladies (*Arum maculatum*). (See D. H. T. Jones, Studying Lords and Ladies, *Arum maculatum* (L.), *Journal of Biological Education*, **11**, 253–260, 1977, who gives fascinating suggestions for project work.)

8 Capture, and etherise carefully and temporarily, a small sample of bees from one specific area (**danger!** stings). Relate the average tongue length of each bee species to the flowers it has visited (as shown by the range of species amongst the pollen grains it has collected) and the average length of the corolla (petal) tube of each flower species.

9 Work out the best pattern of foraging for a bee collecting nectar when it encounters a patch of flowers (those of the Lamiaceae (Labiatae), such as catmint, deadnettles, woundworts or sages, are particularly suitable, but foxgloves will do). Then test your ideas by following individual bees. (See B. La Ferla, Bee–flower interactions: a field test of an optimal foraging hypothesis, *Journal of Biological Education*, **34**, 147–151, 2000.)

10 Investigate the structure and movement of the awns attached to the fruits of grasses such as wild oats, *Avena fatua*. These awns are said to be hygroscopic, altering in shape as the relative humidity of the atmosphere changes. It has been suggested that they facilitate burial of the fruit in soil, or place it at the optimal angle for germination, or, by twisting and turning, enable the fruit to travel over the surface. (See, e.g. J. Q. Hou & G. M. Simpson, The adaptive significance of awns and hairs on grasses, *Journal of Biological Education*, **26**, 10–11, 1992.)

11 Evaluate the hypotheses that the dispersal appendages of wind-dispersed seeds or fruits (a) aid water uptake for germination, (b) place the embryo the right way up when the seed germinates.

12 Investigate the factors that affect the rate at which seeds absorb water before germination.

13 In many species seed germination is inhibited by the presence of leaf canopies above the seeds. Test this assertion with seeds on moistened filter paper in Petri dishes with and without a permanent covering of leaves. Suitable experimental species include lettuce (*Lactuca sativa*) var Grand Rapids, and dandelions. (See E. L. Oxlade & P. E. Clifford, The versatile dandelion, *Journal of Biological Education*, **33**, 125–129, 1999.) With Grand Rapids lettuce, try exposing them to different qualities of light under Lee filters, alternating red and far-red light, and using various periods of exposure to light. (See M. J. Wagner, & A. M. Wagner, A simple and effective filter system for experiments with light-dependent processes in plants, *Journal of Biological Education*, **29**, 170–172, 1995.)

14 Investigate the effects of plant growth substances on the growth of calluses in tissue culture.

15 Determine the region of the coleoptile which detects the stimulus in the experiments in which a germinating seed is mounted in a moist chamber and viewed under the microscope (Practical Exercise 5.21, p. 238) and in which seedlings are exposed to light filters (Practical Exercise 5.22, p. 239). Compare the responses of intact seedlings with those that have had different lengths of their coleoptile tips excised.

16 Investigate one or more of the following responses:

  a the response to the directional illumination of a coleoptile from which the tip has been removed

  b the response of a coleoptile to gravity

  c the response of a radicle to directional illumination

  d the response of a radicle to gravity

  e the response to gravity of a radicle from which the root cap has been removed.

  In each case you will have to think out carefully how best to apply the stimulus. Draw such conclusions as you can, and carry out other experiments of your choice to throw light on how coleoptiles and radicles respond to stimuli. In some experiments, use the technique of mounting a germinating seed in a moist chamber and viewing it under the microscope (Practical Exercise 5.21, p. 238).

17 Examine changes in photosynthetic pigments, and in the concentrations of starch and glucose, in ageing leaves of various ages, and speculate on the value to the plant of these trends. Pigments can be separated by paper or thin layer chromatography (see Practical Exercises 1.6 and 1.7, pp. 25 and 28). Starch concentrations can be estimated with iodine solution and glucose concentrations can be estimated with a Benedict's test. (See Technique 1.4 p. 22, and J. Gill, P. Howell & T. Saunders, The biology of ageing in leaves, *Journal of Biological Education*, **22**, 167, 1988.)

18 Investigate the effects of various treatments intended to prevent the senescence of commercially important crops, such as green bananas, carnations or lettuce. Possible methods of preservation include clingfilm, refrigeration, sealing in polythene bags and, for flowers, anti-bacterial agents in the water. (For background information read G. Hobson, Slowing the deterioration of fruits and vegetables after harvest, *Journal of Biological Education*, **26**, 100–105, 1992.)

6.1 INVESTIGATION — Monohybrid inheritance in tobacco seedlings

I n this investigation you will be provided with a sample of tobacco seeds obtained from one plant. Your job is to grow the seeds to the point where you can identify two **phenotypes** (distinct characters) in the plants, and then predict the **genotypes** (genetic constitutions) of the parent plants.

Guidance

Fungicide

Sow the seeds in flat trays or pots at a density of not more than one seed to $4\,cm^2$. Wash your hands if you have touched seeds (in case they have been treated with fungicide). Keep in a warm, light place and water every 2 or 3 days, but without water-logging the plants. After about 15–20 days, observe and describe any differences between the seedlings with respect to such features as colour of the cotyledons, colour and hairiness of the stems, and the shape of the leaves. Count the number of tobacco plants showing each feature. Calculate the ratio between them and draw such conclusions as you can.

For consideration

1   From your results, predict the *genetic* constitution of the parent plants and calculate what *phenotypic* ratios you would expect among the offspring.
2   How close are your actual ratios to those predicted? Use the chi-squared test (χ^2-test) to analyse them statistically (see p. 312).

Reference

Barker, J. A. Practical genetics with tobacco. *Journal of Biological Education*, **30**, 179–170, 1996.

Requirements

Tray of soil approx. 40×20 cm *or* small pots
Potting compost
Seeds of monohybrid tobacco (*Nicotiniana tabacum*)

Assessment

• **Plan** your investigation. What is your hypothesis? Justify the number and types of measurements you make.

• **Implement** your plan. Did you damage any of the seedlings? How can you be sure that your measurements were valid?

• **Analyse your evidence** and **draw conclusions**. Would graphs or tables be more suitable for the presentation of your results? What do your statistical findings tell you? Interpret your findings in terms of your knowledge of chromosome structure and meiosis.

• **Evaluate** your investigation. Are your conclusions clear cut or tentative? Were there any limitations as far as your methods went? Can you suggest one further investigation to provide additional relevant information?

6.2 PRACTICAL EXERCISE — Monohybrid and dihybrid inheritance in maize

In maize, *Zea mays* (corn), a single cob (ear) is covered with several hundred kernels which represent the fruits. Each kernel contains a single seed. Each seed contains a diploid embryo formed as a result of a single fertilisation. The fertilisations which created the different seeds are independent of each other.

Maize kernels display a number of easily recognised characteristics such as colour and shape: thus they may be purple or yellow, smooth or shrunken, etc. In this practical it is suggested that you examine the phenotypes of the kernels on a number of cobs and make deductions about the genotypes of the parent plants.

Procedure

Monohybrid inheritance (one pair of alleles)

1. Examine cobs **A** and **B**. For each cob, count the number of yellow and purple kernels and determine the ratio between them. Do you think it is sufficient to count the kernels in one (or several) rows, or should all the kernels in the cob be counted?
2. Which is the genetically dominant colour, yellow or purple?
3. What can you say about the genotypes of the yellow and purple kernels on cob **A**?
4. What can you say about the genotypes of the yellow and purple kernels on cob **B**?
5. Consider the parents of the kernels on cob **A**. What is the genotype of each for kernel colour?
6. Consider the parents of the kernels on cob **B**. What is the genotype of each for kernel colour?
7. Construct genetic diagrams to illustrate the crosses involved in the production of cobs **A** and **B**.
8. Examine cob **C**, and notice that some kernels are more shiny than others. Determine the ratio between the two types.
9. The shiny and non-shiny kernels in cob **C** differ in their starch content. Carefully shave off the top of a kernel of each type with a razor or scalpel and stain the cut surfaces with iodine solution. Notice any differences. A blue-black colour indicates starch; a red colour indicates dextrin. Dextrin is a carbohydrate intermediate in size between maltose and starch.

Razor blade

Dihybrid inheritance (two pairs of alleles)

1. Examine cobs **D** and **E**. The kernels differ from each other with respect to *two* pairs of characteristics: each is yellow or purple, *and* wrinkled or smooth.
2. In each of cobs **D** and **E**, estimate or count the number of kernels that are:
   a yellow and wrinkled
   b yellow and smooth
   c purple and wrinkled
   d purple and smooth
3. Construct genetic diagrams illustrating the possible crosses involved in the production of cobs **D** and **E**.

For consideration

1. In terms of relationships within a human family, describe the relationship between two kernels belonging to the same maize cob.
2. Which of the five cobs could have been the result of self-pollination?
3. What tentative conclusions about the way genes work can you draw from your study on cob **C**?

Requirements

Maize (corn) cobs showing segregation for the following kernel characters:
  Cob **A**: yellow, purple (monohybrid)
  Cob **B**: yellow, purple (a different monohybrid ratio)
  Cob **C**: non-shiny (starchy), shiny (waxy) (monohybrid)
  Cob **D**: yellow, purple, wrinkled, smooth (dihybrid)
  Cob **E**: yellow, purple, wrinkled, smooth (a different dihybrid ratio)
Razor or scalpel

Handling *Drosophila*

Drosophila, the fruit fly, is an ideal animal for experimental genetics. It can be kept easily in the laboratory, and at 25 °C the life cycle takes only 10–14 days.

Moreover, a single female lays between 80 and 200 eggs, so it does not take long to produce a large population, and genetic ratios can be determined with a fair degree of precision. The species most often used in the laboratory is *D. melanogaster*.

Before you can do any genetic investigations using *Drosophila*, you need to learn how to handle the flies, recognise the different strains and tell males from females.

Rearing the flies

Fruit flies used in experimental work are descendants of wild species that feed on yeasts and plant sugars such as are found on damaged fruits. In the laboratory, fruit flies can be cultured in bottles containing a suitable nutrient medium.

The **life cycle** is summarised in Illustration 1. After mating, the female stores sperm in a sperm store known as a spermatheca, from

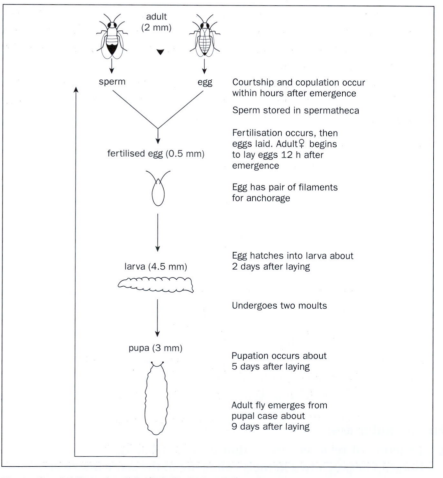

Illustration 1 Life cycle of the fruit fly, *Drosophila melanogaster*. The times apply to fruit flies kept at 25 °C.

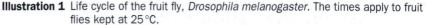

which a large number of eggs can be fertilised. Once laid, the eggs develop into larvae which burrow into the nutrient medium.

After two moults the larvae leave the medium and crawl up into drier parts of the bottle, usually onto the sides and up a roll of filter paper provided for the purpose. They then pupate and after a few days the adults emerge and the cycle starts again.

Examination of live flies

Examine a culture bottle containing a **pure line** of flies – that is, a population of flies that are homozygous at one or more key loci. Adult flies of both sexes should be present. It doesn't matter whether or not larvae and pupae are present.

In order to examine the adult flies in more detail, they must first be **anaesthetised**. One technique is as follows (Illustration 2):

1   Extinguish all naked flames and pipette a few drops of ether onto the cotton wool of an 'etheriser'. Return unwanted ether to the bottle and replace the stopper immediately: ether fumes are dangerous.
2   Tap the culture bottle so that any adult flies are dislodged from the mouth of the bottle and from the cotton-wool bung.
3   Quickly remove the cotton-wool bung and place the funnel of the etheriser over the open mouth of the culture bottle. Leave for 20 seconds to allow the ether to take effect. Now turn the etheriser and culture bottle upside down and tap the culture bottle gently until at least 10 flies have entered the etheriser. Then right the culture bottle and quickly replace its top.
4   Occasionally tap the etheriser while the flies are still moving. This will help prevent the flies from coming into contact with the cotton wool soaked in ether, which can kill them.

Ether   Ether

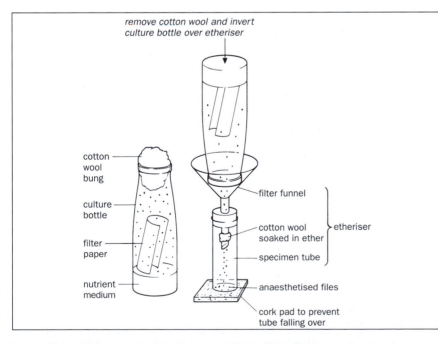

remove cotton wool and invert culture bottle over etheriser

cotton wool bung

culture bottle

filter paper

nutrient medium

filter funnel

cotton wool soaked in ether

specimen tube

anaesthetised files

cork pad to prevent tube falling over

etheriser

Illustration 2 Method of anaesthetising *Drosophila*. (The official name for ether is ethoxyethane, and it is also known as diethyl ether.)

Alternative ways of anaesthetising fruit flies

Because ether (also known as ethoxyethane and diethyl ether) is extremely flammable, an alternative is to use a product called 'FlyNap'. FlyNap contains 50% triethylamine (highly flammable; corrosive; harmful to the eyes, in contact with the skin and if swallowed), 25% ethanol (highly flammable) and 25% 'fragrance' (to mask the smell of the triethylamine). If using this product, be sure to follow the manufacturer's instructions.

A simpler approach is to use ice packs with a smooth, flat surface. Place these in a freezer to solidify. Place the tubes or bottles with fruit flies to be anaesthetised in a refrigerator, on their sides. When the flies have cooled down to the point at which they stop moving, remove the ice packs from the freezer and cover them with handkerchiefs. Tip the flies out onto the ice packs for identifying, counting and sexing.

FlyNap   FlyNap   FlyNap

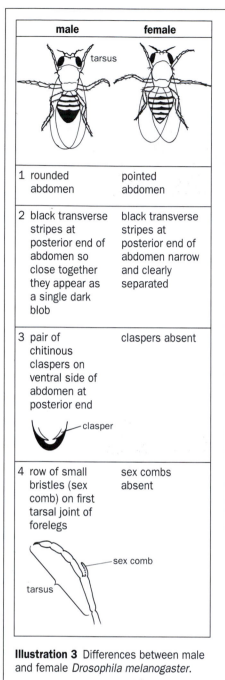

male	female
1 rounded abdomen	pointed abdomen
2 black transverse stripes at posterior end of abdomen so close together they appear as a single dark blob	black transverse stripes at posterior end of abdomen narrow and clearly separated
3 pair of chitinous claspers on ventral side of abdomen at posterior end	claspers absent
4 row of small bristles (sex comb) on first tarsal joint of forelegs	sex combs absent

Illustration 3 Differences between male and female *Drosophila melanogaster*.

5 As soon as the flies in the etheriser stop moving, remove the top of the etheriser and tip the flies onto a while tile or piece of paper.

6 Examine the flies under a hand lens or binocular microscope and identify their gender and strain as explained below. A fine paint brush can be used to move unconscious flies. Anaesthetised *Drosophila* usually remain unconscious for 5–10 minutes. Avoid giving them too much ether, or you will kill them.

Sexing fruit flies

Male and female *Drosophila* can be distinguished as shown in Illustration 3. Note that, shortly after emergence from the pupae, adult flies are pale-coloured and have incompletely expanded wings.

Recognising different strains

Normal *Drosophila* have red eyes, grey bodies, and wings that are slightly longer than the abdomen. Most of the common **mutants** show differences in these characteristics. For example: vestigial-winged *Drosophila* have very short wings; ebony *Drosophila* have black bodies; and white-eyed *Drosophila* have white eyes.

Examine at least two strains of *Drosophila* and ensure you can distinguish the adult males and adult females of each strain.

Requirements

Hand lens *or* binocular microscope
White tile or white paper
Fine paint brush
Etheriser (Illustration 2)
At least two, preferably more, strains
   of *Drosophila*, including wild type

6.4 PRACTICAL EXERCISE | **Monohybrid inheritance in *Drosophila***

This practical exercise requires four laboratory sessions over a period of 4 weeks.

To perform a simple **monohybrid cross** between two different strains, you will need virgin females. Females do not mate until at least 8 hours after they have emerged from their pupae. The simplest way, therefore, to obtain virgin females from a culture bottle with a large number of pupae is to remove all the adult flies early in the morning (say, 8.30 a.m.) and then later on the same day (say, 3.30 p.m.). You then anaesthetise the adult flies that have emerged during the day and separate them into males and females. The females will be virgins and can be used as outlined in the procedure below.

In this practical it is suggested that, working in pairs or a small group, you cross normal (often referred to as **wild type**) and vestigial-winged flies and follow the results through the F_1 generation into the F_2 generation.

Setting up a parental cross

1 Transfer five virgin pure-breeding normal females and five pure-breeding vestigial-winged males into a new bottle containing culture medium. To do this, anaesthetise the flies, taking care not to over-anaesthetise them, and tip them onto a white surface. Then gently lift them, one by one, into the new culture bottle, which should be placed on its side. Leave the bottle on its side until the flies recover, so that they do not become stuck in the medium.

2 Label the bottle with your name, indicating the cross which you have set up as follows:
P: ♀ normal × ♂ vg (date)

3 When you are sure that at least two female and two male flies have recovered from the anaesthetic and are moving freely, put your labelled bottle in an incubator at 25 °C.

4 *One week later*, when the eggs have hatched into larvae, remove the parent flies. The F_1 adult flies should emerge over a period of several days, approximately 10–14 days after the cross was set up.

Examining the results of the parental cross and setting up an F_1 cross

1 Anaesthetise all the F_1 flies that have resulted from your parental cross, taking care, as before, not to over-anaesthetise them. Tip them onto a white surface and count the number of flies in each of the following four categories:
    a female normal
    b female vestigial-winged
    c male normal
    d male vestigial-winged

Produce a hypothesis to explain your results. Predict the result of crossing the F_1 flies amongst themselves.

2 Now cross the F_1 flies among themselves by transferring five female and five male flies to a new culture bottle and incubating at 25 °C. In this case it doesn't matter whether or not the females are virgins. Label your culture bottle so that it records the details both of the new cross and of the original parental cross from which the F_1 flies came.

Examination of F_2 flies

1 One week after the F_1 cross was set up, remove the adult flies from the culture bottle.

2 Allow a further 1 week to elapse and then anaesthetise all the adult flies, examine them carefully and classify them into the same four categories, namely:
    a female normal
    b female vestigial-winged
    c male normal
    d male vestigial-winged

3 Produce a hypothesis to explain your results. Is this hypothesis the

same as the one you suggested before setting up the F_1 cross? Use the χ^2-test (see p.312) to test whether your observed results differ significantly from your expected results.

For consideration

1 Why were pure-breeding flies used for the parental cross?
2 Should the reciprocal cross have been set up – that is, vestigial-winged females and normal males? If not, explain why not.
3 When the parental cross was set up, it was important that the adult females were virgins. However, this was not the case when the F_1 cross was set up. Why the difference?
4 Why was it never necessary for the males to be virgins?
5 Why was it necessary to remove the parent flies before the F_1 flies emerged from their pupae?

Requirements

Hand lens or binocular microscope
White tile or white paper
Fine paint brush
Etheriser
Culture bottles with medium
Pure-breeding normal (wild type) flies
Pure-breeding vestigial-winged flies

Key skills

✓ **Working with others:** Plan your work with others, agreeing objectives, responsibilities and working arrangements (note that some work may have to be carried out outside the course of the usual school/college day). Establish and maintain (these are not the same thing!) cooperative working relationships over the duration of the practical. If necessary, agree changes to achieve the objectives. At the end of the practical, review your work with others and agree any possible ways of improving future collaborative work.

✓ **Application of number:** Justify the methods for obtaining the results. Use a χ^2-test to see if your observed results differ significantly from your expected results. Check your calculations to help ensure any errors are found and corrected. Select appropriate methods of presentation and justify your choice.

6.5 PRACTICAL EXERCISE

Genetic constitution of maize pollen

Gametes formed by an organism that is heterozygous at a particular locus differ in their genetic constitution: approximately half contain one of the alleles; the other half contain the other allele. Although the results of monohybrid crosses provide excellent evidence in support of this, the assertion is difficult to test directly, as genetic differences seldom reveal themselves in gametes. However, an exception to this is provided by the inheritance of starchiness in maize.

Theoretical background

In maize, a distinction can be made between starchy and non-starchy plants. Non-starchy plants contain dextrin instead of starch – dextrin being a carbohydrate intermediate in size between maltose and starch. Fortunately for our purposes, dextrin stains red with iodine solution whereas starch, of course, stains blue-black. This allows us to distinguish the two phenotypes.

Consider a heterozygous maize plant resulting from a cross between starchy and non-starchy parents. Starchiness is controlled by a single gene, so the heterozygous plant will have one allele for starchiness and one for non-starchiness. The alleles responsible for this condition determine the presence or absence of starch in maize pollen grains as well as in adult plants, so pollen grains produced by a heterozygous plant should be starchy and non-starchy in approximately equal numbers. In this practical you can test this prediction.

Procedure

1 You are provided with a floret of a heterozygous maize plant. With mounted needles, tear off the enveloping bracts and remove one of the anthers.

2 Place the anther in a drop of iodine solution on a microscope slide. With your needles, break the anther open and tease out the pollen grains. Put a coverslip on and wait for the iodine solution to react with the starch and dextrin.

3 View the pollen grains under the medium power lens of a microscope. If they appear uniform, alter the illumination. Don't illuminate too brightly: the most common reason for finding it difficult to see the difference between the two types of pollen grain is because there is too much light.

4 Count a large sample of pollen grains (at least 50). Do your results confirm or refute the prediction that the heterozygous plant produces two types of gametes in approximately equal numbers?

For consideration

1 Which of Mendel's laws is given considerable support by the results of this practical? Explain fully.

2 What significance, if any, is there for the conclusions you have drawn, given that, strictly speaking, pollen grains are not gametes but spores?

3 Do you consider that a failure to demonstrate the existence of genetically distinct types of gametes would seriously undermine Mendel's theory? Explain your answer.

> ### Requirements
> Microscope
> Slide and coverslip
> Mounted needles
> Iodine solution
> Floret from a maize plant heterozygous for starchiness

Relationship between genes and chromosomes in *Drosophila*

Unfortunately, it is not possible to look at an organism's chromosomes under the microscope and say which particular genes occur on each one. However, it is possible to draw certain conclusions about the relationship between genes and chromosomes by carrying out breeding experiments. Once again we shall rely on *Drosophila*. You will need to use the procedures described in Technique 6.3 on p. 250. Remember, when using ether, to extinguish all naked flames and minimise the amount of ether fumes.

Ether   Ether

Experiment 1

1 Set up a cross between normal virgin females and brown-eyed, vestigial-winged males. Remember to label your culture bottle. After 1 week, remove the parent flies, and after a further 1 week examine the F_1 offspring.

2 Now cross the F_1 flies amongst themselves and carry the study through to the F_2. Don't forget to remove the F_1 flies before the F_2 flies emerge.

3 Examine the F_2 flies, recording the number of individuals showing each combination of characteristics.

4 Try to explain your results.

Experiment 2

1 Set up a cross between white-eyed, yellow-bodied virgin females and normal (i.e. red-eyed, grey-bodied) male flies. Remember to label the culture bottle. After 1 week, remove the parent flies, and after a further 1 week examine the F_1 offspring. There could be up to eight possible phenotypes, namely:

    a white-eyed, yellow-bodied female
    b white-eyed, grey-bodied female
    c red-eyed, yellow-bodied female
    d red-eyed, grey-bodied female
    e white-eyed, yellow-bodied male
    f white-eyed, grey-bodied male
    g red-eyed, yellow-bodied male
    h red-eyed, grey-bodied male

2 Produce a hypothesis to explain your results. What results would you expect to get if you crossed the F_1 flies among themselves?

3 Now cross the F_1 flies among themselves, and carry the study through to the F_2. As before, do not forget to remove the F_1 flies.

4 Examine the F_2 flies, recording the different phenotypes. Is your hypothesis confirmed or refuted?

Experiment 3

1 Set up a cross between white-eyed yellow-bodied males and normal females. Proceed exactly as in Experiment 2.

2 Record, and attempt to explain, the results obtained in both the F_1 and F_2 generations.

For consideration

1 What do your results tell you about the relationship between the genes responsible for the brown eye and vestigial wing conditions?

2 What conclusions can you draw regarding the relationship between the genes responsible for white eye, yellow body and sex?

3 What further experiments would need to be done to build up a complete picture of *Drosophila's* chromosomes and the genes they carry?

Requirements

Hand lens or binocular microscope
White tile or paper
Fine paint brush
Etheriser
Culture bottles
Pure-breeding normal (wild type) flies
Pure-breeding brown-eyed, vestigial-
  winged flies
Pure-breeding white-eyed, yellow-
  bodied flies

6.7 INVESTIGATION

Making models to illustrate DNA, RNA and protein synthesis

If you think that research necessarily means using sophisticated techniques and complicated apparatus, it is sobering to reflect that Watson and Crick found that building models, using little more than stands, clamps and pieces of wire, was an essential step in unravelling the structure of **DNA** and understanding how it works (Figure 6.1). In this investigation you will have a modest opportunity to follow in their footsteps.

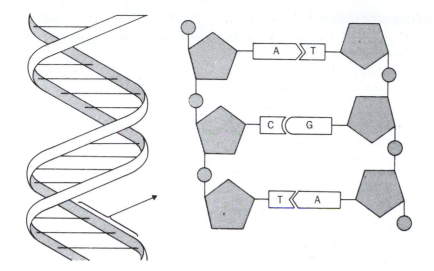

Figure 6.1 The Watson–Crick model of DNA. Shaded polygons represent deoxyribose sugars, and shaded circles represent phosphate.

Procedure

Using matchsticks, plasticine of different colours, pipe cleaners and any other suitable materials of your choice, construct two-dimensional models (i.e. models which lie flat on a table) to illustrate each of the following:

The molecular structure of DNA

Show the relationship between the **sugar**, **phosphate** and **organic bases**, the molecular basis of the helical configuration and the complementary relationship between the bases.

How DNA replicates

Build a short length of DNA made up of, say, five pairs of **nucleotides**. Construct 10 further nucleotides with the appropriate bases. Now make your DNA **replicate**.

Formation of messenger RNA

Show how DNA is **transcribed** into **messenger RNA** – one of the two strands of the DNA serving as the **template** for the whole synthesis of the RNA.

How messenger RNA controls the assembly of a protein

Make models of **amino acids**, **transfer RNA** molecules and a short length of messenger RNA. Show how the sequence of bases in the messenger RNA is **translated** into **protein** structure.

The action of polyribosomes

Make models of two or more **ribosomes**. Move a strand of messenger RNA through the ribosomes in convoy and show how **polypeptides** are formed.

The three-dimensional structure of DNA

If time and opportunity allow, try building a three-dimensional model of DNA or generating your own computer graphics. Represent the shapes of the individual nucleotides as accurately as possible.

For consideration

1 Why do you think Watson and Crick found it necessary to build models of DNA?

2 When Watson and Crick built their model of DNA, they paid particular attention to the shape (stereochemistry) of the four bases. Why?

3 Modify your models to show how cells cope with **introns**, the unexpressed portions of DNA within genes that are excised after transcription and before translation.

References

Jackson, M. E. Kit for making models of DNA. *School Science Review*, **78** (283), 114–115, 1996. (For a 'home-based' approach to the construction of models of DNA.)

van Loon, B. *DNA, The Marvellous Molecule*. Tarquin Publications, Diss, Norfolk, 1999. (For a professionally produced set of cut-out models with which you can construct models of DNA.)

Madden, D. *Illuminating DNA*. NCBE, Reading/Unilever, London (www.ncbe.reading.ac.uk/EIBE), 2000. (Another professionally produced set of cut-out models with which you can construct models of DNA.)

Requirements

Eight different colours of plasticine (modelling clay)
Matchsticks
Pipe cleaners
Other materials as requested by individual students

6.8 PRACTICAL EXERCISE

Distribution of DNA and RNA in root-tip cells

One piece of evidence supporting the DNA–RNA theory of genetic control is that RNA is found in the cytoplasm as well as in the nucleus, but that DNA is mainly confined to the nucleus. In this practical, the distribution of DNA and RNA in undifferentiated cells is investigated by staining with chemicals specific for each nucleic acid. Two techniques can be tried: the **Feulgen technique** stains only the DNA; the **methyl green–pyronin technique** stains both DNA and RNA – but different colours. For both techniques, root-tip cells of bean provide suitable material.

Testing for DNA with Feulgen reagent

The technique involves hydrolysing the DNA with acid. This liberates aldehydes, which restore the red colour to bleached Feulgen reagent.

Hydrochloric acid

Goggles must be worn

Carmine acetic

1 Transfer the bean roots from the acetic ethanol to *either* $1.0\,mol\,dm^{-3}$ hydrochloric acid at 60°C for 6 minutes in an oven, *or*, wearing eye protection, 50% hydrochloric acid at room temperature for 15 minutes. This treatment hydrolyses the DNA and macerates the tissue.

2 Transfer the root to a watch glass of Feulgen reagent for 1–2 hours. If time is short, the reaction can be accelerated by placing the watch glass on a warm surface.

3 Cut off and discard all but the terminal 3 mm of the root. Transfer the root tip to a microscope slide and add carmine acetic (which intensifies the Feulgen stain).

4 Put a coverslip over the stained root tip. Place a piece of filter paper on the coverslip and press gently so as to spread out the tissue and soak up surplus stain.

5 Examine under low and high power. Where is the DNA distributed in the cells?

Testing for DNA and RNA with methyl green–pyronin solution

The stain is a mixture of methyl green and pyronin. DNA takes up methyl green, and RNA the pyronin. This enables the two types of nucleic acid to be distinguished, at least in good preparations.

1 With a sharp razor blade, cut thin *longitudinal* sections of the terminal 3 mm of a root. Place the sections on a slide and cover with methyl green–pyronin stain for 30 minutes.

Razor blade

2 Draw off the stain with a pipette and replace with distilled water. Change the water several times so as to wash the sections thoroughly.

3 Mount the sections in distilled water and view under low and high powers. DNA should be stained blue-green, RNA red.

For consideration

1 From your observations in this practical, what predictions can be made about the way the nucleus communicates with the cytoplasm in controlling the development of the cell?

2 DNA is not entirely confined to the nucleus; small amounts occur in the cytoplasm. Whereabouts in the cytoplasm is DNA found and what is it doing there?

Fungicide

Requirements

Microscope
Oven at 60 °C
Thermostatically controlled hot plate (if available)
Slides and coverslips
Watch glasses
Razor blade
Filter paper
Hydrochloric acid (1.0 mol dm^{-3} or 50%)
Feulgen solution
Methyl green–pyronin solution
Distilled water
Carmine acetic
Eye protection
Bean roots which have been fixed in acetic ethanol for 2 hours
Bean roots which have been fixed in absolute ethanol for 30 minutes

Note: To obtain roots:

Germinate broad bean seeds 10 days before the practical. When the radicle is 1.5 cm long, cut off the tip to stimulate the growth of lateral roots.
   Beware of fungicide-treated seeds. Wash hands after handling.

Plasmid infection of sunflower seedlings[BM]

6.9 PRACTICAL EXERCISE

This practical exercise extends over more than one practical session.

Genetic engineering has the potential to revolutionise our lives. At the same time, it is fraught with both ethical and safety considerations. Unfortunately, these greatly limit the work that can be done in schools and colleges. In this extended practical, it is suggested that you follow *exactly* the following instructions in conjunction with Philip Harris' *Plant Tumour Kit*. These will enable you to inject sunflower seedlings with *Agrobacterium tumefaciens* and observe the results. In doing this, you will be carrying out some of the basic practical steps in the genetic engineering of plants.

A. tumefaciens is a bacterium which is common in soil. It is a serious plant pathogen and can attack many plant species. Having entered a plant through a wound, the bacterium releases a piece of extra-chromosomal DNA known as a **plasmid**. This plasmid inserts itself into the plant DNA and then starts to make its own messenger RNA. This messenger RNA codes for proteins which result in the formation of a plant **tumour** or **gall**. In this practical, infection of sunflower seedlings with *A. tumefaciens* is followed by excision of the galls and re-isolation of the bacterium. Further plants can then be inoculated with the re-isolated bacteria.

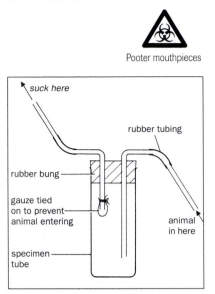

Pooter mouthpieces

suck here

rubber tubing

rubber bung

gauze tied on to prevent animal entering

animal in here

specimen tube

Illustration 1 A pooter, used to suck up small arthropods. There they can be anaesthetised if necessary, identified and counted.

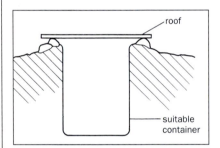

roof

suitable container

Illustration 2 A cross section through a pitfall trap, used to sample arthropods moving over the soil surface. A wooden or glass roof can be supported above the jam jar on stones to prevent rainfall from flooding the trap.

or a sand dune system, or towards a lake or pond margin. Select a starting point at random. Stretch a rope across the habitat. Arrange quadrats at equal intervals along it. Estimate by eye the percentage cover of all the species in each quadrat. An alternative is to measure the length covered by each species which the line crosses, and then to express the data in histograms. Replication can be achieved by sampling three or more parallel transects.

Point quadrats. These are used for plant sampling in short grassland. Pointed needles, usually pushed through a horizontal wooden or metal frame in groups of 10, are lowered one by one through the vegetation. Each plant touched by the point of the needle is recorded. The results are converted to **percentage cover** (the proportion of points at which a species occurs) or **cover repetition** (the total number of touches on a species expressed as a percentage of the number of points sampled). Useful for regular recording in long-term experiments.

Sweep netting. This is used for sampling invertebrates from tall grassland. Take a standard number of sweeps with the open face of a net. Trap the organisms in a pooter (Illustration 1) and anaesthetise them. Identify and count the animals in the sample.

Beating. Used for sampling invertebrates from shrubs and the lower branches of trees. Lay a sheet or beating tray beneath the branches. Give the branches a standard number of thumps of the same intensity. Quickly capture the relevant organisms, for example with a pooter, and identify and count them.

Light sampling. A light trap, containing a tungsten or ultraviolet lamp, is used to attract and catch flying insects at night. The insects fly against a vertical metal plate and fall into a collection jar.

Pitfall trapping. This is used to capture arthropods walking over the soil surface. An empty jam jar, yoghurt carton or similar receptacle is inserted in the soil so that its rim is flush with the surface, and camouflaged (Illustration 2). Passing arthropods fall into the containers and cannot escape. Place several jars in each habitat. Examine each jar at frequent intervals, to reduce the likelihood that carnivores eat other arthropods, and remove the live organisms for counting and identification.

Tullgren and Baermann funnels. These devices (Illustration 3) are used to sample the organisms which inhabit the air spaces (Tullgren) and water-filled spaces (Baermann) in soil and leaf litter.

Kick sampling. This method is used to sample invertebrates from streams. Hold a fine net downstream from the place in which you intend to sample. Use a standard sideways motion of your Wellington boots to disturb the creatures on the bottom so that they swim or drift into the net. Count the individuals of each species obtained from a certain number of kicks. For comparison, repeat the procedure in exactly the same way in different habitats.

Drift netting. Long vertical poles at each end of a net are pushed into the stream bed. After a standard period of time, the organisms caught in the net are identified and counted. This is valuable in comparing different parts of a stream, assessing seasonal changes or comparing animal movements at different times of day and night.

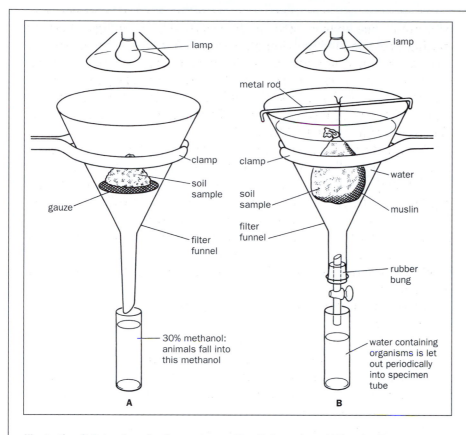

Illustration 3 Extraction of soil organisms with a Tullgren funnel (**A**) and a Baermann funnel (**B**).

Pond sampling. In your mind's eye, divide the pond into a series of microhabitats – the sides, beneath plant leaves, open water, muddy bottom and so on. Use a simple net to remove a certain number of samples from each microhabitat. Turn each set of samples into a separate white bowl and identify and count the individuals.

Earthworm sampling. Arrange quadrats at random, or at various distances from the centre of a tree. A dilute solution of mustard (1 g of mustard per litre of water) or detergent is the cheapest, safest, most effective way to bring worms to the surface (see Project 3, p. 293). It is better still to sample at night, when the earthworms are on the surface.

Sampling of individuals. If you wish to collect a sample of, say, flowers or plants, the most unbiased procedure is to number all the plants, randomly select numbers, and then sample the plants with these numbers.

Diversity can be estimated on the basis of any data collected by the techniques described above, provided that the numbers of individual organisms belonging to each species (or group of species) have been recorded.

The species diversity of samples taken from two contrasting habitats can be compared by using the **Simpson Index** of diversity:

$$N(N-1)/\Sigma n(n-1)$$

where N is the total number of individuals in the sample, Σ means 'sum of', and n is the number of individuals in each species.

References

Further details of these and other sampling techniques can be found in:

Adds, J., Larkom E., Miller, R. and others. *Tools, Techniques and Assessment in Biology*. Nelson, Walton-on-Thames, 1999.

Dowdeswell, W.H. *Ecology, Principles and Practice*. Heinemann, London, 1984.

Slingsby, D. & Cook, C. *Practical Ecology*. Macmillan, London, 1986.

Williams, G. *Techniques and Fieldwork in Ecology*. Bell & Hyman, London, 1987.

The **Projects** section of this chapter (p. 293) mentions several investigations which require these techniques to be selected and put into practice.

7.2 INVESTIGATION

Investigating the microhabitats in a pond or aquarium

Weil's disease

A pond or aquarium is a self-supporting ecosystem, but even within its limited volume, the species are not distributed at random. This investigation allows you to work out the microhabitats occupied by each species (it also links with Investigations 7.4, p. 271 and 7.7, p. 274). A **microhabitat** is a small patch of habitat which provides a distinctive microenvironment, for example, the underside of water lily leaves, or the mud at the base of the pond. Such microhabitats often contain distinctive clusters of species.

Guidance

List as many microhabitats within the pond as possible.

Sample each microhabitat with a small net, identifying and counting the organisms (see Technique 7.1, above).

If you are studying an aquarium, watch some individuals (e.g. fish, snails, water shrimps, water lice) through the glass walls, and quantify the proportion of the time which they spend in different places.

Use the relevant probes, and data-logging equipment (Technique 7.15, p. 287), to measure the physical variables in each microhabitat.

Devise your own experiments in which representatives of a species are provided with the choice of two distinct environments. Where do they spend their time?

For consideration

1 Summarise the ways in which particular environmental factors vary from place to place in the water; in particular, light intensity, oxygen concentration, pH and the availability of living and dead plant food.

2 Does a pond provide more microhabitats than an aquarium? If so, why? How could you alter an aquarium so that it provides more microhabitats?

3   You have worked out the places in the pond, or aquarium, in which each species is most often found. For each species in turn, suggest why it 'prefers' this particular microhabitat. As well as abiotic factors, such as oxygen availability, you must consider other aspects of its niche, its role in the community. What does it eat, where can its food be found, and what eats it? Do these factors influence its distribution pattern?

4   Some species are restricted to one microhabitat, but others are jacks of all trades, flitting from one microhabitat to another. What are the advantages and disadvantages of each lifestyle?

Soil analysis   7.3 TECHNIQUE

Soil is a complex mixture of six components: **mineral particles** (sand, silt, clay); **water**; dead **organic matter** (**humus**); **nutrients**; **organisms**; **air**. Soil analysis is time-consuming and the particular analysis you undertake must be discussed with your teacher or lecturer, and carefully planned. Simple, rather than sophisticated, methods are usually satisfactory enough to obtain significant results.

Soil texture

The proportions of different sizes of soil particles in a soil are known as its texture. It can often be worth determining a soil's texture, for example when you want to relate the distribution patterns of animals living in estuaries to the proportion of sand, silt and clay in the substrate. Particles more than 2 mm in diameter are **stones**, sand particles are 0.02–2 mm, silt particles are 0.002–0.02 mm and clay particles are less than 2 μm across. Particle sizes can be found by pounding dry soil into powdery form and forcing it through a series of sieves of smaller and smaller mesh size. The following method, however, is sufficient for most purposes.

  Add soil to a boiling tube until it fills one-third of the volume. Then add water until the boiling tube is four-fifths full. Mix the contents of the tube with a glass rod. Cork the tube and shake vigorously for 1 minute (but not too vigorously, because the bottom might break off the boiling tube). Place the boiling tube in a rack and allow the soil to settle. The heavier particles settle first, and distinct layers can usually be seen once the finer particles have settled, with any stones at the base, sand above them, silt on top of that and clay at the very top. Organic particles float on the top of the water surface. Measure and record the thickness of each layer in millimetres.

Water content

Weigh a metal crucible. Put some moist soil in it, soon after sampling from the field, and re-weigh. Then place the crucible and soil in an oven at 105 °C for 24 hours and re-weigh. Replace the crucible and soil in the oven and re-weigh whenever possible until they reach constant mass. The difference between the initial and final measurements is assumed to be the mass of the water lost, and this is usually expressed as a percentage of the original mass of the moist soil.

Organic matter

You need dry soil for this – it could be the dry soil from the determination of water content (see above). Heat a known mass of soil in a metal crucible over a roaring flame, preferably in a fume cupboard because of the smell, for 2 hours. Allow the crucible to cool before transferring it, using tongs, to a balance. Continue to heat and measure the mass again in half an hour. When constant mass is achieved, calculate the difference between the initial mass of the soil and the final mass and express it as a percentage of the initial mass of the dry soil. This percentage is assumed to be the organic content of the soil sample.

Mineral nutrients

Conductivity, determined with a conductivity meter or a conductivity probe attached to a data-logger (see Technique 7.15, p. 287), provides the most convenient method of comparing the salinity of water samples taken from marine or estuarine environments. Inland, the calcium carbonate content ('hardness') of water in rivers and streams is also highly correlated with conductivity.

Garden soil test kits, or NPK kits available from biological suppliers, provide estimates of the pH and total nitrogen (N), phosphorus (P) and potassium (K) in soils. These measures are sufficient for many ecological purposes, particularly when the soils to be compared are very different.

More precise kits are expensive, but particularly useful for project work. The Merckoquant, Aquaquant and Aquamerck kits contain dipsticks not only for pH, nitrogen, phosphorus and potassium, but also for ammonium, nitrate (see Practical Exercise 7.12, p. 284), various metal pollutants and even dissolved oxygen.

Soil organisms

Earthworm counts are mentioned in Project 3 (p. 293). The Tullgren and Baermann funnels (Technique 7.1, p. 265) allow soil-dwelling invertebrates to be extracted. We recommend that you do not attempt to grow soil bacteria or fungi, because this yields results which are often too variable to interpret.

Soil air

The air content of soil is seldom worth estimating. The simplest method is to extract a soil core without altering its air content (difficult!), and to add a known volume of core to a known volume of water. If you then break up and stir the soil with a glass rod, bubbles of air will appear and rise to the surface. Measure the final volume of water with the soil in it. Subtract this from the initial volume of the soil and the initial volume of the water. The difference is the volume of air that has been displaced. This can be expressed as a percentage of the initial volume of the soil.

For consideration

List the sources of error in the techniques which you have used.

Requirements

Boiling tubes and corks
Boiling tube rack
Marking pen
Ruler
Balance
Crucible, metal
Oven set at 105 °C
Tripod
Pipe-clay triangle
Tongs
Conductivity meter and data-logger
Test kits or reagent strips
Glass rod
Beaker, large
Soils to be analysed

The zonation of organisms on a rocky shore or a salt marsh

Between the low and high tide marks on a salt marsh or rocky shore live species which are subjected regularly, twice a day, to rapid changes in sunlight, salinity, oxygen supply, food supply and predation. Whilst some species are mobile and move up and down with the tides, others are sedentary. This investigation allows you to compare the distribution patterns of these sedentary species and to speculate on reasons for the differences.

Guidance

At low tide, run a transect line up the shore (see Technique 7.1, p.265, for sampling techniques). Starting at the seaward end, sample $1 m^2$ quadrats at appropriate intervals. In each quadrat record the percentage cover of each seaweed species. Assign each of these seaweed species to the category red, green or brown. In each quadrat, count the numbers of each recognisable animal species (barnacles, topshells, whelks and so on). Express your data in the form of histograms.

For consideration

1   The main factors that vary from the top to the bottom of a rocky shore or salt marsh, and which might affect the distribution patterns of the species growing there, are listed in the introduction to this investigation. How and why does each change from low tide mark to high tide mark?
2   Can you generalise about the distribution patterns of red, green and brown seaweeds?
3   Use reference books, or use direct observation, to find out what each species of animal eats. How does their food supply vary up and down the shore, and how much do food supply and predation affect the distribution pattern of each animal species?

> ### Requirements
> Rope, chain or plastic washing line
> Quadrats
> Identification guides
> Clip-boards
> Recording sheets, tape recorders or
>   palm data-loggers

Key skills

✓ **Application of number:** Calculate the average percentage cover of each species at each level of the zonation.
✓ **Information technology:** Import the data into a spreadsheet and print out histograms showing the distribution patterns of the organisms.

The distribution patterns of woodland herbs in relation to light intensity

The intensity of shade cast by the canopy of trees in a wood may influence the distribution pattern of herbs growing beneath. Obtaining data to test this hypothesis is an interesting sampling problem! In this investigation you are invited to sample woodland herbs and measure the incident light energy which lands upon them.

This investigation should be performed in summer, when deciduous trees are leafy. Even within the same quadrat, the light intensity may vary from hour to hour, even minute to minute. Sampling the plant species is relatively easy. To sample light intensity it is best to mark the sampled sites and return to them one after the other, taking light intensity readings from all the plots within as short a time as possible, at regular intervals throughout the day.

Guidance

Select an area of woodland with a range of tree species and a range of herb species on the woodland floor, say an area $100\,\text{m} \times 100\,\text{m}$. Sample with randomly arranged $1\,\text{m}^2$ quadrats, recording the percentage cover of up to five selected species of herb and the tree species above them. Mark each plot for a light reading later. A large sample size is necessary to provide reliable results.

After the sampling, wait for the light intensity to be fairly constant, and then rapidly tour the plots, recording light intensity with a light meter at each plot as many times as possible through the practical session. Convert these to relative light intensities (how much are they above and below the average light intensity for that sampling session?), and average the results for each site.

In the absence of a light meter, you could use a semi-automatic camera which has a display in the viewfinder of speed and aperture. Set the shutter to a fixed speed. Then each stop in the direction f-11, f-8, f-5.6, f-4 doubles the light intensity.

Rank the light intensities from the lowest to the highest. Divide the light intensities into five equal groups. Work out the average percentage cover of each species in each of the five groups and exhibit the results in histogram form.

For consideration

1   How could you alter your sampling technique so as to allow areas with a wide variety of light intensities to be adequately (equally?) represented in the sample?
2   Review your data. Suggest why some species are more shade-tolerant than others. What factors other than light intensity appear to influence the distribution patterns of your woodland herbs?
3   Some woodland herbs (e.g. bluebell, *Hyacinthoides non-scriptus*), grow and flower before the trees come into leaf. What effect might this have on your conclusions?

Key skills

✓   **Application of number:** You need to express your light meter readings on a linear scale and relate them to the average percentage cover of your species. Are the percentage covers significantly different by a t-test (see Statistical Analysis Appendix, p.304)?
✓   **Information technology:** Use a computer program to express graphically the relationship between the cover of a species and the light intensity.
✓   **Working with others:** If this is a class exercise, and you have only one or two light meters to pass round, you will need to cooperate to organise a reliable sampling technique for each pair of students.

The distribution patterns of seaweeds, mosses and liverworts can often be related to evaporative stress more easily than can the distribution patterns of flowering plants.

Seaweeds, and the gametophytes of many mosses and liverworts, usually lack the waxy cuticle which prevents water loss in many other plants. Different species differ in their resistance to desiccation, and this may affect their distribution patterns. On a salt marsh or rocky shore, the further away from the sea a species occurs, the shorter is the time during which it is submerged and the longer the time during which it is exposed to the air. Similarly, a moss on one side of a wall may receive more direct sunlight, and be exposed to far greater temperatures, than one on the other side. The rate at which a seaweed or bryophyte loses mass in the laboratory provides a rough guide to its desiccation resistance.

In this investigation you are invited to investigate the distribution patterns of two or three species in their natural habitats, and to relate the patterns to their desiccation resistance in the laboratory.

Guidance

Your teacher or lecturer will help you to choose a suitable habitat which contains two or three species which you investigate.

Quantify the distribution patterns of the species using one or more appropriate techniques from Technique 7.1, p. 265.

If the species are abundant, take small samples from the habitat into the laboratory (care, conservation!); hang them on a 'washing line' to dry in similar conditions, and weigh them at intervals.

If you have a balance which is linked to a sensor, and suitable sofware in a computer, you may be able to link the balance to the computer, and allow the computer automatically to store the changes in mass.

Draw graphs of mass against time, and relate the distribution patterns of the species to their resistance to desiccation.

In a parallel investigation, determine the time of death of individuals of each species as they dry. A cell is regarded as dead when it remains irreversibly shrunken after being immersed in water for half an hour.

For consideration

1 How might water on the surface of the organisms at the start of the experiment affect the results?
2 How might the state of dehydration of each species when you removed it from the habitat affect the results? What precautions could be taken to ensure that each species starts at a comparable starting point?
3 What precautions did you take to ensure that your estimates of water loss in the different species were comparable and accurate?
4 What other factors apart from resistance to desiccation might affect the distribution patterns of the species you have investigated?
5 Define the cycles of wetting and drying to which each of your

Quadrats
Clip-board
Recording sheets
String
Clamp stands
Sensitive electrical balance
Seaweeds, mosses or liverworts
   exhibiting zonation (e.g. on rocky
   shore, salt marsh or wall)

species is exposed. In general, photosynthesis stops when a plant is slightly dehydrated and resumes only slowly on rewetting. Bearing in mind that the species continue to respire when slightly dehydrated, what effect might the wetting–drying cycle have on the species you have investigated?

6   Many mosses and liverworts have leaves only one cell thick, in which every cell is photosynthetic. What are the advantages and disadvantages of this arrangement, compared with that in the leaves of flowering plants?

Key skills

✓   **Information technology:** Use a computer program to produce graphs of the decline in mass, with time, of mosses which are drying in experiments in the laboratory.

7.7 INVESTIGATION

Analysis of the food web in a pond

Many textbooks contain diagrams of food webs, showing what organism eats what in a community. How is a food web diagram arrived at? This investigation introduces the difficulties of constructing food webs, using a pond or aquarium.

Guidance

Sample the organisms in the pond or aquarium and identify them (see list of identification manuals in Investigation 7.11, p. 281). Find out as much as you can about the feeding habits of each species. You can (a) look up their likely foods in reference books, (b) observe each organism feeding, (c) examine the feeding apparatus of each species and draw conclusions about the nature of its food, and (d) look at the gut contents under a microscope.

Place together – in pairs – in Petri dishes, beakers or small aquaria, a predator and a likely prey species (e.g. fish and water fleas). Observe their behaviour and note whether or not predation takes place. You can also set up beakers containing an intact plant and a possible herbivore, and find out if the plants are eaten.

Draw a food web for the pond, including the plants; some of the feeding relationships will be definite and others only tentative. Show this uncertainty in your diagram.

Requirements

Pond or aquarium, well established
Pond dipping nets
Teat pipettes
Microscopes, binocular and monocular
Microscope slides and coverslips
Identification guides   .
Petri dishes
Beakers or small aquaria
Reference books (for feeding habits) –
   see Investigation 7.11, p. 281

For consideration

1   How could you modify your techniques to estimate the dry mass of food eaten by each organism, and the proportion of its food derived from various sources?

2   What proportion of the food entering the guts of pond organisms is lost in egesta?

3   Have you included detritus, detritivores and decomposers (such as bacteria and fungi) in your web? Where would they fit in?

4   Sketch approximate pyramids of numbers and biomass for the pond or aquarium.

✓ **Working with others:** You will need to co-operate within a pair to devise and carry out sampling techniques, and between pairs to organise the laboratory predator–prey experiments, and collect together all the results for the class.

✓ **Problem solving:** You will need to assess all the data collected, decide on firm evidence for feeding interactions in your food web, and express these relationships in an elegant diagram.

✓ **Information technology:** Use an appropriate method to produce a diagram of the food web, distinguishing between firm and tentative links.

✓ **Communication:** Devise a presentation, incorporating visual aids, to explain the food web and the evidence on which it is based.

Determination of pyramids of number and fresh biomass

7.8 TECHNIQUE

In order to determine ecological pyramids, you need to know what the various organisms in a community eat. The diets of organisms are most easily discerned in a **freshwater ecosystem** such as an aquarium, and this exercise follows on naturally from Investigation 7.7, in which the feeding relationships in a pond or aquarium community are worked out. A freshwater ecosystem has a clear-cut volume and the number and biomass of plants is much easier to determine than in a terrestrial community. Moreover, most of the plants are small and rootless, and there is little soil to complicate things.

It is more difficult to determine these pyramids in a **grassland ecosystem**. In grasslands, though, the numbers of major decomposer animals can be quite easily estimated. The numbers and biomass of earthworms per unit area can be found by sampling in quadrats of known area and weighing the worms collected (see Project 3, p. 293). Similarly, the numbers of organisms collected in Tullgren and Baermann funnels, from soil samples of known surface area, can be determined. Most of these organisms will be detritivores (animals which eat detritus by mouth and hence are placed in the decomposer trophic level). It is when we get to the herbivores and carnivores that the biggest difficulties arise. All sorts of assumptions have to be made when estimating the number of herbivores and carnivores, big and small, per unit area. The producers (plants) present problems too, for much of their biomass is underground. To estimate it correctly requires soil to be washed off root samples.

To analyse **forest ecosystems** is the most formidable task of all. It requires you to make all sorts of difficult assumptions about the numbers and biomass of trees and tree roots. This is when analysing ecological pyramids becomes really difficult!

Procedure

Preamble

Use a mature pond, a mature water trough or a mature aquarium set up for the purpose. It may be possible to sacrifice the contents of the whole aquarium, but if you use a pond, you will have to work out a pyramid of numbers for a particular part (i.e. volume) of the pond, defined in advance, so as not to destroy too much wildlife. Collecting the visible plants in that part of the pond will present no problems, and the soil or detritus can also be sampled, provided that the pond is shallow. However, relating the mobile animals (water fleas, water boatmen, fish, etc.) to a particular part of the pond is a difficult sampling problem, and merits **class discussion** before you begin.

1   Collect the animals from detritus or soil at the base of the aquarium or pond. Place them in a small, weighed net colander, allow the water to drain off, and re-weigh, recording the mass. Then count the individuals. Assume that these are detritivores, assigned to the decomposer trophic level.

2   Collect the plants. While removing them, transfer any animals (e.g. snails, eggs) on the surface of the plants to a container representing the herbivore trophic level (see step **3** below). Place the plants in a weighed net colander, allow the water to drain off, and re-weigh. Record the mass. Then count the individuals. Assume that these are producers.

3   Collect the animals from the water volume itself. Add these to the animals collected from the surfaces of the plants. Place them in a small weighed net colander, allow the water to drain off, and re-weigh, recording the mass. Then count the individuals. Assume at first that these are herbivores (primary consumers).

4   Look around the pond for other potential carnivores, such as dragonfly nymphs or fish. Catch and weigh them, and decide what numbers, and proportion of their mass, to assign to the primary consumer trophic level, and the secondary consumer level, in the area you are studying.

5   Now you have the basis for constructing a pyramid of numbers, and a pyramid of biomass. If you have time, refine your investigation by finding out more precisely what each type of animal eats. Many of the animals will eat a mixture of algae, plants and detritus. If you have carried out Investigation 7.7 (above), you will have a firm foundation for assessing the feeding habits of the animals you have collected. Otherwise, use reference books (see Investigation 7.11, p.283) or the preliminary list provided by J. Adds, Larkom E., Miller, R. and others, *Tools, Techniques and Assessment in Biology*, Nelson, Walton-on-Thames, 1999. You will also need to separate the animals you have collected into species, and – where they occupy more than one trophic level – to assign some of their numbers and biomass to one trophic level and some to another.

6   Estimate the numbers of photosynthetic algae by using a haemocytometer (Technique 2.45, p.122). Their biomass is more difficult to assess! Any ideas as to how you could do it?

Limitations

In freshwater, the organisms must be kept moist if they are not to be killed. As it is impossible to eliminate the water which clings to the organisms, much of the 'fresh mass' determined will be external water. Furthermore, by concentrating on large mature plants, the numbers and biomass of the photosynthetic single-celled algae will be ignored.

In both a freshwater ecosystem and grassland, the numbers and biomass of decomposers will be grossly underestimated by restricting sampling to animals. In grassland, for example, it has been estimated that the biomass of decomposing bacteria beneath the soil may be 20 times that of the cows grazing above it. Bacteria and fungi can, of course, be sampled on agar plates, but the numbers of fungi, growing from spores, provide little indication of the numbers and biomass of the fungi in the field.

For consideration

1   Read the 'limitations' mentioned above. Make a thorough list of all the other sources of error in your investigation.
2   Is biomass equivalent to energy content? If not, why not? Suggest the practical techniques which you would need to use to determine a pyramid of energy flow for your ecosystem.

Requirements

Pond dipping nets (e.g. net colanders)
Sink access
Teat pipettes
Microscopes, binocular and monocular
Microscope slides and coverslips
Balance
Petri dishes
Beakers
Identification guides
Reference books (for feeding habits)
Pond or aquarium, well established

The energetics of a stick insect or a desert locust   7.9 PRACTICAL EXERCISE

The energy budget of a primary consumer can be determined in the laboratory for the Indian stick insect (*Carausius morosus*), a herbivore which can be fed on the leaves of privet (*Ligustrum* sp.). The individuals in normal laboratory populations are all females. The energy in the food they eat is egested and excreted (in faeces and uric acid), released in metabolism as heat energy, or devoted to eggs and growth in body mass.

The experiment can equally well be done with a desert locust (*Schistocerca gregaria*) provided with grass. Locusts eat more voraciously than stick insects, and need be left with food for only 2 days before the energy budget is determined. Locusts respire more rapidly than stick insects, and are less likely to produce eggs during the experiment, but they are more difficult to handle.

Locust-allergies

Procedure

1   Select a healthy shoot of privet with 4–10 leaves. Without detaching them from the shoot, trace the outlines of all the leaves onto squared paper. Make sure that you record the position on the shoot which the leaf occupied.
2   Weigh the shoot and record its mass (P1).
3   With clingfilm, cover the top of a McCartney bottle or small beaker containing water. Push the base of the privet shoot through the clingfilm into the water. Place the bottle in the centre of half a Petri dish and stabilise it with plasticine (Figure 7.1).
4   Weigh a stick insect (to the nearest 0.01 g) and record its mass (ST1). Put it onto the privet.
5   Add to the Petri dish base a humidifier consisting of a McCartney bottle containing water with pieces of paper towelling stuck into it. Stick it to the base of the Petri dish base with plasticine.

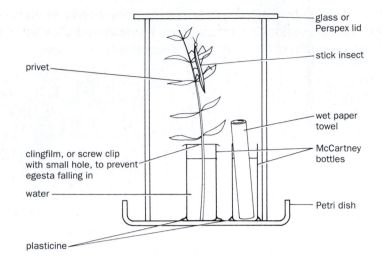

Figure 7.1 An apparatus suitable for investigating the energetics of a stick insect. If the experiment is to be performed on a locust, substitute a known fresh mass of grass for the privet.

6 Cover the privet, the stick insect and the humidifier with a bell jar or coffee jar. Leave the set-up for 1 week.

After a week you will need to collect the stick insect, its eggs, its egesta and the uneaten leaves. You will also have to measure the respiration rate of the insect. Proceed as follows:

7 Remove the insect and determine and record its mass (ST2).
8 Place the insect in a **respirometer** (see Practical Exercise 2.18, p. 80) and determine its metabolic rate as the volume of oxygen absorbed per unit time at room temperature. Measure its respiration rate over as many minutes as possible.
9 Weigh a cavity microscope slide (E1). Carefully collect all the egesta you can find (distinguishing them from eggs), place them in the cavity of the slide and re-weigh (E2).
10 Weigh another cavity microscope slide (EGS1). Carefully collect all the eggs you can find, place them in the cavity of the slide and re-weigh (EGS2).
11 Extract the remains of the privet shoot from the water. Blot it dry. Re-weigh it (P2).
12 Remove each leaf from the shoot in turn. Place it on its original outline on the graph paper. Draw round the edge of the leaf.
13 The masses determined so far are all fresh masses. If you have time, determine the dry masses of the leaf blades (to provide a more accurate estimate of energy content per unit mass), egesta and eggs. Dry them by heating in an oven at 105 °C for at least 48 hours.

Processing the results

The masses you have determined (in grams) can be converted into energy contents (in kiloJoules (kJ)) by applying simple conversion factors. For the stick insect:

$$FE = E + R + P$$

where *FE* is the energy in the food eaten, *E* is the energy in egesta, *R* is the heat lost in metabolism (crudely, respiration) and *P* is the energy content of the eggs and the extra mass of the insect.

14 To calculate the energy deposited in insect and eggs (*P* in the equation above), add the fresh mass of eggs (EGS2 − EGSl) to the increase in fresh mass of the insect (ST2 − ST1). Calculate their energy contents by assuming that 1 g of fresh eggs or insect contains 5 kJ.

15 The fresh mass of the privet eaten is P2 − P1. Calculate its energy content, assuming that 1 g of fresh privet contains 3 kJ.

16 As a check, count squares on the graph paper to estimate the area of leaf eaten by the insect. Weigh leaves of known area to calculate the mass per cm² of the leaf. Then convert the area of leaf eaten to the equivalent mass, and calculate its energy content, assuming that 1 g of fresh privet contains 3 kJ of energy.

17 The fresh mass of egesta produced is El − E2. Calculate its energy content, assuming that 1 g of fresh egesta contains 10 kJ.

18 Calculate the heat energy lost in metabolism in 1 week. Assume that, as a consequence of the uptake of 1 cm³ of oxygen, 0.02 kJ of energy is released. Convert your respirometer measure to 1 hour and multiply by 168 (the number of hours in a week).

19 Put together your energy budget equation. Does it balance?

For consideration

1 List all the possible sources of error in the experiment.
2 Suggest three reasons why you placed clingfilm over the bottle which held the privet stem in water.
3 What effect would a change in mean temperature have had on the energy budget?
4 How might you expect the energy budget to differ in a carnivorous insect of the same size?

References

Monger, G. (Ed.). *Revised Nuffield Biology, Practical Guide 7*, Investigation 29B. Longmans, Harlow, 1986.

Slatter, R. G. The energy budget of the stick insect. *School Science Review*, **62** (219), 312–316, 1980.

Requirements

Bell jar or coffee jar
Petri dish base
McCartney bottles or small beakers
Clingfilm or parafilm
Paper towel or cotton wool
Plasticine
Graph paper
Balance (weighing to ± 0.001 g)
Drying oven
Cavity microscope slides
Pen for marking glass
Respirometer
Indian stick insect (*Carausius morosus*) or desert locust (*Schistocerca gregaria*)
Privet (*Ligustrum* sp.) shoots or handful of grass

Key skills

✓ **Application of number:** There are several accurate weighings to be made. In the calculations involving energy content per gram, you need to use and rearrange formulae. The detailed calculations explained here require considerable understanding and care.

7.10 INVESTIGATION

Preparing a management plan for a habitat

Every area managed for nature, such as a nature reserve, should have a management plan; this investigation provides you with the opportunity to write one. The plan should explain the aims of preserving an area of suitable habitat and the ways in which it should be managed over the next few years to achieve these objectives. It may also suggest how new habitats might be created to increase the range of species which the reserve supports. An example is given in Figure 7.2.

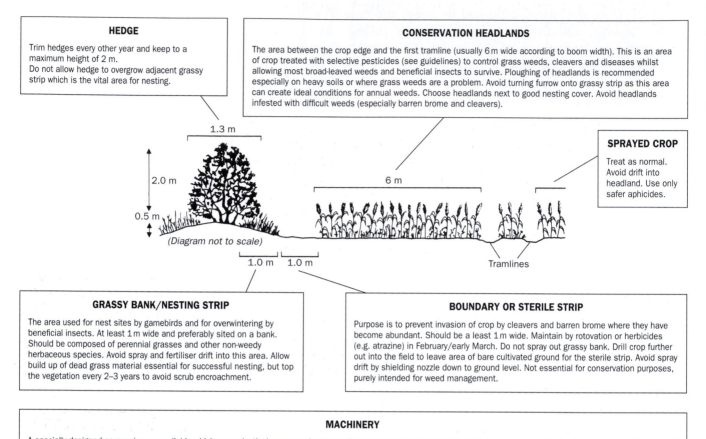

HEDGE

Trim hedges every other year and keep to a maximum height of 2 m.
Do not allow hedge to overgrow adjacent grassy strip which is the vital area for nesting.

CONSERVATION HEADLANDS

The area between the crop edge and the first tramline (usually 6 m wide according to boom width). This is an area of crop treated with selective pesticides (see guidelines) to control grass weeds, cleavers and diseases whilst allowing most broad-leaved weeds and beneficial insects to survive. Ploughing of headlands is recommended especially on heavy soils or where grass weeds are a problem. Avoid turning furrow onto grassy strip as this area can create ideal conditions for annual weeds. Choose headlands next to good nesting cover. Avoid headlands infested with difficult weeds (especially barren brome and cleavers).

SPRAYED CROP

Treat as normal. Avoid drift into headland. Use only safer aphicides.

1.3 m
2.0 m
0.5 m
6 m
(Diagram not to scale)
1.0 m   1.0 m
Tramlines

GRASSY BANK/NESTING STRIP

The area used for nest sites by gamebirds and for overwintering by beneficial insects. At least 1 m wide and preferably sited on a bank. Should be composed of perennial grasses and other non-weedy herbaceous species. Avoid spray and fertiliser drift into this area. Allow build up of dead grass material essential for successful nesting, but top the vegetation every 2–3 years to avoid scrub encroachment.

BOUNDARY OR STERILE STRIP

Purpose is to prevent invasion of crop by cleavers and barren brome where they have become abundant. Should be a least 1 m wide. Maintain by rotovation or herbicides (e.g. atrazine) in February/early March. Do not spray out grassy bank. Drill crop further out into the field to leave area of bare cultivated ground for the sterile strip. Avoid spray drift by shielding nozzle down to ground level. Not essential for conservation purposes, purely intended for weed management.

MACHINERY

A specially designed sprayer is now available which can selectively spray a six-metre strip along the headland while treating the main crop with standard chemicals. Each part of the machinery is independent of the other, thus saving the need for a separate run along the Conservation Headland.
    While spraying sterile strips it is vital to prevent drift into crop and hedge bottom. A very useful device, which applies the chemical safely and accurately from the tractor, has been designed for this purpose.
    For futher information on these two pieces of equipment contact the Conservation Headlands Field Officer.

Figure 7.2 Ways in which a field margin might be treated to make it ideally suitable for wildlife conservation.

Rarely can a wildlife reserve be managed adequately by merely leaving it alone. The vegetation may naturally undergo succession, resulting in a predictable change in the plant and animal species present at a site. This may make conditions less and less suitable for particular species, the preservation of which was intended when the reserve was set up. In addition, alien species may invade the habitat, visitors or holiday-makers may destroy it or disturb the animals, and pollution may deplete the diversity of species. A management plan must suggest policies to cope with all such factors.

Guidance

Select an area which might be suitable as a potential nature reserve. This may be part of your school grounds, a local copse or hedgerow, a churchyard, a pond or stream, or even an existing nature reserve. Ideally, it should be an area where you have already carried out some ecological sampling, so that you are familiar with many of the species.

First survey the whole area, and make an annotated sketch plan showing the main types of habitat into which your nature reserve might be divided. Make a note of any interesting features or unusual species.

On this basis, think carefully about the aims of setting up the reserve, and write down your objectives. This is most important, and may require advice from your teacher or lecturer.

- Which plant communities do you wish to preserve?
- Which animal species should you conserve?
- Are there any species you wish to eliminate?
- Can you create any new conditions and introduce any new species?

Then you must write your management plan. On the basis of your ecological understanding, explain how you should treat each segment of the potential reserve to conserve the communities and species you wish. Bear in mind that communities, if left alone, may change away from the species composition you wish to preserve – short grassland becomes tall grassland, and tall grassland becomes scrub, for example. You might need to mow, introduce grazing animals, cut out shrubs or even apply a herbicide to achieve the vegetation and associated animals you want. The whole suite of measures should be costed.

For consideration

1   How should access to the reserve by humans be managed? Should you confine visitors to a small number of paths? Should access be banned at certain times of the year (e.g. the breeding season for birds)?
2   Examine the reserve from the point of view of 'wildlife corridors'. Can species migrate freely into and out of the reserve along ribbons of suitable habitat, such as streams or hedgerows, to other suitable areas?

Requirements

Clip-board
Identification guides
Local maps, high scale
Patch of suitable habitat

Key skills

✓   **Problem solving:** Once you have defined the features of your area which are worth preserving, you must work out management techniques which will preserve and enhance these features.
✓   **Working with others:** You need to discuss the area with others who know it well, or who are responsible for it, to glean information and ideas.
✓   **Communication:** Prepare a talk giving a detailed justification for the management plan which you have devised.

| Comparing pollution levels in freshwater using a biotic index | 7.11 INVESTIGATION |

Well-oxygenated freshwater rivers, streams, ponds and lakes support a wider range of animal species than poorly oxygenated water bodies (Table 7.1). The addition of too much organic matter or inorganic fertiliser ultimately causes the water to become at least partially deoxygenated, owing to the respiration of an expanding population of bacteria. Some water animals are more sensitive than others to depletion of oxygen, and the more sensitive ones die out when the water is polluted in this way.

The range of animal species which occurs at a freshwater site can therefore provide a sensitive indication of the degree of pollution. In this investigation, you can compare the animal species at different sites along the same river or stream, or compare different ponds, canals or cattle troughs, and relate the differences to oxygen concentrations in the water and possible sources of pollution.

Table 7.1 Freshwater animals as indicators of pollution

Class of waterway	Fauna	Biochemical oxygen demand (mg O_2 absorbed dm^{-3} water at 20°C in 5 days	Waterway used for:
I	Diverse; salmon, trout, grayling, stonefly and mayfly nymphs, caddis larvae, *Gammarus*	0–3	Domestic supply
II	Trout rarely dominant; chub, dace, caddis larvae, *Gammarus*	3–10 (increased in summer at times of low flow)	Agriculture. Industrial processes
III	Roach, gudgeon, *Asellus*; mayfly nymphs and caddis larvae rare	10–15	Irrigation
IV	Fish absent; red chironomid larvae (bloodworms) and *Tubifex* worms present	15–30 (completely deoxygenated from time to time)	Very little. Unsuitable for amenity use
V	Barren, or with fungus or small *Tubifex* worms	>30	None

Water downstream of discharge

Effluent

Guidance

Your teacher or lecturer will select two ponds for comparison, one polluted and the other unpolluted. Alternatively, find a river, stream or canal into which effluent flows. You could sample both upstream and downstream from the outflow.

Produce a sketch map of the site, and establish as precisely as possible the volume and timing of the addition of the organic matter to the water.

Using standard sampling techniques, sample the animals present at each site and identify and count them as far as possible (see Technique 7.1, p. 265).

If an oxygen meter (electrode) is available, measure the oxygen content of the water, at a variety of depths, at each sampling point.

Alternatively, take water samples at each point and determine the **biochemical oxygen demand** using the **Winkler method**. The biochemical oxygen demand is the volume of oxygen (in cm^3) absorbed by the organisms in 1 litre of water incubated for 5 days at 20°C. To determine this, you will need to collect a water sample from each site with the minimum possible disturbance. Add to each sample a known volume of aerated 'dilution water'. This contains nutrient salts, so that bacterial activity will not be inhibited during the incubation by lack of nutrient ions. Pour each sample into a 250 cm^3 sample bottle and incubate in the dark for 5 days at 20°C, together with control bottles which contain only dilution water.

Determine the concentration of dissolved oxygen in each flask at the beginning and end of the 5 day period by the Winkler procedure. This involves the titration of a sample of the solution against dilute sodium thiosulphate.

Relate your information about the source of the pollution to the species composition of the animal life (Table 7.1) and to your measurements of the oxygen saturation of the water.

For consideration

1   Does the pollution have a significant effect on the animal life in the water and, if so, what could be done to prevent the pollution in future?

2   Explain in detail why the addition of fertiliser to a stream might ultimately cause deoxygenation of the water.

3   How does the oxygen content differ with depth? How does this affect both the distribution of animal species, and the suitability of your sampling techniques?

4   As a conservationist, what steps might you take to increase the range of species present in the water?

References

Identification guides:

Clegg, J. *The Observer's Book of Pond Life, 3rd edn*. Warne, London, 1980.

Macan, T. T. *A Guide to Freshwater Invertebrate Animals*. Longmans, Harlow, 1959.

Mellanby, H. *Animal Life in Freshwater, 6th edn*. Methuen, London, 1963.

Quigley, M. *Invertebrates of Streams and Rivers. A Key to Identification*. Arnold, London, 1977.

Techniques:

Hewitt, G. River quality investigations, Part 1: some diversity and biotic indices. *Journal of Biological Education*, **25,** 44–52, 1991. (Provides more details about biotic indices.)

Lock, R. & Collins, N. Freshwater studies using cattle drinking troughs. *Journal of Biological Education*, **30**, 166–168, 1996. (How to set up cattle troughs in the school grounds, if there are none nearby.)

McClusky, D. S. *Ecology of Estuaries*. Heinemann, London, 1971. (For Winkler technique.)

Maidment, C., Mitchell, C. & Westlake, A. Measuring aquatic organic pollution by the permanganate value method. *Journal of Biological Education*, **31**, 126–130, 1997. (An alternative to the Winkler technique for biological oxygen demand.)

Requirements

River or stream with discharge into it of water or organic matter, e.g. from a factory, farm or sewage works
Plankton nets
Plastic bowls
Wellington boots
Oxygen meter, or chemicals for the Winkler method of oxygen determination involving titration of incubated samples of water against sodium thiosulphate

Key skills

✓ **Application of number:** You have to collect and record numerical data on measured volumes of liquids. You should compare the oxygen concentrations in the two water bodies by using a t-test (see Statistical Analysis Appendix, p. 304).

The nitrogen cycle in an aquarium

This exercise extends over more than one practical session.

A well-established aquarium should contain a range of bacteria which are involved in its **nitrogen cycle**. They will include **decomposers** which release ammonia from the proteins, and **nitrifying bacteria** which process the ammonia to nitrite and then to nitrate. This practical involves putting in a pulse of protein and determining whether you can detect the nitrite or nitrate produced.

Sensitive 'dip-sticks', such as Merkoquant reagent strips, provide rapid colour tests for ammonia and nitrate concentrations. Follow the instructions provided.

Requirements

Merkoquant reagent strips to detect ammonium or nitrate (or the equivalent solutions sold by aquarium shops)

Aquarium tank, set up 4 weeks before, containing water weed, pond snails, small crustaceans, fish and plenty of substrate

Casein hydrolysate, 1 g

Note to technicians: Aquaria differ in their levels of nitrifying bacteria. Unfortunately, with low levels of these bacteria this practical can result in a burst of toxic ammonia, killing organisms and stinking out the laboratory. We suggest that you should subculture your aquarium into a smaller tank, making sure that you transfer a considerable amount of the substrate, a month before the experiment is due to start.

Procedure

1. Test the water in the aquarium for ammonium and nitrate. If the concentrations of either of these ions are near the maximum which the test will detect, dilute the water with de-ionised water, and test it again before proceeding. Record the results.

2. Add to the water 0.25 g per litre of casein hydrolysate (amino acids and short-chain peptides). Straight away, test the water again for ammonium and nitrate. Record the resuts.

3. Test the water again, at intervals of 12 hours at first, for up to 1 week, or until the concentrations return to those at the start. Record the results. Note any responses of organisms in the aquarium which might be the result of the added pulse of amino acids.

4. Plot a graph of ammonium and nitrate concentrations against time.

For consideration

1. How did the relevant bacteria get into the aquarium in the first place?

2. At the end of the experiment, did the nitrate return to its previous concentration? if so, can you suggest how?

3. Imagine that a farmer dumps some protein-rich effluent into a slow-flowing river. On the basis of your results, what might happen?

Effect of eutrophication on the growth of duckweed and algae

Many waterways, lakes and ponds are polluted by excess nitrates and phosphates, a phenomenon known as **eutrophication**. Nitrates may be mainly derived from fertiliser run-off, phosphates from sewage and detergents. What effects do these compounds have on plant growth, separately and together?

This practical exercise allows you to investigate the effect of added nitrates and phosphates on the growth of photosynthesising organisms in a controlled experiment in the laboratory or glasshouse.

Procedure

1. Place 250 cm^3 of water from the same source (e.g. tap water) into each of 20 beakers. Do not use water from a source which may already have been enriched with nutrients.

2 Four control beakers (labelled C) have no nutrient additions. There are eight nutrient addition treatments, each applied to two beakers. Label each beaker with its appropriate treatment symbol: Nl, N2, P1, P2, N1P1, N1P2, N2P1, N2P2. In this code, N1 is a small addition of nitrate (as 1g of $NaNO_3$), N2 is a large addition of nitrate (5g of $NaNO_3$), P1 is a small addition of phosphate (0.1g of $CaHPO_4$) and P2 is a large addition of phosphate (0.5g of $CaHPO_4$).

3 Add to each beaker the appropriate mass of salt(s) and stir thoroughly.

4 To each beaker add 10 plants of a duckweed (*Lemna*) species (e.g. *L. gibba*). Count and record the total number of leaves on the plants in each treatment at the start of the experiment.

5 Arrange the beakers in a glasshouse in a 4×5 pattern. Their positions should be randomised and recorded on a plan.

6 At weekly intervals, examine the beakers. Count and record the total numbers of leaves on the plants in each beaker. Then randomise the positions of the beakers again.

7 After 4 weeks, the growth of algae in some beakers may become obvious as a green colouration in the water or on the sides of the beakers. At each sampling date, estimate by eye the relative densities of algae in each beaker. Carefully pour some of the water from each beaker into a clean test tube or colorimeter tube and use a colorimeter to determine how much light the chlorophyll in the sample can absorb. Pour the sample back into the beaker once you have measured its light absorption.

8 Draw graphs of the numbers of leaves per treatment, and the chlorophyll absorption, in each treatment with time.

For consideration

1 What were the effects of the addition of nutrient on the duckweed and the algae?

2 Which was the more effective at promoting growth on its own, the nitrate or the phosphate?

3 Often, the addition of nitrate and phosphate together increases growth far more than might be expected from the effects of nitrates or phosphates alone. Did such an 'interaction' occur in your experiment, and can you explain it?

4 The salts were added as sodium nitrate and calcium phosphate. Design an experiment to confirm that the growth effects in this experiment are due to the nitrate and phosphate rather than to the sodium and calcium (not so easy!).

5 What was the reason for randomising the bench positions of the beakers from time to time?

6 How did the growth conditions in the beakers differ from those which the duckweed might encounter in a waterway enriched with nutrients?

7 Speculate on the influence which lush plant growth in a river or stream might have on the other organisms in the community.

Sodium nitrate

Sodium nitrate

Requirements

Glasshouse or laboratory bench
Beakers (250 cm³ or larger), ×20
Colorimeter and tubes
Measuring cylinder
Marker for writing on glass
Balance
Sodium nitrate(V)
Calcium monohydrogen phosphate (a commercial fertiliser such as phostrogen is a suitable alternative)
Duckweed plants (*Lemna* sp.)

✓ **Information technology:** Become acquainted with the use of sensors and a data-logger. Present your results graphically, using a computer program.

7.14 INVESTIGATION

Effect of organic matter on oxygen depletion in freshwater

When organic matter, such as sewage or leaf litter, falls into ponds, rivers or streams, it is decomposed by bacteria and fungi, which take up oxygen from the water for their aerobic respiration. This may reduce the oxygen concentration in the water to a level at which it is impossible for some aquatic animals to survive.

In this investigation you can add leaf litter or cattle dung to fresh water in a controlled experiment, and investigate its effect on the survival and reproductive success of an aquatic animal species.

Gloves should be worn   Cattle dung

Guidance

Ideally, you need 16 tall beakers. This enables you to set up four different litter or dung treatments, each with four beakers.

Weigh out the leaf litter or cattle dung, place it in the beakers, label them, add fresh water and then add to each beaker a fixed amount of culture of *Daphnia* or a similar aquatic arthropod. At daily intervals, measure the oxygen concentration at the base of each beaker with an oxygen probe (see Technique 7.15, below), make notes on the appearance of each beaker and assess the numbers of live *Daphnia*.

For consideration

1 Under what circumstances, in real life, are waterways likely to have organic matter added to them on a scale similar to that in this experiment, and what might be the consequences?
2 What effect did the addition of nutrients (or toxins) in the organic matter have on the results of the experiment?
3 Why are ponds frequently dredged in autumn?

Requirements

Tall beakers or aquaria
Tap water which has been left standing for a few days
Abundant leaf litter, grass clippings or cattle dung
Pen for marking on glass
Electronic balance
Oxygen meter, with data-logging equipment if possible (see Technique 7.15, below)
Culture of *Daphnia* or similar aquatic arthropod

✓ **Information technology:** Become acquainted with the use of sensors and a data-logger. Express your results graphically, using a computer program.

Data-logging in ecology

The different data-logging systems available all have in common that sensors – capable of detecting environmental changes – are linked to, and powered by, data-loggers or card-loggers, which store the signals. The signals are then outputted to a computer equipped with suitable software, which enables the environmental measurements to be recorded, printed out, expressed as graphs, or analysed. It is easy to accumulate data in this way (e.g. Practical Exercise 2.41, p. 117). You must, however, critically assess how relevant the data are to the organisms themselves, and their distribution.

These data-logging systems are used in schools and colleges for investigations of a few hours' to a few days' duration and, in particular, for project work. The most useful sensors in ecology are those that detect **temperature** (thermistors), **light intensity, pH** and **oxygen** concentration. They are often used to measure changes over the 24 hour daily cycle. In ponds or aquaria, for example, temperature and light intensity increase during the day. Oxygen concentrations may increase in the day, as plants photosynthesise faster than all the organisms respire, and decline at night because aerobic respiration outstrips photosynthesis. Water pH generally exhibits an equivalent pattern, increasing during the day as slighly acidic carbon dioxide is used up, and decreasing at night, when the net carbon dioxide output acidifies the water. These diurnal fluctuations can all be measured with sensors linked to data-logging equipment.

Pressure and **humidity** sensors are sometimes useful in studies of plant transpiration. A pressure sensor can be used to collect the measurements of mass from a balance, in investigations of water loss from leaves or small animals.

Reference

Frost, R. *Datalogging in Practice*. Association for Science Education, Hatfield, Hertfordshire, 1998.

Requirements

Sensors
Data-logger or card-logger
Electricity supply (or spare batteries, if logger is to be used remotely)
Computer
Appropriate software on computer for processing stored signals and analysing them graphically

Note: Several different systems are available, for instance from Philip Harris Educational (sales@education.philipharris.co.uk), DataHarvest Education (sales@dharvest.demon.co.uk), Scientific and Technical Supplies, Bilston (scs@scichem.co.uk), the Pasco system (Instruments Direct, Unit 4, Brentford Business Centre, Commerce Road, Brentford TW8 8LG) or the Carolina systems (www.carolina.com).

Lichens as indicators of atmospheric pollution

There are more than 1300 species of lichen in the British Isles and some are more sensitive than others to atmospheric pollution, particularly to sulphur dioxide. In fact the range of lichen species present at a site provides the best indication of the average concentration of sulphur dioxide in the air in winter. In general, there are fewer lichen species in cities than in the countryside. As one moves further from a road or a polluting factory, the range of lichen species increases. In this investigation you will use a standard scale (Table 7.2), involving a few easily recognisable and widespread species, to compare the pollution levels at several sites. Although most of the species mentioned in Table 7.2 are lichens, *Grimmia pulvinata* is a moss and *Desmococcus* is an alga.

Guidance

Always sample lichens in areas with broad-leaved trees and old stonework (conifers and new stonework usually lack lichens). Old

Table 7.2 A biological scale, based on the occurrence of *Pleurococcus* and various lichens and mosses, which can be used to estimate the mean winter level of sulphur dioxide in the atmosphere. The key beneath the table provides some hints on the identification of species.

Zone	Lichens, mosses and algae	Mean winter SO$_2$ (μg m^{-2})
0	Only *Desmococcus* (green alga) growing on bark	over 170
1	*Lecanora conizaeoides* (lichen) on trees and acid stone	150–160
2	*Xanthoria parietina* (lichen) appears on concrete, asbestos and limestone	about 125
3	*Parmelia* (lichen) appears on acid stone and *Grimmia pulvinata* (moss) occurs on limestone or near mortar	about 100
4	Grey leafy flat lichen species (e.g. *Hypogymnia physodes*) begin to appear pressed to tree bark	about 70
5	Shrubby lichens (e.g. *Evernia prunastri*) begin to appear on trees	about 40–60
6	*Usnea* (lichen) becomes abundant	about 35

Desmococcus is a bright green, unicellular alga which frequently forms a green film over the moist bark of trees.

Lecanora is a lichen which forms grey-green dots, 2 mm across, closely pressed to stone or the bark of living or dead wood.

Xanthoria is a bright yellow lichen (can be orange, red) which forms distinct circular or oval patches, lobed at the edge and usually with yellow dots on the centre.

Parmelia species of lichen occur on stones and trees. They form flat grey plates. They are dark beneath and often attached to the substrate by means of root-like threads.

Grimmia pulvinata is a moss which occurs in small rounded, neat, dense cushions, 1–2 cm high, grey appearance from the 'hair points' of leaves, on rocks or stones.

Hypogymnia physodes is a lichen which is found on trees and fences as grey-green flat plates with the edges strongly lobed. The lobes are 2–4 mm wide and tend to stick up into the air; there are no root-like threads beneath, unlike *Parmelia*.

Shrubby lichens are erect and bush-like, or hanging and tassel-like.

Usnea lichen species are usually grey-green, intricately branched, long and trailing, hanging like long tassels from tree branches. They are known as 'beard lichens'.

churchyards are ideal. The lichens in Table 7.2, which are characteristic of the least polluted areas, are found only on trees.

Only a few resistant lichens are found at the most polluted sites. These lichens may well be present at all the sites you sample. The 'lichen zone' of an area is determined by the lichen with the least pollution resistance. Thus a site with *Desmococcus*, *Xanthoria* and *Parmelia* would be in zone 3, because of the presence of *Parmelia*.

Select a range of sites to test a hypothesis. A possible hypothesis might be that a certain power station produces polluting gases. At each site, examine the lichens and record those present; record also the likely pollution sources and their distance away. Do not remove lichens or mosses; lichens only grow very slowly and must be conserved. Write a report on your findings.

For consideration

1 Suggest two ways in which lichens (and mosses) absorb nutrient ions. Suggest why these organisms are more sensitive to atmospheric pollution than flowering plants.
2 What are the advantages and disadvantages of using organisms as indicators of pollution (see also Investigation 7.11, p.281), rather than chemical analysis?
3 Do lichens growing on walls or trees have any value? Why should they be conserved?

Key skills

✓ **Working with others:** If this is a class exercise, you will need to work in pairs (for safety!), discuss identification difficulties and pool your data with your classmates.
✓ **Communication:** Once you have collected all the data, obtain extra research data on this topic using at least two sources. Produce a written research report. Then plan a talk, with appropriate visual aids, to communicate the results, and their implications, clearly to others.

Using the Lincoln Index to estimate population sizes

INVESTIGATION 7.17

There are various ways of estimating population sizes, depending on the species concerned. The most direct is simply to attempt to count all the individuals in the population. However, this is only feasible for populations made up of large, relatively immobile individuals.

A useful technique which can be used for mobile species is the capture–recapture method, also known as the **mark–release–recapture method**. The principle is straightforward. First, a sample of individuals is caught, counted and marked in some way. Then these individuals are released back into their original location. After they have been allowed to mix with the unmarked individuals, a second sample is caught and counted and the number of marked individuals noted. An estimate of the total population size can then be made by calculating what is called the **Lincoln Index**, thus:

Population size $= n_1 n_2 / n_m$

where:
$n_1 =$ number of individuals marked and released
$n_2 =$ number of individuals caught in the second sample
$n_m =$ number of marked individuals caught in the second sample.

Guidance

You will need to catch individuals, mark them in some way and then return them unharmed. Choose a species that is suitable for this method. Different methods of capture and marking may be needed for different species. For instance, ground beetles can be caught in **pitfall traps** (see Technique 7.1, p.265) and marked by placing a minute drop of waterproof paint on one of their hardened front wings (elytra).

Small mammals can be trapped in **Longworth traps** (Figure 7.3) and marked by clipping off a small piece of their fur. However, any

Longworth, or other, trap used for catching small mammals must be adjusted so that it does not catch any shrews. It is illegal to capture shrews without a licence, the reason being that their metabolic rate is so high that they die within a few hours unless able to feed.

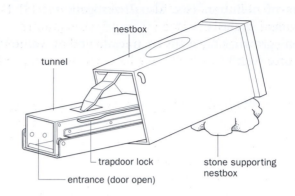

Figure 7.3 A Longworth trap, primed and baited to catch small mammals.

Other possible species for the mark–release–recapture method include, in the laboratory, flour beetles and, in the field, woodlice, pond skaters, whirligig beetles (see G. Dussart, Mark–recapture experiments with freshwater organisms, *Journal of Biological Education*, **25**, 116–118, 1991), grasshoppers or snails. Within a school, to demonstrate the principle, the technique can be used to estimate the numbers of year 7 or year 8 pupils.

Conduct a small pilot investigation to ensure that you can catch and satisfactorily mark individuals of your chosen species (Figure 7.4). For your main investigation, you will need to mark sufficient individuals to recapture at least half a dozen marked individuals. You will also have to decide how long to wait between returning the marked individuals and obtaining your second sample. Once you have carried out your investigation, estimate the size of the population using the Lincoln Index given above.

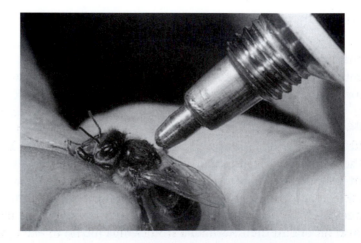

Figure 7.4 A student using a permanent marking pen to mark a honeybee *(Apis mellifera)* queen.

For consideration

1   Using the Lincoln Index to estimate population sizes involves making a number of assumptions. One assumption is that marked individuals are as likely as unmarked individuals to die or to emigrate from the population before the second sample is obtained. Can you suggest at least three other assumptions made? Do you think these assumptions are realistic for your investigation?
2   Suggest ways in which your procedures could be improved.
3   In what ways might this technique be of use in ecological research?

References

Department for Education and Science. *Animals and Plants in Schools: Legal Aspects*. Administrative Memorandum No. 3/90, Department for Education amd Science, London, 1990. (Spells out the illegality of shrew capture without a licence.)

Advice on both legal and technical aspects of mammal trapping is available from the Mammal Society, Department of Zoology, University of Bristol, Woodland Road, Bristol BS8 1UG.

Requirements

Oil paint (any bright colour)
Paint brushes (size 00 for marking individuals and size 1 for moving them) or fine scissors
Longworth traps, pitfall traps or suitable nets
Other items may be required by individual students

Key skills

✓   **Application of number:** The calculations in the Lincoln Index are not easy for everyone. After you have worked out the population size for yourself, construct some imaginary data and calculate the population size to check that you fully understand the method.

The relationship between a predator and its prey   7.18 PRACTICAL EXERCISE

In a natural community, one animal species preys upon another. From this we can predict that the feeding relationship between these two species may influence their relative abundance.

In this investigation the predator–prey relationship between two common pond animals is analysed. The two animals are the damselfly or dragonfly nymph (predators) and the water flea *Daphnia* (prey).

Biting dragonfly nymphs

Procedure

1   Label six jars A–F and place an equal volume of pond water in each; they should not be more than two-thirds full.
2   Place one nymph (damselfly or dragonfly) in each jar, providing it with a short twig on which to cling.
3   After 10 minutes to allow the nymph to settle down, transfer a known number of *Daphnia* specimens to each jar: to jar A add five *Daphnia*, to B add 10, to jar C add 15, to D add 20, to jar E add 30 and to F add 50. Leave each jar for 40 minutes.
4   After the 40 minutes has elapsed, remove the predator from each jar and count the number of *Daphnia* still remaining.
5   Record your results, pool them with the class results and calculate the average number of *Daphnia* eaten (vertical axis) in each jar.
6   Plot the average number of *Daphnia* eaten (vertical axis) against the number of *Daphnia* in each jar before predation (horizontal axis).

Six jars or beakers of the same size
Wide-mouthed teat pipette
Pond water
Rich culture of water fleas
Dragonfly or damselfly nymphs, ×6
    (starve them for 24 hours beforehand
    and, after the experiment, return them
    to their natural habitat)
Short twigs, ×6

For consideration

1 What can you say about the relationship between the rate of predation and prey density?

2 In the wild, could this particular predator have a significant effect in controlling the numbers of the *Daphnia* species?

3 Predict what might have happened if you had included a second prey species, at a variety of densities, in your experiment.

Key skills

✓ **Application of number:** Calculation of the average number of *Drosophila* eaten should be accompanied by calculation of the standard errors of the means (see Statistical Analysis Appendix, p.304), so that the means can be meaningfully compared.

✓ **Information technology:** Ideally, you should use a computer program to calculate the means and their standard errors, and to draw the graphs.

7.19 INVESTIGATION

Effect of different conditions on the growth of yeast cells[BM]

Microorganisms grow better under certain environmental conditions, just as animals and plants do. In this investigation we suggest that you should use a **haemocytometer,** as described in Technique 2.45 on p.122 and Technique 5.17 on p.231 to study the optimal conditions for the growth in numbers of a yeast population.

Guidance

1 Make a list of the various environmental factors which might affect the growth in numbers of a yeast population (e.g. temperature, availability of nitrogen).

2 Predict how you might expect one of these factors to affect the growth in numbers of a yeast population.

3 Investigate the effects of this one factor.

Requirements

Microscope
Haemocytometer
Graduated cylinder (50 or 100 cm³)
Conical flask (250 cm³)
Cotton wool
Pipette
Linear (usual, arithmetical) graph paper
Semi-logarithmic paper
Nutrient medium for yeast (e.g. cider,
    2% sucrose solution or malt broth)
Suspension of brewer's yeast
Other items may be requested by
    individual students

For consideration

Was your prediction confirmed or refuted? How could you extend your study to build up a picture of the niche of a microorganism?

Reference

Mills, J. & Jackson, R. Analysis of microbial growth data using a spreadsheet. *Journal of Biological Education*, **31**, 34–38, 1997. (For spreadsheet analysis of microbial growth data.)

Key skills

✓ **Information technology:** For spreadsheet analysis, see *Reference* above. Use a computer program to plot a graph of the increase in microbial numbers with time.

Before starting a project, as on p. 57 assess the risks inherent in your intended procedure and discuss your intended procedure with your teacher/lecturer. Teachers should verify the safety of any site to be visited. (The various safety considerations are covered in *Safety in Biological Fieldwork*, Institute of Biology, London, 1999.)

1 Use some of the sampling techniques outlined in Technique 7.1 (p. 265) to compare the animal or plant species of two or more contrasting habitats. Possiblities include hedge and roadside verge, slow-flowing and fast-flowing parts of a stream, or shady woodland and clearings.

2 Investigate the distribution pattern of nettles (*Urtica dioica*) in relation to soil nitrate or phosphate. (See G. Monger (Ed.), *Revised Nuffield Biology, Practical Guide 7*, Longmans, Harlow, 1986.)

3 Examine the pattern of earthworm distribution in relation to shade, soil pH and soil organic matter content. (See T. J. King, *Ecology*, Nelson, Walton-on-Thames,1989.) Mustard in water seems a particularly efficient non-toxic worm-disturbing compound. (See A. Gunn, Estimating earthworm populations, *School Science Review*, **72**, 86–88, 1991; the relative advantages of mustard and detergent are discussed by D. East & D. Knight, Sampling soil earthworm populations using household detergent and mustard, *Journal of Biological Education*, **32**, 201–206, 1998.) Investigate, for example: (i) the abundance of earthworms with distance from the trunks of trees; (ii) their relative abundance in limed and unlimed soil; (iii) their relative abundance under broad-leaved and coniferous trees. The results can be followed up by choice chamber experiments in the laboratory. (See T. Pearce, V. Robinson & P. Ineson, Earthworms and soil pH, *School Science Review*, **70**, 63–68, 1988.)

4 Compare the distribution patterns of any two species of woodlouse, and then explain them as far as possible by laboratory experiments to investigate the environmental preferences of the species, with choice chambers or by providing a range of microhabitats within a glass jar.

5 Investigate the effects of different soil water table levels on plant growth in turves. (See G. Monger (Ed.), *Revised Nuffield Biology, Practical Guide 7*, Longmans, Harlow, 1986.) Turves can be cut from a lawn or a playing field (care!) and kept in large plastic bowls in which different water levels are maintained by watering or a siphon system. The effects of these treatments on plant growth can be monitored and related to the natural microhabitats of the species.

6 Examine the relationship between earthworms and seeds. Collect faecal pellets and germinate the seeds; estimate the survival rates of different species of seed in the gut. (See T. G. Piearce, N. Roggero & R. Tipping, Earthworms and seeds, *Journal of Biological Education*, **28**, 195–202, 1994.)

7 If you have a site near you with abundant ant-hills or mole-hills, compare the relative abundances of five selected plant species on the ant-hills/mole-hills with their abundances in the surrounding vegetation, using the methods in Technique 7.1 (p. 265). Are the abundances of any of these species significantly different on and away from the mounds? Carry out statistical tests to find out. (See Statistical Analysis Appendix, p. 304.) If so, suggest reasons. (See T. J. King & S. R. J. Woodell, The use of the mounds of *Lasius flavus* in teaching some principles of ecological investigation, *Journal of Biological Education*, **9**, 109–113, 1975.)

8 Examine the distribution patterns of mosses on walls or gravestones in relation to aspect, or algae up a salt marsh or rocky shore, and relate the patterns of different species to their desiccation tolerances. The green protoctist, *Pleurococcus*, widespread on tree trunks and fences, is also worth investigation.

9 Investigate factors affecting the distribution patterns of barnacles, limpets and mussels on a rocky shore, or freshwater shrimps and planarians in a freshwater stream.

10 Compare the effects of different salinities on the growth of two plant species, one of which normally grows on salty soils near the sea, and the other which is usually found on inland soils. (A suitable method, using multicompost or perlite, and investigating both seed germination and growth, is given by E. Whitaker, The effects of salt on the growth of ryegrass, *Journal of Biological Education*, **28**, 13–16, 1994.)

11 Investigate the effect of different salinities on the hatching success and growth of the brine shrimp, *Artemia salina*. Eggs are available from most aquarists or aquatic centres. (See K. Ward-Booth, & M. J. Reiss, *Artemia salina*: an easily cultured invertebrate ideally suited for ecological studies, *Journal of Biological Education*, **22**, 247–251, 1988. For further ecological projects on brine shrimps, consult M. Dockery, Investigating the feeding behaviour of brine shrimps, *Journal of Biological Education*, **34**, 211–213, 2000, S. Tomkins, A review of the use of the brine shrimp, *Artemia* spp., for teaching practical biology in schools and colleges, *Journal of Biological Education*, **34**, 117–122, 2000 or even the book M. Dockery & S. Tomkins, *Brine shrimp ecology*, British Ecological Society, London, 2000.)

12 Using a pH probe attached to a data-logging device (see Technique 7.15, p. 287), record the fluctuations in pH in the same place in an aquarium over a period of one day. Alter the position of the probe and read the pH in different parts of the aquarium. Interpret your observations in terms of the balance between photosynthesis and respiration, and fluctuations in temperature. Can you test your conclusions experimentally by altering the environmental conditions and predicting the effects of your changes on the pH fluctuations?

13 Measure the growth of duckweed (*Lemna* sp.) at different concentrations of added detergent to simulate pollution in an experiment designed rather like Practical Exercise 7.13 (p. 284). Other possible pollutants are copper (use copper-containing coins) and female sex hormones, such as ethynyloestradiol, commonly used in contraceptive tablets, and they can be tested on *Lemna* sp., *Elodea canadensis* or *Spirodela polyrhiza*. (See S. Kawakami, T. Oda & R. Ban, The influence of coins on the growth of duckweed, *Journal of Biological Education*, **31**, 116–118, 1997 or M. Walker, L. Read, K Jackson and others, The effects of oestrogenic substances on two components of freshwater ecosystems, *Journal of Biological Education*, **32**, 226–229, 1998.)

14 The effects of acid rain can be investigated by watering seedlings of cress (*Lepidium sativum*) or mustard (*Brassica nigra*) in a replicated experiment with simulated rainfall of buffer solutions of different pH, using a range of pH 1–7. Similar investigations can be performed on seed germination and early seedling growth of a variety of species. To test the effects of acid rain on leaves, different, marked leaves on large plants kept in the laboratory, a frame or a greenhouse can be exposed to artificial rainfall of different pH.

15 The predator–prey experiment (Practical Exercise 7.18, p. 291) can also be carried out with small fish provided with prey at differerent densities – for example water fleas or midge larvae (bloodworms). Altenatively, investigate the effects of providing the insect predator with a choice of two different prey, at a variety of densities.

16 Competition experiments between two different plant species can be carried out by growing them at different relative numbers in pots in a greenhouse. This is easiest to set up from the seedling stage. Mustard (*Brassica nigra*) and cress (*Lepidium sativum*) can be sown together, and a range of densities achieved by removing some of the seedlings which emerge. Experiments are more convincing if the competing species normally occur together in nature, for example a crop plant and a weed which is found with it, or two species of duckweed (*Lemna* spp.) which can be competed in water-filled beakers. (See G. Monger (Ed.), *Revised Nuffield Biology, Practical Guide 7*, Longmans, Harlow, 1986.) Alternatively, it is fascinating to compare the outcomes of sowing seeds of competing species at different relative times.

If you perform such experiments, it is important to reproduce each treatment three or four times. At the end of the experiment, the best measure of relative growth is usually the dry mass of the harvested plants.

17 Investigate the growth rates of white clover (*Trifolium repens*) and grass in turves containing both, exposed to different fertiliser treatments. Clover is a legume, and therefore likely to have an independent source of nitrogen through nitrogen fixation by bacteria in its root nodules. Carefully map the relative positions of clover and grasses, on squared paper, in six turves collected from a grassland. Leave two of the turves as controls, add a low dose of nitrogenous fertiliser to two more, and a high dose to the other two. Keep the turves in shallow trays in a glasshouse and, at intervals, map the areas covered by grass and clover.

18 Using the technique suggested in Practical Exercise 7.9 (p. 277), compare the energy budgets of stick insects (or desert locusts) of different sizes and ages. To what extent does the pattern which occurs during the development of a stick insect resemble that of a human as (s)he grows from childhood to adulthood?

19 Determine the energy budget of a domestic mammal, such as a guinea pig. It can be fed weighed amounts of food. Note that the energy content per gram of lipids is about twice that of carbohydrate and protein, and so it is desirable to know the proportion of these various constituents in the diet.

20 Investigate the early stages of succession on bare rock by looking at the lichens and mosses on gravestones of different ages. Are some surfaces more resistant to colonisation than others by virtue of their texture and composition? Can you relate the diameters of certain lichen species to the ages of the gravestones on which they are growing? Can you work out the successional sequence by recording whenever one species is growing on top of another? Relate the speed of colonisation to aspect and slope.

21 Obtain data from tombstones or national newspapers to see whether women and men live to different ages. Data from tombstones will also enable you to see whether life spans have increased over the past few hundred years.

22 Use pitfall trapping (Technique 7.1, p. 265) to compare the species diversity of the ground fauna in two different habitats – for example grassland and woodland. (See M. L. Burchfield, Using pitfall traps to investigate species diversity, *Journal of Biological Education*, **27**, 217–219, 1993.)

23 Investigate succession on herbivore dung.

24 Estimate the pyramid of biomass or energy flow on a mixed farm (with the farmer's permission!). (Some useful background data, and an example to start you off, are given by D. C. J. Maidment, Energy studies in dairy farming, *School Science Review*, **77** (279), 63–65, 1995.)

25 Devise a project to study some aspect of biological control. For example, do ladybirds control the numbers of aphids?

26 Investigate the efficiency of different compounds in controlling the populations of mosquito larvae in water. If you cannot find them in the wild, first rear your mosquitoes. (See S. A. Corbet & G. W. Danahar, Rearing mosquitoes – pets or public enemies? *Journal of Biological Education*, **27**, 253–259, 1993.)

27 Study some aspect of the population biology of an introduced species, for example grey squirrel (*Sciurus carolinensis*), rabbit (*Oryctolagus cuniculus*), Japaese knotweed (*Fallopia japonica*), rhododendron (*Rhododendron ponticum*) or swamp stonecrop (*Crassula helmsii*). How abundant is the species in a given area? How many offspring can each individual produce? How old are individuals before they can reproduce?

28 Do different species of slugs or snails occupy the same feeding niche? Collect the faecal pellets by keeping the individuals in separate containers for 24 hours. Estimate the proportions of various constituents under the microscope: living (green) flowering plant tissue; living moss; dead moss; fungi; pollen grains; arthropods; the rest. Do the diets of species differ? Do the species compete with one another for food?

29 Follow the development of frog or toad spawn in a pond. Can you work out what causes death at different stages of the life cycle?

The fitness of the white-eyed allele in *Drosophila*   8.1 INVESTIGATION

As discussed in Handling *Drosophila* (Technique 6.3, on p. 250), numerous **mutants**, or different forms, are known in the fruit fly, *Drosophila melanogaster*. In this investigation it is suggested that you study whether individuals with white eyes are fitter or less fit than individuals with red eyes.

Guidance

In order to see whether or not the allele for white eyes is fitter than the allele for red eyes, you will need to set up breeding colonies of *Drosophila*, using the methods described in Technique 6.3 on p. 250, and then follow the resulting populations for at least two generations. The principle is to set up colonies in which there is competition between white-eyed and red-eyed individuals. Here are two possible starting breeding colonies, though you may think of others:

- Three red-eyed males, three white-eyed males and six red-eyed females.
- Six red-eyed males, three white-eyed females and three red-eyed females.

However you proceed, the important thing once the colonies are set up is to count the number of individuals with different phenotypes over at least two generations. You should then be in a position to:

1 Work out whether one allele is dominant or whether they are codominant.
2 Determine whether the alleles occur on the autosomal or sex chromosomes.
3 Predict the ratios of phenotypes you would expect to see in successive generations from your answers to (1) and (2) and your knowledge of Mendelian genetics.
4 Compare your observed phenotypic ratios with your expected phenotypic ratios (if necessary using the χ^2 test explained on p. 312).
5 Determine whether the allele for white eyes has the same fitness as the allele for red eyes.

For consideration

1 Is red-eyed dominant to white-eyed, or *vice versa*, or are the two alleles codominant? Explain your answer.
2 Are the alleles autosomal or sex-linked? How do you know?
3 Did you find that the allele for white eyes has the same fitness as the allele for red eyes?
4 Why was it necessary to follow the breeding colonies for at least two generations?

Ether   Ether

Requirements

Hand lens or binocular microscope
White tile or paper
Fine paint brush
Etheriser
Culture bottles
Pure-breeding male red-eyed
   Drosophila
Pure-breeding virgin female red-eyed
   Drosophila
Pure-breeding virgin female white-eyed
   Drosophila

✓ **Application of number:** In 'Guidance' 5, above, choose an appropriate significance test from the Statistical Analysis Appendix (p.304) with which to analyse your results, identify the null hypothesis, calculate the averages, carry out a significance test to estimate the degree of confidence to be placed in this hypothesis, present your findings and explain their relevance to evolution.

8.2 PRACTICAL EXERCISE

Selective predation of coloured prey

The peppered moth, *Biston betularia*, spends much of the day resting on tree trunks, a dangerous pastime as birds find the moths very palatable. The normal speckled white form of the moth does best in unpolluted parts of Britain, where tree trunks are often covered in pale-coloured lichens. In such areas, the dark form is conspicuous. The dark form does best in industrial areas, where pollution kills off the lichens and darkens tree trunks. In these areas, the speckled white form is the more obvious.

In this practical it is suggested that you make pastry 'baits' as prey and see whether students, acting as predators, find some colours easier to find than others.

Procedure

1 Sort washed river gravel into paler ('white') and darker ('brown') piles. Put each type onto a separate tray.
2 Make pastry 'baits' using one part lard (or vegetarian equivalent) to three parts plain flour. Add edible colouring dyes and firm the pastry into pellets approximately 7 mm × 5 mm. Try to get white baits the same colour as the white river gravel, and brown baits the same colour as the brown river gravel.
3 Randomly place the same number of white and brown baits in the tray with white gravel. If the tray is 30 cm × 20 cm, a total of 24 baits would he suitable. You can half-bury the baits, provided you treat the two colours the same.
4 Ask a fellow student to choose the first 10 baits they see. Make a note of how many baits of each colour they choose.
5 Replace the baits and repeat step 4 with another student. Again, record your results. Continue until you have results from 10 students.
6 Carry out steps 3 to 5, but using the tray with the brown gravel.

Requirements

Washed river gravel (average maximum diameter approx. 10 mm), 10 kg (obtainable from builders' merchants)
Cooking lard (or vegetarian equivalent), 100 g
Plain flour, 300 g
Edible colouring dyes – brown, black and orange (obtainable from certain supermarkets or from wholesalers)

For consideration

1 What can you conclude from your results?
2 Explain the significance of your results for the maintenance of genetic polymorphisms in the wild.
3 What difference do you think it would have made if you had carried out the practical with only one student instead of 20 different ones? After you have made your prediction, you might like to carry out the practical with only one student and see whether your prediction is correct.

Reference

Allen, J. A., Anderson, K. P. & Tucker, G. M. More than meets the eye –
a simulation of natural selection. *Journal of Biological Education*, **21**,
301–305, 1987. (See also Project 1, p.303.)

Key skills

✓ **Application of number:** After obtaining the relevant information, choose
an appropriate significance test from the Statistical Analysis Appendix
(p.304) with which to analyse your results, identify the null hypothesis,
calculate the degree of confidence to be placed in this hypothesis, present
your findings and explain their relevance to evolution.

The vertebrate pentadactyl limb: an exercise in homology

8.3 PRACTICAL EXERCISE

Homologous structures are features of different organisms believed by
biologists to share a common ancestor, even though they may differ in
function. So, for example, the spines of cacti are believed to be homologous with the leaf stalks of other flowering plants. On the other hand, the
wings of insects and birds are not thought to be homologous; they are
described as analogous, meaning that they share the same function, but
differ in their ancestry.

A further example of homology is thought to be provided by the
pentadactyl limb of vertebrates, so called because, typically, it terminates
in five digits. It is possessed by amphibians, reptiles, mammals and birds.
However, in the course of evolution, the pentadactyl limb appears to
have undergone considerable modification in different groups. These
modifications have involved enlargement, fusion, degeneration or, in
some cases, total loss of certain components.

In this practical exercise, you will examine the limbs of various
tetrapods (four-limbed animals) and observe the extent to which they
conform to, or depart from, the typical structure of a pentadactyl limb.
In each case, try to correlate the structure of the limb with the function
it performs.

Procedure

Study Figure 8.1. This shows the anatomy of a generalised pentadactyl
limb. Notice that the diagram shows both a forelimb and a hindlimb.
How many bones are shown in each wrist and each ankle?

Rabbit

1   Examine the forelimb and hindlimb bones of a rabbit. Identify the
    component parts, regarding the carpus and tarsus as single units for
    the moment. To what extent does each limb depart from the gener-
    alised pentadactyl pattern?
2   Now examine the carpus and tarsus in detail. Are all the component
    bones present? If not, what do you think has happened to them?
    What functional explanation would you suggest for the modifica-
    tions seen in the carpus and tarsus?

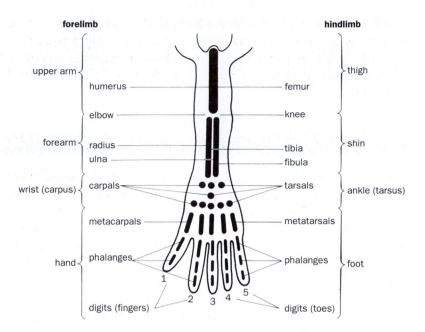

Figure 8.1 A generalised pentadactyl limb of the type possessed by amphibians, reptiles, mammals and birds. The left-hand side points towards the body.

Frog

1   Examine the forelimb and hindlimb bones of a frog. Again, regarding the carpus and tarsus as single units, identify the component parts of each limb. To what extent do the fore- and hindlimbs differ from each other, and how do they depart from the generalised pentadactyl pattern? How would you explain the differences?
2   Now examine the carpus and tarsus in detail. How would you explain the structure of the carpus and tarsus in this animal?

Bird

1   Examine the hindlimb of a bird. This is more modified than that of either the rabbit or the frog. Try to work out what has happened in the course of evolution. What are the likely functional reasons for the modifications?
2   Now examine the forelimb. This is even more modified. Again, try to work out what may have happened in the course of evolution and suggest functional reasons for these modifications. If you have access to an intact wing with the skin and feathers in position, this may help you in your interpretations.

Other tetrapods

If they are available, examine the forelimbs and hindlimbs of other mammals, or photographs of them – for example human, monkey, pig, mole, bat, etc. In each case, how much do their bones depart from the generalised pentadactyl limb, and what advantage might this confer on the individuals in the species?

For consideration

1   Are you convinced that the pentadactyl limbs which you have examined share a common ancestor, or are you sceptical or unsure? What further information, if any, would you need to be more certain?

Requirements

Hand lens
Microscope
Skeleton of forelimb and hindlimb of rabbit
Skeleton of forelimb and hindlimb of frog
Skeleton of forelimb and hindlimb of bird (e.g. pigeon)
Intact wing of bird
Other limb skeletons of tetrapods (or photographs thereof) as available
Feather

2 Birds' wings are covered with feathers. With what structures in other vertebrates might feathers be homologous? How might you test your suggestion? If time permits, examine a feather under the microscope. What functions do feathers perform and how do these relate to their structure?

Variation in leaf and flower morphology in daisies · 8.4 INVESTIGATION

Variation within a species provides the 'raw material' for **natural selection**. Darwin and Wallace independently realised that inherited variation could lead to evolutionary change over time. Suppose, to take a hypothetical example, a species of bee shows variation in its hairiness, and suppose that the climate changes so that it becomes colder. The hairier bees may now be more likely to survive and so, on average, produce more offspring. Over time, natural selection will cause the species to become more hairy.

In this investigation we suggest that you look at variation in daisies with a view to assessing its possible evolutionary significance.

Guidance

Daisies are found growing in lawns or other short grassland and all belong to the one species, *Bellis perennis* (daisy) (Figure 8.2). Daisies are convenient for our purposes, because you can be sure that all the individuals you examine come from the one species. This is important, because natural selection works within species, as some individuals survive and reproduce more than the rest.

Figure 8.2 Daisies *(Bellis perennis)* in flower.

The first thing to do is to find a population of daisies. Ideally, you should have access to at least 50 individuals and they should not all come from a single clump. Having found some daisies, examine them carefully, noting their growth form, leaves and flowers.

Now look at one daisy in detail and describe it as fully as you can. Think about every part of the plant above ground. (There is no need to dig any daisies up.) Most of your description will be **quantitative** – for example, the number of white 'petals', the number of leaves, the length and width of each leaf. However, some of your descriptions may be **qualitative** (e.g. colour). Make a particular effort to record any characters which you suspect show some variation. Keep a record of where each plant is. This will help prevent you from measuring the same plant twice; later, you can see whether any of the characters you have measured vary from place to place.

Once you have collected some data, make a preliminary analysis and presentation of your results. Try, for example, plotting a **frequency distribution histogram** with frequency (i.e. number of individuals) up the vertical axis and variation in a character (e.g. number of petals) along the horizontal axis (see p.4). Is there much variation? What sort of distribution have you found? Does the variation appear to be **discrete** (so that there are only a few classes of individuals, as in the number of fingers humans have) or **continuous** (as in human height)?

Your preliminary analysis may cause you to think of new ways of collecting or recording data before you complete your survey.

For consideration

1 Comment on the amount of variation you found.
2 Suggest what possible evolutionary significance, if any, such variation might have.
3 Do some characters appear to be correlated with others? For example, is leaf length correlated with leaf breadth? If some correlations are found, why do you think this might be?
4 Did you find any evidence that there is more variation between different clumps of daisies than within a clump? Whether you did or didn't, suggest two hypotheses to explain your findings.
5 Do you think daisies reproduce vegetatively or sexually, or both? What significance does this have for your findings?

Key skills

✓ **Communication:** Write an account of this investigation which synthesises the key information into a clear account which can be easily understood by any of your classmates. Plan a talk to the others, with visual images, which is structured, easily understood and concise.
✓ **Application of number:** Present your data clearly in histograms and tables and carry out appropriate correlations (see 'For consideration' 3, above, and the Statistical Analysis Appendix on p.304).
✓ **Information technology:** The histograms can be drawn, and the correlations performed, on a computer.

| 8.5 INVESTIGATION | **Colour and banding in the European field snail (*Cepaea nemoralis*)** |

In the Europaean field snail (*Cepaea nemoralis*), individuals differ greatly in the appearance of their shells (Figure 8.3). This is the result of genetically determined differences in the colours and banding patterns of the shells. The background colour of the shell may be yellow, pink or

Figure 8.3 A group of snails (*Cepaea nemoralis*) on a plant stem on a sand dune. Some of their shells have prominent black bands; banding is genetically determined.

brown. In addition, the number of black bands on the shell varies from no bands at all to as many as five.

You can investigate the reason for this variation. You will only have time to scratch the surface of variation in *Cepaea nemoralis*. The species has been intensively studied since the 1950s and hundreds of papers have been written about its population genetics.

Guidance

First, find some snails, and observe their appearance and distribution. Field snails are widely distributed in woods, hedges and grassland throughout the British isles except northern parts of Scotland. You will need to devise an unambiguous way of describing and categorising the snails' shells (Figure 8.4). Then generate some hypotheses in an attempt to explain the variation in shell colour and banding pattern. For example, you might predict that some forms are more visible to birds, and therefore more likely to be eaten. Visibility will be a feature both of a snail's shell and of the background colour and appearance of its habitat. Or you might predict that some forms warm up more quickly, and are therefore at an advantage in cooler places. Or you might predict that some form of sexual selection is going on, in which individuals either avoid, or are attracted to, other individuals of similar shell appearance.

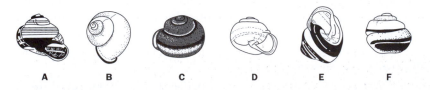

Figure 8.4 Some examples of variation in the European field snail. **A** Yellow shell with five bands and a dark lip (opening to the shell). **B** Pink shell with a dark lip but no bands. **C** Brown shell with only the central band present. **D** Yellow shell with the bands present but unpigmented, making them translucent, and with an unpigmented lip. **E** Yellow shell with five bands but an unpigmented lip. **F** Pink shell with only the central and two lower bands present.

Having generated one or more hypotheses, think carefully how you can test your ideas and then carry out an investigation to test at least one of them. You will probably want to work in an area with two or more contrasting habitats (e.g. grassland and woodland).

For consideration

1 What tentative conclusions can you draw from your investigation?
2 Do you feel that the frequencies of the different forms you have determined are likely to be accurate, in view of the fact that some forms will be more camouflaged than others to your eyes? In what ways might this problem have affected your results, and how could you eliminate it?
3 Try to find out about the range of colours visible to birds. Are birds likely to see the shells in the same way as you do?
4 How could you investigate the genetic basis of any differences that you have observed?

Requirements

Access to a site with European field snails (*Cepaea nemoralis*). Species-rich grassland with adjoining hedges is often suitable.

Key skills

✓ **Application of number:** After obtaining the relevant information, choose an appropriate significance test from the Statistical Analysis Appendix (p.304) with which to analyse your results, identify the null hypothesis, calculate the degree of confidence to be placed in this hypothesis, present your findings and explain their relevance to evolution.

8.6 INVESTIGATION

The struggle for existence among seedlings

Inherited variation between individuals is not enough for natural selection to occur. For natural selection to take place, one **genotype** must be **fitter** than another. Fitter genotypes become more frequent in succeeding generations. In other words, they outcompete less fit genotypes. In this investigation, we suggest that you follow the fortunes of two forms of the same species to see if one sort is fitter than the other one.

Guidance

Fungicide

You need to sow seeds of two forms within a species. These forms must belong to the same species, as natural selection operates within species. One possibility is to sow seeds of two different varieties (e.g. lettuce). Different commercial varieties of the same species can be obtained from garden centres. Choose varieties that differ in leaf shape, so that you can distinguish them without too much difficulty as they grow. Another possibility is to sow seeds of different genotypes within a variety of tomato. These can be chosen with differences in such characters as cotyledon colour, stem colour and stem hairiness.

Sow the seeds in flat trays or pots. Ensure that you sow equal numbers of each variety in each tray or pot, but vary the densities. For example, you might have 10 pots, each with two plants of one form and two plants of the other form (i.e. four plants in total in each pot); 10 pots, each with five plants of one form and five plants of the other form; 10 pots, each with 10 plants of one form and 10 plants of the other form;

10 pots, each with 20 plants of one form and 20 plants of the other form. You may want to use toothpicks to mark the presence of each form, in case it is difficult to distinguish the different forms as they grow.

Keep in a warm, light place and water every 2 or 3 days, but without water-logging the plants. At weekly intervals, observe and describe any differences between the seedlings. Count the number of plants showing each feature. Calculate the ratio between them each week. Continue the investigation for as many weeks as is feasible.

For consideration

1 Did you find any evidence that one genotype is fitter than the other?
2 From your observations, can you suggest why this might be?
3 What effect, if any, did density have?
4 How could this investigation be improved?

▶ Projects

Before starting a project, as on p. 57 assess the risks inherent in your intended procedure and discuss your intended procedure with your teacher/lecturer.

1 Make pastry 'caterpillars' from one part lard (or vegetarian equivalent) to three parts plain flour. Add edible colouring dyes to make various colours of caterpillars (e.g. green and yellow). Place the differently coloured caterpillars on grass. Does the colour of the pastry caterpillars affect the chances of their being eaten by a bird? How does the orientation of the bait affect its chances of being eaten? Interpret your findings with reference to camouflage and predation. (See P. E. Sellers & J. A. Allen, On adapting the right attitude: a demonstration of the survival value of choosing a matching background, *Journal of Biological Education*, **25**, 111–115, 1991, and J. A. Allen, J. M. Cooper, G. J. Hall and others, 'Evolving pastry': a method for simulating microevolution, *Journal of Biological Education* **27**, 274–282, 1993, for further ideas.)

2 Germinate seeds of different species on blotting papers with different concentrations of salt (NaCl). Are there differences between species in salt tolerance?

3 Germinate seeds of a species which has a short life cycle, such *as Brassica campestris* (p. 216), on blotting papers with different concentrations of salt, distinguishing between the seeds derived from each plant. Is there any variation in salt tolerance within the species? If there is, try growing the plants which are most tolerant through to reproduction and see if the seeds they produce are, on average, more tolerant to salt.

4 Lead produced by anti-knock agents (lead tetra-ethyl) in petrol has contaminated roadsides throughout Britain. The concentration of lead in the soil decreases with distance from a busy road. If you have permission from the landowner, select individual plants of the same species from various distances away from a main road and test their tolerance, in culture, to various concentrations of lead chloride solution. Explain how this tolerance could have been selected for. Alternatively, the study can be carried out on different varieties of the same species grown from seed. A suitable species is creeping red fescue (*Festuca rubra*); seeds of the varieties Merlin and Dawson can be obtained from Philip Harris Educational.

5 Carry out a survey to see if there is any relationship in humans between height and the number of children a person has. Investigate males and females separately. Does natural selection appear to be acting on human height? Explain your results.

6 If you have a wild (feral) cat colony near you, record the colours and coat lengths of all the individuals which you can find. Then repeat the exercise on the same number of domestic cats. What do the results show, if anything, about natural and artificial selection?

7 Examine entire skeletons of different vertebrates. What other structures beside the limbs appear to be homologous with each other? Compare such structures and try to explain the differences between them in functional terms.

8 It has been suggested that, when white-eyed male *Drosophila* individuals are very rare in a population dominated by red-eyed individuals, they may actually enjoy greater reproductive success than red-eyed males. Test this hypothesis by setting up breeding colonies with different ratios of white-eyed to red-eyed males, using methods such as those in Technique 6.3, p. 250 and Practical Exercise 6.4, p. 252. Think carefully about your experimental design before starting.

9 Investigate whether the fitness of vestigial-winged *Drosophila* individuals relative to normal-winged individuals depends on the population density. You will need to set up breeding colonies with different densities, either by using containers which differ in size, or by setting up and maintaining colonies with different numbers of individuals. For methods, see Technique 6.3, p. 250. (A similar investigation has been suggested by S. P. Downes, The practical investigation of selection: an A level experiment using *Drosophila melanogaster*, *Journal of Biological Education*, **26**, 37–40, 1992.)

Appendix

Statistical analysis

Much biological work produces data which need to be analysed. The aim of this appendix is to help you to carry out your analysis of data, and to make it easier for you to draw conclusions from your results and understand what is going on.

What are data?

Data are facts like the heights of plants, the number of species growing in a wood and the colours of flowers. Most data are **quantitative**. This means that they are measured in numbers, for example height in centimetres or mass in kilograms. However, some data are **qualitative**, for example flower colour. We shall concentrate on quantitative data because having data in the form of numbers makes analysis more feasible. Sometimes qualitative data can be converted into quantitative data, making analysis easier. For example, colours can be represented by numbers that are the wavelengths of light of these colours. Thus blue is approximately 450 nm, green 510 nm, yellow 570 nm, and so on.

Analysing your data

Analysis of data means doing something with the numbers to help you interpret your findings and draw conclusions. Here is an example based on real data. Suppose you determine the densities of five pieces of wood belonging to a species of tree which we will call species A. You then repeat the exercise with five pieces of wood from another species, species B. All in all you finish up with 10 bits of data, as follows:

Density of wood of species A: 0.76, 0.74, 0.75, 0.72, 0.71

Density of wood of species B: 0.68, 0.67, 0.72, 0.69, 0.66

After getting these results, the best thing to do is to look at them and think about them. By inspection, it seems likely that the density of the wood of species A is greater than that of species B, but how can we be sure? In this case, the first thing to do is to calculate the **mean**.

Calculating means

You have almost certainly calculated means before. All you have to do is to add up the individual values and divide by the total number of measurements. So, in this case, the mean is:

$$(0.76 + 0.74 + 0.75 + 0.72 + 0.71) \div 5 = 0.736$$

The general formula for calculating a mean is:

$$\bar{x} = \Sigma x / n$$

where:
$\bar{x}$ is the mean
Σ stands for 'sum of'

x refers to the individual values of the sample

n is the total number of individual values in the sample

Repeating this exercise with species B, we find that the mean density of the wood of species B is 0.684. Now 0.684 is less than 0.736, so we might feel confident in concluding that species A has denser wood than species B. However, it is worth thinking about these data a bit more carefully.

For a start, note that *some* of the individual measurements of the density of the wood of species A are equal to, or even less than, certain of the individual measurements of the density of the wood of species B. How can we be *certain* that the difference between 0.736 and 0.684 isn't just the result of chance? The answer is that we *can't* be certain. However, we can use statistics to see how *confident* we can be about our conclusions. This is an important distinction. Statistics is not about certainties; it is about what statisticians call **degrees of confidence**.

Degrees of confidence

The easiest way to explain what is meant by degrees of confidence is to give an example. Suppose a bag contains a large number of marbles, some of which are red and some of which are yellow. Imagine now that 10 marbles are drawn at random from the bag, and that eight are red and two yellow. We conclude that the bag may well contain more red than yellow marbles, but we can't be certain of this. Imagine now that a further 10 marbles are drawn at random from the bag and that this time nine are red and one yellow. By now we are even more confident that there are more red than yellow marbles in the bag, but just *how* confident would we have to be to satisfy ourselves that this really is the case?

By convention, statisticians like to be at least 95% certain of something before drawing any conclusions! Another way of saying this is that statisticians like to draw conclusions only if the chance of their being wrong is less than one in 20 – that is, 5%. Let us return to our earlier example of the density of the wood of two different species, A and B. For a statistician to be satisfied that the average density of the wood of the two species *really* is different, we need to show that the probability of the *observed* difference being due to *chance* is less than 5% – that is, less than 0.05. Finding that the probability of the observed difference being due to chance is less than 5% is sometimes referred to as being *confident at the 5% level*.

Another way of putting this is to say that we first *assume* that the densities of the woods of the two species are *not* different. This is our **null hypothesis**, so called because our assumption (hypothesis) is that there is *no* difference between the two woods. We then *reject* this null hypothesis only if we are 95% sure it is wrong.

The statistical tests that follow involve making calculations to determine how confident we can be about drawing conclusions, in other words about *rejecting* a null hypothesis. Some of these tests are made much easier if a calculator with certain statistical functions is available. These requirements are explained under the description of each test. If you have access to a computer with a statistical package, this will save you time, but you will need to refer to the next few pages both to decide which test to use and to interpret the results.

Different sorts of statistical tests

There are hundreds of different statistical tests, and each makes certain assumptions. For our purposes, we can concentrate on three different tests. These tests are widely used in biology and the assumptions they make are valid for most sorts of biological data.

To decide which test you want, answer the following questions:

1 *Are you interested in seeing whether there are significant differences between the means of two sets of data?* (For example, does one species of animal grows faster than another, or does adding fertiliser make a difference to the height of plants?) If the answer to this question is 'yes', go to the section below on '**Testing the difference between two means**'. If, however, the answer to this question is 'no', go to question 2.

2 *Are you interested in seeing whether the ratio of your results is what you expect?* (For example, does a genetics ratio differ significantly from the 3:1 ratio you expected?) If the answer to this question is 'yes', go to the section below on '**Seeing if observed numbers differ from expected numbers**'. If, however, the answer to this question is 'no', go to question 3.

3 *Are you interested in seeing whether two sets of data are correlated?* (For example, do plants with bigger flowers attract more insects, or are people who smoke less fit than other people?) If the answer to this question is 'yes', go to the section below on '**Finding out if a correlation exists**'. If, however, the answer to this question, as to questions 1 and 2, is 'no', then unfortunately we can't help you. You might like to consult your biology teacher/lecturer, a mathematics teacher/lecturer or one of the books on statistics listed on p. 317. As we said earlier, there are hundreds of different statistical tests and we've chosen only three.

Testing the difference between two means

To test the significance of the difference between two means, we need first to calculate **standard deviations.** The standard deviation is a measure of the extent to which individual measurements *vary* around the mean. The greater the variation among the individual measurements, the bigger the standard deviation; the less the variation among the individual measurements, the smaller the standard deviation.

It helps to have a calculator that works out standard deviations. If you *don't* have such a calculator, read the next section entitled '*Calculating standard deviations*'. If you *do* have a calculator that works out standard deviations, you may want to skip this section and go to the section entitled '*Using a calculator to obtain standard deviations*'.

Calculating standard deviations

The standard deviation, s_x, is given by the following formula:

$$s_x = \sqrt{\frac{\Sigma x^2 - \frac{(\Sigma x)^2}{n}}{n-1}}$$

where:

Σ stands for 'sum of'

x refers to the individual values of the sample

n is the total number of individual values in the sample

An example may help. We will go back to our earlier data on the density of the wood of species A. The five individual values – that is, values of x, were: 0.76, 0.74, 0.75, 0.72 and 0.71. The sum of these five values, Σx, equals 3.68. Using these values of x and Σx in the above formula, we have:

$$s_x = \sqrt{\dfrac{(0.76^2 + 0.74^2 + 0.75^2 + 0.72^2 + 0.71^2) - \dfrac{(3.68)^2}{5}}{4}}$$

$$= \sqrt{\dfrac{2.7102 - 2.7085}{4}}$$

$$= 0.021$$

Using a calculator to obtain standard deviations

You may need to have your calculator in standard deviation mode, and type the data into a memory. Then there will be a key, often labelled $\bar{x}$. This key gives you the mean of the data. Another key, often labelled s or σ, gives you the standard deviation. If you have the key σ_{n-1} or s_{n-1} use it in preference to σ_n or s_n for working out the standard deviation.

Using standard deviations to calculate the significance of the difference between two means

If you have a very posh calculator (or access to a statistical package) you may have a key labelled t. This stands for **t-test**, because that is the name of the test we are going to carry out. If you do have such a key, use it as instructed by the calculator or statistical package and go to step 8 below. If you don't have a key labelled t, proceed as follows:

1   Work out the means of each of the two sets of data.
2   Subtract the smaller mean from the larger one.
3   Work out the standard deviation of one set of data. Multiply this number by itself (i.e. square it) and divide it by the number of pieces of data in that set of data.
4   Work out the standard deviation of the other set of data. Multiply this number by itself (i.e. square it) and divide it by the number of pieces of data in that set of data.
5   Add together the figures you calculated in steps 3 and 4.
6   Take the square root of the figure calculated in step 5. You have now calculated what is called the **standard error**.
7   Divide the difference between the two means (step 2) by the figure calculated in step 6. This is your **t value**.
8   Now use Table A.1 to see whether your value of t could be expected by chance. Note that you need to know something called the **degrees of freedom**. For a t-test, the degrees of freedom are simply two less than the total number of individual measurements in the two samples.

Table A.1 Table of t values

Degrees of freedom			t			
1	1.00	3.08	6.31	12.71	63.66	636.62
2	0.82	1.89	2.92	4.30	9.93	31.60
3	0.77	1.64	2.35	3.18	5.84	12.92
4	0.74	1.53	2.13	2.78	4.60	8.61
5	0.73	1.48	2.02	2.57	4.03	6.87
6	0.72	1.44	1.94	2.45	3.71	5.96
7	0.71	1.42	1.90	2.37	3.50	5.41
8	0.71	1.40	1.86	2.31	3.36	5.04
9	0.70	1.38	1.83	2.26	3.25	4.78
10	0.70	1.37	1.81	2.23	3.17	4.59
11	0.70	1.36	1.80	2.20	3.11	4.44
12	0.70	1.36	1.78	2.18	3.06	4.32
13	0.69	1.35	1.77	2.16	3.01	4.22
14	0.69	1.35	1.76	2.15	2.98	4.14
15	0.69	1.34	1.75	2.13	2.95	4.07
16	0.69	1.34	1.75	2.12	2.92	4.02
17	0.69	1.33	1.74	2.11	2.90	3.97
18	0.69	1.33	1.73	2.10	2.88	3.92
19	0.69	1.33	1.73	2.09	2.86	3.88
20	0.69	1.33	1.73	2.09	2.85	3.85
21	0.69	1.32	1.72	2.08	2.83	3.82
22	0.69	1.32	1.72	2.07	2.82	3.79
24	0.69	1.32	1.71	2.06	2.80	3.75
26	0.68	1.32	1.71	2.06	2.78	3.71
28	0.68	1.31	1.70	2.05	2.76	3.67
30	0.68	1.31	1.70	2.04	2.75	3.65
35	0.68	1.31	1.69	2.03	2.72	3.59
40	0.68	1.30	1.68	2.02	2.70	3.55
45	0.68	1.30	1.68	2.01	2.70	3.52
50	0.68	1.30	1.68	2.01	2.68	3.50
60	0.68	1.30	1.67	2.00	2.66	3.46
70	0.68	1.29	1.67	1.99	2.65	3.44
80	0.68	1.29	1.66	1.99	2.64	3.42
90	0.68	1.29	1.66	1.99	2.63	3.40
100	0.68	1.29	1.66	1.99	2.63	3.39
Probability (p) that chance alone could produce the difference	0.50 (50%)	0.20 (20%)	0.10 (10%)	0.05 (5%)	0.01 (1%)	0.001 (0.1%)

- If your value of t is *bigger* than the critical value highlighted in Table A.1, you can be at least 95% confident that the difference between the means is significant. Your result is said to be **statistically significant** and you can reject the null hypothesis that there is no difference between the means.
- If your value of t is *smaller* than the critical value highlighted in Table A.1, you are less than 95% confident that the difference between the means is significant. Your result is not statistically

significant and you cannot reject the null hypothesis that there is no difference between the means.

All this may look rather formidable, so perhaps an example will help. We will use the data listed earlier on the density of the wood of two different species, A and B. Our null hypothesis is that there is no difference between the densities of the woods of the two species.

1   Mean density of species $A = 0.736$; mean density of species $B = 0.684$.
2   Difference between the means $= 0.052$.
3   Standard deviation of the density of species A multiplied by itself divided by the number of pieces of data in that set of data $= 0.021 \times 0.021 \div 5 = 0.0000882$. (Note that your calculator may well display this number as '8.82–05'. This means 8.82×10^{-5}.)
4   Standard deviation of the density of species B multiplied by itself divided by the number of pieces of data in that set of data $= 0.023 \times 0.023 \div 5 = 0.0001058$.
5   The sum of the figures calculated in steps 3 and $4 = 0.0000882 + 0.0001058 = 0.000194$.
6   The square root of the figure calculated in step $5 = 0.0139$.
7   The difference between the two means (step 2) divided by the figure calculated in step $6 = 0.052 \div 0.0139 = 3.74$.
8   It is obvious that 3.74 is much greater than the critical value of t, which for a total number of pieces of data of 10 – that is, 8 degrees of freedom – equals 2.31. This means that we are at least 95% confident that the mean density of the wood of species A differs from the mean density of the wood of species B.

We can sum up the way to calculate the value of t by these steps as follows:

$$t = \frac{\text{mean of X} - \text{mean of Y}}{\text{standard error}}$$

$$= \frac{\bar{x} - \bar{y}}{\sqrt{\dfrac{(s_x)^2}{n_x} + \dfrac{(s_y)^2}{n_y}}}$$

where:
$\bar{x}$ equals the mean of sample X
$\bar{y}$ equals the mean of sample Y
s_x is the standard deviation of sample X
s_y is the standard deviation of sample Y
n_x is the number of individual measurements in sample X
n_y is the number of individual measurements in sample Y

The degrees of freedom are equal to $n_x + n_y - 2$.

One final point. Note that, if there really is a difference between the means of X and Y, the greater the values of n_x and n_y, the greater will be the value of t. This means that the larger your sample sizes, the more likely you are to detect a significant difference, if one exists. You really need an absolute *minimum* of half a dozen individual measurements in each sample.

So far we have given no explanation as to *how* calculating t enables us to decide whether the difference between two means is significant or not. There is no need to know this to be able to carry out a t-test. Indeed, there is no requirement for you to understand why any statistical test works. However, if you are interested in understanding how a t-test works, this box gives a *partial* explanation. A full explanation would take us into complex mathematics beyond the scope of this book.

The normal distribution

When measurements of a particular characteristic showing continuous variation, such as the height of people or the density of pieces of wood, are made on a large number of individuals in a population, a graph of frequency against the characteristic often falls approximately on a **normal distribution curve**. An example of a normal distribution curve is shown in Illustration 1. The curve is bell-shaped. Its position and its shape depend solely on its mean and standard deviation. The larger the standard deviation, the flatter and more spread out the curve will be.

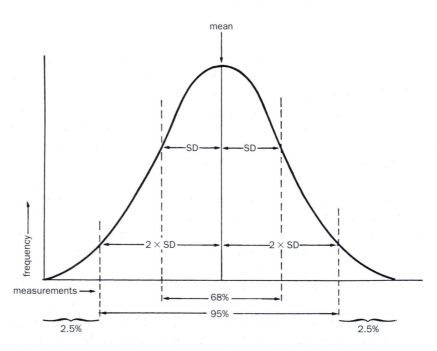

Illustration 1 Diagram of the normal distribution curve. SD, standard deviation.

The useful feature of the normal distribution curve for our purposes is that one standard deviation on either side of the mean encloses some 68% of the area under the curve. Two standard deviations (to be more exact, 1.96 standard deviations) on either side of the curve enclose 95% of the area under the curve. The two curves labelled A and B in Illustration 2, and drawn with continuous lines, show the curves we should expect if we had measured and plotted the densities of hundreds of individual pieces of wood from species A and B.

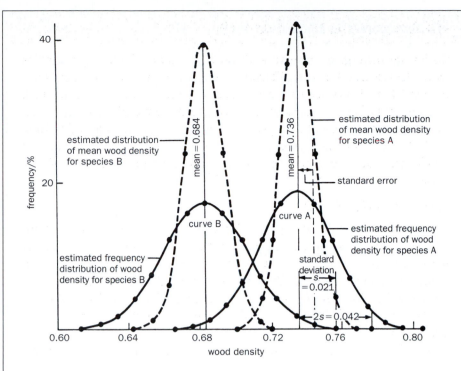

Illustration 2 Normal distribution curves for the wood density data.

Standard error

We used a total of five measurements of wood density to calculate the mean density of the wood of species A, and we obtained a value of 0.736. Obviously this value, calculated from a mere five measurements, is unlikely to equal precisely the *actual* mean density of the wood of species A. Now, the more measurements of wood density we made before calculating the mean, the closer we would expect our calculated mean to be to the actual mean.

This is where the argument gets a bit tricky. Suppose we made a large number of estimates of the mean density of the wood of species A, each time using n individual measurements to calculate each mean (in the example we worked out earlier, n equalled five). In such a case the estimates of the mean lie on a normal distribution. As you might expect, the mean of these estimates will lie close to, but will probably not exactly equal, the actual mean. If we calculate the standard deviation of the estimated means we find that this equals $s/\sqrt{n}$, where s, as before, equals the standard deviation of the individual measurements. The standard deviation of the estimated means is generally referred to as the standard deviation of the mean, or simply the **standard error**. As it equals $s/\sqrt{n}$, it is always smaller than the standard deviation of the individual measurements, by a factor $\sqrt{n}$.

In the case of the densities of woods of species A and B we have:

$s_A = 0.021$

$n_A = 5$

$s_A/\sqrt{n_A} = 0.021/\sqrt{5} = 0.009$

$s_B = 0.021$

$n_B = 5$

$s_B/\sqrt{n_B} = 0.023/\sqrt{5} = 0.010$

The two curves in Illustration 2 drawn with broken lines show the curves which we should expect if we had calculated the mean densities of hundreds of samples of wood from species A and B where each sample contained five individual measurements. These curves show the normal distributions for the means. They are taller and more pointed than curves A and B, which show the normal distributions for the individual measurements. It is because they are taller and more pointed that they overlap less, and it is because they overlap only very slightly that we can be confident that the means are different.

Seeing if observed numbers differ from expected numbers

To see if observed numbers differ from expected numbers, you need to work out exactly what your expected numbers are. An example will help. Suppose you cross two plants each of which is heterozygous at the same locus. We can represent this as Aa × Aa. Now if A is dominant to a, you might expect to get a 3:1 ratio of phenotypes among the offspring, for example for the ratio of red flowers to white flowers. Let us suppose you actually classify 50 offspring and find that the ratio is 40 red:10 white. The question is, does this ratio of 4:1 differ *significantly* from the expected one of 3:1?

The first thing to do is to work out the expected numbers. In this case we expect one-quarter of the 50 offspring (i.e. $50 \times 0.25 = 12.5$) to have one set of characteristics (white flowers), and three-quarters (i.e. $50 \times 0.75 = 37.5$) to have the other set of characteristics (red flowers). It may look odd expecting non-whole numbers, but this is the only way to get a ratio of exactly 3:1 (i.e. 37.5 red:12.5 white).

Now we complete the following table:

	Red	White
Observed (O)	40	10
Expected (E)	37.5	12.5
O−E	2.5	−2.5
(O−E)^2	6.25	6.25
(O−E)^2 ÷ E	0.17	0.5
Sum of {(O−E)^2 ÷ E} = 0.17 + 0.5 =	0.67	

Here 0.67 is called the **chi-squared value** or χ^2 **value**. The bigger it is, the greater the chance that the observed results differ significantly from the expected ones. To see if the difference is significant, use Table A.2. Note that you need to know the number of classes of data to work out the **degrees of freedom**. For a χ^2 test, the degrees of freedom are simply one less than the number of classes of data. In our example, the number of classes of data equals two (because each offspring fell into one of two classes), and the degrees of freedom equals 1. If the expected ratio had been 1:2:1 (e.g. red:pink:white), the number of classes of data would have been three and the expected numbers would not have been 37.5 and 12.5, but 12.5, 25 and 12.5. In this case the degrees of freedom would equal 2.

Table A.2 Table of χ^2 values

Degrees of freedom	Number of classes	χ^2						
1	2	0.016	0.46	1.64	2.71	3.84	6.64	10.83
2	3	0.21	1.39	3.22	4.61	5.99	9.21	13.82
3	4	0.58	2.37	4.64	6.25	7.82	11.34	16.27
4	5	1.06	3.36	5.99	7.78	9.49	13.28	18.47
Probability (p) that chance alone could produce the deviation		0.90 (90%)	0.50 (50%)	0.20 (20%)	0.10 (10%)	0.05 (5%)	0.01 (1%)	0.001 (0.1%)

If your value of χ^2 is bigger than the critical value highlighted in Table A.2, you can be at least 95% confident that the difference between the observed and expected results is significant. Your result is said to be **statistically significant**. You can see that, in our example, the value of χ^2 (0.67) is much smaller than the critical value (3.84). This means that the ratio of 40:10 is not significantly different from a 3:1 ratio.

The general formula you need to carry out this sort of test, called a **chi-squared test** (or χ^2 **test**), is given by:

$$\chi^2 = \Sigma \frac{(O - E)^2}{E}$$

and, as explained above, the degrees of freedom are equal to one less than the number of classes.

As always in statistics, the more data the better. For technical reasons, a χ^2 test needs each expected value to equal at least 5.

Finding out if a correlation exists

To find out if a significant correlation exists between two variables, you first need to know the **correlation coefficient**. The most sensitive test to find out if a significant correlation exists requires you to work out the **Pearson product–moment correlation coefficient**, abbreviated to **r**. Unfortunately, it is extremely long-winded to calculate r, which means that you really need a calculator (or a statistical package) that works it out for you.

A slightly less sensitive test to find out if a significant correlation exists requires you to work out the **Spearman rank correlation coefficient**, abbreviated to **r_s**. If you *don't* have a calculator or statistical package that works out r, use the section below titled *'Calculating the Spearman rank correlation coefficient'*. If you *can* calculate r, skip this section and go straight on to the section entitled *'Interpreting correlation coefficients'*.

Calculating the Spearman rank correlation coefficient

Although, for small sample sizes, calculating the Spearman rank correlation coefficient is less likely to reveal the existence of a correlation, it makes fewer mathematical assumptions than the test based on the Pearson product–moment correlation coefficient. So, although you are less likely to conclude that a correlation exists, if you *do* conclude that one exists, your conclusion is more likely to be valid.

Body mass/g	Gill mass/mg
14.4	159
15.2	179
11.3	100
2.5	45
22.7	384
14.9	230
1.4	100
15.8	320
4.2	80
15.4	220
9.5	210

The test based on the Spearman rank correlation coefficient has one other advantage. This is that, as its name suggests, it can be used on *ranked* data. For example, you could use it to see if people are less fit if they smoke heavily, even if you can't *quantify* their fitness or the amount they smoke, provided you can *rank* their fitness and the amount they smoke.

Here is an example to show you how to calculate the Spearman rank correlation coefficient, r_s. The data in the margin show gill mass and body mass in the crab *Pachygrapus crassipes*:

Our null hypothesis is that there is no correlation between body mass and gill mass. It's always best to plot your data on a scattergram (see pp. 4–5) to see if a correlation seems to exist before embarking on any calculations of correlation coefficients. In this case plotting the data, or visualising them in your mind's eye if you are can do that sort of thing, shows that it is likely that a significant correlation does exist.

To calculate r_s, we need to *rank* the data. (This is why r_s is referred to as the Spearman *rank* correlation coefficient.) For each column, rank the data from 1 (the largest value) downwards. Applied to our example, we get the following ranking:

Body mass/g	Rank	Gill mass/mg	Rank
14.4	6	159	7
15.2	4	179	6
11.3	7	100	8.5
2.5	10	45	11
22.7	1	384	1
14.9	5	230	3
1.4	11	100	8.5
15.8	2	320	2
4.2	9	80	10
15.4	3	220	4
9.5	8	210	5

Notice that, because there are two gill masses the same (100 mg), they are given a rank of 8.5, on the grounds that they share ranks 8 and 9.

The two ranks (body mass and gill mass) are given the labels R_1 and R_2 – it makes no difference which is which. The Spearman rank correlation coefficient is given by:

$$r_s = 1 - \frac{6\Sigma(R_1 - R_2)^2}{n(n^2 - 1)}$$

In the above example we have:

$$\Sigma(R_1 - R_2)^2 = (6-7)^2 + (4-6)^2 + (7-8.5)^2 + \ldots + (8-5)^2 = 29.5$$
$$n = 11$$

So:

$$r_s = 1 - \frac{6 \times 29.5}{11(11^2 - 1)} = 1 - \frac{147}{1320} = 0.87$$

Interpreting correlation coefficients

The value of a calculated correlation coefficient lies between -1 and $+1$:

- A correlation coefficient of close to -1 means that there is a strong *negative* relationship between the two variables: an *increase* in one variable (e.g. height of a tree) is accompanied by a *decrease* in the other variable (e.g. amount of light reaching the ground).
- A correlation coefficient of close to $+1$ means that there is a strong *positive* relationship between the two variables: an *increase* in one variable (e.g. mass of an animal) is accompanied by an *increase* in the other variable (e.g. amount of food consumed each day).
- A correlation coefficient of close to 0 means that the relationship between the two variables is weak or non-existent.

Having obtained a value for your correlation coefficient, use either Table A.3 or Table A.4 to see if it differs significantly from 0. Use Table A.3 if you have calculated the Pearson product–moment correlation coefficient, r, and Table A.4 if you have calculated the Spearman rank correlation coefficient, r_s. Note that in neither case are degrees of freedom required to use these Tables, simply the number of points used to calculate the correlation coefficient.

Table A.3 Table of r values

Number of points	r					
3	0.71	0.95	0.99	1.00	–	–
4	0.50	0.80	0.90	0.95	0.99	1.00
5	0.40	0.69	0.81	0.88	0.96	0.99
6	0.35	0.61	0.73	0.81	0.92	0.97
7	0.31	0.55	0.67	0.76	0.88	0.95
8	0.28	0.51	0.62	0.71	0.83	0.93
9	0.26	0.47	0.58	0.67	0.80	0.90
10	0.24	0.44	0.55	0.63	0.77	0.87
12	0.22	0.40	0.50	0.58	0.71	0.82
14	0.20	0.37	0.46	0.53	0.66	0.78
16	0.18	0.34	0.43	0.50	0.62	0.74
18	0.17	0.32	0.40	0.47	0.59	0.71
20	0.16	0.30	0.38	0.44	0.56	0.68
25	0.14	0.27	0.34	0.40	0.51	0.62
30	0.13	0.24	0.31	0.36	0.46	0.57
40	0.11	0.21	0.26	0.31	0.40	0.50
50	0.10	0.18	0.24	0.28	0.36	0.45
60	0.09	0.17	0.21	0.25	0.33	0.41
70	0.08	0.16	0.20	0.24	0.31	0.39
80	0.08	0.15	0.19	0.22	0.29	0.36
90	0.07	0.14	0.17	0.21	0.27	0.34
100	0.07	0.13	0.17	0.20	0.26	0.32
Probability (p) that chance alone could produce the correlation	0.50 (50%)	0.20 (20%)	0.10 (10%)	0.05 (5%)	0.01 (1%)	0.001 (0.1%)

For example, if data on the heights of different meadow buttercup plants and the number of flowers they produce were obtained from 10 plants, r would have to exceed 0.63 for the relationship to be significant at the 5% level, while r_s would have to exceed 0.65.

A final important piece of information. At low sample sizes you need more points on your scattergram to reveal a significant correlation if your test is based on the Spearman rank correlation coefficient than if it is based on the Pearson product-moment correlation coefficient. Get *at least* 10 points if using the Spearman rank correlation coefficient, and *at least* six if using the Pearson product-moment correlation coefficient.

Table A.4 Table of r_s values

Number of points	r_s					
4	0.60	1.00	—	—	—	—
5	0.50	0.80	0.90	—	—	—
6	0.37	0.66	0.83	0.89	1.00	—
7	0.32	0.57	0.71	0.79	0.93	1.00
8	0.31	0.52	0.64	0.74	0.88	0.98
9	0.27	0.48	0.60	0.70	0.83	0.93
10	0.25	0.46	0.56	0.65	0.79	0.90
12	0.22	0.41	0.50	0.59	0.73	0.85
14	0.20	0.37	0.46	0.54	0 68	0.80
16	0.18	0.34	0.43	0.50	0.64	0.76
18	0.17	0.32	0.40	0.47	0.60	0.73
20	0.16	0.30	0.38	0.45	0.57	0.70
25	0.14	0.27	0.34	0.40	0.51	0.63
30	0.13	0.24	0.31	0.36	0.47	0.58
40	0.11	0.21	0.26	0.31	0.41	0.51
50	0.10	0.18	0.24	0.28	0.36	0.46
60	0.09	0.17	0.21	0.26	0.33	0.42
70	0.08	0.16	0.20	0.24	0.31	0.39
80	0.08	0.15	0.19	0.22	0.29	0.36
90	0.07	0.14	0.17	0.21	0.27	0.34
100	0.07	0.13	0.17	0.20	0.26	0.33
Probability (p) that chance alone could produce the correlation	0.50 (50%)	0.20 (20%)	0.10 (10%)	0.05 (5%)	0.01 (1%)	0.001 (0.1%)

References

Cadogan, A. & Sutton, R. *Maths for Advanced Biology*. Nelson, Walton-on-Thames, 1994.

Coolican, H. *Research Methods and Statistics in Psychology, 2nd edn.* Hodder & Stoughton, London, 1994.

Dytham, C. *Choosing and Using Statistics: A Biologist's Guide.* Blackwell Science, Oxford, 1998.

Edmonson, A. & Druce, D. *Advanced Biology Statistics*. Oxford University Press, Oxford, 1996.

Heath, D. *An Introduction to Experimental Design and Statistics for Biology*. UCL Press, London, 1995.

Parker, R. E. *Introductory Statistics for Biology*. Edward Arnold, London, 1979.

Powell, S. *Statistics for Science Projects*. Hodder & Stoughton, London, 1996.

Webb, N. & Blackmore, R. *Statistics for Biologists*. Cambridge University Press, Cambridge, 1985.

Preparation of reagents

Note that preparation of some of these reagents is hazardous. Preparations should never be undertaken by students and only by appropriately qualified technicians, teachers or lecturers using appropriate precautions and protection.

Danger

Details of how to make up some reagents, when the reagents are only mentioned once in the book, appear under the Requirements for individual Practical Exercises or Investigations.

Acetic ethanol (ethanoic ethanol)

Three parts of ethanol to one of pure ethanoic acid.

Acetocarmine

Add 1 g of carmine to 45 cm³ of pure ethanoic acid. Mix. Add 55 cm³ of distilled water. Boil. Cool and filter.

Benedict's reagent

Dissolve 173 g of hydrated sodium citrate and 100 g of hydrated sodium carbonate in approximately 800 cm³ of warm distilled water. Filter, and make the filtrate up to 850 cm³. This is solution **A**. Dissolve 17.3 g of hydrated copper sulphate in approximately 100 cm³ of cold distilled water. This is solution **B**. Add **B** to **A**, stirring as you do so. Make up to 1 dm³ with distilled water.

Chloral hydrate

Dissolve 128 g of chloral hydrate in 80 cm³ of distilled water.

Fabil stain

First make up lactophenol. To do this mix, in equal parts by mass, the following compounds: phenol (crystals), glycerol, lactic acid, distilled water.

Then mix the following three solutions:

A Aniline blue: 0.5% in lactophenol
B Basic fuchsin: 0.5% in lactophenol
C Iodine, 3 g; potassium iodide, 6 g; lactophenol, 1 dm³.

To make up the stain, mix the stock solutions in the ratio of 4 parts **A** : 1 part **B** : 5 parts **C**. Allow to stand for 12 hours, then filter. The stain will keep indefinitely.
(From Noel, A. R. A., *School Science Review*, **47**, 156–157, 1965.)

Feulgen's reagent

Dissolve 1.0 g of basic fuchsin in 200 cm³ of boiling distilled water. Filter. Add 30 cm³ of hydrochloric acid (1.0 mol dm⁻³) and 3.0 g of potassium metabisulphite to the filtrate. Allow to bleach for 24 hours in the dark. If the solution is still coloured, the residual colour should be absorbed on carbon. Filter. Store in tightly stoppered bottle in the dark.

Glycerine, dilute

For mounting botanical sections, use a 5% concentration. Prepare by making up 5 g of pure glycerine to 100 cm³ with distilled water.

Iodine solution

Dissolve 1.0 g of iodine crystals and 2.0 g of potassium iodide in 300 cm³ of distilled water.

Methanolic HCl

A 1% solution of concentrated HCl in methanol.

Methylene blue

Mix 1 g of methylene blue, 0.6 g of sodium chloride and 100 cm³ of distilled water.

Methyl green (in ethanoic acid)

Make up 100 cm³ of 1% ethanoic acid in distilled water. Add 1 g of methyl green.

Methyl green–pyronin solution

Add 2.5 cm³ of ethanol to 20 cm³ of glycerol. Mix in, stirring, 0.15 g of methyl green and 0.25 g of pyronin. Make up to 100 cm³ with 0.5% phenol solution.

Ninhydrin

Prepare 200 mg of ninhydrin in 100 cm³ of propanone.

Orcein, ethanoic

Dissolve 3.3 g of orcein in 100 cm³ of glacial (undiluted) ethanoic acid by gently boiling under reflux for about 6 hours. Filter. This gives a stock solution which can be stored. When required for staining, dilute 10 cm³ of stock solution with 12 cm³ of distilled water. The diluted stain deteriorates quickly.

Phloroglucinol, acidified

Phloroglucinol is benzene-1,3,5-Triol.
Dissolve 5 g of phloroglucinol in 100 cm³ of 95% ethanol. Stir. Add concentrated hydrochloric acid dropwise until the phloroglucinol begins to precipitate.

Schultze's solution (chlor-zinc iodide)

In a fume cupboard, dissolve 110 g of zinc in 300 cm³ of hydrochloric acid (hydrogen is evolved). Evaporate to half the volume, using an evaporating dish over a low flame. In the course of the evaporation, add a little more zinc to ensure complete neutralisation of the acid. Dissolve 10 g of potassium iodide, in the least possible quantity of water, and add 0.15 g of iodine crystals. Mix thoroughly and, if necessary, filter through glass wool. Keep in a tightly stoppered bottle in the dark.

Acknowledgements

The authors and publisher wish to acknowledge, with thanks, the following sources.

Photographs
Biophoto Associates: **1.11, 2.13, 2.25, 2.34, 4.5a, 4.13, 4.20a, 4.21a, 5.2a**; Gene Cox: **6.4**; Holt Studios International: **8.3** (Bob Gibbons); Institute of Biology, London: **7.4** (from the Journal of Biological Education); Rex Features: **4.28**; Science and Plants for Schools, Homerton College, Cambridge: **5.7**; Science Photolibrary: **1.12** (Dr Kari Lounatmaa), **2.33** (D. Phillips), **3.3a** (CNRI), **4.7a** (Professor S. Cinti, CNRI), **5.1** (L. Williatt, East Anglian Genetics Service), **6.3** (Sinclair Stammers); TRIP: **8.2** (J. Ringland). Picture research by John Bailey.

Artworks and other material
Figure 1.1 Adapted from J. Hewitson & R. Price, Plant mineral nutrition in the classroom: the radish, *Raphanus sativus* L. is a good plant for such studies, *School Science Review* 76 (274) 44–5, 1994. **Figure 2.5** After P. W. Freeland, *Focus on Biology: Micro-organisms in Action. Investigations*, Hodder & Stoughton, London, 1990. **Figure 2.6** Based on *GCSE Biology*, D. G. Mackean (John Murray) 1995. **Illustration** (p.141) Based on G. Monger (Ed.) *Revised Nuffield Biology, Practical Guide 3*, Longmans, Harlow, 1985. **Figure 2.48** After P. W. Freeland, Problems in Practical Advanced Level Biology, Hodder & Stoughton, London, 1985. **Figure 7.1** From G. Monger (Ed.), *Revised Nuffield A-level Biology, Practical Guide 7*, Longmans, Harlow, 1986. **Figure 7.2** From Dr N. D. Boatman, *Game Conservatory Review*, 1989. The Game Conservatory Trust, Fordingbridge, Hampshire, 1989.

Colleagues
Dr J.L. Chapman
The Master and Fellows of Sidney Sussex College, Cambridge, for a Schoolteacher Fellow Commonership during the tenure of which Tim King wrote his contribution to the book
Sonia Clark
Sally Cullen
Dr Tim Gunn
Heather King
Stephen Tomkins
John Tranter

Index

Bold page references refer to illustrations, figures or tables.